WELLINGTON'S WAR

WELLINGTON'S WAR

Or

'ATTY, THE LONG-NOSED BUGGER
THAT LICKS THE FRENCH'
[unknown Irish soldier]

Peninsular Dispatches
presented by

JULIAN RATHBONE

Foreword by Field Marshal Lord Carver

MICHAEL JOSEPH
LONDON

MICHAEL JOSEPH LTD

Published by the Penguin Group
27 Wrights Lane, London W8 5TZ
Viking Penguin Inc., 375 Hudson Street, New York, New York 10014, USA
Penguin Books Australia Ltd, Ringwood, Victoria, Australia
Penguin Books Canada Ltd, 10 Alcorn Avenue, Toronto, Ontario, Canada M4V 3B2
Penguin Books (NZ) Ltd, 182-190 Wairau Road, Auckland 10, New Zealand

Penguin Books Ltd, Registered Offices: Harmondsworth, Middlesex, England

First published in Great Britain 1984
First published in this paperback edition 1994

Copyright © 1984 by Julian Rathbone

Printed in Great Britain by Clays Ltd, St Ives plc

ISBN 0 7181 3841 4

CONTENTS

LIST OF MAPS

LIST OF ILLUSTRATIONS

All the illustrations are taken from engravings of Captain Andrew Leith-Hay's drawings done during the war, while he was A.D.C. to General Leith. They first appeared in Leith-Hay's *Narrative of the Peninsular War* and are reproduced by permission of the British Library.

Many such drawings were made, by many different artists, and for practical reasons: for yesterday's commanders they served the same purpose as satellite photographs do for today's.

FOREWORD
by Field Marshal Lord Carver

Julian Rathbone's choice of extracts from the letters and dispatches of my great-great-great-great uncle confirms to me the fervent admiration which I have always entertained for him. They show, beyond all doubt, that he was a complete master of his profession. The prescience and subtlety of his strategy are as impressive as his grasp of the details of administration. They reveal the clarity and quickness of his mind, as they do his never-failing, pragmatic common sense. He was no romantic. He did not expect much of his fellow men – politicians, generals, officers or soldiers – but he knew how to get the best out of them. His human concern for those who suffered death, wounds, illness, or simply lack of funds, may surprise those who have been led to think of the Iron Duke as harsh and arrogant. Of his personal courage and disregard of danger, there has never been any doubt.

He welded the army of the Peninsula into a team which raised the reputation of the British army to the level which it had gained under Marlborough, but from which it had fallen in the long years of neglect in the eighteenth century. Not until the twentieth was it to reach those heights again. Readers will find many similarities between Wellington's army in the Peninsula and Montgomery's Eighth Army in the Second World War, as they will between those two masters of their profession. The principal difference was that Wellington was not only commander-in-chief, but also his own chief of staff – indeed, he personally carried out all the activities of the general staff. The pages which follow vividly portray the astonishing range of his ability and activity.

INTRODUCTION

This book consists of a selection of the Duke of Wellington's dispatches, orders, general orders, and correspondence between July 1808 and November 1813, that is, from his first landing in Portugal to his invasion of the south-west of France. The printed material from this period comes to something a little under 2,000,000 words, that is, the equivalent of 400 modern novels. My selection runs to about 55,000 words – it is therefore an eclectic, possibly idiosyncratic choice. I have provided an equally eccentric, but I hope explanatory commentary that fills in background, narrative links, and descriptions of the places and countryside through which the campaigns moved. I have visited every major site, and most of the minor ones between Mondego Bay and the Grande Rhune, apart from Badajoz and Albuera.

The chief aim of this book is to entertain. I hope a second may also have been achieved: to demonstrate the largeness, subtlety and prescience of Wellington's mind; the complexity and depth of his personality; and, of course, his extraordinary capacity for work organised by an intelligence that is little less than miraculous.

The sources for the extracts are *The Dispatches of Field Marshal the Duke of Wellington, K.G.*, edited by Lieutenant-Colonel Gurwood, which were printed in thirteen volumes between 1834 and 1839; and *Supplementary Despatches, Correspondence, and Memorandu of Field Marshal Arthur Duke of Wellington, K.G., 1794–1818*, edited by his son, the Duke of Wellington, printed in fifteen volumes, between 1858 and 1872. The latter also includes most of the quoted letters written by his correspondents. I have not included page references, nor an index – it is not my wish that this book should be thought to have academic pretensions – but I have, in almost every case, given date and addressee, so the interested reader with access to the Dispatches should be able to trace the source readily enough.

The principal source for my commentary, apart from my own travels in the Peninsula, is *The History of the Peninsular War* by Charles Oman. I have also used often *A History of the Peninsular War* by William Napier, *Wellington's Army* by Charles Oman, *Wellington's Headquarters* by S. G. P. Ward, *Wellington as Military Commander* by Michael Glover, *Wellington in the Peninsula* by Jac Weller, *The Duke* by Philip Guedalla,

The Life of Wellington by W. H. Maxwell, *The Years of the Sword* by Elizabeth Longford, and *Wellington's Masterpiece* by J. P. Lawford and Peter Young.

I have also attempted at times to catch the flavour and atmosphere, the experience of the British Army in the Peninsula, and for this I have drawn on many of the diaries and memoirs of the period, but particularly, and deliberately for the sake of contrast, on those of private soldiers, most notably *The Vicissitudes of a Soldier's Life* by Private Green, and the *Letters of Private Wheeler* edited by Captain Lidell Hart.

At this point I would like to express my gratitude for the help and many kindnesses I have received from the staff of Southampton University Library, particularly the archivist Mr Christopher Woodgar, and to Russel Billington for drawing the maps in this book.

The book is, nevertheless, Wellington's. As I have said, I have finally settled on about one fortieth of what he actually wrote during the period. Most of what I have excluded is, first of all, repetition. He had several regular correspondents, both official and private, so obviously several different letters will often cover the same events in much the same language. Similarly four or five commanders on a particular occasion would receive similar orders. I have also excluded, apart from a few typical examples of each, most of the literally voluminous correspondence on the buying and distribution of provisions and *matériel*, on pay for the troops, on the economics of Portugal, on the intrigues within the Portuguese Regency, within the Spanish Juntas and Cortes, on Courts Martial, on the endless bickering about promotion and the pecking order amongst the officers of his army, and so on. But it is all there in the original Dispatches, witness to the meticulousness, energy, patience and intelligence that Wellington brought to seemingly chronic and intractable problems.

What remains I hope will do justice to what Walter Bagehot said of the Dispatches when they were first published: 'There are people in the world who cannot write the commonest letter on the commonest affair of business without giving a just idea of themselves. The Duke of Wellington is an example. You may read a dispatch of his about bullocks and horse-shoe nails and yet you will feel an interest – a great interest, because somehow among the words seems to lurk the mind of a great general.'; and justice also to the Duke's own comments (not the least of his great qualities was a just opinion of his own worth): 'I have been much amused at reading them over – the energy and action are quite as great as ever . . .' and, 'They are valuable, more so than

Caesar's Commentaries because Caesar wrote afterwards for effect. These are a Collection of the Instruments used at the Time – They were all written in my own hand.'

Wellington's words are throughout printed in roman characters; my commentary is in italics. Quotations whether written or verbatim are in quotation marks. Omissions within a particular document are signified thus . . . When those three dots occur in front of a name it is almost always a repetition of rank and title that has been dropped. The spelling of Portuguese and Spanish place names has been a vexing business. Generally speaking Wellington's own usage is closer to that now current than that invented by most nineteenth century historians, and I have tried to keep either his or what is now current. Accents were not used in Spanish in his day and I have left them off throughout. The tilde ˜ was used in both languages much as it is now, and it is used here. I doubt I have maintained consistency to these principles, and I apologise in advance for any deviance from them. The maps are based on those that appear in Oman's *History of the Peninsular War*, in Fortescue's *History of the British Army*, and on Kummerley and Frey's Map of Iberia, 1973.

Finally I should mention, not because I have forgotten them but because I wish to give them grateful emphasis, Sir Arthur Bryant's *The Years of Victory* and *The Age of Elegance*. They were given to me when I was fourteen years old and from them I caught the obsession with the Duke that lies behind the present work. It remains unexorcised.

JULIAN RATHBONE

PROLOGUE

Following Trafalgar and the scrapping of his invasion plans in 1805 Napoleon's main thrust against Britain was through the Berlin Decrees by which he attempted to close off all European ports to ships carrying cargoes to and from Britain. By 1808 only a few Scandinavian and Portuguese ports remained open. He invaded Portugal and threatened Sweden.

The British Government determined on a military expedition to keep or re-open these ports – the question was, whether to send it to the Peninsula or the Baltic. On 1st May the Spanish rose against the French, who had kidnapped both King Charles IV and his son Ferdinand, and placed Joseph, Napoleon's elder brother, on the throne. This rising was ruthlessly suppressed in Madrid but was more successful almost everywhere else – especially in Galicia, on the Portuguese borders, in Estremadura, and Andalusia, where armies were raised against the intruders. This made up the Government's mind and a small expeditionary force was put together under Lieutenant-General Sir Arthur Wellesley, K.B. with instructions to land in Spain or Portugal, as he saw fit.

At this time Sir Arthur was Britain's most successful general. He had won India from possible French influence in a brilliant campaign which had culminated in a victorious general action at Assaye. However, he was only just thirty-nine years old with many generals on the list senior to him, and the military establishment (the Horse Guards) set a low value on colonial campaigns. Sir Arthur was, however, connected by family and friendship to the chief grandees of the tory party, particularly the Duke of Richmond, under whom he had served as Secretary in Ireland, Lord Castlereagh who was Secretary of State for War, Lord Liverpool, and others.

1808

PRELUDE

THE LANDING

THE MARCH

THE BATTLE

THE AFTERMATH

OUR HERO

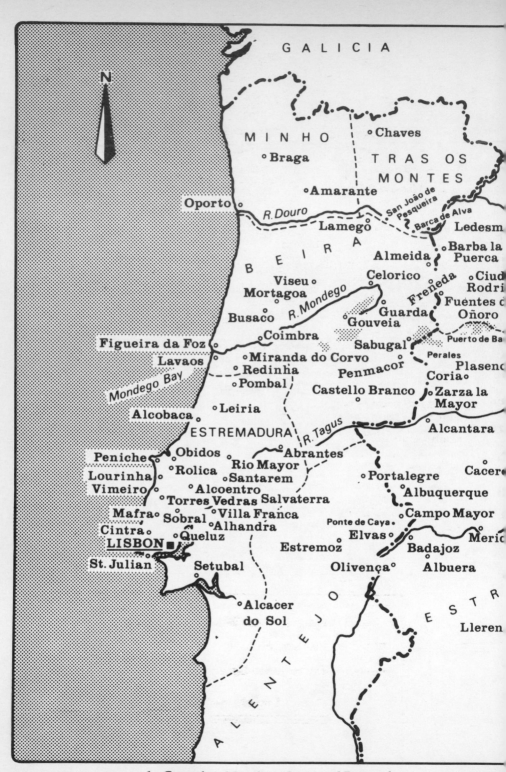

1. Central and Southern Spain and Portugal

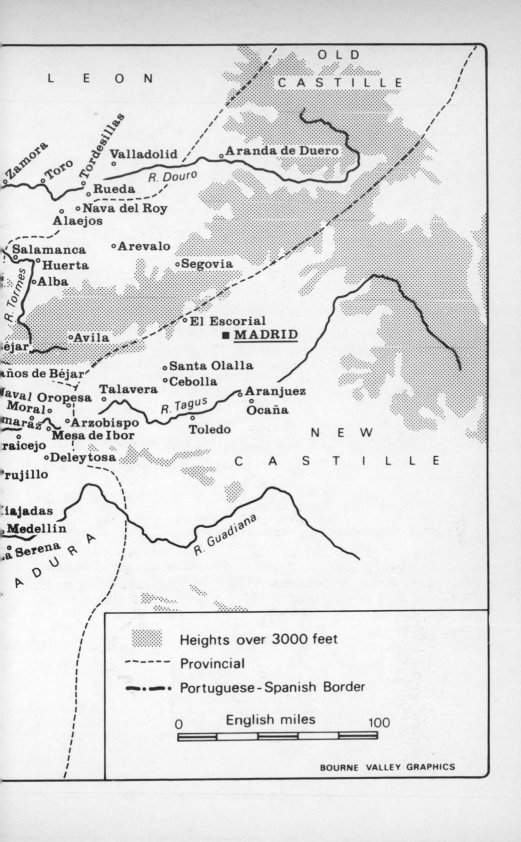

LEON

OLD CASTILLE

Zamora
Toro
Tordesillas
Valladolid
Aranda de Duero
R. Douro
Rueda
Nava del Roy
Alaejos
Arevalo
Salamanca
Huerta
Segovia
Alba
R. Tormes
El Escorial
■ **MADRID**
éjar
Avila
ños de Béjar
Santa Olalla
Cebolla
Naval Oropesa
Talavera
Aranjuez
Moral
R. Tagus
Ocaña
maráz
Arzobispo
Toledo
NEW
raicejo
Mesa de Ibor
Deleytosa
CASTILLE
rujillo
iajadas
Medellin
ADURA
á Serena
R. Guadiana

Heights over 3000 feet

------- Provincial

—·—·— Portuguese-Spanish Border

English miles

0   100

BOURNE VALLEY GRAPHICS

PRELUDE

———— ⋙ ————

The Grand Old Duke of York appoints a commander.

> The Hon. Sir A. Wellesley, K.B.   Horse Guards, 14th June 1808.
> Sir,
> His Majesty having been graciously pleased to appoint you to the command of a detachment of his army, to be employed upon a particular service, I have to desire that you will be pleased to take the earliest opportunity to assume the command of this force, and carry into effect such instructions as you may receive from His Majesty's Ministers . . .
> I am, &c.
>
> Frederick, Commander in Chief.

The Secretary of State for War confesses to some uncertainty on the part of the cabinet as to the nature of the 'particular service'.

> Viscount Castlereagh, Secretary of State, to Lt. General the Hon. Sir A. Wellesley, K.B.   Downing Street, 21st June, 1808.
> Dear Sir,
> . . . The Cabinet are desirous of postponing, . . . their final decision on your instructions, being unwilling that you should get too far to the southward, whilst the spirit of exertion appears to reside more to the northward . . .
> I am, &c.
>
> Castlereagh

Sir Arthur welcomes an old friend as one of his general officers.

My Dear Hill,   Dublin Castle, 23rd June.
I rejoice extremely at the prospect I have before me of serving again with you, and I hope we shall have more to do than on the last occasion on which we were together . . .
   Believe me, &c.

Arthur Wellesley

The Cabinet makes up its collective mind. Castlereagh to Wellesley, 30 June:

> Sir,
> The occupation of Spain and Portugal by the troops of France, and the entire usurpation of their respective governments by that power,

6

has determined His Majesty to direct a corps of his troops . . . to be employed under your orders in counteracting the designs of the enemy, and in affording to the Spanish and Portuguese nations every possible aid in the throwing off of the yoke of France . . .

The entire and absolute evacuation of the Peninsula by the troops of France is after what has lately passed the only security for Spanish independence . . .

At Cork, to embark his troops. To Castlereagh, Cork, 10 July: The wind is still contrary, but we hope it will change so as to sail this evening. We are unmoored, and shall not wait one moment after the wind may be fair . . .

THE LANDING

Wellesley to Castlereagh, H.M.S. Crocodile, Coruña, 21 July: . . . I deemed it expedient to quit the fleet containing the troops under my command, as soon as it was clear of the coast of Ireland, and I arrived here in this ship yesterday . . . It is impossible to convey to you an idea of the sentiment which prevails here in favour of the Spanish cause. The difference between any two men is whether the one is a better or a worse Spaniard, and the better Spaniard is the one who detests the French most heartily . . . It will be necessary that you should assist all the Spanish provinces with money, arms and ammunition. Notwithstanding the recent defeat of the Galician army, *at Medina de Rio Seco, and a much more disastrous thrashing, indeed rout, than the Junta let on,* the Junta have not expressed any anxiety to receive the assistance of British troops . . . I think this disinclination is founded on the objection to give the command of their troops to British officers.

. . . The three northern provinces of Portugal are in a state of insurrection, and there is a Portuguese army at Oporto . . . I now intend to look for the fleet this night, and if we should not find it, I shall leave one of Captain Hotham's *(builder of Hotham House, Bognor Regis)* squadron upon the rendezvous . . .

Wellesley to Castlereagh, H.M.S. Crocodile, off Oporto, 25 July: I arrived here yesterday . . . the fleet are now coming on. *To Spencer, on the Crocodile, off the Tagus, 26 July:* . . . as I am convinced that the most effectual mode in which Great Britain can serve the Spanish cause is by driving the French out of Portugal . . . I cannot avoid urging you to embark the troops under your command *10,000 of them originally at Gibraltar, now, since the Spanish rising against the French, at Cadiz* as soon as you shall receive this letter, and to proceed to the Tagus.

To Castlereagh, 26 July: Admiral Sir Charles Cotton . . . thought it probable that it would be deemed advisable that the troops should land at Mondego Bay, or at Peniche *(See map page 4).*

To Castlereagh, H.M.S. Donegal, off the Mondego River, 1 August, 1808: The enemy's position in the neighbourhood of the Tagus appears so strong, that it is considered impractical to make a landing in that quarter . . . There is no place to the northward of Lisbon which would at all answer for a place of disembarkation nearer than Mondego . . . I shall consider the possession of the harbour and city of Lisbon as the immediate object of our operations . . . I have this day commenced my disembarkation in the river of the Mondego . . . The landing is attended with some difficulties and would be quite impossible if we had not the cordial assistance of the country, notwithstanding the zeal and ability of the Officers of the Navy.

. . . the surf on the whole of the coast of Portugal is great . . .

MEMORANDUM FOR DISEMBARKATION

The infantry will be directed to be landed from the transports in the roads, and to be rowed in the boats up the river and landed on the south bank of it. In the meantime . . . havresacks *(sic)* and canteens are to be given out to the men, . . . tin camp kettles are to be issued . . . the men to land, each with one shirt and one pair of shoes, besides those on them, combs, razor, and a brush . . . the men will land with three days' bread and two days' meat cooked . . . The Commanding Officer of Artillery . . . will also land 500,000 rounds of musket ammunition *each round consisted of a cylindrical paper cartridge containing ball and powder, sixty packed in a weather-proof pouch were normally carried, trained men could fire their muskets four times in one minute* . . . Each soldier will have with him three good flints . . . Three days' oats to be landed with each of the horses . . .

If you stand on the southern bank of the estuary of the Mondego you see to your left a long, long sweep of white-gold sand, stretching for miles, and building up behind it, an equally long line of dune, crowned with samphire and long coarse grasses that squeak if you walk in them. The estuary itself is narrow and the tip of the opposite point is marked by a low fort. To the right of this and still in front is Figueira – in 1808 an unpretentious fishing village and minor market town, now a quite jolly resort not unlike Selsey or the Witterings. The sea approach was variable according to tides and weather, and so it had never developed into any sort of a port to rival Oporto, or even Peniche. The fort had been occupied by a small French detachment which had been driven out by armed students from nearby Coimbra University. Marines now landed to take their place.

In fine weather, such as existed on 1 August, 1808, the whole scene is vigorous and exciting: the Atlantic breeze stirs the white sand into a permanent haze above the dunes, the rollers march in, white-crested over the bar from the indigo blue of deep water beyond, roar up the greener shallows and crash on the bleached sands on your left, or swirl in vicious eddies up the estuary in front of you; beneath everything is the continuous roar of the surf, a never-ending roll on a bass drum whose integument is the Earth itself.

Now add to the scene, beyond the bar where the rollers are crested with spume, way out on the heaving indigo, five or six ships of the line, as stately as Queens as solid as castles (think of Turner: The Fleet off Spithead, the Trafalgar sketches) undisturbed by the enormous swell, black and yellow with gilded figureheads and sterns, and soaring masts with reefed scraps of sail to keep them hoved-to in station, decked with shifting pennants, and every now and then emitting puffs of white smoke a heart-beat or two before the thud of cannon-fire reaches your ears . . . a signal will be made to Captain Malcolm, when it will be settled at what period it may be proper to move the horse ships, and the ships having the ordnance on board, into the river; *then the wallowing transports further in and nearer you, with bustling activity all about them, as soldiers in red coats and the just newly issued blue-grey trousers clamber down their sides on rope nets. Below them wait fearless sailors who stand in open rowing boats – each soldier is handed down and made to sit on the thwarts, his musket clutched between his knees, his pack between his feet.*

Inevitably the surf upsets some and before sunset a dozen drowned bodies are pushed up the sands by the insensate waves, but most, almost all, get through, some actually carried through the eight-foot breakers on the shoulders of the sailors. The crowd on the foreshore thickens – horses, neighing with terror or perhaps exhilarated to be on land again, break loose and career through the dunes; the camp ladies (six washerwomen were allowed to each company of a hundred men) stretch out the sodden red coats to dry, light fires from the sea-shaped flotsam and set the kettles going for . . . tea.

Soon the General himself is on shore and for much of the time barefoot; with breeches rolled up he strides along the edge of the surf, issuing his orders, giving advice, instruction, peremptory, sharp, decisive, to the point, impatient with fools. He is of middling height, well-built, not quite forty years old; no badges of rank save the star of the Bath sewn to his tunic, yet his appearance instantly commands respect – especially his eyes. These are blue, clear, deepset beneath

9

high brows. But of course it is the nose you notice first – large, arched high up near the bridge, and from three weeks at sea, already red and peeling.

The next day he moved his headquarters a mile or so inland to Lavaos while the landing continued. All together it took nine days, the last batch being 5,000 men under Brent Spencer from Cadiz.

Meanwhile it was necessary to make it clear to all concerned, the people of Portugal and the troops themselves, just why they were there.

PROCLAMATION
PEOPLE OF PORTUGAL

The time is arrived to rescue your country, and restore the government of your lawful Prince . . .

The English soldiers, who land upon your shore, do so with every sentiment of friendship, faith, and honour.

The glorious struggle in which you are engaged is for all that is dear to man – the protection of your wives and children; the restoration of your lawful Prince; the independence, nay, the very existence of your kingdom; and for the preservation of your holy religion . . .

Lavaos, 2nd August, 1808   **Arthur Wellesley**
                                                Charles Cotton

---

General Order: H.M.S. Donegal, 31st July
The troops are to understand that Portugal is a country friendly to His Majesty, that it is essentially necessary to their own success that the most strict obedience should be preserved, that properties and persons should be respected . . . The Lieutenant-General declares his determination to punish in the most exemplary manner all who may be convicted of acts of outrage and of plunder . . . the religious prejudices and opinions of the people of the country should be respected . . . when an officer or a soldier shall sit in a church from motives of curiosity he is to remain uncovered . . . When the Host passes in the streets, officers and soldiers are to halt and front it; the officers to pull off their hats, and the soldiers to put their hands to their caps . . . the guard will turn out and present arms.

Here, right at the very beginning, for that General Order is dated 31 July, we have what was to be a continuing theme, treated with mortification, anger, even rage, right through to the battle of Vitoria in 1813 and beyond: the propensity, given the slightest excuse, of many of the soldiers to plunder and even rape and

10

murder the people they had come to free; and on the other side, equally galling and in some ways even more frustrating, the inability of the Portuguese and later the Spaniards to give their liberators the welcome they thought they deserved.

Another recurring theme, particularly in the first years, was the failure of the Commissariat to supply the troops. The Commissaries were civilian clerks answerable to the Treasury; they were meant to deal with local shopkeepers, farmers and so on, supply all the regulations demanded, and convey it in locally-hired waggons. Frequently the Commissaries were inefficient; often they had to pay in bills on London which local peasants and shopkeepers would not accept; and of course a criminal few had endless opportunities for lining their own pockets. The result was that often the troops went unfed and resorted to plunder, which in turn alienated the locals . . . and so on.

And what did the regulations demand? The same G.O. is explicit:

The troops will receive rations from the Commissary. The rations will consist for each day of 1lb of bread or biscuit, (*biscuit was bread baked twice – it was thus lighter, dryer, lasted longer*) and 1lb of meat, salt or fresh. If the soldiers should have fresh meat, they are not entitled to spirits or wine; if they should have salt meat . . . they shall have one quarter of a pint of spirits, or a pint of wine (*in fact this allowance quickly became standard whether or not the meat was salt*). The troops are also entitled in camp to 3lbs of wood each man.

The women, that is to say six for each company of a 100 men will receive half a ration per diem, and the children a quarter, but no spirits or wine . . .

Horses will receive a ration of 10lbs of hay and 10lbs of oats . . . or 14lbs of Indian corn or barley, and 10lbs of straw.

Sir Arthur goes on in meticulous detail, and with unanswerable clarity to set out how returns should be made so detachments could draw their entitlement, how receipts should be drawn up and who should sign them, and when, in triplicate *(his emphasis), and so on, concluding:*

The officers and soldiers are to understand that they are to pay for every thing they require from the country, excepting provisions, forage, wood . . .

Not an easy matter if you were a private on a net pay of one shilling and sixpence a week, out of which you had to contribute to the washerwomen's soap; or an ensign on £62,10s,8d per year, out of which you paid for your uniform, accoutrements, and horse; and even more difficult when pay was normally two months in arrears and often more.

As noted – in spite of Sir Arthur's minutely careful instructions – it took less than a week for the Commissariat to make a cock-up of just about everything.

11

To Castlereagh, Lavaos, 8 August, 1808: I have had the greatest difficulty in organizing my commissariat for the march, and that department is very incompetent . . . deserves your serious attention. The existence of the army depends upon it, and yet the people who manage it are incapable of managing anything out of the counting house.

I shall be obliged to leave Spencer's guns behind for want of means of moving them . . . Let nobody ever prevail upon you to send a corps to any part of Europe without horses to draw their guns. It is not true that horses lose their condition at sea.

He was now very anxious indeed to be off, for on the very day he landed he had heard he was to be superseded in his command, not once but six times. The letter just quoted closes by alluding to his monstrous disappointment.

I have received your private letter of the 21st July, for which I am obliged to you. I shall be the junior of the Lieutenant Generals; however, I am ready to serve the government wherever and as ever they please.

He had first heard the news from his brother William Wellesley Pole, Secretary to the Admiralty. Pole and Bughersh have apprised me of the arrangement for the future command of the army . . . All that I can say on the subject is that whether I am to command the army or not, or am to quit it, I shall do my best to ensure its success; and you may depend upon it that I shall not hurry the operations, or commence them one moment sooner than they ought to be commenced in order that I may acquire the credit of the success.

What had happened was this: Spencer had sent a paper both to Sir Arthur and to England, saying that he believed there to be 20,000 French troops in Portugal. Sir Arthur takes up the tale in a letter to his old boss in Ireland, the Duke of Richmond, written on 1 August when he was still on board the Donegal.

He sent this same account to England, where they took the alarm, and ordered out 5,000 men, and Moore's corps of 10,000 men, with several General Officers senior to me, and Sir Hew Dalrymple to command the whole army. I hope I shall have beat Junot before any of them arrive, and then they will do as they please with me . . .

Which doesn't exactly chime with his later more moderate statement, already quoted: 'I shall not hurry the operations . . . in order that I may acquire the credit of the success.'

Of course he didn't: no matter how intemperate his first reaction to the news, he was characteristically quick to control it – the preparations plodded on, meticulously. He went to visit the Portuguese General Freire and arranged for 5,000 stands of arms to be delivered to him; his own troops were all ashore, and

Spencer's too. Most of the problems with the Commissariat were sorted out. On 10 August they marched.

THE MARCH

G.O.   Lavaos, 9th Aug., 1808.
The army will march to-morrow by the right; the mounted dragoons to lead, followed by the 3rd, 5th, and 4th brigades of infantry . . . all guards, piquets, and other duties to be called in at an early hour in the morning; and the tents to be struck and packed in their cases . . . in sufficient time to enable the whole line to move off at 4 o'clock . . .

How big an army was it then that moved off through the pearly Portuguese dawn? They were: 14,180 infantry formed in fifteen and a half battalions, and including 1,500 riflemen; only 372 cavalry, light dragoons, of whom only 215 had horses . . . the dismounted dragoons to go to Lavaos as a guard to the Commissariat; *18 guns drawn by draught horses from Ireland* . . . Our artillery horses are not what we ought to have . . . cast horses of dragoons and Irish cart horses bought for 12*l* each! but not fit for an army that, to be successful and carry things with a high hand, ought to be able to move; *and at the end of the column* The reserve artillery and depôt mules, &c. will follow the infantry; then the baggage of the head quarters and General Officers, the baggage of brigades in successions, the medical stores, the Commissariat mules, &c., depots . . .

That cryptic '&c.' includes one hundred and fifty Portuguese bullock carts that the Commissariat had at last contrived to hire. Their descendants may still be seen in Galicia and northern Portugal, though then they were current over most of the west of the Peninsula. Each consists of a flat floor or chassis, boat shaped, with posts set at the edges to secure the load, and is mounted on solid axles with solid wheels turning in wood journals. Two bullocks are harnessed on either side of a pole protruding in the front. They are not large, not above ten feet long and four feet across at the squared off rear. Their main feature, that was remarked on by almost every diarist, was the hideous screech of the wooden axles. So, if you were at all near the rear it was not to the noise of the bands, the drums, the pipes, the jingle jangle of high-stepping cavalry, but to this ear-splitting cacophony that your campaign, like all those that succeeded it, got under way.

And towards what? Four or five days' march away 6,000 French under Delaborde were across the coast road at Obidos; and further into the interior

13

9,000 under Loison were plundering and looting the small towns and villages up the Tagus. Further off still, at Lisbon itself, were a further 12,000 under General Junot, Duc d'Abrantes, and Buonaparte's intruded viceroy: but before these latter could become a danger Sir Arthur expected to be reinforced – a dubious benefit, since, with the reinforcements, would come one if not more of the Generals who would supersede him.

They made tolerably good speed the first day, twenty miles, rather less the next, arriving at Leiria only another eight miles on. The roads had been passable, and flat at first, through the sandy irrigated fields that lie to the south of the Mondego estuary, fields of wheat stubble with larks, and ripening Indian corn. At Leiria the countryside changes – craggy hills, chain after chain, rise up out of the plain, crowned with pines and ilex, terraced for vines, and with orchards nestling about the villages. Small windmills with cloth sails are perched here and there to catch the Atlantic breeze. At Leiria they paused, to sort out some of the problems that had arisen.

G.O.   Leiria, 11th Aug.
A pint of wine per man to be issued this evening, at five o'clock . . . and such corps as did not receive meat yesterday for today will be supplied with it immediately. Meat for to-morrow to be issued to the army as soon after daylight in the morning as possible.

To Lieutenant Sir H. Burrard, Bart., the senior officer most likely to reach him first: In the present season of the year, you cannot depend upon the country for bread. Portugal never fed itself for more than seven months out of twelve. The common consumption of the country is Indian corn . . . you must therefore depend upon your transports for bread. Wine and beef you will get . . . *He then goes on in the most detailed fashion to outline what he thinks Burrard should do on his arrival: it's very easy to read into this doubts about his superior's competence.*

At Leiria he inspected the Portuguese army under Freire, and did not like what he saw, nor did he like Freire's proposed plan of campaign. The upshot was that he moved on leaving the greater part of the Portuguese behind him, but taking 1,600 light troops who were commanded by Colonel Nicholas Trant, an Irish officer in the Portuguese service – a colourful if erratic figure who will appear frequently until he suffers a serious wound at Salamanca in 1812. When he died in 1839 Wellington remarked: 'Trant, poor fellow! A very good officer, but as drunken a dog as ever lived.'

To this Trant, then, on 13 August, 1808, he wrote: I have written to General Freire upon the subject of his supplies, upon which I have nothing further to say. As to his plan of operations, I do not see what purpose it is to answer . . . and I can certainly never give my sanction to

14

Abrantes

anything which appears so useless, and so crudely digested, so far as even to promise to communicate with or aid the person who is carrying it into execution.

I have one proposition to make to General Freire, that is, that he should send me his cavalry and his light infantry . . . to be employed as I choose, and I engage to give these men their bread; and for meat, wine, and forage, they shall fare as well as our troops.

The events of the next three days are described in his official dispatch to the Secretary of State, dated Caldas, 16 August, and his private letter of the same day. Throughout the next six years this was his almost unvaried custom – a pair of letters at weekly or fortnightly intervals if nothing of importance intervened: the first is formal, matter of fact, almost without emotion, quite often obscures facts, especially the blunders of his generals, and almost never makes comments. These were made public and were often printed in the English newspapers. The second is almost always shorter, franker, and passes judgements – each succeeding Secretary of State was a more or less close personal friend, and Castlereagh more so than later ones.

On this occasion he spends the first three pages detailing what has happened between him and Freire; then he comments again on the supply situation, which was not as bad as he had thought. In fact he had made an uncharacteristic mistake about the country he was in. There was little flour round Mondego in August because the rivers were low and the water-mills were not working. It had all been moved further south to the hills where those tiny windmills were turning briskly in the Atlantic breeze.

Having found the resources of the country more ample than I expected, I should certainly have undertaken to feed his army according to his desire; as I consider it of importance, on political rather than on military grounds, that the Portuguese troops should accompany our march; only that I have found the British Commissariat to be so ill composed as to be incapable of distributing even to the British troops the ample supplies that have been procured for them . . .

And so at last to the first shots of the campaign.

I marched from Leiria on the 13th . . . and I arrived here yesterday. The enemy, about 4,000 in number, were posted about ten miles from hence at Roliça; and they occupied Obidos, about three miles from hence, with their advanced posts. As the possession of this last village was important to our future operations, I determined to occupy it . . . I directed that it might be occupied . . . by four companies of riflemen of the 60th and 95th regiments.

Obidos is a tiny village, with sketchy Moorish fortifications and a windmill or two perched on a crest that interrupts a wide broken valley of fields, lime-stone

16

outcrops, orchards and terraces. To the south the valley widens and in the centre is the large village of Roliça in front of which Delaborde had posted his 6,000 men – more than Sir Arthur had reckoned on. Officially, in public as it were, he consistently underestimated the forces opposing him. Obidos was clearly important as a post from which to observe the whole valley.

Four hundred men, those of the 95th in dark green jackets braided in black, with black caps, moved in open order up the steadily steepening slopes towards Obidos, clambering up terraces, pushing under ripening apples, snared with melon vines. They were armed with the Baker rifle, a formidable weapon, being accurate at 300 yards and more. Little surprise that the handful of French at the top withdrew as the first shots were fired.

Since this weapon is to play such an important role, it's worth considering its history. In 1800 the Board of Ordnance, learning belatedly from the lessons of the American War of Independence, convened and tested forty rifles and chose this one. Designed by one Ezekiel Baker it weighed nine and a half pounds, had a two-and-a-half-foot barrel, twenty bore (i.e. twenty balls weighed one pound) with seven grooves each giving a quarter turn. Its main disadvantage was that, being rifled, it took longer to load than the conventional Tower Musket or Brown Bess. However, they complemented each other perfectly. The rifle companies skirmished ahead of the infantry, firing at will from a substantial distance, with accuracy, and using whatever cover was available. As the distance between the masses of infantry closed they fell back through the infantry lines and handed over to the smooth bore but fast loading gun of the line which could maintain a continuous fire through the rolling volley – see below at Vimeiro, page 22.

One may note that not the least mistake made by that over-rated military intelligence, Napoleon Buonaparte, was to withdraw rifles from the French Republican army. His tirrailleurs who also skirmished, like our riflemen, ahead of his columns used smooth bore weapons. They were therefore always outgunned by the British rifles and their effectiveness, which had been so great at Austerlitz, Wagram, and Jena, was reduced virtually to nil in the Peninsula.

The enemy, consisting of a small piquet of infantry and a few cavalry, made a trifling resistance and retired; but they were followed by a detachment of our riflemen to the distance of three miles from Obidos.

One can imagine: first blood and they run – after the anxiety of the first few hundred yards up those terraces, the sudden surge of fear as the first shots rattled round the crags, then the sight of their backs, and some cantering off on horses too, must have been exhilarating. No doubt whooping and hallooing and even jeering the Green Jackets galumphed after them down the southern slope, less steep than the north, for all of three miles . . .

The riflemen were there attacked by a superior body of the enemy, who attempted to cut them off from the main body of the detachment to which they belonged, which had now advanced to their support; larger bodies of the enemy appeared on both flanks of the detachments; and it was with difficulty that Major General Spencer, who had gone out to Obidos when he heard that the riflemen had advanced in pursuit of the enemy, was enabled to effect their retreat to that village . . .

The judgement was passed in the second, private letter.

The affair of the advanced posts of yesterday evening was unpleasant, because it was quite useless; and was occasioned, contrary to orders, solely by the imprudence of the officer, and the dash and eagerness of the men: they behaved remarkably well, and did some execution with their rifles.

Overall he was now well pleased with the way things were turning out.

We are going on as well as possible; the army in high order and in great spirits. We make long marches to which they are becoming accustomed . . . I have every hope of success.

To the Duke of Richmond he added: I am perfectly well. The troops very healthy, notwithstanding that they are in the sun all day and in the dew all night, for they have no tents . . . *Left behind at Mondego Bay? No, at this time an army marching was expected to do without tents which were large, heavy, and needed valuable draught animals. The army normally bivouacked – that is they cut down branches to make small, very temporary huts and wrapped themselves up in their blankets and great coats. It was not satisfactory. For years Wellington fought the Horse Guards on the subject before he got the small, lighter tents he wanted in 1813.*

The next day, the seventeenth, saw the first major engagement, not of the Peninsular War, there had been several score between the French and Spanish, but of Wellington's War.

On the night before the situation was as follows. The allied army, some 15,000 strong was at the northern end of the Roliça valley, based round Obidos. The valley is a horseshoe, surrounded by higher hills to the south, east, and west, but the floor of it is broken country: towers of limestone rock rise up out of the undulating fields and orchards, it is laced with rivulets and shallow ravines. Near the southern end lies the village of Roliça, and in front of it, using the advantages of the broken terracing, Delaborde had placed what had now become, according to Wellington's revised estimate, 6,000 men. Beyond the village the hills rise quickly to steep escarpments, pierced by four gullies choked with boulders which Sir Arthur later referred to as 'passes'. Beyond this ridge the hills slope down again towards the south, but still rocky and broken, and the

18

only easy way out is by a steadily narrowing ravine to the south of the hamlet of Zambugeira.

A final complication was that Loison's 5,000 marauders were now known to be only a day's march away at Rio Mayor to the east. Nevertheless, Sir Arthur resolved not only to push Delaborde out, but if possible to surround and annihilate him.

The plan of attack was formed accordingly, and the army, having broken up from Caldas this morning *17 August* was formed into three columns. The right, consisting of 1200 Portuguese infantry, 50 Portuguese cavalry, destined to turn the enemy's left, and penetrate into the mountains in his rear. *These were commanded by Trant, and were operating on the Atlantic and therefore safer side of the position.* The left, consisting of . . . Ferguson's and . . . Fane's brigade of infantry, three companies of riflemen, a brigade of light artillery, and twenty British and twenty Portuguese cavalry, was destined to ascend the hills at Obidos, to turn all the enemy's posts on the left of the valley . . . This corps was also destined to watch the motions of General Loison on the enemy's right who had moved from Rio Mayor towards Alcocentre last night. *This was in fact a withdrawal towards Lisbon – Loison had become less of a threat than he had been. The centre column consisting of 9,000 men with a brigade of nine pounders and a brigade of six pounders was destined under Sir Arthur's personal command to attack General Laborde's position in the front.*

. . . Nightingall and Craufurd moved with the artillery along the high road, until at length the former formed in the plain immediately in the enemy's front, supported by the light infantry companies, and the 45th regiment of . . . Craufurd's brigade; while the 50th and 91st . . . were kept up as a reserve in the area.

The centre column in fact halted two miles short of the French and opened out into battle line with parade ground precision in spite of the broken countryside. One French officer wrote later that the display was magnificent. The lines, two deep now, moved forward with the riflemen in open order in the front and on the flanks. Next the artillery unlimbered and opened fire at an ineffectually long range. Through their glasses the French would see the horses (which they would not have admired) led off to the rear of the guns, the business of the gunners, the flash of a sword and the puff of white smoke. A second later the pop of the report, and just behind it, and if you were stationed in its line of flight you could actually mark its progress, the plop of a nine-pound ball in the fields below them or a shower of stones if it hit a dry stone dyke. The fact is it was a display, and intended as such, to hold Delaborde's attention until the pincer movements had encircled him.

. . . at the same moment . . . Fane's riflemen were in the hills on his right, and . . . Ferguson's column was descending from the heights into the plain. *But Delaborde was no slouch. And anyway he had his cavalry out in the hills trying to make contact with Loison – instead they fed back reports that he was menaced, not reinforced on his right.* From this situation the enemy retired by the passes into the mountains *the high ridge to the south of Roliça* with the utmost regularity and the greatest celerity; and notwithstanding the rapid advance of the British infantry, the want of a sufficient body of cavalry was the cause of his suffering but little loss on the plain.

It was then necessary to make a disposition to attack the formidable position which he had taken up.

Very formidable. Delaborde had chosen an escarpment about a thousand yards long with a dry stone wall running along most of its length. In his front he deployed the famed sharpshooters who had ample cover on the rock-strewn slopes, and his immediate flanks were protected by the gullies where the slopes were even steeper.

. . . Fane's riflemen were already in the mountains on his right . . . The Portuguese infantry were ordered to move up a pass on the *(allied)* right of the whole . . .

The Portuguese never really made contact, because what happened next was in fact a blunder – carefully concealed in Sir Arthur's dispatch. Moving up one of the gullies the 1st 29th, commanded by Lieutenant-Colonel Lake, got too far ahead of the rest of the line, came under murderous fire, attempted to form a line – this was gallant, most foreign troops would by now have broken and fled – and was almost annihilated. Hill brought forward the 9th in support, but it was not enough. Sir Arthur now realised that a general engagement was inevitable and that it would have to be started before his second flanking movement was complete. He ordered a general advance.

These passes were all difficult of access and some of them were well defended by the enemy, particularly that which was attacked by the 29th and 9th regiments. These attacked with the utmost impetuosity, and reached the enemy before those whose attacks were to be made on the flanks.

The defence of the enemy was desperate; and it was in this attack principally that we sustained the loss which we have to lament, particularly of that gallant officer, the Hon. Lieut. Colonel Lake, who distinguished himself upon this occasion. The enemy was, however, driven from all the positions he had taken in the passes of the mountains and our troops were advanced in the plains on their tops. *That is, they had a precarious foothold on the flat ground at the top of the escarpment.* For a considerable length of time the 29th and 9th regiments alone were advanced to this point, and they were afterward supported by the 5th regiment, and by the light companies of Hill's brigade, which had come upon their right, and by the other troops ordered to ascend the mountains, who came up by degrees.

The enemy here made three most gallant attacks upon the 29th and 9th regiments . . . with a view to cover the retreat of his defeated army, in all of which he was, however repulsed; but he succeeded in effecting his retreat in good order, owing principally to my want of cavalry . . . *Sir Arthur pressed this point whenever he could. In fact at this stage it is unlikely that cavalry against well-disciplined troops would have done much. However, as the French entered the narrowing ravine, they came at last in contact with the allies on their flanks. They broke, and ran, 'good order' forgotten. It was now that if they had been pursued by cavalry they would have suffered much heavier losses than they did. Nevertheless* . . . The loss of the enemy has been very great, and he left three pieces of cannon in our hands . . .

The enemy's positions were formidable, and he took them up with his usual ability and celerity, and defended them most gallantly. But I must observe, that although we had such a superiority of numbers . . . the troops actually engaged in the heat of the action were, from unavoidable circumstances (*Lake's impetuosity, my emphasis*) only the fifth, 9th, 29th, the riflemen of the 95th and 60th, and the flank companies of Hill's brigade; being a number by no means equal to that of the enemy. Their conduct therefore deserves the highest commendation.

To Captain Malcolm, who commanded the flotilla that protected his right and ensured his supplies, and could even take him off if necessary: I fought an action yesterday . . . The French received a terrible beating; I am informed they lost 1500 men. Our loss is 489 killed, wounded and missing, officers included; of that number about 70 are killed. *His figures after battles are meticulous – the Horse Guards required that they should be so. The losses of the French throughout the war are still a matter of dispute. French generals feared their superiors who feared Buonaparte and almost always minimised their losses.*

That day he also wrote the first of many letters of condolence to relatives of killed officers. These were always generous, and, however formal the language, communicate sincerity. To Lake's brother-in-law: I do not recollect the occasion upon which I have written with more pain to myself than I do at present, to communicate to you the death of your gallant brother-in-law. He fell in the attack of a pass in the mountains, at the head of his regiment, the admiration of the whole army, and there is nothing to be regretted in his death . . . he deserved and enjoyed the respect and affection of the world at large . . . he was respected and loved by the whole army . . . he fell, alas! with many other, in the achievement of one of the most heroic actions that have been performed by the British army.

THE BATTLE

Meanwhile, what of General Androche Junot, Duc d'Abrantes, Buonaparte's Governor of Portugal? Although two years younger than Sir Arthur and in his youth undoubtedly a dashing officer with great personal loyalty to his master, he had become, since receiving a wound in the head, unreliable, capricious, and a voluptuary. He was reluctant to leave Lisbon where he lived like an oriental satrap. If he had acted with the speed and élan that characterised most French generals when the boss was nearby he could possibly have concentrated sufficient numbers near Mondego before all of Spencer's men were landed, but he feared that if he left the capital it would rise behind him. As General Foy (then a colonel) commented later: 'Portugal was Lisbon, and Lisbon was all that was worth having in Portugal.'

On 15 August he did at last move to go to the aid of Delaborde, but leaving a much larger force behind him. Nevertheless, he took with him his military chest of a million francs, much of his loot, and most of the food in his possession. Of course, he moved slowly. On 17 August he heard the guns of Roliça. He fell back on Torres Vedras where he was joined by Loison from the east a day later and where Delaborde finally completed their concentration on 19 August.

Sir Arthur pushed south, but keeping always to the indirect coastal roads, not wanting to lose contact with the sea and the reinforcements he daily expected. Where to land them? Peniche was the obvious place, but was held by a small garrison in a well-constructed fort. A delaying siege operation would be necessary to make the harbour safe. There was a beach twelve miles south at the mouth of the Maceira river which looked viable, at any rate no worse than Mondego. Behind it was a system of steep hills which would provide sound defensive positions to cover the landings.

There is a small village amongst these hills called Vimeiro and there he made his headquarters on the 19 August. The Maceira, which is little more than a rivulet at this time of year, meanders up from the south, leaves a low hill and then the village to its right, is joined by an even smaller brook, enters a short but precipitous gorge between two steep ridges, and then turns sharply left for the

22

last mile and a half to the sea. At this point there is a natural spring where Vimeiro water, a very pleasant drink on a hot day, is now bottled. The river widens into a shallow creek between two headlands. Round the southern one is a long crescent of sandy beach with dunes behind, and then the steep hills or ridges. These are and were cultivated on the southern slopes with vines, Indian corn, with bamboo wind shields facing the sea. The northern slopes which are almost precipitous are covered with holly-leaved myrtle, small gorse, and a thyme-like shrub. Down in the dunes, until the end of August, one of the rarer migratory shore birds, the swallow-like, daintily-marked pratincole, runs slickly over the sand or swoops above the long coarse grass. On an early morning when the tide is going out and the sand is still wet you can dig up quite large clams. Back in the hills buzzards and red kites soar, and Vimeiro itself is haunted with house-martens and swifts.

Wellington pitched his camps, or the men built their bivouacs, on the long western ridge covering the beach, and on the lower hill south of Vimeiro.

From there, on the twentieth, he wrote to Castlereagh: Anstruther is on shore *with 2,703 men, but suffered losses in the heavy surf* and I expect him in camp every moment . . . The enemy have their advanced guard in front of Torres Vedras, and the main body of their army collected in the rear of that town. I understand that they have gotten (sic) together everything that Portugal can afford. *To Captain Bligh, not the Mutiny one, on H.M.S. Alfred:* I have just been down at Maceira, where I hope that you will land the bread, ammunition, &c., and the saddles . . . If General Acland should join you, keep him with you, and desire him to let me know it immediately. *Most of Acland's brigade were gotten ashore in the dusk that day and this increased the allied numbers by a further 1,332. They slept on the beach, as I have, it's really rather a good spot to camp.*

Not so another and less welcome figure – Lieutenant-General Sir Harry Burrard, up from Gibraltar. He was now nominal Commander-in-Chief, but he chose to remain on shipboard. There Sir Arthur paid his respects and pressed the case for a further push next day to Mafra. Sir Harry did not like the idea at all. He wanted to wait until Sir John Moore's corps arrived – it was due in a day or so – and after insisting that the army stayed put, retired to bed, or hammock, or whatever.

Sir Arthur was furious. His letter penned to Castlereagh at six o'clock on the morning of 21 August, clearly shows it.

My Dear Lord,

Sir Harry Burrard will probably acquaint your Lordship with the reasons which have induced him to call Sir John Moore's corps to the assistance of our army, which consists of 20,000 men, including the

Portuguese army . . . and is opposed, I am convinced, by not more than 12,000 or 14,000 Frenchmen, and to halt here until Sir John's corps shall join. You, will readily believe, however, that this determination is not in conformity with my opinion, and I only wish Sir Harry had landed and seen things with his own eyes before he had made it.

This was written under particularly galling circumstances. The French cavalry had been feeling round the British positions all through the day before; at midnight the rumble of Junot's guns on the wooden bridge at Villa Facaia could be heard; Sir Arthur expected a dawn attack and had every one under arms an hour before dawn – and several hours before the leisurely Sir Harry need be expected ashore. But dawn came and no sign of the French. It was then Sir Arthur wrote this frustrated letter.

Two hours later his heart must have lifted when he was called to the east of his position and saw large bodies of cavalry on our left, upon the heights on the road to Lourinha; and it was soon obvious that the attack would be made upon our advanced guard and the left of our position. *Yet it was not easy to be sure just where the French were and in what strength – the ground is broken and hilly with trees and scattered orchards – only the dust and noise indicated where each column was threading its way through tracks and lanes towards the British positions.*

But as soon as he was sure of what the French were up to – an attempt to turn or roll up his left flank – Sir Arthur calmly redistributed his forces, moving the greater weight of them from the western ridge, where most had bivouacked and which covered the beaches, across the gorge of the Maceira and on to the eastern ridge. He also reinforced the height that lies to the south of the village, leaving Hill on the eastern end of the west ridge as reserve from where he could reinforce either of the other positions. By this swift but precise redistribution Sir Arthur quite brilliantly turned what might have been a catastrophic tactical disadvantage into quite the opposite. Moreover, by keeping the major part of his men on the reverse slope of each crest he concealed his movements from the French.

The enemy's attack began in several columns upon the whole of the troops on this height *the hill to the south of the village;* on the left they advanced, notwithstanding the fire of the riflemen *who were deployed in skirmishing order in front of the main line* close to the 50th regiment and they were checked and driven back only by the bayonets of that corps.

This conceals rather than reveals what happened – which was to be typical of the whole war and the major reason, apart from Wellington's ability as a general, for the repeated defeats of the French, even when attacking with vastly superior numbers. It is therefore worth analysing what happened. The French came in two columns – each of thirty men across and forty-two ranks deep. The

24

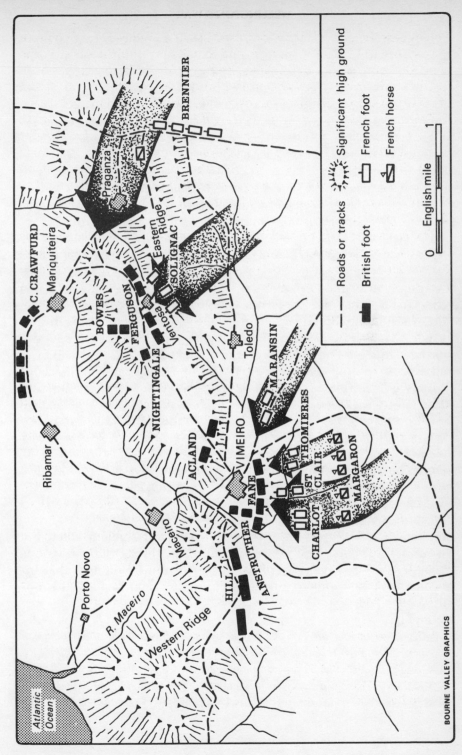

Legend:
- Roads or tracks
- Significant high ground
- British foot
- French foot
- French horse

0 — English mile — 1

Atlantic Ocean

Porto Novo
Ribamar
R. Maceiro
Maceiro
Western Ridge
HILL
ANSTRUTHER
FANE
VIMEIRO
ACLAND
NIGHTINGALE
Ventosa
FERGUSON
BOWES
Mariquiteira
C. CRAWFURD
Praganza
Eastern Ridge
SOLIGNAC
BRENNIER
Toledo
MARANSIN
ST THOMIERES
CLAIR
MARGARON
CHARLOT

2. The Battle of Vimeiro, 21 August 1808

BOURNE VALLEY GRAPHICS

allies were deployed in a two deep line. They fired their first volley at 100 yards and from then on a volley came every fifteen seconds. The British line was using every one of its 900 muskets, the French less than 200 of their 1,200. As the advance slowed, the ends of the British line wheeled in a deadly pincer, still firing every fifteen seconds, but now into the flanks of the French as well as the front of the column. General Thomières attempted to deploy his columns into lines, but the confusion in the French ranks only increased. The bayonet charge was thus the coup de grâce to what had been achieved by superiority of formation and musketry.

It seems a simple enough business, but what must be remembered, always, is that it depended entirely on the individual steadfastness, even heroism, of each separate British soldier. It must, at least to begin with, have required incredible grit to stand only two deep in the face of such coordinated machine-like masses, drums beating, tricoleurs billowing, knowing that every other European army had broken in front of them.

The second batt. 43rd regiment was likewise closely engaged with them in the road which leads into Vimeiro; a part of that corps had been ordered into the churchyard, to prevent them from penetrating into the town. On the right of the position they were repulsed by the bayonets of the 97th regiment . . . supported by the 2nd batt. 52nd which by an advance in column took the enemy in flank. *The fighting in the streets was vicious – the British were here yet more heavily outnumbered and lacked the advantage of formation, but the French still broke, perhaps fearful that the attack on their flank would cut them off. But another feature of the whole war was also demonstrated here for the first time, the devastating rolling volley here used by the 97th. Still in two-deep line they fired by turn in half companies, fifty muskets at once. As the volley passed down the line muskets were reloaded above it and thus a completely continuous fire was maintained.*

At length, after a most desperate contest, the enemy was driven back in confusion . . . with the loss of seven pieces of cannon, many prisoners and a great number of officers and soldiers killed and wounded. He was pursued by a detachment of the 20th light dragoons, but the enemy's cavalry were so much superior in number, that this detachment has suffered much, and Lieut. Colonel Taylor was unfortunately killed.

And this too proved to be characteristic – the uncontrollability of the British cavalry in pursuit: again and again over the years they could not be called back once they had been released; they could not reform and withdraw. Inevitably they ended up with blown horses amongst the enemy's reserves.

It was now eleven o'clock and Sir Harry appeared, no doubt splashed and shaken by his boat-ride through the surf, and thoroughly bemused by what must

26

have seemed appalling noise, confusion, and horror around him. Magnanimously perhaps, but certainly with good sense, he allowed Sir Arthur to continue what had been so well begun, and placed himself with Hill's reserve on the inland end of the western ridge, where he would have had as good a view of what was still to happen as the broken nature of the ground allowed.

Nearly at the same time the enemy's attack commenced upon the heights on the road to Lourinha *the eastern ridge*: this attack was supported by a large body of cavalry and was made with the usual impetuosity of French troops. It was received with steadiness by Major General Ferguson's brigade *which had been posted in three lines by Sir Arthur himself, with the light companies in open order on the military crest and the main line behind on higher ground, but concealed by the lower ridge, and – another feature to be used again and again, and most notably of all at Waterloo – lying down.* These corps charged as soon as the enemy approached them, who gave way, and they continued to advance upon him . . . *Again 'charge' is not really what happened. The lines, 3,000 strong, strode down the hill, again maintaining the continuous fire of rolling volleys by seventy-two half companies.* In the advance six pieces of cannon were taken from the enemy, with many prisoners, and vast numbers were killed and wounded.

The enemy afterwards made an attempt to recover part of his artillery, by attacking the 71st and 82nd regiments, which were halted in a valley in which it had been taken. These regiments retired from the low grounds in the valley to the heights, where they halted, faced about, and fired, and advanced upon the enemy, who had by that time arrived in the low ground, and they thus obliged him again to retire with great loss.

Again this is a bald and even misleading statement. The very last of Junot's columns, led by General Brennier, had taken a circuitous route round the north-east corner of the British position which brought them into the battle later than the rest. They came over the crest of a hill and saw the British below them – apparently at their mercy. But while they came down one side of the valley the British managed to withdraw up the other in tolerably good order although taken in the flank. Meanwhile the 29th, who had been held in reserve, took a wide sweep round behind the re-forming British line and took Brennier's force on his right. Again a horseshoe of muskets poured lead into French columns. They broke, fled, or surrendered.

It is odd that this action of the 29th is not mentioned in Sir Arthur's dispatch – odd, but possibly explained by the fact that he was on the spot and led them himself. Not only were the original French guns recaptured, but Brennier's were taken as well, and Brennier too.

Everywhere now, the French ran. Six more or less simultaneous assaults had been turned into massive defeat.

In this action, in which the whole of the French force in Portugal was employed, under the command of the Duc d'Abrantes in person, in which the enemy was certainly superior in cavalry and artillery, and in which not more than half of the British army was actually engaged, he has sustained a signal defeat, and has lost thirteen pieces of cannon, twenty-three ammunition waggons, with powder, shells, stores of all descriptions, and 20,000 rounds of musket ammunition. One General Officer has been wounded and taken prisoner, and a great many officers and soldiers have been killed, wounded and taken.

And that was it, though of course it should not have been. Sir Arthur drove his tired horse up the western height to where Sir Harry was no doubt chewing his finger nails. 'Sir Harry, now is your time to advance, the enemy is completely beaten, and we shall be in Lisbon in three days.' *But Sir Harry said the army had done enough for one day – he'd wait for Moore, Junot might have a reserve, his cavalry was too dangerous to be meddled with, three miles separated the British left from its right, things might get out of control. Sir Arthur countered: Hill's brigade were fresh, the French could be cut off from their line of retreat, Ferguson had 1,500 of them in a corner of the hills they could not escape from, every British soldier had a day's cooked food in his haversack . . . But Sir Harry was obdurate. With the French in full retreat he ordered the British back to camp. They returned with colours flying and bands playing, dragging the captured French guns in their midst, and all utterly puzzled at the tame and inconsequent end to such a day.*

THE AFTERMATH

To H.R.H. the Duke of York, Vimeiro, 22 August: I cannot say too much in favour of the troops: their gallantry and discipline were equally conspicuous . . . this is the only action I have been in in which everything passed as it was directed *(including the pursuit of the 20th light dragoons?)* . . . I think if General Hill's brigade . . . had moved upon Torres Vedras . . . the enemy would have been cut off . . . and we should have been at Lisbon before him. But Sir Harry Burrard . . . thought it advisable not to move . . . and the enemy made good their retreat.

Sir Hew Dalrymple arrived this morning and has taken command of the army.

To Viscount Castlereagh: . . . I believe he will march to-morrow. Indeed, if he does not, we shall be poisoned here by the stench of the dead and wounded *(my emphasis)*; or we shall starve, everything in the neighbourhood being already eaten up. *No-one noticed the pratincoles now – only the kites feeding on corpses.*

But no march was necessary. For on that same day a party of French galloped into the British camp (a sudden flurry – was this a surprise attack?) led by General Kellerman, a horrendously ugly personage, but gifted with serpentine cunning. They brought with them terms for an armistice whereby the French would give up Portugal, but only if they were evacuated in British ships and put down on French soil, with arms, baggage, cannon and loot.

To Castlereagh, 23 August: Although my name is affixed to this instrument I beg that you will not believe that I negotiated it, that I approve of it, or that I had any hand in wording it . . . Sir Hew Dalrymple desired me to sign it . . . I object to its verbiage . . . *which entirely sums up what was to be his consistent stance on the vexed issue of what was later redrafted as the Convention of Cintra. There was public outcry in England – the clauses that stipulated that British ships should repatriate the French, and that the French returned under arms and with no commitment not to fight again, being the main objections – which led to a public enquiry the following winter. Throughout, Sir Arthur's criticism of his superiors remained confined to their failure to follow up the victory with a vigorous pursuit, and the wording of the Convention, which he knew very well would stir up the opposition at home. As to the actual terms he approved of* allowing the French to withdraw from Portugal. *Having lost the chance of annihilating them it was the very best that could be hoped for.*

To his brother William he wrote: The General has no plan, or even an idea of a plan, nor do I believe he knows the meaning of the word plan. These people are really more stupid and incapable than any I have ever met with; and if things go on in this disgraceful manner I must quit them.

It was, indeed, time to be off. At the end of the previously quoted letter to Castlereagh of 21 August comes this appreciation of his position. I will not conceal from you, however, my dear Lord, that my situation in this army is a very delicate one. I never saw Sir Hew Dalrymple till yesterday; and it is not a very easy task to advise a man on the first day one meets with him. He must at least be prepared to receive advice. Then I have been successful with the army, and they don't appear to me to like to go to anybody else for orders or instructions upon any subject. This is another awkward circumstance which cannot end well; and to tell you the truth I should prefer going home to staying here . . .

It appears that General Spencer and Sir Hew did not agree very well when they were at Gibraltar together; and poor Spencer is very low indeed. I wish you could confer upon him some mark of the King's favour. There was never a braver officer, or one who deserves it better.

Nothing could have been more generous, since it was Spencer's over-estimate of the French in Portugal that had brought all these 'chiefs' down around them both.

And to Richmond, the final words: I am not very well pleased, between ourselves, with the way in which things in this country are likely to go on, and I shall not be sorry to go home, if I can do so with propriety . . . But I don't like to desire to go, lest it should be imputed to me that I am unwilling to serve where I don't command.

A P.S. *comments:* Lord Fitzroy has been very useful to me . . . *which is worth mentioning since this was the twenty-year-old Lord Fitzroy Somerset. He remained on Wellington's staff throughout the war, became his military secretary, was wounded twice and lost an arm at Waterloo. He later married Wellington's niece. As Lord Raglan he died of dysentery and despair in the Crimea.*

On 1 September, also to Richmond, he wrote: I shall wait till I see the French fairly off . . .

On the ninth: I am sick of all that is going on here, and I heartily wish I had never come away from Ireland.

OUR HERO

In the Autumn of 1808, at the age of 39, Sir Arthur suffered from that particular arrogance that arises in those of us who know we are very superior in every respect, who know that most of the world has yet to recognise this, but that there is a close circle of acquaintance that does have some inkling of our greatness, both innate and achieved. If this sounds ironic – well then, the irony is defused by the facts.

Even on the physical level Arthur Wellesley was very fit indeed: he could ride seventy-five miles in less than a day over open country; get his horses up and down slopes, over obstacles and through country that make the most savage of modern three day events look like pre-teen gymkhanas.

As a politician, or at any rate a holder of posts politically appointed, he had proved himself a sensitive, intelligent, and above all uncorrupt administrator, who put the interests of the ruled above those of party – and this in Ireland at that. As a general he had already done better than any in Britain since the Duke of Marlborough.

All this was evident, on record. What was not was that he had a mind whose grasp, spread, capacity equalled the best of his age, of any age – a mind that could attend to the minutest, most transitory detail at the same time that it organised all the facts available to it into a model (to use the current jargon) that fitted the global reality of things as they were, in a way that worked.

That this 'model' was inevitably coloured, was indeed deeply conditioned by the ideology of his class, in no way vitiates it: his was the dominant class, though a threatened one, and its world view was the one that most nearly fitted reality, especially when it expressed itself in a mind like Sir Arthur's – whose appreciation of the importance of the economic base on which the hegemony of his class depended was entirely clear: private property, particularly as land – with the surplus income from land accumulated as capital invested in trade and manufacturing, which in turn generated a need for empire, was far nearer the truth than the vapourings of, say, a Burke. It was a mind which saw with unerring clarity both how this hegemony needed a monarchy and was threatened by any form of republicanism, yet knew equally clearly that, if it was to be maintained, power-sharing, compromise with the bourgeoisie was essential. It eventually acknowledged, what few of his class could encompass, that limited parliamentary reform was inevitable though unfortunate; that the refusal for ever of catholic emancipation was a position that could not and should not be maintained.

Finally he had exorcised two demons. The first one, both endemic and epidemic in his class as it was also in the lowest orders, was alcoholism. From six bottles of claret a day he had cut down to one, with a glass or two of brandy in the evening. The other, perhaps more sadly, was artistic creativity. His father had indeed been the Earl of Mornington (though rather fortuitously – his grandfather was born Richard Colley, was adopted by his matrimonial uncle, and became Richard Wesley, first baron) but he had also been professor of music at Trinity College, Dublin. His third surviving son was and always remained a very keen amateur of music, and showed very early a talent far in advance of his father's. But in 1793, at the age of twenty-four, Arthur burnt his fiddle and addressed himself to the career that had been chosen for him.

After Vimeiro he knew he was the best, with only one possible rival on the scene – the charismatic Sir John Moore, who was now in Lisbon with his 10,000 men. Sir John's military record did not include major engagements like Vimeiro or Assaye, but it was a good one. Moreover, he was tremendously popular with the army in general, and with the light regiments in particular. These he had trained on entirely new lines, encouraging initiative and skill rather than automaton-like, rum-inspired stolidity. He had also attempted to humanise the horribly brutal disciplinary system. His disadvantage was that he was a whig – had sat on the opposition benches in the House of Commons – and was therefore deeply distrusted by both government and Horse Guards. Dalrymple and Burrard had been sent out specifically to deny him the command, and because of this he remained Achilles-like, reluctant to assume their place.

But now there was no question that the 'chiefs' could remain: public clamour against the Convention demanded their presence in London, and Sir Arthur's too. What he did now was typical in both its generosity and its sound appreciation of the needs of the situation.

He wrote to Sir John on 17 September: My Dear General . . . It appears to me to be quite impossible that we can go on as we are now constituted; the Commander-in-Chief must be changed, and the country and the army naturally turn their eyes to you as their commander . . . *He goes on frankly to suggest that Sir John might decline on the grounds that he had not the complete confidence of the government: Sir Arthur begs to talk to him to remove any trace of this effect; he pleads that he is not a party man, but a friend of those in power . . .* and I think I have sufficient influence over them, that they may listen to me upon a point of this description, more particularly as I am convinced that they must be as desirous as I can be to adopt the arrangement for the command of this army which all are agreed is the best.

In these times, my dear General, a man like you should not preclude himself from rendering the services of which he is capable by any idle point of form . . .

Next day he rode over to Queluz where Moore was stationed, and reiterated: 'And you are the man – and I shall with great willingness act under you.'

Thus with a touch not unreminiscent of a Ulysses urging an Achilles back to the field, he scotched several snakes with one stick: no-one could now say that he did not wish to serve where he could not command; he had ensured that, at least until the storm over the Convention had blown over, the army was led by much the best of the senior generals available; and that that general could act with a confidence in the support of his masters that he had hitherto lacked. And of course he had left the door open for his return to the scene of action if the findings of the inquiry exonerated him.

Which of course they did. Although he feared to be hanged, drawn and quartered, or roasted alive . . . *or shot like Byng, and although the Board of Inquiry dragged on to 18 January, the result was a rap over the knuckles for Dalrymple for the terms of the Convention and acceptance that the failure to pursue after Vimeiro was no fault of Sir Arthur's. The seal of public approval was set on 27 January, 1809, when* <u>nem con</u>, *the House of Commons passed a vote of thanks to the Victor of Roliça and Vimeiro. The recipient made his point in his answer with a sincerity I do not detect in the rhetoric of his latterday successors:* No man can value more highly than I do the honourable distinction which has been conferred upon me – a distinction which it is in the power of the representatives of a free people alone to bestow.

1809

———◆◆◆———

OPORTO

HIATUS

TALAVERA

ON THE GUADIANA

———◆◆◆———

OPORTO

Two days before the Board reported, Sir John was killed at Coruña. A brief resumé of what happened will fill in the gap. Junot and his force were duly given a free passage to La Rochelle on British ships. The way ahead into Spain seemed open. Working, he thought, in conjunction with efficient Spanish armies Sir John led his troops into Castille, arriving at Salamanca on 13 November, where he stayed ten days. It was so cold that troops bivouacking in the open found their hair frozen to the earth. There followed a period of indecision made yet more indecisive by the fact that Buonaparte himself had appeared on the scene: 'Il faut que j'y suis!' First he reinstated his brother in the new royal palace at Madrid: 'Mon frère, vous serez mieux logé que moi!' Then he moved south, apparently to conquer Andalusia, so Sir John moved north and east to cut the great road from Bayonne at Burgos. Buonaparte back-tracked and with enormous determination got his soldiers over the Guadarramas in a blizzard, and reciprocated by cutting Sir John's communications with Portugal. Sir John could now only fall back on Coruña and evacuate – the forces against him were too huge, since in the midst of everything else Buonaparte or his marshals had contrived to defeat every Spanish army within several hundred miles.

Fortunately perhaps, Buonaparte felt he had done enough. He handed the army over to Soult and took himself back to the well-heated palaces of Paris. At Sahagun on 21 December and at Benevente a week later the British cavalry under its best commander, Lord Henry Paget, inflicted minor defeats on the French, but the retreat went on. Under appalling conditions discipline broke down, which did little for Moore's reputation as a humanitarian, but miraculously reappeared before Coruña. There they stood, and after a stubborn and inconclusive battle Soult withdrew, badly mauled. The British, allowed to board their transports virtually unmolested, claimed the victory. They had lost their leader.

In March Soult entered Portugal and occupied Oporto. The Portuguese Empire at this time was ruled by a Regent, Don John, whose mother, Queen Maria, was mad. Both resided throughout the war in Brazil, and Portugal was ruled by a Regency junta led, in 1809, by the Bishop of Oporto. This Regency again asked for support and even asked Sir Arthur himself to lead their army in their own employ. They accepted, at his suggestion, his friend Lieutenant-General William Beresford, the illegitimate son of the Marquess of Waterford. Mean-

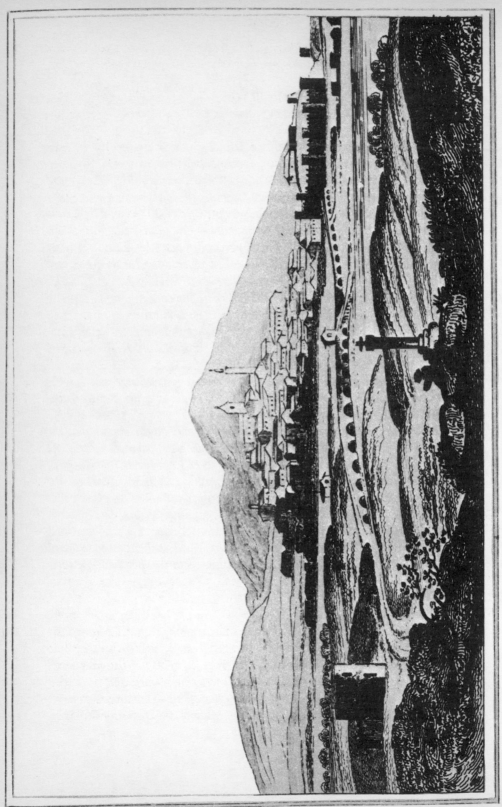

Merida

while it was clear that he would soon be chosen to return to take overall command of both British and Portuguese forces, but responsible only to the British Government.

Moore had said that Portugal could not be held once Spain was defeated. Sir Arthur, unwittingly subscribing to Foy's view that 'Portugal was Lisbon' knew better, and on 7 March wrote to Castlereagh: I have always been of the opinion that Portugal might be defended, whatever might be the result of the contest in Spain; and in the meantime the measures for the defence of Portugal would be highly useful to the Spaniards in their contest with the French . . . *He went on to argue the point in detail, showing how a force of 20,000 British troops, including about 4,000 cavalry which of course he had lacked in 1808 but whose usefulness had been fully proved by Moore, acting in conjunction with 40,000 Portuguese militia (locally raised defence volunteers) and 30,000 regulars would siphon off over 100,000 French from Spain.*

On 2 April he was given his orders:

> . . . to prepare and equip the British army for the field . . . to direct his utmost exertions to the bringing forward of the Portuguese army . . . to cooperate with Beresford. The defence of Portugal you will consider as the first and immediate object of your attention . . .

Sir Arthur was back in Lisbon on 22 April, 1809. Five long years lay ahead during which he left the Peninsula only to pursue the French into the South of France. I have found no record of any other person whose service in the Peninsula was unbroken throughout the whole war.

On the twenty-seventh his first public dispatch to Castlereagh outlined the situation and what he intended to do about it.

I have assumed command of the army. The whole of the British army are assembled at Leyria and Alcobaca, with the exception of the 2nd batt. 30th regiment, in garrison at Lisbon . . .

The corps of Marshal Soult is still in the north of Portugal, occupying the city of Oporto . . . The corps of General Lapisse . . . has marched along the frontiers of Portugal to Alcantara where it crossed the Tagus; and it is now joined with that under the command of Marshal Victor, at Merida, upon the Guadiana . . .

General Cuesta is at Llerena; and I understand that the Spanish government are taking measures to reinforce that General; and that he will move into Portugal, if Victor should take advantage of the absence of the British army engaged in operations to the northward of Portugal.

Under these circumstances, I have determined forthwith to move to the northward . . . As soon as the enemy shall have evacuated the north of Portugal, it is my intention to return to the Eastern frontier of the kingdom, and to co-operate with the Spanish General Cuesta, against the army of Marshal Victor.

By 1 May he was at Leiria, a day later at Coimbra. He wrote to Villiers, the British Minister in Lisbon, that the force he had left there under Major-General Mackenzie would be sufficient to cover the capital. . . . no corps will make any impression by the Tagus at this season of the year, if the Government will look well after the boats on that river . . . We mean to fortify all the fords on the river at and above Salvaterra.

All of which is prophetic in its way of what was about to happen in Oporto and of the defence of Lisbon eighteen months later in the Autumn of 1810. This particular letter ends with a most interesting sidelight on the composition of these letters and dispatches. He had asked Villiers to send back copies of previous letters and in reply Villiers had offered to lend him clerks. I am much obliged to you for your offer to procure me assistance to copy my dispatches; but I have plenty of that description. The fact is, that, excepting upon very important occasions, I write my dispatches without making a draft, and those which I sent out to you were so written before I set out in the morning, and I had not time to get them copied before they were sent . . . *They were almost always written in his own hand and 'off the top'.*

He stayed at Coimbra for nearly a week, collecting his forces; arranging for the landing of reinforcements at Mondego . . . the best mode we found to be to send into the river all the vessels whose draft of water would permit their passing the bar . . . for the rest we disembarked the horses from them with the boats of the country . . . ; *reviewing Beresford's Portuguese* . . . your troops made a bad figure this morning . . . and the officers worse than anything I have seen . . . ; *trying to cope with inevitable failures in the Commissariat and particularly the Regency's chronic failure to feed, let alone pay its own troops; and, more romantically, maintaining contact with a French dissident, a mole, a spy called Argenton* . . . Our friend came to Aveiro yesterday; and I saw him last night at a fire on the road between Fornos and Martede. *This last is a complicated story, but it hinged on whether or not Soult would declare himself King of Portugal – if he did, then, the mole said, the more republican of his officers would lead the army back to France* . . .

By 7 May he was buoyant. To Castlereagh: I think I shall soon settle this part of the country . . . and I shall then turn my attention entirely to Victor. I think it probable that Cuesta and I shall be more than a match for the French army on the Guadiana, and we shall force them to retreat. The tenor of my instructions will then become important; and unless they are altered I shall be obliged to halt at the moment I shall

3. North Portugal, May 1809

have removed from the Portuguese frontier the danger by which it is threatened . . . I wish the King's Ministers to consider this point, and to give me latitude to continue my operations in Spain . . .

On the eighth he moved. To Frere, the British Minister at Seville where the Spanish Junta then was: The troops under my command have commenced their operations against Marshal Soult, one column marched by Vizeu towards Lamego *this the Portuguese under Beresford aiming to cut off Soult's likeliest line of retreat*, and another, under my own command being on its march towards Oporto. This last will cross the Vouga, on which are the enemy's outposts, to-morrow morning.

He had been in Portugal sixteen days and during this time had formulated the strategy that was to be followed for the next six months, coped with a hundred tiny and stupid details, and planned the immediate campaign ahead of him. But also he had effected three major innovations which were to have a most significant, indeed crucial influence on the next five years. Firstly, he organised the infantry in divisions rather than brigades – this meant that up to 6,000 men, later sometimes more, were commanded by one man, and fed and maintained as one unit, instead of units of 2,000. Secondly, he placed Portuguese battalions in the British army at a ratio of about five to one, and vice-versa: and thus accelerated enormously both the effectiveness of the Portuguese, and the respect with which they were treated by the British. The Portuguese were also drilled and trained by British N.C.O.s and quite largely officered by British officers, especially above company level. Thirdly, he increased the proportion of skirmishing light infantry, usually armed with rifles, from one third of each brigade to one half.

On 10 May the first skirmishes took place and on the following day a more serious affair. In both cases the significant thing is that the French were manoeuvred out of strong defensive positions with little loss, and, more important, no delay (see map page 41). Sir Arthur reported both events to Villiers that day – the first at 6.00 a.m., the second at 6.00 p.m. He is concerned here to demonstrate to the Portuguese Regency, through Ambassador Villiers, the usefulness of the Portuguese troops. What he omits, though of course included in the London dispatch, was that Rowland Hill had landed at Aveiro, and was leading the division on the left.

I have just time to tell you that we drove in the enemy's cavalry, and other posts, north of the Vouga yesterday, and gained ground as far as Oliveira. We attempted to surprise the cavalry, which attempt failed, for causes into which it is not necessary to enter (*it was dark, the maps were bad, they got lost*). They tell me the Portuguese riflemen, the students I believe, behaved remarkably well . . .

And the second letter: . . . we have been still more successful this day.

We have completely beaten a corps of about 4000 infantry . . . Colonel Doyle's battalion of the 16th Portuguese regiment behaved remarkably well. Recollect that in talking about this subject, you do not forget to mention the name of the Colonel of the regiment, who was in the field I know, for I had given him a piece of my mind in the morning . . . *Apropos of getting lost – a piece of Sir Arthur's mind reduced even generals to tears on occasion.* I do not know whether they propose to give us another field day on this side of Oporto, but I should think not, as they did not shew their cavalry this day. If they should do so, I shall have my whole corps upon them . . .

My goodness – but isn't he glad to be back, and properly in command? A field day, indeed! And of course he was right – that night the French scuttled across the Douro and into Oporto, and blew up the bridge behind them.

The alegría, the élan of this opening to the campaign was brought to a brilliant conclusion the very next day.

Oporto, apart from a few suburbs, lies on the north bank of the Douro, some two miles or so from the open sea, at just that point where the river widens into a

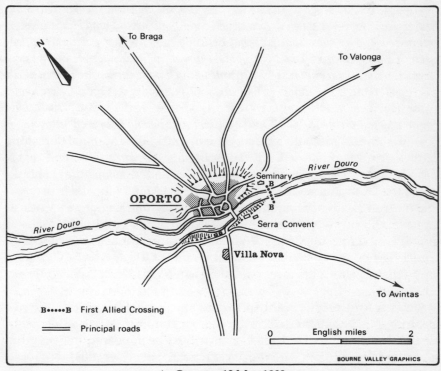

4. Oporto, 12 May 1809

deep water estuary after the ravines and gorges that have marked most of its serpentine journey through Spain, where it is the Duero, and Portugal. As the name suggests Oporto is a port of some consequence – then as now the centre of the trade in port wine.

The town is hilly, with cobbled streets, and much of it, especially near the old port and quays, is now as it was then. Tall, timbered tenement buildings rise above dark alleys which climb the hills where convents and palaces brood over the city below. Baskets of sardines scattered with salt are traded at every street corner, the dark people are handsome and poor – the children and women go bare foot and not by choice. Down by the river, in the shadow of the high modern bridge which spans the last cliffs of the gorge, small naked boys dive off the old quays into the brown water and old men drag in large grey mullet on improvised lines cast at the sewage outlets. On this quay is a bronze plaque which proudly represents in low relief what happened next – though possibly it exaggerates the part played by the populace.

Soult had 10,000 men in the town, most of them in the large buildings on the heights, and a division on the coast a few miles away. In the interior Loison operated on what was the French left. Soult was certain that the Douro could not be crossed. He had ordered all the boats to be moored on the north quays, and the bridge was down. What he feared was that Sir Arthur would land Hill's division on the coast above the estuary, or that Beresford and another Portuguese army under General Silveira would cut off his retreat into Spain. For retreat he knew he must – the allies could now concentrate a much larger army than his in north Portugal, though the numbers that actually faced him at Oporto were about equal, if you include the division on the coast. So, he began to make preparations for an evacuation on 13 May – his heavy baggage had already been sent off.

It was important, with a view to the operations of Marshal Beresford *because he had to out-rank all the Portuguese Generals, Beresford was a Marshal – and thereby hangs many a tale to be touched on later* that I should cross the Douro immediately; and I had sent Major General Murray in the morning with a battalion of the King's German Legion, a squadron of cavalry, and two 6 pounders, to endeavour to collect boats, and if possible, to cross the river at Avintas, about four miles above Oporto; and I had as many boats as could be collected brought to the ferry, immediately above the towns of Oporto and Villa Nova *the suburb on the south bank.*

The ground on the right *(north)* bank of the river at this ferry is protected and commanded by the fire of cannon, placed on the height of the Serra Convent at Villa Nova; and there appeared to be a good position for our troops on the opposite side of the river, till they should be collected in sufficient number.

44

The enemy took no notice of our collection of boats, or of the embarkation of the troops, till after the first battalion (The Buffs) were landed, and had taken up their position, under the command of Lieut. General Paget, on the opposite side of the river. *This was Edward Paget, not the Paget who had been with Moore.*

In fact it was not Murray who found the boats. Probably he marched right past the first of them. What happened was that a Colonel Waters who worked as a sort of private reconnaissance unit often well behind enemy lines, and was actually in the Portuguese service, met up with a Portuguese barber who lived on the south side but whose shop was in the city. Not wishing to lose the trade of the French dandies but loving his family too, he had kept his boat, a small rowing skiff, hidden from French eyes. With this, and the help of four or five working men, Waters succeeded in hijacking four wine barges from the north quays. All this was done at or about dawn, under the eyes of the French sentinels, who did not realise what had happened until the 600 Buffs were established on their north side bridgehead, covered by the British guns in the Villa Nova convent.

They then commenced an attack upon them, with a large body of cavalry, infantry, and artillery, under the command of Marshal Soult, which that corps most gallantly sustained, till supported successively by the 48th and 66th regiments belonging to Major General Hill's brigade . . .

Lieut. General Paget was unfortunately wounded soon after the attack commenced, when the command of these gallant troops devolved upon Major General Hill.

Although the French made repeated attacks upon them they made no impression; and at last *(my emphasis)* Major General Murray having appeared on the enemy's left flank on his march from Avintas, where he had crossed; and Lieut. General Sherbrooke, who had by this time availed himself of the enemy's weakness in the town of Oporto, and had crossed the Douro at the ferry between the towns of Villa Nova and Oporto, having appeared on their right with the brigade of guards and the 29th regiment, the whole retired in the utmost confusion towards Amarante, leaving behind them five pieces of cannon, eight ammunition tumbrils, and many prisoners.

'Crossed the Douro at the ferry' – *but in scores of boats. The inhabitants, seeing the way things were going, swarmed down those cobbled alleyways and on to the quays, unmoored their boats and ferried the allies across. This is the incident that bronze plaque represents.*

Brig. General the Hon. Charles Stewart *Castlereagh's half-brother* then directed a charge by a squadron of the 14th Dragoons, under the command of Major Hervey, who made a successful attack on the enemy's rearguard *which had, unaccountably, managed to get past the unenterprising Murray's infantry.*

In Lieut. General Paget . . . I have lost the assistance of a friend, who has been useful to me in the few days which had elapsed since he had joined the army. He had rendered a most important service at the moment he received his wound . . . *commanding the Buffs on the bridge-head. This, reading between the lines and after the event, seems to me to combine coolness with sincerity. The fact was that the Pagets had indeed been good friends, that is until, only just over two months earlier, this Paget's elder brother Henry, whose brows were wreathed with the laurels of Sahagun and Benavente, made off with Sir Arthur's sister-in-law Charlotte née Cadogan, the wife of his younger brother also called Henry. All this, which was quite a mess, deprived Wellington of the best cavalry general available, until Waterloo by when the scandal had somewhat receded. Edward Paget lost an arm at Oporto and did not return until Autumn 1812.*

Sir Arthur wrote less formally and more succinctly to Beresford, concluding: the infantry went off towards Valongo and Amarante in the utmost confusion. Some of the cavalry went the same way.

I am much afraid we shall not be able to march till the day after to-morrow . . . keep Villa Real if you can do so with safety and depend upon my being close upon the heels of the French.

In this lies the explanation of why Soult apparently got off lightly from the desperate fix he was in – far more desperate than either he, Sir Arthur, or Beresford realised. Amarante lies north of the Douro valley but almost due west of Oporto at the end of about forty miles of winding mountainous roads. Villa Real, where Beresford was, is another twenty miles beyond that. What all supposed was that Loison, with a fresh corps of 6,500 was waiting at Amarante. If Soult combined with him they would be a match for either of the allied armies if they were given an opportunity to take them in detail. Moreover, Sir Arthur's troops were knocked up after a hectic week, and stores and artillery had to be ferried across the Douro.

But Loison was not at Amarante. Unaccountably he had moved his troops off from an impregnable position into the inhospitable north-west, towards Braga. Soult, of course, knew of this before Beresford or Sir Arthur. On the thirteenth he abandoned his artillery and also headed north instead of west, but Sir Arthur knew nothing of this until late that day.

Meanwhile the troops rested, the ferries plied to and fro across the Douro, and he wrote letters, and proclamations:

INHABITANTS OF OPORTO!

The French troops having been expelled from this town by the superior gallantry and discipline of the army under my command, I call upon the inhabitants of Oporto to be merciful to the wounded and prisoners . . . they are entitled to my protection . . . these unfortunate persons . . . can only be considered as instruments in the hands of the more powerful who are still in arms against us . . . I have appointed Colonel Trant to command in this town.

To H.R.H. the Grand Old Duke of York, who was no longer Commander-in-Chief – his mistress, Mary Anne Clark having been caught selling army commissions:
Although your Royal Highness unfortunately is no longer at the head of the army, I am convinced that you cannot but be interested in their success . . . *he then describes the taking of Oporto, and ends:* It is impossible to say what induced Soult to be so careless about the boats on the river; or to allow us to land at all at a point so interesting to him . . . I rather believe we were too quick for him . . .
In fact when Soult was woken and told that the British were over, he dismissed the information as false: what had been seen was a party of red-coated Swiss having a bathe.

Towards the end of the day came the news that Soult's retreat was not turning out as expected. Sir Arthur scribbled a note to Murray: Information is just arrived that the enemy have burnt their artillery, and have retreated precipitately to the left and are gone towards Valença and the Minho *that is, north and west rather than east.* I wish you immediately to send a patrole *(sic)*, either of cavalry or mounted riflemen, if you can get mules or horses, and ascertain whether this information is correct . . . General Silveira is said to be at Amarante *that is, where everyone expected Loison to be.*
Next day, to Beresford: The enemy are certainly off to Braga . . . Mellish saw fires last night near Penafiel *half way between Oporto and Amarante;* therefore it is not impossible that Loison may have remained there last night to cover the retreat of Soult . . . If Loison is not there, Murray is to proceed to Braga . . . and I recommend you to proceed to Chaves.
Soult destroyed his guns and blew up his ammunition yesterday morning . . . and then went off towards Braga . . .

47

The next five days were hectic. Communications over the rough, mount-
ainous, largely unmapped provinces of the Minho and Tras os Montes, took
far longer than usual, General Silveira lost his way, and Beresford's corps were
forced to wade across rivers up to their shoulders and rest in water up to their
knees – for it rained and rained and rained as only it can rain in those Atlantic
provinces of Europe that are also mountainous. Sir Arthur moved more quickly,
got his advanced guard to Braga ahead of the French, and so convinced Soult
that the way to Vigo was barred. He moved north-east, Sir Arthur hoped into
the arms of Beresford and Silveira, but he got to Chaves just ahead of them,
scuttling out leaving behind roast pig on the fire for Beresford's advance guard.

They disappeared into the mountains – a completely routed, indisciplined
mob, a prey for the partisans of both countries as they crossed the border into
Spain. They left behind horrors. To Castlereagh, 18 May: The enemy
commenced this retreat . . . by destroying a great proportion of his
guns and ammunition. He afterwards destroyed the remainder of both
and a great proportion of his baggage, and kept nothing excepting
what the soldiers or a few mules could carry. He has left behind him his
sick and wounded; and the road from Penafiel to Montealegre is
strewed with the carcases of horses and mules, *many actually not dead,*
but merely hamstrung, waiting for the British to put them out of their misery,
and of French soldiers, who were put to death by the peasantry before
our advanced guard could save them.

This last circumstance is the natural effect of the species of warfare
which the enemy have carried on in this country.

Their soldiers have plundered and murdered the peasantry at their
pleasure; and I have seen many persons hanging in the trees by the
sides of the road, executed for no reason that I could learn, excepting
that they have not been friendly to the French invasion and usurpation
of the government of their country; and the route of their column on
their retreat could be traced by the smoke of the villages to which they
set fire . . .

I hope your Lordship will believe that no measure which I could take
was omitted to intercept the enemy's retreat. It is obvious, however,
that if an army throws away all its cannon, equipments, and baggage,
and everything which can strengthen it, and can enable it to act
together as a body; and abandons all those who are entitled to its
protection, but add to its weight and impede its progress; it must be
able to march by roads through which it cannot be followed, with any
prospect of being overtaken, by an army which has not made the same
sacrifices.

It is impossible to say too much of the exertions of the troops. The weather has been very bad indeed. Since the 13th the rain has been constant, and the roads in this difficult country almost impracticable. But they have persevered in the pursuit to the last, and have generally been on their march from day-light in the morning till dark.

In two weeks the army that pursued Moore to Coruña had been destroyed. Soult lost 4,000 men, all his transport, baggage and artillery. The survivors were useless as a fighting force until the late summer. The allies lost 300 killed and wounded, 200 sick and straggled.

Sir Arthur's is the last word, again to the Duke of Richmond:

My Dear Duke   Oporto, 22nd May, 1809.
I have just returned from the most active and severe service. I have been on the pursuit, or rather chace *(sic)* of Soult out of Portugal. We should have taken him if Silveira had been one or two hours earlier at the bridge of Melgaço, or if the Captain of the militia of the province had allowed the peasants, as they wished, to destroy it. We should have taken his rearguard on the 16th, if we had had a quarter of an hour's more daylight; but in the dark our light infantry pursued by the road to Rivaes instead of by that of Melgaço. But as it is, the chace out of Portugal is a <u>pendant</u> for the retreat from *(sic)* Coruña. It answers completely in weather: it has rained torrents since the 12th.

I am now moving the army as fast as possible to the Eastern frontier by which a corps of Victor's army has entered. I hope soon to be able to force them out also.

Remember me kindly to the Duchess.

Believe me, &c.

Arthur Wellesley

HIATUS

Victor made his gesture towards Castello Branco. The bad weather had delayed the appearance of green forage on which the French were now dependent – he was probably simply looking for food and fodder. To Mackenzie, who had obviously panicked: I observe that the enemy has carried the bridge of Alcantara, and has advanced as far as Castello Branco. I do not think it clear, however, that a column will enter Portugal on the side of the Alentejo; but if one should enter, and you have taken up the bridge at

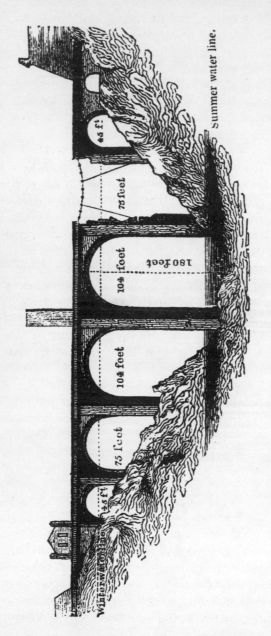

ROMAN BRIDGE AT ALCANTARA, BUILT BY THE EMPEROR TRAJAN.

(*View looking down the stream.*)

The Bridge of Alcantara

Abrantes, and secured the boats on the Tagus, I do not see what you have to apprehend from it at this season of the year, more particularly after the late heavy fall of rain . . . Look at your instructions, my dear Mackenzie, act boldly upon them, and I will be responsible for all the arrangements.

Throughout the war Wellington's generals, though all of them were personally foolhardy to the point of madness, acted indecisively, even timorously when left to themselves, with the notable exceptions of Hill and Craufurd. They always needed stiffening, pats on the back and raps on the knuckles judiciously mixed.

No column appeared south of the Tagus. Victor was feeling north, not only for forage but also perhaps to find out what had happened to Soult, for it was already the case that the French could not control an inch of Spain beyond musket range of a soldier: the guerrilleros had made it almost impossible for one army to talk to another.

But Sir Arthur too had his problems. To Villiers, 22 May: I cannot be certain of the subsistence of this army, unless the Portuguese Governor will let us have 300 or 400 good mules, with saddles and drivers. It is ridiculous that in Portugal that number cannot be found.

24 May: We are sadly in want of shoes; and the carts upon the road from Lisbon to Coimbra have been so ill-used, that I fear we cannot depend upon the communication; and if we could I believe we should receive them sooner by sea.

It will require forty carts to bring up 20,000 pairs of shoes . . . ask the Admiral to allow one of his ships of war to take them on board . . . we cannot depend upon the transports making way against the wind at this season . . .

G.O.   Coimbra, 31st May, 1809.
1. There being now 6,000 pairs of shoes, the officers will . . . make a requisition to the assistant commissary attached to each brigade for the number of pairs of shoes they will require to complete the men; but no regiment is to require more than one pair of shoes for each man. These shoes are to be paid for at the rate of 6s 6d per pair. *Uniforms and shoes were the responsibility of colonels in command of regiments. At home they were entitled to negotiate with local contractors, and then sell, by docking pay at source, to their men, making an entirely legitimate if small profit out of the transaction which would then be spent on such amenities as replacing the band's instruments. Abroad Sir Arthur is shortening the process by ordering the bulk himself from England and setting the price.*

Green forage was at last appearing, so . . .

51

2. The regiments are to make a requisition . . . for bill-hooks . . . one for every ten men.

3. Those regiments in want of camp kettles will make a requisition . . . deficiencies must, however, be accounted for in a satisfactory manner . . .

Arthur Wellesley

At about this time another continuing story raised its ugly head.

The question of rank between the English and English/Portuguese officers is one of a very delicate nature; and it arises entirely out of the practice of giving to Officers going into the Portuguese service a step of Portuguese rank beyond that which they held in the service of the King. *This was done to attract officers to take the step. It gave rise to all sorts of bad feeling. Should an English captain defer to a Portuguese major who was his English junior, having been made a captain after him? And what about pay? And what happens when the English/Portuguese become merely English again? The English officer caste treats pecking order with a reverence rational people reserve for lovable things, and bickering continued throughout the war. At the top of the tree was that very junior Lieutenant-General (English rank) William Beresford, who was Marshal no less, in Portugal, and dressed himself in gold braid (the Portuguese expected it) and rode, or even, damn it, drove about Lisbon with a feathery staff behind him, expecting the guard to turn out every time he passed.*

I wish to God that Beresford would resign his English Lieutenant General's rank. It is inconceivable the embarrassment and ill-blood which it occasions. It does him no good; and if the army was not most successful, this very circumstance could probably bring us to a standstill. *That is, all the Lieutenant-Generals senior to Beresford, and most of them were, would bugger off home. But only a fool or a rich man would resign an English commission, which had probably cost him a penny or two in the first place and was still an insurance against the day the Portuguese sacked him.*

I find all this boring and it will only reappear when it becomes important. But believe me, there's an awful lot of the Dispatches *and* Supplementary Despatches *devoted to it in the next four years.*

A far more serious and equally recalcitrant problem was the ineradicable tendency of many of the British troops to plunder. To Villiers, Coimbra, 31 May: I have long been of the opinion that a British army could bear neither success or failure, and I have had manifest proofs of this opinion . . . They have plundered the country most terribly . . .*Success or failure? Why not simply because they were two months in arrears in pay, and owed the best part of another month for shoes?* They have plundered the people of bullocks, among other property, for what reason I am sure I do not know, except it be, as I understand it is their practice, to sell them to the people again. I shall be much obliged if you will beg the Ministers to issue a proclamation forbidding the people . . . to purchase anything from the soldiers of the British army.

We are terribly distressed for money. I am convinced that 300,000*l*. would not pay our debts; and two months pay is due to the army. I suspect that the Ministers in England are very indifferent to our operations in this country.

I rather suspect that Sir John Cradock has detained the <u>Surveillante</u> at Cadiz, and that this is the reason why that ship has not returned with the dollars in exchange for our gold. *The dollar was the principle unit of Spanish currency at the time.*

He took up the plundering problem in his private letter to Castlereagh, of the same day: The army behave terribly ill. They are a rabble who cannot bear success any more than Sir John Moore's could bear failure . . . They plunder in all directions.

A rabble? But scarcely more than a week earlier it had been impossible to say too much for them. Wellington is usually presented as a phlegmatic, unemotional man, with an iron grip on himself. This simply is not true. He responded emotionally and psychologically in a most marked way to every stimulus that came his way – victory, retreat, sunshine, rain. Particularly he always went through an 'up' even reached a 'high' during the preparations for an offensive and in its early stages, and suffered a 'down', often a very bleak 'down' in its aftermath, however successful the outcome. No doubt this was in part due to exhaustion, but it was also related to his deeply-felt revulsion from the horrors of war which inevitably followed any major fighting: deep sorrow and then melancholy for the fallen amongst his own men, and a more general disgust for the whole business. This expresses itself in these letters, which are all official, or near it, in a testiness, a rattiness, sometimes real fury, during these black periods. The strength of the man, and perhaps the reason for the myth of his coldness, shows itself in the fact that he never allowed these emotions to endanger the efficacy of what he was doing: indeed the reverse – no doubt his ebullience was infectious and promoted enthusiasm, just as his black moods put people on their toes, sharpened their attention to detail at times when things could go wrong.

A rabble? And later, more than once 'the scum of the earth', though that phrase was never applied to the army as a whole, he always said that the army had the scum of the earth in it. Nevertheless, looked at from his ideological standpoint there was a lot of truth in it.

For what sort of man would volunteer for this sort of army? The pay was meagre, the conditions of service harsh, the likelihood of being horribly killed, maimed, or dying of disease so very high that only those enlisted who knew life at home was even worse. Thus they were the unemployed with no hope of employment, and no families, for no extra allowance was paid for dependants – though Wellington pleaded with successive administrations that such a payment should be made to encourage steady family men to enlist. There were many on the run from the law; that is, they were already criminals – often no doubt decent folk driven to crime by poverty, but in many cases people for whom poverty and therefore crime had been their way of life and that of their forefathers. No doubt some joined for adventure, and even out of patriotism, but again one should ask oneself what sort of youth it is will put himself in the way of extreme horror and hardship for such motives: at all events not the steadiest of young men, nor those most susceptible to discipline.

And it was after all easy enough to turn this rabble into an efficient fighting machine. Once the men trusted the efficacy of the way they were taught to fight, and knew that if they obeyed battlefield orders they would win battles and suffer few losses, they quickly responded. The problem was that, unlike the French who were not only told to plunder but told how, and could not survive if they didn't, the allies were operating on friendly territory, depended on the support of the locals, paid for everything they used or took, and relied for their survival on their reputation for doing so.

In the first week of June Sir Arthur was ahead of his army, at Abrantes on the Tagus, in the middle of Portugal. On the eighth he wrote to Lieutenant-Colonel Bourke, an Assistant Quarter Master General who had been seconded to the Spanish General Cuesta to act as liaison officer between the two armies. As usual he saw and planned his operations not in isolation but always as one factor in a continuously changing, contradictory, dynamic situation. The troops have not yet arrived from the northward; and when they reach the Tagus, which will not be until the 11th or 12th, they will require a day or two's rest, before I can put them in motion again for another operation . . . I have heard and believe that Marshal Ney, joined by Kellerman with 8,000 or 9,000 men has invaded the Asturias *the mountainous region on the north coast of Spain between Galicia and the Basque Country.* In proportion as the French spread themselves, they certainly do mischief in the country, which is always to be regretted, but they at the same time weaken themselves . . . it is very obvious that Ney, Soult and Kellerman will have more work upon their hands than they will be able to manage in the Asturias and Galicia: and if they should venture to detach, they will lose both those kingdoms; or if they do detach one or

Distant Castello Branco

even two of these corps to the assistance of Victor, General Cuesta and I shall be strong enough for them.

This is followed next day by a long letter, not easy to follow, outlining all the possible moves Cuesta had suggested, giving his own view on each, and then asking again for Cuesta's opinion. He had yet to learn what sort of person he was dealing with. His main conclusion is clear: Of the three propositions made to me I decidedly prefer that which takes the British army to Plasencia *via Castello Branco, ending up fifteen miles or more north of the Tagus.* By this movement, if it should be concealed from the enemy for a sufficient length of time, we must cut off his retreat by the bridge at Almaraz, and possibly by Arzobispo and Talavera.

If it should not be concealed, at all events the enemy cannot pretend to defend the Tagus. It *(the plan)* is unattended by risk, as both armies are, I conceive, sufficiently strong to defend themselves separately against any attack which Victor might make upon them; and the probability of want is lessened for both armies, as we shall be in a country that has hitherto been untouched.

On 10 June he heard that Cuesta had apparently accepted this plan which was basically an attempt to encircle Victor somewhere between the Tagus and the Guadiana where he then was; and on the same day he received his authority to go into Spain. The black mood began to lift. Reinforcements too were on the way in the shape of the Light brigade under Craufurd. However, the money problem remained. He wrote to Villiers in Lisbon, on the same day: So the ball is now at my foot and I hope I shall have strength enough to give it a good kick. I should begin immediately, but I cannot venture to stir without money. The army is two months in arrears; we are over head and ears in debt; and I cannot venture into Spain without paying what we owe, at least in this neighbourhood, and giving a little money to the troops.

Had a French Marshal read that, he would probably have done himself an injury. Pay the troops? Well, sometimes, but not really a consideration. Not move until you have paid the locals what you owe? 'C'est un fou à lier, il est d'un ânerie!'

While he was waiting for his money and an answer from Cuesta another recurring theme, that was not to be resolved until 1813, made its first appearance. To Frere, 12 June: I am much flattered by some persons of authority at Seville, of appointing me to the command of the Spanish armies . . . I believe it was considered an object of great importance in England, that the Commander in Chief of the British troops should have that situation, but one more likely to be attained by refraining from pressing it, and by leaving it to the Spanish Government themselves to discover the expediency of the arrangement. *As the reader and*

Sir Arthur are about to find out, Spanish sensitivity to Holy Pecking Order surpasses even that of the English, and it took them four years to discover that expediency.

Although it was Cuesta himself who had first proposed that the British should move by Plasencia on Almaraz, it was he who now decided that his own position in front of Victor was insecure and he pleaded instead that Sir Arthur should move south. It was the first real indication of the sort of man Sir Arthur was dealing with. Nevertheless, as a young general to a very old one, as an intrusive ally to the home team, as someone already becoming aware of Spanish pride, he gave way. To Bourke, 13 June: Notwithstanding that I am convinced that the most effectual way of destroying the French army would be to adopt the line I at first proposed; more particularly if General Cuesta could be prevailed upon to place his army in a situation of security, till the British army should be so far advanced on its march as to render it impossible for the enemy to attack without being exposed to certain destruction . . .

To Frere, same day: I can only say that the obstinacy of this old gentleman is throwing out of our hands the finest game that any armies ever had.

Next day the whole thing became academic. Victor caught some sense of the danger he was in, blew up the fort at Merida, and moved briskly back across the Tagus, establishing his army at the bridges of Almaraz, Arzobispo, and Talavera. The fact that his men were now starving on the Guadiana possibly concerned him too.

The money moved nearer. To the Commissary General, 16 June: I am happy to hear of the arrival of the Surveillante . . . I have settled with Mr Villiers that he is not to have any of the money . . . The Paymaster at Lisbon and the Paymaster of the Artillery must have those sums which are absolutely necessary and no more. I do not think any demands can be more pressing than those of the service of the army . . . *But still several days were needed to unload it and get it up the Tagus.*

During this pause he was able to catch up on less immediately important correspondence. At Vimeiro, the year before, spherical case-shot, filled with musket balls fired from howitzers and fused to explode above the heads of infantry, was used for the first time. He now wrote to the inventor of this ingenious device. I have the satisfaction to acquaint you that the spherical case shot were used by the artillery with the army under my command last year in Portugal, and I have every reason to believe that they had the best effect in producing the defeat of the enemy at Vimeiro on the 21st August. *The recipient of this was Lieutenant-Colonel Shrapnell.*

The days trickled by and there was time to check that his generals were up to the mark. To Beresford, 19 June: It appears to me that you have omitted to require carriages for the carronades; and you might as well alter your letter and ask for them. I also think you had better have another copy made of the list of intrenching tools required, and leave out the remarks at the end. You can get plank and timber in Portugal. I also think you might get –

artificers' tools	steel
iron wedges	tarpaulins
coils of rope	chests of tools
junk	sand bags
iron	ballast baskets

in Portugal, and you had better omit them in your list altogether; as it only swells it, and will delay the transmission of other articles more necessary to you.

Believe me, &c.,

Arthur Wellesley

P.S. When you shall have made these alterations, forward the letter to Lord Castlereagh.

('Junk' was pieces of old cable used for making fenders, gaskets, oakum, and so on. He rewrote Beresford's letters to even more effect after Albuera in 1811.)

On 21 June he blasted to pieces the findings of a Court Martial on a private of the 29th who had been acquitted of mutiny and of attempting to shoot an ensign (subaltern) of the 88th. Sir Arthur meticulously summarises the recorded evidence and finds the charges proved – a complication remains, however, that the prisoner had pleaded insanity.

In respect to the fact stated to me by your Surgeon that the prisoner is insane, I have to observe that there is no proof whatever of its existence. It might not be necessary to prove it, the prisoner being acquitted; but if the Court should agree in opinion with me, upon the revision of their sentence, that the prisoner ought to be convicted of one or both of the crimes charged against him, it will be necessary that means should be taken to ascertain whether he is insane or not.

On the twenty-third he had to report that his younger officers had taken to shooting at each other instead of at the enemy. To Villiers: I am sorry to have to inform you that Lieut. B, of 66th was shot in a duel some days ago by Lieut. D of the same regiment . . . Captain M, Lieut. D, &c. are now in arrest; and if the Government . . . think . . . they should be tried by the tribunal of the country, they shall be given up: if not, I shall give directions that they may be tried by a General Court Martial.

But at last the money arrived. To Bourke (with Cuesta), 26 June: I have the pleasure to inform you that the army will march to-morrow morning, the money having arrived yesterday; the advanced guard will be at Zarza la Mayor on the 2nd July, and the infantry of the army on the 4th and 5th . . . the whole will move forward to Plasencia as soon as possible: indeed I do not propose to make any halt till I shall arrive at that place.

I strongly recommend to General Cuesta to risk nothing till I shall be at hand to give him assistance.

Next day he wrote to Castlereagh: We shall not go into Spain quite so strong as I could wish; but when Craufurd's brigade arrives I think we shall have nearly 20,000 rank and file of infantry, and about 3,000 cavalry. *This is not a lot: the whole army could fit into Trafalgar Square, nothing compared with the vast armies the Europeans were even then shunting towards Wagram, near Düsseldorf. A Griffon's vulture soaring five hundred feet above them, would have been aware of some dust, some noise, even some music beneath the pines and amongst the flowering gum cistus and the broom, and then they were gone.* I shall desire that a weekly state may be sent to your Lordship . . . for I observe that it is frequently imagined in England that armies are much stronger than they really are . . . It is a most difficult task to keep up numbers, particularly of cavalry, in this country and climate. The brigade of heavy cavalry, which has not yet done a day's duty, is obliged to leave here nearly 100 horses . . .

Apropos of which, General Order for 1 July: Great care must be taken when rye is given to the horses that they are not watered two hours before, or two hours after they are fed; the same rule should be observed when they are fed Indian corn or barley . . . *which any pre-teen member of the Pony Club could have told them, but, as we shall see, the British Cavalry seemed to know a lot less about the Care of the Horse than one might have expected.*

And so, with only occasional interruptions – to reprimand Mackenzie for allowing a cart to break down through overloading, to arrange the disposal of yet more money arrived at Lisbon, to order a sick, and possibly incompetent general back to Lisbon: I cannot conclude without expressing my concern to lose your assistance; but I am convinced that, if you were to stay, you would be unable to afford me any, and that you will become worse instead of better . . . , *he, and his army, followed the winding tracks through the Portuguese uplands, away from the cooling breezes off the Atlantic, and down into the wide bowl of the Tagus – which in July and August must be one of the hottest, bleakest, nastiest places in Europe (see map pages 4–5). The wheat would have been ripe already, the harvest under way if not complete – dust from the stubble, dust from the threshing and flailing, papery red poppies by the* *waysides, brilliant blue daisy-like flowers on spiky stems and, occasionally, tall fennel whose chewed stalks provided instant refreshment of a sharp aniseed flavour. There would too have been flocks of larks scurrying over the stubble, handsful of goldfinches flitting round the bushes in those <u>ramblas</u> that still held water, and, on the horizon, shimmering in the heat, the broken arches of a Roman aqueduct, mute reminder of the transitory nature of empires. Above, as always, red kites drifted and lurched like sheets of brown paper, and above them soared the eagles, the buzzards, and the vultures above the lot.*

To Don Martin de Garay, Secretary of State for War to the Spanish Junta, Zarza la Mayor, 3 July, 1809: I have the pleasure to inform your Excellency, that the advanced guard passed the frontier this day; the army will follow to-morrow and the following days; and no time shall be lost in placing ourselves in communication with General Cuesta.

TALAVERA

To the Junta of Plasencia: Gentlemen . . . I shall, on my part, do everything in my power to maintain the discipline of the army; and I have no doubt but the people of Plasencia will have no reason to complain of the troops; and, in order that they may put the inhabitants of the towns, through which they pass, to as little inconvenience as possible, they construct huts for themselves, and lodgings will be required only for the General Officers and Officers of the Staff.

Beresford and the main Portuguese army remained on the frontier to the north. As Sir Arthur moved into Spain he began to show signs of nervousness. From Plasencia, 9 July: I have not forgotten either the Puerto de Baños or the Puerto de Perales *the two passes which connect New Castille and the Kingdom of Leon with Estremadura. Both lie between Salamanca and Caceres. A French threat from the north would have to come through one of these or deviate to the east via Madrid* and have called upon Cuesta to occupy both. The former is already and the latter will be in a day or so.

I have no apprehension that Soult will be able to do anything for some time with his whole corps . . .

On the tenth Sir Arthur duly went to pay his respects to the Spanish Capitán General, Commander-in-Chief, Cuesta, who was at Almaraz. The word 'duly' is perhaps not the mot juste. Because of poor maps and an incompetent guide Sir Arthur was five hours late, and arrived after dusk. He reviewed the Spanish troops by torchlight and did not like what he saw – the officers appeared

60

unprofessional, and men who could not drill properly would not be able to manoeuvre in the face of an enemy. Cuesta was even less confidence-inspiring.

Don Gregorio Garcia de la Cuesta was sixty-nine years old; as befitted one of his generation he still affected a bob-tail wig and principles of warfare that Frederick the Great had made obsolete fifty years before. He had been routed at Cabezon and Medina de Rio Seco in 1808. Already in 1809 he had been beaten by Victor at Medellin where he had been ridden over by his own routed cavalry. Since then he travelled in a huge waggon drawn by nine mules. If or when he got out he had to be held up by his A.D.C.s. Before a battle he never inspected the ground or reconnoitred the enemy but, to quote Sir Arthur Bryant, 'like a true countryman of Don Quixote based his actions on strong imaginative hypotheses that had little relation to reality'. He feared that Sir Arthur Wellesley and J. Hookham Frere were plotting to get him removed, and he was right. He judged Sir Arthur to be an upstart stripling, a pretender to the arts of war, and he was wrong.

During the rest of the night the two Generals faced each other, talking in dubious French or through interpreters, and disagreed on every possible point. However, Sir Arthur got on well enough with Cuesta's Adjutant General who was of Irish descent. To Frere, 13 July: I settled the plan of operations with General O'Donoju who appears to me to be a very able officer, and well calculated to fill his station. It is impossible for me to say what plans General Cuesta entertains.

However, Sir Arthur could not quite bring himself to back Frere's plot to have Cuesta removed: The general sentiment of the Spanish army, as far as I can learn it from the British Officers, *again catholics who served abroad because they were debarred from holding commissions in Britain,* appears to be contempt of the Junta and of the present form of the Government; great confidence in Cuesta, and a belief that he is too powerful for the Junta, and that he will overturn the Government . . . and if this be true, I do not know whether there are not some advantages to be derived from the employment of Cuesta.

The opaqueness of the language, the double negatives, reveals how uncomfortable Sir Arthur was in this sort of intrigue.

The plan he had agreed with O'Donoju, if not with Cuesta, was that the armies should combine (35,000 Spanish and 20,000 British with the Light brigade still to come) and move against Victor who had only 20,000 men at Talavera and possibly was still not aware that the British had come up.

To Beresford, 17 July: The infantry of the army moved this day, and the whole will cross the Tietar to-morrow, to co-operate with Cuesta in an attack upon the French upon the Alberche *a small tributary of the Tagus about four miles east of Talavera.* It is not quite certain yet whether they intend to retire, or to wait for us, but I am inclined to think they will do the former. . . . I asked Cuesta to secure for me the passes of Baños and Perales, and he has occupied the former, but has left the latter *(to the west)* to be occupied by the Duque del Parque *a young and energetic Spaniard who was putting an army together at Ciudad Rodrigo.* I wish that you would send somebody to see how the pass is occupied, and that, at all events you should have an eye to that pass.

On 21 July the British and Spanish armies combined at Oropesa, twenty miles west of Talavera.

G.O.: The army will parade this evening in marching order, at five o'clock . . . to be seen by General Cuesta . . . The troops will be in open ranks, and will present arms, and officers salute; drums and bands to play a march.

On the next day the Spanish skirmished with the French advance guard, and had to be helped out by Anson's British and German cavalry. This was the first intimation that Victor had that he was faced by anything more serious than a Spanish army he had already beaten once.

By dusk the British, on the right, were in the hills to the north of Victor, while Cuesta had marched through Talavera and faced the bridge on the fordable Alberche. He promised to attack at dawn. At 3.00 a.m. Sir Arthur was ready, his troops covered by hills wooded with cork and olive trees. Daylight came. From Talavera nothing, not a sound. At ten o'clock Sir Arthur rode over to the Spanish camp and found Cuesta asleep. On being woken he announced that his army, having marched two days running, was too tired to fight that day. Mañana *was soon enough. But when tomorrow became today Victor had slipped twenty miles away down the main road to Sta Olalla.*

Refreshed by his day of rest – it had been a Sunday – Cuesta rushed off in pursuit, but Sir Arthur now refused to follow. To Frere, 24 July: We intended to attack the enemy this morning at daylight in his position on the Alberche, and all the arrangements had been made . . . but the enemy retired to Sta Olalla in the night.

General Cuesta has since marched to Cevolla; and I do not know whether he intends to halt there, or what are to be his future operations. I have been obliged to intimate to him . . . that I could attempt no further operation till I should be made certain of my supplies, by being furnished with proper means of transport and the requisite provisions from the country . . . although my troops have been on forced marches, engaged with operations with the enemy, the success of which I must say depended upon them, they have had nothing to eat, while the Spanish army have had plenty . . . I can only say that I have never seen an army so ill-treated in any country . . . It is ridiculous to pretend that the country cannot supply our wants – *the wheat harvest was now well gathered in and this is wheat country*. The French army is well fed, and the soldiers who are taken in good health, and well supplied with bread . . . This is a rich country in corn, in comparison with Portugal . . . The Spanish army has plenty of everything, and we alone, upon whom everything depends, are actually starving.

I am aware of the important consequences which must attend the step which I shall take in withdrawing from Spain . . . But no man can see his army perish by want without feeling for them, and most particularly . . . when he knows they have been brought into the country in which the want is felt by his own act, and on his own responsibility.

The enemy had their rearguard in Sta Olalla this day; and I have just heard that General Cuesta was marching to that place. I am only afraid that he will get himself into a scrape: any movement by me to his assistance is quite out of the question.

In fact, had Victor realised that the Spanish alone were after him he could have smashed them even more completely than the allies might have defeated him the day before.

At midday on 25 July Cuesta learnt that Sebastiani was bringing another corps to Victor's assistance from the south and that King Joseph was at last on the move from Madrid. The Spanish army swarmed back towards Talavera even more quickly than they had left it. In spite of what he had said Sir Arthur did move forward to support this retreat and was then confounded yet again when, on the twenty-seventh, Cuesta refused to withdraw across the Alberche, but insisted on making his stand with his back to the river – the old fool had been caught in just that way the year before at Cabezon, but had learnt nothing. Sir Arthur had literally to go down on his knees and plead with him to withdraw to a far stronger position. As he did so the British covered his retreat with Sherbrooke's and Mackenzie's divisions, and one consequence was that Sir Arthur himself was, as near as damn it, captured or shot. General Cuesta having consented to take up his position on the morning of the 27th, I ordered General Sherbrooke to retire with his corps to its station in the line, leaving General Mackenzie with a division of infantry and a brigade of cavalry as an advanced post in the wood, on the right *that is, west bank* of the Alberche, which covered our left flank.

Here stood a solid building, half farmhouse half fort, the sort of place Don Quixote mistook for a castle, the sort of affair one finds all over Europe where minor landlords once had to fear marauders or bandits. It still stands, though the ugly ribbon development of suburbs along the main road to Madrid has long since engulfed it. Sir Arthur climbed its tower to get a view over the undulating country which was wooded, not closely but much like an English park, with cork and olives. As he got to the top French skirmishers entered the eastern end of the complex. He scampered down the stairs and just escaped, with musket balls whistling about his ears.

The horrid farce continued. More French light troops caught two battalions of British actually asleep under the cork trees, and they suffered serious losses before Sir Arthur himself took command of Mackenzie's brigade and brought the survivors off safely.

These were the opening shots of what came to be known as the Battle of Talavera. All battles are bloody, nasty, horrible and usually muddled affairs – and this was worse than most. Waterloo was worse and it was of Waterloo that Wellington said: Nothing except a battle lost can be half so melancholy as a battle won. *It was his invariable reaction even after his more exhilarating victories. His Talavera dispatch is therefore more than usually brief, laconic, and, unlike other dispatches of great battles, it is not supplemented by less formal, more buoyant notes to friends and relations penned in the succeeding days, for, in this case, as we shall see, these were almost more hellish than the battle itself.*

By the late afternoon of 27 July the allies were in the positions they were meant to be in – or thought they were.

The position taken up by the troops at Talavera extended rather more than two miles: the ground was open upon the left, where the British army was stationed, and it was commanded by a height *(El Cerro de Medellin)* on which was placed, as the second line, a division of infantry under Major General Hill.

There was a valley between the height and a range of mountains still further to the left . . . which appeared too distant to have any influence on the expected action.

The right, consisting of Spanish troops, extended immediately in front of the town of Talavera, down to the Tagus. This part of the ground was covered by olive trees, and much intersected by banks and ditches. The high road . . . was defended . . . by a heavy battery in front of a church, which was occupied by Spanish infantry.

All the avenues of the town were defended in a similar manner . . .

In the centre, between the two armies, there was a commanding spot of ground, on which we had commenced to construct a redoubt *a simple field fortification placed in front of the main line* with some open ground in its rear. Brig. General Alexander Campbell was posted at this spot with a division of infantry, supported in his rear by General Cotton's brigade of dragoons and some Spanish cavalry.

At about 2 o'clock on the 27th the enemy appeared . . . *and there follows his account of the affair at the Casa de Salinas and that of the sleeping battalions, neither of which are overtly gone into:* the troops withdrew in good order, but with some loss particularly by the 2nd batt. 87th . . . and the 2nd batt. 31st . . . in the wood. *Second battalions were not usually sent abroad. They were maintained at home to train up replacements for the first battalions. These were therefore only partially trained and wholly inexperienced.*

In the late evening occurred the one muddle which, without being callous, we might describe as funny. The enemy commenced his attack . . . by an attempt with his cavalry to overthrow the Spanish infantry . . . This attempt entirely failed. *Well, almost entirely. In the dusk a force of French dragoons reconnoitred the Spanish position, which, protected by ditches, hedges, walls, farm buildings and trees, was virtually unassailable. They loosed off their pistols at shadows which perhaps they mistook for Spanish piquets. Without orders, and at the entirely harmless range of 1,000 yards, the Spaniards fired off a thunderous volley at them, and they cantered off. Four Spanish battalions in Talavera heard the noise and ran in the opposite direction, believing their front line had been overwhelmed.*

In a letter written four weeks later (see page 74) Sir Arthur described what happened: Nearly 2,000 ran off . . . not 100 yards from the place where I was standing, who were neither attacked nor threatened with attack, and who were frightened only by the noise of their own fire: they left their arms and their accoutrements on the ground, their officers went with them; and they and the fugitive cavalry, plundered the baggage of the British army which had been sent to the rear. *Two days later Cuesta ordered one in ten of these (which is what decimation really means) to be shot. Sir Arthur interceded but could not get him to drop the figure below forty. The executions took place, which goes to show there is no such thing, after all, as a funny story at war.*

The tragedy of errors continued into the night. Early in the night he pushed a division along the valley on the left of the height occupied by . . . Hill, of which he gained a momentary possession; but . . . Hill attacked it instantly with the bayonet, and regained it. *In the dusk, with some battalions badly shaken by the earlier skirmishing, and all exhausted after fifteen hours of marching and fighting, the alignment on the Medellin was not as it should have been and the French were able to attack a brigade of Germans who had been allowed to go to sleep without piquets since their commander believed they were in the second line. The French gained the summit between Hill to the north and Donkin to the south. Hill went to see who these troops were – he rather thought they were 'the old Buffs as usual making some blunder', and rode right up to them. A voltigeur sprang at him, nearly had him off his horse, his brigade major was killed, and he only just escaped. He then organised two counter attacks – the first, hurriedly put together out of detachments, failed; the second, made by the 29th who had done so well at Vimeiro, pushed double their numbers off the height.*

We lost many brave officers in the defence of this important point in our position; among others, I cannot avoid mentioning Brigade Major Fordyce. . . . Hill was himself wounded, but I am happy to say but slightly.

Sir Arthur, who had ridden over as soon as he heard the musketry, now corrected the alignment on the Medellin, and then snatched one of his famous catnaps, wrapped in his cloak on the hill-side. An hour before dawn he had his troops under arms again.

This attack was repeated . . . at daylight on the morning of the 28th, by two divisions of infantry, and was again repulsed by Major General Hill.

It started at 5.00 a.m. A single French gun popped its puff of white smoke from the summit of the Cascajal: it was the traditional Buonaparte opening to a battle – a barrage, in this case of fifty or sixty guns concentrating their fire on one area, the Medellin. But Sir Arthur made the men withdraw behind the crests or lie down, smoke and drifting morning fog obscured the targets, and the damage done was negligible.

The attacks that followed were a re-run on a larger and more confused scale of those at Vimeiro. The French came on in columns behind screens of light troops, always attacking the English lines, first on the Medellin through to seven o'clock and then, after a lull, concentrating on the line further south up to the redoubt. They ignored the virtually entrenched Spanish whom Sir Arthur did not dare ask to move, and thus were always attacking with odds of at least two to one in their favour. Because of the smoke and fog the superior range of the Baker rifles was less of an advantage than usual, and the British light companies skirmishing in front of the line suffered heavily, but maintained their slow, deliberate withdrawal, following the movements developed by Sir John Moore, so courageously that the head of the French columns was often as close as a hundred yards before they had withdrawn through the line. At one point they were so slow they masked Hill's field of fire. Most uncharacteristically he swore – there is only one other recorded instance. 'Damn their filing. Let them come in anyhow.'

The long lines held their fire until the range had dropped to a matter of sixty yards or less – then a single volley, followed by the rolling volley by half companies. The French columns, on a broader front than at Vimeiro, and so with increased fire power, sixty men across, twenty-four deep, looked solid, indestructible, but again and again reached the point where they could no longer

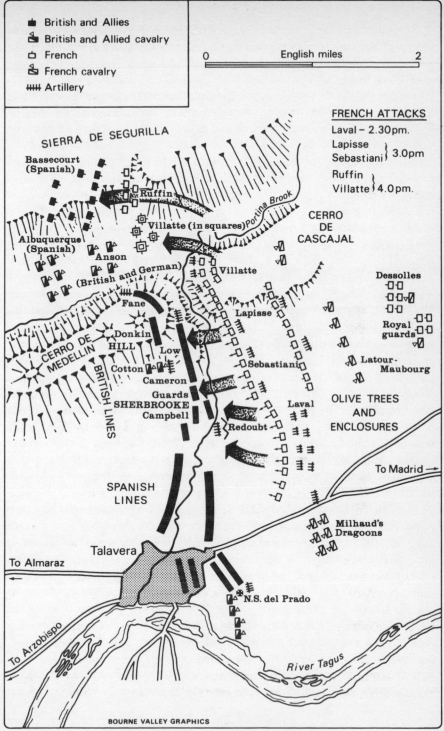

Legend:
- British and Allies
- British and Allied cavalry
- French
- French cavalry
- Artillery

0   English miles   2

FRENCH ATTACKS
Laval – 2.30pm.
Lapisse
Sebastiani } 3.0pm
Ruffin
Villatte } 4.0pm.

SIERRA DE SEGURILLA

Bassecourt (Spanish)

Ruffin

Villatte (in squares)

Portina Brook

CERRO DE CASCAJAL

Albuquerque (Spanish)

Anson (British and German)

Villatte

Fane

Lapisse

Donkin

CERRO DE MEDELLIN HILL

Low

Cotton

Cameron

Guards

SHERBROOKE

Campbell

BRITISH LINES

Sebastiani

Dessolles

Royal guards

Latour-Maubourg

Laval

OLIVE TREES AND ENCLOSURES

Redoubt

To Madrid →

SPANISH LINES

Milhaud's Dragoons

Talavera

To Almaraz ←

N.S. del Prado

To Arzobispo

River Tagus

BOURNE VALLEY GRAPHICS

5. The Battle of Talavera, 3.00–5.00 p.m., 28 July 1809

hold together. All dissolved and broke. I know of no case when a French column broke a British line: if it had happened once history would have been different. By how much, who can say?

By seven o'clock in the morning the day was already appallingly hot – in late July temperatures can get well into the hundreds in the Tagus Basin – and a truce was agreed. The British immediately buried their dead on the Medellin, the French held a council of war. Joseph was now on the scene with Jourdan, his Chief of Staff, and they were for retreat. Victor wanted one more big push. Meanwhile the men of both sides fraternised across the tiny brook that trickled between their lines. They shook hands across it, helped each other to swigs of its brackish water. Sir Arthur, Wellington, unlike his coarser, more brutalised successors in the wars of our century, actually encouraged this sort of practice.

At eleven o'clock the French pulled back a half mile or so and regrouped. At one o'clock the cannonade began again, and between two-thirty and three o'clock they launched three more assaults on the British line. All failed. The fourth developed into something more serious.

An attack was also made at the same time upon Lieut. General Sherbrooke's division, which was in the left and centre of the first line of the British army. This attack was most gallantly repulsed by a charge with bayonets by the whole division; but the brigade of Guards, which were on the right, having advanced too far, they were exposed on their left flank to the fire of the enemy's batteries, and of their retiring columns, and the division was obliged to retire towards the original position, under the cover of the second line of General Cotton's brigade of cavalry which I moved from the centre, and the 1st batt. 48th regiment. I had moved the last regiment from the height as soon as I observed the advance of the Guards, and it was formed in the plain, and advanced upon the enemy, and covered . . . Sherbrooke's division.

This was the moment when the battle hung. The Guards had left a hole right in the centre of the allied line which the French were threatening to fill with dragoons, artillery, and 10,000 men. Once through they could have rolled up the British and annihilated them. Sir Arthur anticipated the gap when he saw how the Guards had gone too far, but his resources were pitifully small. For a short time 3,000 faced 10,000. But as the rolling volleys settled into a steady roar the Guards were regrouping, although they had lost a quarter of their men. When they came back into the line, probably now little more than 600 muskets strong, the French advance faltered, stood, broke, and fled.

Finally, to the north, a last attempt was made to get round the Medellin. French columns were moving in between it and the mountains to the north; first they came under fire from the long-barrelled nine pounders Sir Arthur had placed on the top; then he saw how they hesitated and ordered the cavalry he had posted on the extreme left of his position to charge.

These columns were immediately charged by the 1st German hussars and 23rd light dragoons . . . and although the 23rd dragoons suffered considerable loss, the charge had the effect of preventing the execution of that part of the plan.

What happened was this: the 23rd light dragoons began at a canter, which they should have maintained, across what appeared to be a grassy plain only thinly dotted with cork and ilex. Unforgivably they broke into a gallop, which became a race, which ended in a concealed ditch with broken necks and legs. The Germans came on more sedately, forced the French into squares, which in turn made them more vulnerable to the artillery on the hill, and they soon pulled back.

Shortly after the repulse of this general attack in which apparently all the enemy's troops were employed, he commenced his retreat across the Alberche, which was conducted in the most regular order, and was effected during the night, leaving in our hands twenty pieces of cannon, ammunition tumbrils, and some prisoners.

Your Lordship will observe, by the enclosed return, the great loss which we have sustained of valuable officers and soldiers in this long and hard-fought action with more than double our numbers. That of the enemy has been much greater. I have been informed that entire brigades of infantry have been destroyed: and indeed the battalions that retreated were much reduced in numbers. I have particularly to lament the loss of Major General Mackenzie . . .

Your Lordship will observe that the attacks of the enemy were principally, if not entirely directed, against the British troops . . . *some Spanish artillery had been on the Medellin and some cavalry in reserve in the north. These, with the volley of a thousand muskets the previous evening, were the Spanish contribution* . . . the ground which they occupied was so important . . . that I did not think it proper to urge them to make any movement on the left of the enemy while he was engaged with us. *Nor even after. As the French withdrew they left only a few hundred dragoons between their battered columns and the 35,000 Spanish troops. It was contemptuous but justified Sir Arthur's refusal to use them in pursuit of a beaten enemy.*

Again to the Duke of Richmond the last word.

29th July, 1809
Talavera de la Reyna

My Dear Duke

You will see the account of the great battle we fought yesterday. Our loss is terribly great. Your nephew *Lord Fitzroy Somerset* is safe. His horse was shot under him on the 27th. Almost all my staff are hurt or have lost their horses, and how I have escaped unhurt I cannot tell. I was hit in the shoulder at the end of the action, but not hurt, and my coat shot through . . .

Remember me kindly to the Duchess and all the little girls.

Believe me, &c.

Arthur Wellesley

ON THE GUADIANA

The French admitted to losing 7,268 men out of 40,000, the British actually lost 5,365 out of 20,000. Naturally both sides claimed a victory, but it was the French who withdrew. Although the dead were buried hastily, the wounded continued to suffer horribly in the heat. When Craufurd's Light brigade arrived late in the evening after heroically long marches, much at Sir John Moore's quickstep, three steps walking, three steps running with sixty-pound packs and temperatures in the upper nineties, they recognised the building where the surgeons were at work from the piles of amputated limbs beneath the windows. On the battlefield cartridge papers had set the dry grass on fire and the stench of burning horses was carried on the thick smoke that drifted through the hot dry town.

Sir Arthur still had a sort of faith in the Spaniards. To Beresford: My intention is to get Cuesta to follow them . . . and I shall follow as soon as my troops are a little rested and refreshed, after two days of the hardest fighting I have ever been party to. We shall certainly move towards Madrid, if not interrupted by some accident on our flank . . .

Which is of course precisely what happened. In spite of everything Cuesta had not held the Puerto de Baños in anything like the strength Sir Arthur had asked for, the French were pushing through from the north after all, and all hopes of Madrid had gone. To Frere, 30 July: We have received this morning accounts that the enemy are threatening the Puerto de Baños, which leads to Plasencia, in which object if they should succeed, they would cut off my communication with Portugal, and may otherwise do us infinite mischief . . .

To O'Donuju, 31 July (he almost never wrote direct to Cuesta now if he could help it): Adverting to the intelligence . . . of movements of a French corps towards the Puerto de Baños, I cannot avoid requesting that you would press his Excellency General Cuesta to detach towards that quarter, on this night, a division of his infantry with its guns, and a Commanding Officer upon whose exertions and abilities he can rely . . . *the correctness is so punctilious as to suggest sarcasm, he is after all only asking again for what he thought had been done a week before.* I certainly never should have advanced so far if I had not had reason to believe that that point was secure . . . if the division should arrive in time . . . it will preclude the necessity of my adopting more effectual measures to re-establish and secure my communication with Portugal . . . *That is, I won't have to leave you to face this* 'pack of marshals', *as he later called them, on your own. Joseph, Jourdan, Victor, Soult, Ney, Kellerman, and Sebastiani, were all now in the hunt, but all as wary as once-bitten dogs.*

But Sir Arthur really had enemies almost as bad under his increasingly lofty nose. To O'Donoju, 1 August: During the action of the 28th many of the horses of our dragoons *the ones who galloped into that ditch* strayed . . . I see English horses with short tails in possession of many of the Spanish troops . . . I also understand, that on the morning of the 29th, when our officers and soldiers were engaged in collecting the wounded and in burying the dead, the arms and accoutrements of both were collected and carried away by the Spanish troops . . .

And to Castlereagh, the same day: I certainly should get the better of everything, if I could manage General Cuesta; but his temper and disposition are so bad, that that is impossible . . . We are miserably supplied with provisions and I do not know how to remedy this evil. The Spanish armies are now so numerous that they eat up the whole country. They have no magazines, nor have we, nor can we collect any; and there is a scramble for everything.

Then came the news, late on 2 August, that Soult was through the Puerto de Baños with 20,000 men. Sir Arthur moved his 18,000 back to Oropesa, leaving his wounded in the care of the Spanish at Talavera. To Beresford: The movement of Soult . . . has deranged all my plans, and I am obliged to return to drive him out. *It was the last optimistic note he struck that summer, for even as he was writing it news of Cuesta's latest enormity came in.* Since I wrote you the letter that goes with this, I have received a letter from General Cuesta . . . he so far thinks Victor will be of the party that he breaks up from Talavera, leaving there my hospital and follows me. Under these circumstances, it is difficult for me to say what I shall do.

In fact, after much anguished debate with Cuesta, Sir Arthur withdrew to the south bank of the Tagus, securing the key bridges at Almaraz, and Arzobispo. Cuesta was to follow, was dilatory, and got caught by Soult's cavalry during the siesta. He lost 6,000 men, his cannon, and the cannon that had been captured from the French at Talavera. But this was the most Soult could do. He could not long maintain any serious concentration without starving; to move as many so far south he had had to abandon vast areas of the north to the guerrillas, and country that had already been 'pacified' once would have to be 'pacified' again. Both British and Spanish armies were in unassailable positions at Deleytosa and Mesa de Ibor. Soult pulled back to the north.

Meanwhile Frere's place at Seville had been taken by Marquess Wellesley, Sir Arthur's eldest brother, under whom he had served as general when the latter was governor-general in India. He almost always addressed Richard in the most formal terms – in truth there was some coldness between them, in part arising from Arthur's disapproval of Richard's flamboyant, indeed licentious life-style. But occasionally fraternal feeling shows through.

You have undertaken an Herculean task; and God knows the chances of your success are infinitely against you . . . I wish I could see you, or could send somebody to you . . . that is to say, if I remain in Spain, which I declare I believe to be almost impossible, notwithstanding that I see all the consequences of withdrawing. But a starving army is actually worse than none. The soldiers lose their discipline and their spirit. They plunder even in the presence of their officers. The Officers are discontented, and are almost as bad as the men; and with the army which a fortnight ago beat double their numbers, I should now hesitate to meet a French corps of half their strength.

. . . Ever yours, most affectionately,

Arthur Wellesley

Three days later, 5 August, Cuesta made the mistake of complaining that the British were looting, and that biscuit designated for the Spaniards had been hi-jacked by their allies. This drew from Sir Arthur the verbal equivalent of a rolling volley.

When troops are starving it is not astonishing that they should go to the villages, and even to the mountains, and look for food where they think they can get it . . . in this very village, I have seen Spanish soldiers, who ought to have been elsewhere, take the doors off the houses which were locked up, in order that they may plunder the houses, and they afterwards burnt the doors.

I absolutely and positively deny the assertion, that any thing going to the Spanish army has been stopped by the British troops or Commissaries . . . I also declare to your Excellency most positively, on the honor *(sic – he nearly always used the '-or' spelling for words currently spelt by the English '-our')* of a gentleman, that the British army has received no provisions since it has been at Deleytosa, excepting some sent from Truxillo by Señor Lozano de Torres; and I call upon the gentleman who has informed his friend that biscuit addressed to the Spanish army has been taken by my Commissaries, to prove the truth of his assertion. *This is fighting talk: let us not forget that while Sir Arthur discouraged duelling amongst his juniors, he called out Lord Winchelsea in 1829.*

But this letter from your Excellency brings the question respecting provisions to a fair issue. I call upon your Excellency to state distinctly, whether it is understood by you that the Spanish army are to have not only all the provisions the country can afford, but all those which are sent from Seville, I believe, as much for the service of the one army as the other . . .

I hope that I shall receive satisfactory answers to these two questions to-morrow morning. If I should not, I beg that your Excellency will be prepared to occupy the post opposite Almaraz, as it will be impossible for me to remain any longer in a country *country, of course means the 'neighbourhood extending several miles around him', as in Jane Austen. He is not, at this point, threatening to withdraw completely from Spain* in which no arrangement has been made for the supply of provision for the troops . . .

In regard to the assertion that the British troops sell their bread to the Spanish soldiers, it is beneath the dignity of your Excellency's situation and character to notice such things, or for me to reply to them. I must observe, however, that the British troops could not sell that which they had not . . .

Consequentially or not, I do not know, Cuesta had a stroke and was replaced by a General Eguia. Whatever hopes Sir Arthur had that things might now improve were soon dashed. To Eguia, 18 August: I am sorry to have to inform your Excellency that the British army under my command have this day no bread *(the prayerful echo was, of course, intended)* instead of receiving the plentiful supply of which your Excellency announced the arrival in the conversation which I had with you yesterday.

On the same day at 6½ P.M.: As the soldiers have not received their provisions for this day . . . I trust you will have ordered troops to relieve my outposts on the Tagus, if you still propose to hold that position. *And again, in the falling dusk:* That which obliges me to move into Portugal is a case of extreme necessity, viz., that description of necessity which an army feels when it has been starving for a month . . .

Eguia was foolhardy enough to accuse him of lying. 19 August: I feel much concerned that any thing should . . . induce your Excellency to express a doubt of the truth of what I have written to you. As, however, your Excellency entertains that doubt, any further correspondence between us appears unnecessary; and accordingly this is the last letter I shall have the honor of addressing to you . . . *but he goes on yet again to recapitulate the state of his army, and how his determination to withdraw is unshaken – even though he must leave behind ammunition* from the want of means of moving it.

He headed for Truxillo – an ambiguous move since it is more or less due south of Jaraicejo and Deleytosa – yet put him in touch with Lisbon. Also at Truxillo was a magazine which the Spanish had hastily put at his disposal. With Soult gone and Venegas operating out of the Sierra Morena with an unbeaten army there was still, even now, a possibility that a move on Madrid was not out of the question. On the Spanish side, they were coming to realise that without the British they were probably doomed, even though they still outnumbered the French.

It was something they could not quite admit – but at least they accepted it to the point of opening that magazine at Truxillo. Not that the magazine was found to be much use after all. After a day there Sir Arthur wrote to the man in charge, Señor Lozano de Torres, in the sort of French that can't be all that wonderful since even I can understand it: Je suis fâché d'avoir à vous annoncer que je me mettrai en marche demain pour la frontière de Portugal . . . Hier ils n'ont eu qu'une demie livre de farine, au jourd'hui que trois quarts d'une livre, et les chevaux absolument rien . . . nous mourons de faim, et je ne peux plus rester.

Next day, 22 August, he was at Miajadas – half way to Merida on the Guadiana where he would be in touch with the supply line from Lisbon. He explained why to Richard: I was unable to co-operate in any movement . . . excepting that which I am now making; having no provisions, no stores, no means of transport; being overloaded with sick; the horses of the cavalry being scarcely able to march, or those of the artillery to draw guns; and the Officers and soldiers being worn down by want of food, and privations of every description.

He reached Merida on 23 August and wrote a long letter to Castlereagh on all that had been suffered, analysing the situation as it stood, and, most particularly, reporting on the state of the Spanish armies as he had found them. It is a terrible indictment, and still causes deep offence to the descendants of his Spanish allies so that I have read in recent Spanish publications articles attempting to prove he was wrong: yet the evidence is clear enough. It should be remembered that he never stinted his praise for the heroism of the partisans and guerrillas; that whenever he could he praised Spanish officers; and that by 1813 when the Spanish armies operated under his command, when they had been reorganised, retrained, and rearmed according to his specifications, he found them as good as any he ever commanded; that even before that he got on excellent terms with those he could respect – de la Romana, Julian Sanchez, Freire, and above all Alava who remained a close personal friend long after the wars were over. It is in this wider context that what follows should be read.

The Spanish cavalry are, I believe, nearly entirely without discipline. They are in general well-clothed, armed, and accoutred, and remarkably well mounted . . . But I have never heard any body pretend that in any one instance they have behaved as soldiers ought to do in the presence of the enemy. They make no scruple of running off, and after an action are to be found in every village, and every shady bottom within fifty miles of the battle.

The Spanish artillery are, as far as I have seen of them *(a battery on the Medellin did well at Talavera)* entirely unexceptionable, and the Portuguese artillery excellent.

In respect . . . to the infantry, it is lamentable to see how bad that of the Spaniards is, and how unequal to a contest with the French. They are armed, I believe, well; they are badly accoutred, not having means of saving their ammunition from the rain; not clothed in some instances at all, in others clothed in such a manner as to make them look like peasants . . . It is said that sometimes they behave well; though I acknowledge that I have never seen them behave otherwise than ill. Bassecourt's corps, which was supposed to be the best in Cuesta's army . . . ran away from the bridge at Arzobispo . . . This practice of running away, and throwing off arms, accoutrements, and clothing is fatal to everything, excepting a re-assembly of the men in a state of nature, who as regularly perform the same manoeuvre the next time an occasion offers. *Here, in a nutshell, is explained one puzzling fact about the whole war – how it was that the French could go on inflicting catastrophic defeats, again and again and again on Spanish armies, only to find that three or four months later, there the defeated army was again, to all appearances alive and well – though perhaps in a state of nature.*

Nothing can be worse than the officers of the Spanish army . . . They are really children in the art of war, and I cannot say they do any thing as it ought to be done.

This long letter (all but 2,500 words) continues with a very characteristic view of the Spanish Government. A word should be filled in about that at this point. After the spontaneous uprisings against the French in 1808, those cities and provinces where the French had withdrawn, or which indeed they had never occupied, formed their own local juntas which were usually made up of the local bishop, the local provincial governor (who was usually a general) and perhaps the senior members of the local bureaucracy, generally supported by professionals: doctors, lawyers and so on. From these had emerged a Supreme Junta, which at this time resided in Seville, and claimed to be the legitimate caretaker government until such time as Napoleon could be induced to remove his elder brother Joseph from the throne and replace him with Ferdinand, who at that time was a prisoner of Napoleon's at Valancay. There he indulged in vulgar vice and applauded the victories of the French over the people whose legitimate ruler he was. Back to Sir Arthur and his views on the Supreme Junta.

They have attempted to govern the kingdom . . . with the aid of what is called enthusiasm . . . and is only the excuse for the irregularity with which every thing is done.

People are very apt to believe that enthusiasm carried the French through their revolution, and was the parent of those exertions which nearly conquered the world; but if the subject is nicely examined, it will be found that enthusiasm was the name only, but that force was the instrument which brought forward those great resources . . . and that a perseverance in the same system of applying every individual and every description of property to the service of the army, by force, has since conquered Europe. *Which may or may not be accurate, which may or may not match with what romantic pro-buonapartists think of the matter, but which clearly and succinctly goes some way towards encapsulating what Sir Arthur thought he was about in devoting his very considerable gifts to the overthrow of a system which he had clearly shown to be, according to the way he saw it, totalitarian, even if that word was not available to him. And now I must add a note myself. A totalitarian state is simply one in which the apparatus of the state reserves to itself the right to control every aspect of its entire population's lives, whether or not it chooses to exercise that right, and whether or not it exercises it in what you or I would think to be a benign or malignant manner. This is the sort of state Napoleon, for whatever reason, was attempting to create, and it is the sort of state that most countries in the world have now become, as certainly in the U.K., the U.S.A., and the U.S.S.R. as in France or West Germany. And it is precisely to the subversion of the emergence of that sort of state that our hero dedicated his life.*

The letter goes on to say that a reinforcement on a large scale of the British troops in the Peninsula would be a mistake at the moment since probably it would not be fed. He then discusses the Portuguese army, how, so far, it was useless to expect it to operate outside Portugal: it must be recollected, that for the last fifty years nearly, the troops have never left their province and scarcely ever their native town. *He is now nearing the nub of the second part of this long letter – the defence of Portugal, which he believed practicable, but where Moore's dictum that it was not still hung around his neck like the albatross.*

What is so interesting is that he is already developing in his mind, but cautiously, the strategy of the Lines of Torres Vedras. My opinion is that we ought to be able to hold Portugal, if the Portuguese army and militia are complete . . . *but* . . . it would be very difficult to prevent the enemy from penetrating; and it is probable that we should be obliged to confine ourselves to the preservation of that which is most important – the capital.

It is difficult, if not impossible, to bring the contest for the capital to extremities, *that is, fight a battle, and lose it,* and afterwards to embark the British army. You will see what I mean by a reference to the map. Lisbon is so high up the Tagus that no army we could collect would be able at the same time to secure the navigation of the river by the occupation of both banks, and the possession of the capital. One of the objects I fear must be given up, and that which the Portuguese would give up would be the navigation of the Tagus; and, of course, our means of embarkation. However, I have not entirely made up my mind on this interesting point. I have a great deal of information upon it, but I should wish to have more before I can decide upon it.

Refer then to the map on page 111. By drawing an impregnable line east-west through Torres Vedras from the sea to the Tagus, you first of all render it impossible for an enemy on the north and western bank operating from, say, Santarem, to communicate or act in conjunction with one operating on the southern, eastern bank, based, say, at Setubal. Make the line a three-fold defence system and even if the enemy look like breaking through on the north side, you have time to embark the greater part of your troops from any of the bays or beaches to the west of Lisbon which are out of reach of the putative enemy on the south bank. Thus by remaking the map you remove the choice between evils that Sir Arthur feared.

To sum up: the experience of 1809, from the end of May onwards, had been appalling. From it Sir Arthur learnt lessons that governed his every move for the next three years. What were these lessons? Firstly, that the Spanish armies were a mess, and that to cooperate with them was to court disaster. In fact, under abler commanders than Cuesta, they were not quite so awful as he imagined and he possibly denied himself opportunities of fruitful combinations as a result of this well-founded, bitterly learnt, but not entirely accurate prejudice. Secondly, that his was, therefore, one small army against several large ones and that a small army that loses a quarter of its men in a victory is a defeated army. Fourteen months elapsed before he risked it again in a general action. Thirdly, that he could not trust his own commissariat, and absolutely must not rely on anyone else's. Fourthly, that even his best troops were not as professional as they should be. There should be no more adventures like those of the Guards and Dragoons at Talavera, and certainly no more siestas in the presence of the enemy. Finally, from his personal tendency to see to everything himself, came the conviction that on the whole he had better see to everything himself. This has been the main criticism made of him as a Commander-in-Chief in the field. God knows how long his army would have lasted if he had managed it otherwise.

On 31 August the Spanish also fell back to the Guadiana. The British, now suffering badly from malaria – another lesson Sir Arthur learnt: from then on he kept his troops away from rivers in hot weather – moved west to Badajoz, and there they stayed until the very end of the year.

Two items remain to be noted.

G.O.   Badajoz, 7th Sept.
1. Notwithstanding the repeated orders given out upon the subject, the soldiers of the 4th division of infantry plundered bee-hives, in the neighbourhood of Badajoz . . .

He hád caught them at it himself: 'Hullo, sir! Where did you get that beehive?' *'Just over the hill there, and by Jasus, if ye don't make haste they'll all be gone.'* *He told the story with a laugh at dinner, and more than one biographer who would attach to him a vulgar sort of humanity that he did not require suggests 'he had not the heart to punish'. She ignores the G.O. of 14 September:* The orders of the 12th inst. respecting the plunder of beehives by the troops of the 4th division are countermanded; the plunderers having been discovered and brought to trial.

There is another, less ambiguously cheerful note to end on. On 12 September, 1809, he read this from the Duke of Portland, First Lord of the Treasury:

Nothing could be more gracious than the King's acceptance of your services, or more immediate and decisive than his approbation of the suggestion of creating you a Viscount.

On the sixteenth, at the end of a routine letter to Villiers, on the subject of Portuguese finances, he wrote:
Believe me, &c.

                                                            Wellington
P.S. This is the first time I have signed my new name.

1810

———⟨⟩———

THE MAKING OF THE LINES

THE FRENCH MOVE

THE FORTRESSES FALL

BUSACO

TORRES VEDRAS

———⟨⟩———

THE MAKING OF THE LINES

For four months the army remained on the Guadiana at or about Badajoz. In the early weeks they suffered terribly from heat and malaria, but as the weather grew cooler, and finally cold, the health of the troops improved. So too did their discipline and training, though their officers had to be badgered into seeing to it.

G.O.   Badajoz, 16th Sept., 1809
2. The officers of the army are much mistaken if they suppose that their duty is done when they have attended to the drill of their men, and to the parade duties of the regiment. The order and regularity of the troops . . . , the subsistence and comfort of the soldiers, the general subordination and obedience of the corps afford constant subjects for the attention of the field officers in particular . . .

Problems of supply remained intractable and Wellington had constantly to nag and even blackmail the Spanish authorities for food.

To the Junta of Estremadura
Gentlemen   Badajoz, 22nd September.
I am concerned to state to you that the supplies of bread for the British army . . . are very scanty and by no means regular . . . whatever may be the cause of deficiency I now inform you that I propose to withdraw the army from Spain entirely, on the first day there may be any failure or deficiency in the supplies of provisions for the troops.

On the same day he received news of an action near Salamanca which he assumed the Spanish had lost. To Richard: I should certainly move immediately, if my movement was not likely to expose the city of Seville to imminent danger . . . *But in fact the Spaniards had done well, and indeed later in the month the Duque del Parque inflicted a quite substantial defeat on the French at Tamames. The danger to the northern frontier and the fortresses that protected it was lifted for many weeks.*

Meanwhile in Seville it was proposed that the Supreme Junta should be legitimated by an elected Cortes. This provoked from Wellington the first of many characteristic letters on the subject.

I acknowledge that I have a great dislike to a new popular assembly. Even our own ancient one would be quite unmanageable, and, in these days would ruin us, if the present generation had not before its eyes the example of the French revolution . . . *However, he saw advantages, the chief being that by taking power from the Junta the main opposition to the British presence would be removed:* your remark being perfectly well-founded, that there is no prejudice or jealousy of us anywhere in Spain excepting by the Government. *Still* . . . Great care should be taken . . . to protect them from the effects of popular fury in the place of their sitting; but still, with all these precautions, I should prefer a wise Bourbon, if we could find one, for a Regent, to the Cortes. *Well, it was to be one of the curses of the country that no wise Bourbons could be found for over a century and a half, until the accession of Juan Carlos in 1976, though there were plenty of near imbecile ones.*

More down to earth problems also demanded careful attention. Tin camp kettles or iron ones? Craufurd, whose light brigade needed to be mobile, wanted the lighter, but smaller cooking pot – for that is what a camp kettle was. There is much to be said on both sides of the question . . . the iron kettle is best for cooking and lasts longest, . . . requires the employment of the fewest men in cooking . . . the choice between them resolves itself into this point: which is most likely to be carried with certainty? . . . In a regiment well looked after, it is certain the tin kettles would answer best, as the officers would oblige the soldiers to take care of them . . . and in actions they would be prevented from throwing them away; and care would be taken that the carrier of the kettle should, above all, not straggle or stay behind his regiment till the hours for cooking should be past, or get drunk and lose the kettle. But in two thirds of the regiments of this army such care would not be taken . . .

On 10 October he slipped into Lisbon almost unnoticed. Only to Castlereagh did he hint what he was about: I am going to Lisbon on Sunday, all being quiet; and I hope in a short time to be able to make a report on the defence of Portugal which will be satisfactory to the Government. *There followed a period of ten days in which he wrote very little, and was very little seen in public, but worked as intensely as at any time of his life, going over every inch of the terrain that was to become the Lines of Torres Vedras. There are many extraordinary aspects to these defence works, not least their complete success. They were kept secret from the French, not even the allies or the Government fully understood their extent. But the most important point is that they were conceived over twelve months before they were needed, and had this not been so they would not have been completed in time.*

What I am trying to get across is Wellington's prescience: his grasp of the situation right across the Peninsula, right across Europe where Buonaparte had subdued the Austrians and Prussians and had, at Tilsit in July, carved up Europe with the young Czar of Russia. For a year at least the entire might of the French armies could be pushed into Spain – if their master so wished.

At the end of ten days of hacking over the rocky hills, down the close valleys, across the occasional flat areas that stretch from the Atlantic and Torres Vedras to Alhandra on the Tagus, with Sobral de Monte Agraco at the centre, Wellington wrote a detailed memorandum to Lieutenant-Colonel Fletcher, commanding the Royal Engineers. Fletcher had accompanied him over most of the ground, and became now the chief instrument of his design. He organised and carried out the work on the spot, but always to Wellington's specifications, and always referring back to his master at every stage. A third extraordinary thing to note is that the final result deviated only in one respect from this memorandum: the right being pulled back three miles nearer Lisbon from Castanheira, where there was a wide plain not easily defended, to Alhandra.

Memorandum for Lieut. Colonel Fletcher,
Commanding Royal Engineers

Lisbon, 20th October, 1809.

In the existing relative state of the Allied and French armies in the Peninsula, it does not appear probable that the enemy have it in their power to make an attack upon Portugal. They must wait for their reinforcements; and as the arrival of these may be expected, it remains to be considered what plan of defence should be adopted for this country.

The great object in Portugal is the possession of Lisbon and the Tagus, and all our measures must be directed to this object. There is another also connected with that first object . . . viz. – the embarkation of British troops in case of reverse.

In the winter season the river Tagus will be full, and will be a barrier to the enemy's enterprises with his left attack not very difficult to be secured. In the summer season, however, the Tagus being fordable . . . even lower than Salvaterra, care must be taken that the enemy does not, by his attack directed from the south of the Tagus, and by the passage of that river, cut off from Lisbon the British army engaged in operations to the northward of the Tagus.

The object of the allies should be to oblige the enemy as much as possible to make his attack with concentrated corps. They should stand in every position which the country could afford, such a length of time as would enable the people of the country to evacuate the towns and villages, carrying with them or destroying all articles of provisions and carriages, not necessary for the allied army; each corps taking care to preserve its communication with the others, and its relative distance from the point of junction.

There follows an outline plan for the gradual withdrawal through the Beira, from Castello Branco, and through the Alentejo, to the actual posting of the men in the lines, and even including their withdrawal through them, enumerating at each point the positions at which stands should be made.

In order to strengthen these several positions, it is necessary that different works should be constructed immediately, and that arrangements and preparations should be made for the construction of others.

Accordingly, I beg Colonel Fletcher, as soon as possible, to review these several positions.

1st. He will examine . . . the effect of damming up the mouth of the Castanheira river; how far it will render that river a barrier, and to what extent it will fill.

2nd. He will calculate the labor required for that work . . .

3rd. He will make the same calculations for the works to be executed on the hill in front, and on the right of Cadafoes . . .

4th. He will examine and report upon the means of making a good road of communication from the plain across the hills into the valley of Cadafoes, and to the left of the proposed position . . .

5th. He will examine the road from Otta . . . to Merciana, and thence to Torres Vedras . . . from Alemquer to Sobral de Monte Agraco . . .

These lateral roads of communication were central to the whole scheme – the actual entrenched positions, forts and redoubts were to be held by Portuguese militia; the British would remain just behind and mobile, ready to move along these roads to any point where the enemy might threaten to break through.

6th. He will entrench a post at Torres Vedras for 5000 men . . . he will entrench a position for 400 men to cover the retreat of the corps from Torres Vedras.

and so on through eleven more positions.

18th. He will fix upon spots on which signal posts can be erected upon these hills, to communicate from one part of the position to the other.

19th. It is very desirable that we should have an accurate plan of the ground.

Briskly he set about providing Fletcher with the means. To Beresford, 26 October: Colonel Fletcher writes to have a corps of militia consisting of 600 men at Torres Vedras, a corps of 500 men at Sobral, and a corps of 800 men at St Julian, in order to furnish working parties to complete the works at these places respectively and I shall be obliged if you will give orders accordingly; *and to John Murray, his Commissary General, five days later:* The Chief Engineer, Lieut. Colonel Fletcher, is desirous to have stores prepared . . . at the stations mentioned . . .

1. 3000 palisades to be provided at Torres Vedras
2. 1500 fascines, at Torres Vedras
3. 3000 palisades } at Sobral
4. 1500 fascines }
5. 13,000 palisades } at Lisbon
6. 7000 fascines }

Preoccupied with this masterpiece though he was he also found time to write to Colonel Peacocke, who commanded the Lisbon garrison.

It has been mentioned to me that the British Officers who . . . are in the habit of going to the theatres . . . conduct themselves in a very improper manner . . . *He had been there himself:* I have been concerned to see officers in uniform, with their hats on, upon the stage during the performance, and to hear of the riots and outrages which some of them have committed behind the scenes; and I can only repeat, that if this conduct should be continued, I shall be under the necessity of adopting measures to prevent it, for the credit of the army and of the country . . . Indeed, officers who are absent from their duty on account of sickness might as well not go to the playhouse . . . *Clearly the manners and breeding of the English upper classes were as unpolished then as now.*

In the first week of November he made his visit to Seville and even found time to take in Cadiz: I have been induced to come on here, partly to arrange money matters with Lord Wellesley, and partly by curiosity to see this place . . . *Curiosity? Hardly. He knew very well that within weeks the Spanish armies would be defeated, that Seville, which was not defensible, would be taken, and that the Junta would have to go somewhere. Cadiz was the obvious place. Set on a peninsula at the end of a narrow isthmus which connected it with the Isla de Léon, which in turn was connected to the mainland by bridges only, it could not be taken from the land. Wellington wanted to be sure that this was the case, but it would have been most undiplomatic to say so.*

He returned to Badajoz to find that there had been a cabinet re-shuffle at home. Castlereagh had resigned, Liverpool was now Secretary for War, his brother Richard, Marquess Wellesley, was to be Foreign Secretary, and his younger brother Henry, who had been on his way to take Villiers' place at Lisbon was re-routed to Seville. In the interim Mr Bart. Frere, brother of J. Hookham Frere, held the Seville post until Henry could arrive. All this involved many long letters from Wellington briefing his new boss. None made direct reference to the Lines, though one of the briefer notes, 21 November, hints at his concern that their creation should remain classified.

The newspapers, *in London,* have recently published an account of the defensive positions occupied by the different English and Portuguese corps, which certainly conveyed to the enemy the first knowledge he had of them; and I enclose a paragraph recently published, describing the line of operation which I should follow in case of the occurrence of a certain event *(embarkation)*, the preparations which I had made for that operation, and where I had formed my magazines . . . if the editors really feel an anxiety for the success of the military operations in the Peninsula, they will refrain from giving this information to the public, as they must know their papers are read by the enemy and that the information is mischievous . . . exactly in proportion as it is well founded and correct.

On the thirtieth the expected news of Spanish defeat arrived. I was at Seville when the General commenced his march from the Sierra Morena; and in more than one conversation with the Spanish Ministers and Members of the Junta, communicated to them my conviction that General Areyzaga would be defeated.

The expectation of success from this large army, stated to consist of 50,000 men, was so general and so sanguine, that the possibility of defeat was not even contemplated. *It was, however, one of the most humiliating defeats ever inflicted on a large army operating in its own country. 56,000 Spaniards were utterly routed by 30,000 mixed French, Germans, Poles at Ocaña, a few miles south of Aranjuez. The Spanish suffered 18,000 casualties, though no doubt many of these reappeared later, in shady bottoms, in a state of nature.*

Wellington, of course, appreciated what the immediate consequence would be. Del Parque's possession of Salamanca can be but momentary, as it must be expected that the enemy will take advantage of the defeat of the army under General Areyzaga, to reinforce their troops in Old Castille to such an extent as to estabish their government in that province . . . I am anxious to cross the Tagus with the British army and to station it on the frontiers of Old Castille, from thinking that the point . . . which will best answer for my future operations in the defence of Portugal . . .

In fact by the time he wrote this Del Parque had been defeated at Alba, and Salamanca was already lost, though the defeat was not crippling. Nevertheless, when Wellington heard of it he decided that the game was up as far as Spain was concerned. His frustration boils over in this letter to Mr Bart. Frere.

To B. Frere, Esq.

My Dear Sir,   Badajoz, 6th December, 1809.

I shall not detain the messenger by any addition to my official letters of this day, excepting to lament that a cause which promised so well a few weeks ago should have been so completely lost by the ignorance, presumption, and mismanagement of those to whose direction it was intrusted.

I declare that if they had preserved their two armies, or even one of them, the cause was safe. The French could have sent no reinforcements which could have been of any use; time would have been gained; the state of affairs would have improved daily; all the chances were in our favour; and in the first moment of weakness occasioned by any diversion on the continent, or by the growing discontent of the French themselves with the war, the French armies must have been driven out of Spain.

But no! Nothing will answer excepting to fight great battles in plains, in which their defeat is as certain as is the commencement of the battle . . .

I wonder whether the Spanish officers ever read the history of the American war; or of their own war in the Dutch provinces; or of their own war in Portugal.

Believe me, &c.

Wellington

He had read all the reliable military histories from antiquity to the day before yesterday, and he took note of what they had to offer.

Three days later the withdrawal into Portugal began, but gradually. He did not leave Badajoz and Spain until Christmas Day.

The Tagus was now in flood and Lisbon could not be threatened, consequently he moved his army into the Beira covering the corridor that runs into Portugal from Ciudad Rodrigo and Almèida down the Douro to Viseu, then across to the Mondego valley to Coimbra and so via Pombal to Lisbon (see map page 4–5). The last small town on the way is Torres Vedras.

For a time it seemed he had got things badly wrong. He had expected Soult and Joseph to go for Portugal, but loot was what they were after and with him out of the way they fell on Andalusia. Seville fell early in the new year and the remnants of the Spanish army, the Junta, and countless refugees scuttled on to the Isla de Leon and in to Cadiz.

Even before that he had to face criticism for his withdrawal. The Spanish hated it, the French made great propaganda gains out of it, and with Seville and its trade doomed the Common Council of the City of London delivered an address to the King.

You see the dash which the Common Council of the City of London have made at me! I act with a sword hanging over me, which will fall upon me whatever may be the result of affairs here; but they may do what they please, I shall not give up the game here as long as it can be played.

But by 31 January, 1810, he seems almost to have lost his nerve about just how long it could be played. With Andalusia going he appeared to recognise that the weight of troops that could be brought against him would be overwhelming. To Liverpool: Adverting, then, to the probability . . . that the whole or greater part of the French army in Spain will be disposable to be thrown upon this country, I should be glad to know whether it is the wish of His Majesty's Government that an effort should be made to defend this country to the last; or whether I shall turn my mind seriously to the evacuation of the country, and to the embarkation of as large a body of people, military as well as others, as I can carry away.

For the next ten months he continued publicly to prepare for evacuation in meticulous detail, considering even the merits of taking off the Portuguese army as well as his own, and so on. No doubt much of this arose from his caution and sense of deep responsibility to the men he commanded, but simultaneously the work on the Lines went ahead and with no publicity at all. It is my belief that he never seriously expected to have to evacuate, but that he very much wanted the French to believe he would, and the more talk of embarkation there was in the English newspapers the better. If information could be mischievous, 'in proportion as it was well founded and correct', then misinformation might well do good. I believe it was his design to lure a French army, the bigger the better, into a hostile, starved environment, facing impregnable lines, to destroy it with the minimum loss to himself. The lesson of Talavera had been learnt: he could beat the French once, but if he was to beat them again and again it had to be done without losing men.

Meanwhile the day-to-day running of the army had to be continued, and, as was often the case during a time of doubt, even of self-doubt, the tone of what he wrote was, to quote Craufurd on a famous occasion eighteen months later, 'damned crusty'.

G.A.O.   Coimbra, 5th Jan., 1810
As the profession of free-masonry is contrary to the law of Portugal, *the suppression had not been for religious reasons, though that of course was the reason given. The Portuguese lodges had in fact been secret societies of liberal*

radicals. Not so the British, where they served then as they do now to promote the class interests of an oligarchical elite, the Commander of the Forces requests that the meetings of the lodges . . . , the use of masonic badges and emblems, and the appearance of the officers and soldiers in masonic processions may be discontinued while the troops will be in this country. The Commander of the Forces is convinced that the officers and soldiers of the army . . . will show their respect for the attachment of the people of Portugal to their own laws by refraining from an <u>amusement</u> (*my emphasis – Wellington had been inducted into the masons as a youth. You can judge what he thought of them*) which, however innocent in itself . . . is a violation of the law of this country, and very disagreeable to the people.

An important figure in the next year or so was Vice Admiral the Hon. G. Berkeley, officer commanding the fleet off the Tagus. It was he who kept open the supply lines from Britain, and elsewhere, on whom much of the possibility of a successful evacuation would fall if the need arose, and who could help in a hundred other ways too. To begin with they did not get on. Berkeley made the mistake of suggesting that his ships could supply the army at Coimbra and Viseu through the estuary of the Mondego rather than overland, and that money would be saved if he did. Wellington knew better.

I am much concerned that you should imagine that measures are adopted for the supply of this army that occasion an useless expense which might be avoided. If ever there was an officer at the head of an army interested . . . in keeping down the expenses of the army, it is myself, for I am left wholly to my own resources, and am obliged to supply the wants of the allies, as well as of the British army from what I can get; and if I fail, God will, I hope, have mercy upon me, for nobody else will.

. . . it will not do for me to depend for what I want upon the navigation of the sea upon the coast of Portugal, during the winter, by victuallers and transports, or upon the passage of the bar of the Mondego by square-rigged vessels, at a season when all the people of the country agree in stating that the bar can scarcely be passed by a schooner drawing little water . . .

But as the months went by the relationship improved until eventually Wellington was really distressed to see the Admiral go.

The anniversary of Moore's retreat to Coruña came and seemed to prey on Wellington's mind. To Liverpool, 24 January: The credit of the British army has been stretched to the utmost; and notwithstanding that we have paid large sums on that account, many debts still remain due on account of Sir John's army . . .

I am concerned to tell you . . . the conduct of the soldiers is infamous. They behave well generally with their regiments . . . but when detached, and coming up from hospitals, although invariably under the command of an Officer, and always well fed and taken care of, and received as children of the family by the housekeeper in Portugal . . . they commit every description of outrage. They have never brought up a convoy of money that they have not robbed the chest; nor of shoes or any other article that could be of use to them, or could produce money, that they did not steal something . . . They are a better army than they were some months ago. But still these terrible, continued outrages give me reason to apprehend that . . . they will slip through my fingers, as they did through Sir John Moore's, when I shall be involved in any nice operation with a powerful enemy in my front.

The Portuguese government continued to make endless difficulties over supply and pay, and now insisted that the army's grain should be bought from Portuguese merchants. To Villiers, 25 January: It is convenient to me to buy Mr Phillip's grain (which, by the bye, he will sell at as cheap a rate as any other can be got) because he will take payment for it in bills upon the Treasury, which he engages not to negotiate at Lisbon, Cadiz, or Gibraltar; and this grain is tantamount to so much money introduced into the military chest. It will probably not be convenient to purchase the grain of another dealer, because he will come into the money market with his bills . . .

The fact was, the western sea-board was now so saturated with bills on the Treasury that banks would only clear them at substantial discounts, which led the merchants either to put their prices up, or demand specie. But no! after a fortnight's consideration, the suggestion is not adopted! But no other plan is adopted or even proposed. The army is still starving . . .

The cavalry too got its share. To Lieutenant General Payne, who commanded it until June, 27 January: Considering that the cavalry do no work, and that they are all in stables, and adverting to the very excellent condition in which the horses of the hussars are which have been most worked, and which I am sorry to say are now fed on rye, I cannot but be apprehensive that there is some deficiency of attention to stable duties. I should recommend to you therefore . . . to resume the use of the curry-comb and brush universally, if they should not be able immediately to supply themselves with the hair gloves which you preferred.

Nothing was going quite as it should. The same letter ends: You will be sorry to hear I lost three horses the other day, smothered in the stable which had caught fire; two of which were my black and the chestnut.

THE FRENCH MOVE

Just over a fortnight later the French began to move, and although it soon became clear that their chief aim at this point was to protect their occupation of Andalusia rather than to threaten Portugal, purpose, urgency, confidence return to the Peer's correspondence. To Beresford, 15 February, 1810: I conclude that you will have heard that the enemy had summoned Ciudad Rodrigo, as well as Badajoz, on the 12th. I cannot believe they are in earnest in intending to attack both these places at the same time. However, we shall see. I enclose a memorandum of the movements which I have ordered . . . I shall continue the movement of these troops forward, if I should find it necessary; and I wish you would come up as soon as you can.

To Craufurd, 18 February, 1810: I do not understand Ney's movement *(on Ciudad Rodrigo)* coupled as it was with a movement upon Badajoz from the south of Spain *(By Soult)*. The French are certainly not sufficiently strong for two sieges at the same time, and I much doubt whether they are in a state even to undertake one.

Nevertheless, although he was already pretty certain that these French moves were diversionary, he felt the work on the Lines should be hurried along. To J. Murray, Commissary General, 18 February: As the works carrying on under Lieut. Colonel Fletcher may require the employment of persons in the country, and the use of materials, without waiting for the employment of those persons or the purchase of those materials by an Officer of the Commissariat, I have to require that all orders . . . drawn by Lieut. Colonel Fletcher . . . may be paid.

I have also to request that the Deputy Commissary General at Lisbon may be directed to supply Lieut. Colonel Fletcher with such numbers of fascines *(a bundle of sticks used to provide cover, much like a modern sandbag)*, palisades and pickets as he may require at such stations as he may point out, without waiting for further orders from me . . .

And to Beresford, same day: I have to request that four Portuguese engineers, who understand French *(generally the lingua franca of the allies)* may be placed at the disposal of Lieut. Colonel Fletcher, chief engineer, with a view to their being employed in the destruction of roads when it may be necessary.

A week later Fletcher wrote to Wellington:

I once more beg to assure your Lordship that nothing shall be left undone that, to the best of my judgement, and with the means that I possess, can be performed; but should the contest come to extremities very soon, I am conscious the system proposed will not be easily completed.

Hill commanded, as he was to for much of the war, the allied right, based in the north of the Alentejo (see map pages 4–5). If the French by-passed Badajoz (held by a Spanish garrison) he was to cross to the north side of the Tagus and then: All the boats from Villa Velha inclusive down to Villa Franca . . . must be ordered down to Alhandra, *downstream of the Lines, and on the north bank – Soult was not to be allowed a revenge for the boats of Oporto.*

And on 28 February he wrote to Liverpool: I hope that you will have attended to my suggestion to send to the Tagus a fleet of ships of the line; a measure which I really think of the utmost importance. Besides the facility which their assistance will give us in embarking . . . the enemy might combine his attack upon the frontiers of Portugal with a movement of his fleet in the Mediterranean to the Tagus. If he should make this movement, you will probably lose your army . . . *For many months Wellington remained less than convinced that he had the new ministry's wholehearted support.*

On 1 March he sent a confidential memorandum to the Governor of the Province of Beira. It is rare that his memoranda were so classified – an indication that he still hoped to keep the extent of his preparations from the French. Arrangements must be made for destroying the bridges over the Coa . . . The bridge at Almeida should also be destroyed . . . *and so on for the Mondego, the Alva, and the Zezere. For the next ten days he continued to issue orders of this sort, and offer advice to Charles Stuart, the new, and from now on permanent Minister at Lisbon, on how the Portuguese should be prepared to cope if the British and Portuguese armies had to embark.*

But at the same time there was to be no question of yielding an inch of country without contention. By 11 March he was massing his centre on the Coa, with Craufurd and what was now the Light division in front and on the Agueda. In case Brigadier General Craufurd should require assistance in infantry . . . I wish Major General Cole to give it to him. I beg . . . Craufurd to inform . . . Picton, and . . . Cole, as well as myself, of all that passes in front.

On the nineteenth his much improved intelligence system, of which more later, began to send in reports of a French build-up. To Cole: There is no doubt that the enemy have . . . collected a large force on the left *(southern)* bank of the Tormes *(near Salamanca)* . . . Junot, with another corps is at Leon . . . and I conclude that the troops between the Tormes and the

Agueda are the corps of Ney, Kellerman, and Loison. I think that the first operation will be to the northward, *that is against Astorga, gateway to Galicia which they had still not regained after Wellington had drawn them off in the previous summer.* If they seriously intend to attack Ciudad Rodrigo it is extraordinary that they should collect a force in the country from which they must draw their subsistence during the continuance of the siege, and keep it there for so many days.

Nevertheless, though he was right in principle, the French were determined to hold him in check while they went north, and they left Ney's considerable force to watch him throughout the spring and early summer, occasionally prodding Craufurd's advance posts on the Agueda with surprise attacks. The first was on 19 March below Ciudad Rodrigo, at a point where the river runs through a steep gorge between two villages – Barba de Puerco on the allied held side, San Felices on that held by the French. The only bridge is at the foot of the very steep but terraced slopes.

The enemy had collected a brigade of infantry at San Felices; and crossed the bridge with 600 men after dark *(having bayoneted the sentinels).* These followed the piquet of the 95th up from the bridge and immediately made their attack; but they were repulsed with the loss of two officers and seven men killed, six prisoners, and thirty firelocks . . . this affair was highly creditable to Colonel Beckwith *(a huge man, who personally rallied his men, bellowing with a bull-like voice, and led them, sword in hand, on the headlong rush back down the pitch-dark terraces and on to, but not over the bridge)* and displayed the gallantry and discipline of the officers and troops under his command.

First blood of the year to the allies, who, however, were still two months in arrears with pay, and, lacking money to buy vegetables in the village markets, resorted to less orthodox and more dangerous practices to get them.

G.O.   Viseu, 23rd March, 1810
1. The soldiers of the army are desired not to eat roots, particularly the onions which they find growing wild in the fields: even in the gardens many of them are poisonous, and a serjeant of the 57th regiment has died of the consequences of eating some.

Daffodils? As far south as this they would be over as flowers and the leaves beginning to wilt.

The next day Wellington was able to pass on almost gleefully the information to Craufurd that: They are bringing a battering train into Spain from France, which looks like an intention to go regularly to work.

On the last day of the month he looked forward with optimism to the campaigning months ahead, the blues of January quite gone. If the main French

93

threat came across the Agueda he had his best troops there to meet them, and two well garrisoned fortresses – Ciudad Rodrigo and Almeida, and behind him the Lines would now be complete. To the north he had Beresford and the Portuguese, to the south Hill. When he retired – and sheer weight of numbers would mean that eventually it would come to that, they would pull in to join him. The Spanish were strong in Galicia and apparently so round Badajoz in Estremadura; both would delay the French and weaken them. He wrote to Lieutenant Colonel Torrens, who had been his Military Secretary from Mondego to Vimeiro, but was now Secretary to the Commander-in-Chief at the Horse Guards, a letter which exactly expresses this quiet but firm confidence.

I can give you no news. The French threaten us on all sides, and are most desirous to get rid of us. But they threaten upon too many points at a time to give me much uneasiness respecting any one in particular, and they shall not induce me to disconnect my army.

I am in a situation in which no mischief can be done to the army, or to any part of it; I am prepared for all events; and if I am in a scrape, as appears to be the general belief in England, although certainly not my own, I'll get out of it.

THE FORTRESSES FALL

For the next six or seven months Wellington was plagued with a particular class of nuisances he always referred to as 'Croakers'. It was his word for people anywhere who doubted that he was doing the right thing, but especially those who expressed the opinion that he might risk a British army out of motives of personal ambition. This slur in part arose as a result of Richard Wellesley's flamboyant life-style as governor-general of India – the conventional wisdom had it that all the family were extravagant and proud overreachers.

Of these croakers whig politicians were the most open and the most easily brushed off – what would you expect from crypto- and not so crypto-buonapartists? Less easily stomached were friends in Government at home, and the elderly military establishment who still could not quite accept the fact that we had a general and an army that actually won battles. The keystone of their position was that statement of Moore's that Portugal could not be defended, and it was backed up by Wellington's known and apparently absurd decision to embark if need be from a small cove called St Julian three miles west of Lisbon, instead of from Peniche some fifty miles to the north where a strong fort protected a safe harbour. But the worst croakers of all were those in the army itself, who in turn fell into two opposed factions: those who took the Moore line, and those who thought the Peer was too cautious, that he should again be co-operating with the Spanish armies to get the French out of the Peninsula instead of kicking his heels on the Coa.

The trouble was that Wellington's attempts to answer his critics always foundered on the fact that he could not use the Lines of Torres Vedras to justify either his actions or his inaction. A long letter explaining and justifying what he was doing without mentioning them, written to Liverpool on 2 April, is almost tortuous in the attempt, though, reading between the lines he almost blows the gaff.

My opinion is that as long as we shall remain in a state of activity in Portugal, the contest must remain in Spain; that the French are most desirous that we should withdraw from the country, but know they must employ a very large force indeed . . . to render it necessary for us to go away; and I doubt whether they can bring that force to bear upon Portugal without abandonning other objects, and exposing their whole fabric in Spain to great risk. If they should be able to invade it, and should not succeed in obliging us to evacuate the country, they will be in a very dangerous situation; *which was precisely the case when Masséna's army came to starve at Santarem in the following winter.* If the enemy should invade . . . with a force less than . . . to create the necessity for embarking, I shall fight a battle to save the country, for which I have made preparations . . . *which refers, I think, to both Busaço ridge where he had had the lateral concealed road renovated and in some of its length actually created six months before the French arrived there, and to the Lines themselves.*

Defending his decision to embark from St Julian without referring to the Lines proved the most intractable problem of all. St Julian lay within the Lines and Peniche outside – it was as simple as that, but he couldn't say so. After waffling through two pages of laborious argument he almost gives in and concludes with this snippet, much loved by almost every doting biographer, and even quoted in books of quotations:

Fourthly; when we do go, I feel a little anxiety to go, like gentlemen, out of the hall door, particularly after the preparations (*not the Lines, but the fortifications at St Julian*) which I have made to enable us to do so, and not out of the back door, or by the area.

Now this was nicely judged. Wellington was already known for his insistence on 'standards' of gentlemanly behaviour, and he knew he was, so it was convincing then, and remains convincing now to those who prefer to fantasise him into a dandy, rather than accept him as the general he was. I am quite convinced that he would never have risked a single life for the sake of such a gesture.

But it was the croakers he was trying to silence, and their influence on Liverpool. The letter concludes: Depend upon it, whatever people may tell you, I am not so desirous as they imagine of fighting desperate battles; if I was, I might fight one any day I please . . . But I have looked to the great result of maintaining our position on the Peninsula . . . I am convinced that . . . the conduct which I have pursued has given us at this moment an efficient army, which is the only hope of the Peninsula . . . All I beg is, that if I am responsible, I may be left to the exercise of my own judgement; and I ask for the fair confidence of Government upon the measures which I am to adopt.

If Government takes the opinion of others . . . then let them give me their instructions in detail, and I will carry them strictly into execution. I may venture, however, to assure you that, with the exception of Marshal Beresford who . . . concurs entirely in all my opinions . . . there is no man in the army who has taken half the pains on the subject as I have.

That Buonaparte would be able now to throw more and more armies into the Peninsula became clearer with his marriage to the daughter of the Emperor of Austria. Europe was, for the time being his, though even the most secure of his satrapies did not always accept his yoke meekly. To Craufurd, one of the bravest of Wellington's generals in a fight, but a croaker behind the scenes, 4 April: The Austrian marriage is a terrible event and must prevent any great movement on the continent for the present. Still I do not despair of seeing at some time or other a check to the Buonaparte system. Recent transactions in Holland show that it is all hollow within, and that it is so inconsistent with the wishes, the interests, and even the existence of civilised society, that he cannot trust even his brothers to carry it into existence.

Thus then the situation at the beginning of April. What happened next was . . . rain, two months of it. The French shifted about, probed the Coa once or twice, seemed for a moment almost weak enough on their side of the Agueda to tempt him into a quick sortie out of his Portuguese fortress, but he thought better of it. In the north Junot laid siege to Astorga, in the south Joseph and Soult plundered Seville.

About now Wellington began to appreciate the full usefulness of the guerrillas: the insurrection is again in a state of organisation and the <u>partidas</u> are beginning to be active . . . The accounts which I receive from all quarters mention the great activity of the parties of guerrillas throughout the country. Some of these accounts are certainly exaggerated, but I have no doubt there is some foundation for them, as I observe that the enemy mention the operations of these parties in the Gazettes published in Madrid. *By the end of the year he was fully alive to the possibilities of fruitful co-operation with them, had learnt to admire and rely on their stamina, the accuracy of their information, the extent to which they controlled almost the entire countryside out of musket shot of the French, and tied down and seriously weakened quite large bodies of troops. In short they restored his faith in Spanish military activity once it was away from the generals and the official military establishment.*

On 1 May came the first significant shift in the situation. To Beresford: Alas! Astorga surrendered on the 22nd April . . . The question is, what they will do now, and what we ought to do. I do not think that Junot will push into Galicia. If he does, they are not equal to the siege of Ciudad Rodrigo; if he does not we are not equal to its relief.

They have not yet moved the heavy guns from Salamanca, and the rain must, for the present stop their operations as well as ours.

If you have driven even a modern vehicle on an unmade-up road in or near Salamanca during wet weather you will appreciate the point. The deep top soil is a thick red clay which, with rain, develops into a vicious pudding that is as slippery as grease and as sticky as treacle at the same time.

By the eleventh it was clear which way Junot was going. To Henry: A great part of Junot's corps, it is said, is gone to Valladolid. It is reported at Valladolid that Masséna is coming to command the army to be employed against this country, and that a General Martinière is coming with 20,000 more men.

I should be very glad at any time to see Alava, who is a very good fellow. I do not know, however, in what manner I could employ him . . .

André Masséna, duke of Rivoli, Prince of Essling was indeed on his way. The son of a village wine-store keeper born near Nice he is judged by many to have been the best of the marshals. Certainly that was Wellington's opinion. He saved the Emperor from a humiliating defeat at Aspern-Essling, and did as much as his master to create the victory of Wagram. His commission now was 'to drive the leopard into the sea' and was proof enough that the French were now indeed to 'go regularly to work'.

Alava too deserves a note: for a start he actually fought at Trafalgar in the Spanish navy where one of his uncles was a Spanish admiral under Villeneuve. Later he transferred to the army, and in Seville and Cadiz worked assiduously for the English interest. He was soon to become first a Spanish Commissary for Wellington, then an A.D.C., and finally a life-long friend.

Behind the Lines work went ahead to prepare the Portuguese for the French invasion, and particularly for the part they would have to play in Wellington's scorched earth policy. He took exception to a proclamation that had been issued on the subject. To Stuart, 13 May: In my opinion, the fault of all these proclamations . . . has been that the writers of them have followed the example of those published by the French . . . they have invariably flattered and deceived the people. What we want is: First an exposition of their danger. Secondly a reference to the existing means of resistance. Thirdly an exposition of their duties. Fourthly an exhortation to perform them: and lastly a declaration that those who should not . . . would be punished without distinction of persons. *Had he not been a general, he would have been a good teacher of English. He goes on:* This ought to be stated in plain language, without bombast, and ought above all to be short . . . Every man in Portugal is sufficiently alive to the danger, and is very anxious to avert it: there is plenty of enthusiasm; *not, as we already know, a commodity the Peer had much time for –* there are cries of 'Viva' and illuminations, and patriotic songs and feasts everywhere: but that which is wanting is the plain simple performance of his duty, each in his station, and obedience to order.

That the Portuguese should love us and hate them was an even more pressing concern than usual. Brigadier Cox, the English commander of Almeida, drew a fierce rebuke for requisitioning carriages to move magazines rather than hiring and paying for them in the proper way. War is a terrible evil, particularly to those who reside in those parts of the country which are the seat of operations of hostile armies; but I believe it will be acknowledged by the people of Portugal, that it is inflicted in a less degree by the British troops than by the others; and that eventually all they get from the country is paid for, and that they require only what is necessary.

The wet, however, continued. To Beresford, 21 May: We have at last got a fine day, and we may expect that the weather will settle, and that the rivers will fall . . . *but it was a false alarm: the rain came back, Masséna returned to Valladolid, and the impasse continued. Not until 2 June could he write:* Some of the guns which left Salamanca on the 28th appear to have arrived . . . *On the fifth:* The enemy have been collecting in our front for some days, but they hitherto have not crossed the Agueda . . .

It was time to grasp the nastiest nettle of the campaign. Ciudad Rodrigo was garrisoned by five thousand brave Spaniards under a particularly competent and valiant governor, General Herrasti. But on three sides, all but the south-west where the river runs under the walls, it faces an undulating plain which was occupied by the French. As Wellington had said five weeks earlier – if the French were equal to the siege, then he would not be equal to its relief, for he could not face an equal or superior French army, in open country, with fewer cavalry, and a river in his rear. He wrote to Herrasti on the sixth: I assure you that I am sincerely interested in the fate of Ciudad Rodrigo, not only on account of Your Excellency, the garrison, and inhabitants, but from a strong sense of the importance of the preservation of that place for the general cause; and I hope you will believe, that if I should not be able to attempt your relief, it will be owing to the superior strength of the enemy, and to the necessity of attending to other important objects.

Within five days, in spite of yet more rain, the French had crossed the Agueda and completed the investment. A bitter note now appears in Wellington's letter to Henry: I think that I might have delayed still longer the complete investment of the place . . . if the Government possessed any strength, or desired to have any thing done but what is <u>safe and cheap.</u>

On 15 June one finishing touch to the defence of Portugal was put into effect – the use of telegraphs, masts on which a system of balls and triangular pennants could be hoisted to communicate over fifteen miles or more. It was a naval system. To Berkeley: I should be very much obliged if you could give us some assistance . . . sober signalmen, one at each station, with one seaman at each, would be a sufficient establishment at present.

To Liverpool, 27 June: The enemy commenced his fire on Ciudad Rodrigo on the 24th and it has continued ever since. That of the place has been well kept up.

Don Julian Sanchez, who commands a party *(that is, of guerrillas)* which had been attached to the garrison for some time quitted it with his party (195 men) without loss, on the night of the 22nd, and brought me a letter from the Governor, in which he states his determination, and that of the garrison, to hold out to the last . . .

Don Julian Sanchez, 'El Charro' (which is the word for the people and country round Salamanca), was a flamboyant figure whose huge black beard and motley followers put one observer in mind of Ali Baba and his Forty Thieves. He started life as a herder of fighting bulls, but over the previous two years (some say as a result of seeing his family butchered by the French) had built up, round a nucleus of his colleagues from the ranches, a flying column of lancers whose numbers fluctuated between 90 and 600 men. He attacked convoys, harassed columns, and above all kept open communications with the 'intelligence people' at Salamanca, of whom more later. His was one of the first detachments to be fully integrated into Wellington's army – soon they wore British uniforms but distinguished them with long yellow or red scarves. The local girls had a song about him which, freely translated, goes something like this:

Any lancer of Don Julian
I must love and cherish
But the one who loves me back
I must have or perish.

Don Julian, your lancers
Look like clouds at sunrise,
Their blood red scarves are streamers
That dazzle female eyes.

A lancer of Don Julian
has impaled me on his lance
I'm sure he'll take me on his crupper
All the way to France.

He was, however, Spanish. To Henry, 25 June: Don Julian . . . says he brought with him 195; he brought in reality about 90.

The siege was marvellously protracted. 29 June: Ciudad Rodrigo is making a capital defence; and I only regret that the enemy have collected such a force that it is impossible for me to attempt the relief of the place. *2 July:* Ciudad Rodrigo held out last night, but I fear they will have surrendered this day . . .

Meanwhile, the harvest was in, and what other commander would have been so aware that his men, though volunteers, were not so by choice but through unemployment.

G.O.   11th July, 1810.
The Commander of the Forces requests that the General Officers commanding divisions will direct that those soldiers who may be inclined to reap the harvest may have leave of absence for that purpose . . . *It was, of course, vitally important that it should be not only safely gathered in but gathered to the rear before the French push came. On the same day, he wrote to Liverpool:* I have received a report that Ciudad Rodrigo surrendered to the enemy yesterday evening . . . I consider the defence to have been most honourable to the Governor, Don Andreas Herrasti and its garrison, and to have been equally creditable to the arms of Spain. I have been most anxiously desirous to relieve the place since it has been attacked; and have been prevented . . . only by the certainty which I had that the attempt must fail.

Almeida remained across Masséna's path into Portugal, and there was no reason to suppose that it would not hold out for as long as Ciudad Rodrigo had.

The main British army remained behind the Coa, but Craufurd was still between the two rivers and in contact with the second fortress (see map page 133). On 11 July he was caught in an untidy little skirmish almost exactly half way between the two towns at Barquilla. It is of little significance but it brought to Wellington's attention a Captain the Hon. C. Somers Cocks, whose detachment of light dragoons were criticised. The young man tried to insist on an inquiry to clear them, which Wellington turned down, but what he saw of Cocks led him now to use him in scouting missions where intelligence as well as bravery were required. Later he became one of his A.D.C.s for a time, that is he joined that select band of young, aristocratic, brave, and unusually intelligent officers that made up 'his family'.

'Black Bob' Craufurd was a difficult person to manage. He was ambitious, relied too heavily on the famed mobility of his Light division, had to be restrained and warned not to take risks.

On 22 July, at 8.00 p.m. Wellington wrote to him: I have ordered two battalions to support your flanks, but I am not desirous of engaging in an affair beyond the Coa. Under these circumstances, if you are not covered from the sun where you are, would it not be better that you should come to this side with your infantry at least? *This, for most people, would have been enough. However, on the very next morning, Craufurd was caught by Ney with an exposed right flank, and the ravine of the Coa and only one narrow bridge in his rear. His only protection was Almeida itself, half a mile beyond his left. News of what happened did not reach Wellington until the afternoon.*

To Craufurd, 24 July, 2.00 p.m.: I have heard there was firing in your front as late as nine this morning; but I conclude I should have heard from you this morning, if it had been serious. *Then at ¼ before 3:* I have just received Captain Campbell's note written at eleven. I think you had better retire upon Carvalhal, holding Valverde, and the heights upon the Coa only by your piquets, and communicate with the left of the Pinhel with General Picton. *Then at 3.00 p.m., to Campbell:* I have just heard General Craufurd was attacked this morning under Almeida, and that he has retired across the Coa.

In fact 300 men were lost, and but for the steadiness of the troops there could have been many, many more. The trouble was that many of the officers, and even many of the men were simply not ready to leave the two fortresses to their fate without a fight, and their commander would not give them a fight until he was sure of a victory with minimal losses. His correspondence with his generals became quite sharp.

To Cotton, commanding the cavalry now in place of Payne, 30 July, 10.00 p.m.: You do not appear to have occupied Juremelha, or to be aware of the advantage of occupying that post. You will see everything from it, and it will of course give you proportionate security . . .

To Cole: I request you to write your communications, notwithstanding that you may think it proper to send an officer; as the mode of stating a circumstance makes a difference in the meaning . . .

To Cotton again, who would not keep his bullock drawn forges sufficiently to the rear: That which the commanding officers do not, or will not understand, is that we shall retreat, and that bullock carts cannot keep up on a retreat with cavalry. I am quite tired of this subject, upon which I have been writing above six weeks.

To his brother William he wrote more in sorrow than in anger. Although I shall be hanged for them, you may be very certain that not only I have had nothing to do with, but had positively forbidden the foolish affairs in which Craufurd involved his outposts . . . In respect to the last . . . I had positively desired him not to engage in any affair on the other side of the Coa . . . I had expressed my wish that he should withdraw his infantry to the left of the river . . . After all this he remained above two hours on his ground after the enemy appeared in his front . . . during which time he might have retired across the Coa twice over . . .

You will say, if this be the case, why not accuse Craufurd? I answer, because if I am to be hanged for it, I cannot accuse a man who I believe has meant well, and whose error is one of judgement, and not of intention.

The enemy are wofully strong; I should think not less than 80,000 men whom they can bring into Portugal: but I don't give the game up as lost, and I think it will be gained, if Government will only land me some infantry to fight the battle near Lisbon.

The enemy have at least 250,000 effectives in Spain.

Masséna moved in on Almeida, but very slowly, very deliberately and another period of phoney war set in. It was not until 17 August that the siege was properly under way. Two days earlier Wellington was able to report to Liverpool the growing success of his scorched earth policy: The inhabitants of the country have generally quitted their villages, and the enemy experience great difficulty in procuring subsistence: they are obliged to send a considerable distance to find it, so that their detachments for this purpose and their patrols are much annoyed by the Ordenanza, and by the light detachments of the army.

Some of the Portuguese peasants did, however, need encouragement. To Cotton: I cannot read the name of the village which the people have not quitted, but let them know that they may stay or not as they please, but that any man that has communication with the enemy shall be hanged.

On the nineteenth he twisted the screw a little tighter. I propose to collect the army again to the front, in order to oblige the enemy to keep his forces collected during the operations of the siege, and thus increase his difficulties as to subsistence, and afford more scope for the operations of the guerrillas.

To Henry: They are removing their women and properties out of the enemy's way, and taking arms in their own defence. The country is made a desert, and behind almost every stone wall the French will meet an enemy . . . If we cannot relieve Almeida, it will, I hope, make a stout defence: the Governor is an obstinate fellow, and talks of a siege of ninety days . . .

Of course not everyone was wholehearted in their support of the war effort. Don Joso Paes, Inquisitor General of Coimbra and something of a notable, had the effrontery to complain that a Major Marston who had been billeted on him had brought his wife and children too. When he received the following no doubt the don disappeared in a puff of smoke. . . . These duties are more peculiarly incumbent up on the rich and high in station, who would be the first victims of, and greatest sufferers from, the enemy's success . . . It is not very agreeable to any body to have strangers quartered in his house; nor is it very agreeable to us strangers, who have good houses in our own country, to be obliged to seek quarters here. We are not here for our pleasure: the situation of your country renders it necessary; and you, a man of family and fortune, who have much to lose, should not be the first to complain of the inconvenience of our presence in the country.

In spite of the Don Josos of this world, things were looking up. It was even possible that the supply problem might land Masséna in a scrape . . . Unfortunately, on the very first day the French opened fire on Almeida a keg of powder carried by a donkey from the magazine in the crypt of the cathedral, sprang a leak, left a trail, and the cathedral itself blew up in one of the biggest explosions the world had yet seen. Every house roof was sheered off by the blast, as if by a knife. Brigadier Cox still wanted to fight on, but the Portuguese officers led their men out on the next day, the twenty-seventh.

To Stuart, 31 August: . . . the explosion of the magazine destroyed the whole town, made a breach in the place, blew all the guns excepting three into the ditch, destroyed all the ammunition . . . killed or wounded the greater part of the artillery men. The major commanding the artillery was the person employed by Cox to settle the capitulation for him. He went out and informed the French of the exact state of the place after the explosion, and never returned!! Masséna has made him a Colonel!!

103

The stones of the buildings killed or wounded forty men even in the enemy's lines.

BUSACO

On 3 September the orderly retreat began behind a screen of Cotton's cavalry. Cocks was even further behind him. To Cotton, 3 September, 8.00 a.m.: . . . I am going to Gouvea. I beg you to attend to the former instructions; observe the enemy's movements, but do not engage yourself in any serious affair. Captain Cocks is upon Prados, with a piquet of observation upon Guarda. Prados is on the hill on the left of the Vale de Mondego . . . I believe Cole has left the English key of the telegraph at Guarda with Cocks; if he has not I shall desire him to send it to him. I shall leave mine with the telegraph officer you have had with you, who shall stay here.

When Guarda and Celorico are finally evacuated, take care that the telegraphs are destroyed; and probably the most effective mode of destruction would be to have straw laid in them ready to burn them.

To Hill, who was near Castello Branco, watching the Tagus, 6 September: I rely upon your prudence and discretion not to engage in any affair of which the result can be at all doubtful. Retire gradually, if you find the enemy threatening you in too great force; and let me hear from you constantly.

If we can avoid any accident before we all join, I have confidence of our final success.

The croakers, however, had Moore's retreat to Coruña too much in mind. To Beresford, 8 September: The croaking which already prevails in the army, and particularly about head quarters, is disgraceful to us as a nation, and does infinite mischief to the cause . . . *To brother William:* There is a despondency among some; a want of confidence in their own exertions; an extravagant notion of the power and resources of the French, and a distaste for the war in the Peninsula, which sentiments have been created and are kept up by correspondence with England, even with Ministers and those connected with them. *Amongst them was Adjutant General Charles Stewart, no connection of the Minister in Lisbon, but a half-brother of Castlereagh. The situation was complicated because he was a close, though scarcely loyal, friend of the Wellesleys.* All this is uncomfortable. With the exception of Beresford I have really no assistance; I am

Guarda

left to myself, to my own exertions, to my own execution, the mode of execution, and even the superintendence of that mode: but still I don't despair. I am positively in no scrape; and if the country can be saved, we shall save it. Government have behaved with their usual weakness and folly about reinforcements . . .

In spite of having to do everything himself he found time to write to Minister Stuart in Lisbon about the dangers of the urban mob in Lisbon, 9 September: I think we cannot employ our time better in accustoming these gentry to the discipline to which it is obvious they must submit as soon as matters become at all critical . . . all coffee houses should be shut up at sunset . . . patrols should go every hour, day and night . . . all disorderly assemblages of people should be immediately dispersed, &c. *It is the way of authority to leave in force regulations passed during an emergency until an interested party makes an effort to get them removed. The sequel to this comes a year later. To Stuart, 15 August, 1811:* I enclose a petition from the keeper of a coffee house in Lisbon, on the subject of a regulation supposed to have been recommended by me, that the coffee houses of Lisbon should be closed at a certain hour every evening . . . I see no reason why the regulations should be continued.

On the tenth Guarda, the highest town in Portugal and a chilly place to be camping in in August let alone September, fell. To Beresford: Cocks sent a dragoon with a message to Cotton . . . to inform him that a column consisting of 3000 cavalry and 5000 infantry were just entering Guarda.

And still the croakers played on his nerves. To Stuart, 11 September: . . . for the first time, whether owing to the opposition in England, or whether the magnitude of the concern is too much for their minds and nerves, or whether I am mistaken and they are right, I cannot tell; but there is a system of croaking in the army which is highly injurious to the public service . . . Officers have a right to form their own opinions upon events and transactions; but officers of high rank or situation ought to keep their opinions to themselves: if they do not approve of the system of operations of their commander, they ought to withdraw from the army. And this is the point to which I must bring some . . . Believe me, that, if anybody else, knowing what I do, had commanded the army, they would now have been at Lisbon, if not in their ships.

On the fifteenth the French began to move in earnest. To Cotton, midnight: . . . I am now apprehensive that the directions I shall give you may not suit the situation in which you may be. I wish you to fall back. *To Beresford, 17 September:* You should order all your sick away from Coimbra . . . and send people down to be in readiness to remove or destroy your ammunition and other stores there without loss of time. I am going to give similar orders. *And so he left Viseu, which, with Celorico, had been his principal head quarters for eight months.*

On 21 September he was still several miles to the north of Coimbra, on a ridge above the Mondego, watching his regiments filing in down the winding defiles of the river, through woods of pine and juniper, toiling up the last mile or so of a steep, rocky hillside. To Cotton, Convent of Busaco, 21 September, 9.30 p.m.: We have an excellent position here, in which I am strongly tempted to give battle. Unfortunately Hill is one day later than I expected; and there is a road upon our left by which we may be turned and cut off from Coimbra. But I do not yet give up hopes of discovering a remedy for this last misfortune . . . *During the next three days he shepherded his forces in – Beresford and the Portuguese from the left, Hill put on a magnificent spurt and joined from the right. By the 26th all 51,000 were in position along the eight mile ridge of Busaco, or lying behind it. Below, French advance guards scouted along the road he had used himself and by evening the full force of 66,000 were massing around the two villages below. That night no camp-fires were lit on the ridge. Apart from riflemen and piquets the allies were invisible to the French.*

At dawn, on the twenty-seventh, with drums beating, they came up the rocky slopes, through a thick white mist.

To Liverpool: The Serra de Busaco is a high ridge which extends from the Mondego in a northerly direction about eight miles. At the highest point of the ridge, about two miles from its termination, is the convent and garden of Busaco. *Nearby is an excellent small museum commemorating the battle, and a cenotaph. The whole area has been re-forested and is now far more thickly wooded than it was in 1810. . . .* the whole army was collected upon the Serra de Busaco, with the British cavalry observing the plain in the rear of its left . . . At six in the morning of the 27th the enemy made two desperate attacks upon our position, the one on the right *(Regnier)*, the other on the left of the highest point of the Serra *(Ney)*. One division of French infantry arrived at the top of the ridge, where it was attacked in the most gallant manner by the 88th regiment *(Connaught Rangers)*, under the command of Lieut. Colonel Wallace, the 45th . . . and by the 8th Portuguese regiment . . . directed by Major General Picton. These three corps advanced with the bayonet and drove the enemy's division from the advantageous ground which they had obtained. The other division of the 2nd corps attacked farther on the right, also in front of . . . Picton's division . . . These were repulsed before they could reach the top of the ridge . . . by the 74th and the brigade of Portuguese infantry of the 9th and 21st regiments . . . Major

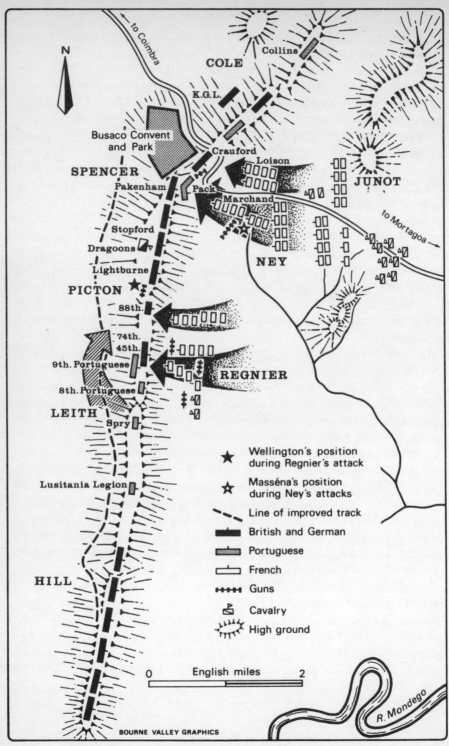

to Coimbra

N

COLE
Collins

K.G.L.

Busaco Convent
and Park

Crauford
Loison

JUNOT

SPENCER

Pakenham
Pack

Marchand

to Mortagoa

Stopford

Dragoons

NEY

Lightburne

PICTON

★

88th.

74th.
45th.

9th. Portuguese
REGNIER

8th. Portuguese

LEITH

Spry

Lusitania Legion

HILL

★ Wellington's position
during Regnier's attack

☆ Masséna's position
during Ney's attacks

– – – Line of improved track

British and German

Portuguese

French

Guns

Cavalry

High ground

0   2
English miles

BOURNE VALLEY GRAPHICS

R. Mondego

6. The Battle of Busaco, 27 September 1810

General Leith also moved to his left to the support of . . . Picton and
aided in the defeat of the enemy . . . I beg to assure your Lordship that I
have never witnessed a more gallant attack than that made by the 88th,
45th and 8th Portuguese regiments. *What he doesn't mention is how all the
British movements were made along the improved road behind the ridge, a
lateral communication which made his defence the dynamic affair it was.*

On the left the enemy attacked with three divisions of infantry on the
part of the Serra occupied by the light division commanded by Brig.
General Craufurd, and by the brigade of Portuguese infantry commanded by Brig. General Pack. One division of infantry only made any
progress to the top of the hill, and they were immediately charged with
the bayonet by . . . Craufurd . . . and driven down with immense loss.
*This was the climax of the engagement. The French struggled up a steep,
broken, partially wooded and shrubbed slope in the face of at least 500
skirmishing riflemen. At the top Craufurd, a small, black-chinned man sitting
in an enormous saddle on a fine heavy horse, waited for them with the guns of
Ross's battery on either side of him. Behind him, behind the ridge, but only
twenty yards away, were a thousand muskets. The guns fired one last round of
canister each, limbered up and moved back, the French, exhausted and deci-
mated though they were, managed a cheer and surged up the last few yards.
Craufurd seemed to be alone. At twenty-five yards he bellowed, in his deep,
organ-like voice: 'Fifty-second, avenge Moore', and they came over the shelf as
one man. All volleyed, the centre charged with bayonets, but the worst damage
by far was done by the flanking companies who lapped round the French
columns firing regular volleys from the two-deep line.*

*The last attack came to the south of Craufurd's position. The French were
forced to deploy 3,500 men to clear Pack's 500 Portuguese skirmishers from a
pine wood on the lower slope. They reformed and came on, cheered by the sight of
the few brown uniforms left in front of them. Pack did not wait. He brought his
line battalions to the crest at a hundred yards and in the face of their steady fire
the French could come on no further.* . . . the 4th Portuguese caçadores,
and the 1st and 16th regiments, directed by Brig. General Pack . . .
showed great steadiness and gallantry.

The loss sustained by the enemy . . . has been enormous. I understand that the Generals of division Merle, Loison, and Maucune are
wounded and General Simon was taken prisoner. The enemy left 2000
killed upon the field of battle, and I understand from the prisoners and
deserted that the loss in wounded is immense. *Total French casualties
were at least 4,500. The allies lost 1,170 shared equally between the Portuguese
and British.*

The enemy did not renew his attack, excepting by the fire of his light troops on the 28th; but he moved a large body of infantry and cavalry from the left of his centre to the rear, from whence I saw his cavalry in march on the road from Mortagoa over the mountains towards Oporto.

Having thought it probable that he would endeavour to turn our left by that road, I had directed Colonel Trant with his division of militia, to march to Sardão, with the intention that he should occupy the mountains, but unfortunately he was sent round by Oporto, by the General Officer commanding in the north, *not the first incompetence General Bucellar had been guilty of,* and he did not reach Sardão till the 28th at night, after the enemy were in possession of the ground.

As it was probable that . . . the enemy would throw the whole of his army upon the road, by which he could avoid the Serra de Busaco . . . I was induced to withdraw.

I should not do justice to the service, or to my own feelings, if I did not take this opportunity of drawing your attention to the merits of Marshal Beresford. To him exclusively, under the Portuguese Government, is due the merit of having raised, formed, disciplined, and equipped the Portuguese army, which has now shown itself capable of engaging and defeating the enemy.

It was a point he made again and again in the next weeks, but perhaps most notably in the General Orders for the thirtieth.

Every friend to his country and to the liberties of the world, and the whole British army, must have observed with the greatest satisfaction the gallantry and steadiness of the Portuguese troops during these days, and that they, equally with their brother soldiers in His Majesty's service have deserved and obtained the approbation of Marshal Beresford, and of the Commander of the Forces.

These words are still read with pride in Portugal, for they are inscribed on the lintels of the museum that is built on just about the spot where Pack's troops were positioned at the beginning of the battle.

TORRES VEDRAS

To Henry, Leiria, 3 October: The allied army is behind this town, and the advanced guard in Pombal. We shall make our retreat to the positions in front of Lisbon without much difficulty, or any loss . . . *apart, inevitably, from those caught plundering or looting. To Cotton:* There is a

BOURNE VALLEY GRAPHICS

N

TRANT AND WILSON – PORTUGUESE MILITIA

Thomar

Torres Novas

Pernes

Rio Mayor

Santarem

R. Tagus

Peniche

HILL, BERESFORD

Torres Vedras

Merciana

Alemquer

Sobral

Salvaterra

Pero Nero

Cadafoes

Castanheira

Alhandra

Villa Franca

Mafra

Calandriz

Alverca

Bucellas

LISBON

St. Julian

Setubal

Alcacer do Sol

Main fortified areas

Area to which Masséna was constricted 15th. Nov., 1810 – 6th. March, 1811

0   25

English miles

7. The Lines of Torres Vedras, 15 October 1810 – 6 March 1811

report that there are some stragglers, Portuguese as well as English, in the villages on the right and left of the road where you are cantoned, and I shall be much obliged to you if you will send out patroles, and take up all men of this description, and send them in here as prisoners. *General Orders:* Major General Picton is requested not to allow the troops of his division to enter any town unless necessarily obliged to pass through it, until further orders. *To which was added, at the end of the same day:* a British and a Portuguese soldier have . . . been hanged this day for plundering in the town of Leiria.

To William, on the fourth: The croakers about useless battles will attack me again on that of Busaco, notwithstanding that our loss was really trifling . . . the battle has had the best effects in inspiring confidence in the Portuguese troops both among our croaking officers and the people of the country. It has likewise removed an impression that had begun to be very general, that we intend to fight no more but retire to our ships; and it has given the Portuguese troops a taste for an amusement to which they were not before accustomed.

At the rear of the rearguard was the excellent Cocks. In retiring the British cavalry from Fornos . . . Captain Cocks of the 16th light dragoons charged the enemy. *It all looked good.* The enemy suffer great distress. The inhabitants of the country have fled from their houses universally, carrying with them everything they could take away which could be deemed useful to the enemy. *In short:* My opinion is that the French are in a scrape.

As the armies grew nearer to Lisbon less sanguine souls showed signs of panic. The Regency presumed to instruct Wellington on where he should make his stand, and, amazingly, demonstrated just how good the security had been. To Stuart: I believe . . . the government do not know where the lines are. Those round Lisbon are not those in which I shall place the army, but those extending from Torres Vedras to the Tagus . . . I know best where to station my troops, and where to make a stand against the enemy, and I shall not alter a system, framed upon mature considera- tion, upon any suggestion of theirs. I am responsible for what I do, and they are not; and I recommend to them to look to the measures for which they are responsible . . . viz., to provide for the tranquillity of Lisbon, and for the food of the army, and of the people.

By the fifteenth the army was safely within the first lines, the fortified positions of which were now held by Portuguese militia, and, to the east, by the Marques de la Romana's Spanish army that had pulled in from Merida and Badajoz. A few skirmishes developed in front; the French seemed to concentrate at Sobral, but no attack developed. Masséna demanded of his officers why he had not been told about the lines. They answered – Wellington made them. 'Que diable, Wellington n'a pas construit ces montagnes!'

Indeed he had not – but what he had done is, in many places, as imposing now as it was then: hills crowned with the flat, functional forts of the period, one hundred and forty of them in the first line alone, slopes denuded of trees and bushes, dry stone dikes and terraces levelled to form pitilessly clear glaçis; trench systems ringing hill-sides where vineyards had strutted up the slopes before. At both ends lakes, inundations, had been formed by damming rivers and everywhere, always in sight, was one telegraph at least – the weird gallows-like structures up and down which pennants and globes rose and fell, no doubt reporting Masséna's progress as he hacked his way along, sullen, then angry, with his frightened A.D.C.s jangling behind. And then of course, above those low but steep and menacing hills, the grey storm clouds rolled in off the Atlantic and the curtains of rain swept past between him and those blank low forts, and mud and cold settled round the French to complete their despair. Surely he must attack – and be defeated – or withdraw! But no: to everyone's growing bewilderment he did neither. Masséna and the French, 60,000 of them, sat down in that wretched corner and, to the Peer's growing irritation, contrived not to starve.

They were cut off, surrounded. To the north Colonel Trant arrived near Coimbra on the 7th . . . and took possession of it . . . he took 80 officers and 5000 men (principally sick and wounded) . . . and . . . Waters *(he of the Oporto wine barges)* with small detachments of cavalry and infantry, also in the enemy's rear, has taken many prisoners. *So. There was no hope of succour from the rear.*

But: At this moment the enemy are living upon grain found close to the lines; and they grind it into flour with the mills in our sight, which the Government were repeatedly pressed to order the people to render useless, and which could have been rendered useless only by taking away their sails. *To Stuart, 31 October:* The French could not have stayed here a week if the provisions had been removed; and the length of time they can now stay depends upon the quantity remaining . . . all military arrangements are useless, if they can find subsistence on the ground they occupy.

For aught I know to the contrary, they may be able to maintain their position till the whole French army is brought to their assistance. It is heartbreaking to contemplate the chance of failure from such obstinacy and folly.

After all the situation began to look depressing and frustrating, if not immediately dangerous – the nearest French armies were some way off and well occupied either with plunder or with guerrillas. Nevertheless it was disappoint-

113

ing. What was needed was a party, a feast – and the excuse was at hand. Pero Nero, 3 November, 1810, 10.00 a.m.: My dear Beresford, It gives me the greatest satisfaction to inform you that I have received the King's commands to invest you with the Order of the Bath . . . I rather believe it had better be . . . in the presence of as many officers of the army and other individuals as I can collect at a feast . . . *The invitations went out.* To Vice Admiral the Hon. G. Berkeley: My Dear Sir, I propose to invest Marshal Beresford on Wednesday at Mafra, and intend to give a great feast . . . at which I hope to have the pleasure of your company, and that of Lady Emily Berkeley and the Miss Berkeleys . . . I propose to invest the Marshal at about five o'clock, and we shall dine afterwards, and then the ball . . . *and all the captains of the squadron were invited too. All accepted: for a moment Wellington faltered –* We shall all appear in our best attire, but I fear that, with many, bad is the best; and we shall be highly flattered by your company, and that of the Captains of the Fleet, whether in full or frock uniform.

It all went off very well, a good time was had by all – a bare fifteen miles from the French outposts.

And then at last . . .
To Brigadier General R. Craufurd. On the Hill in front of Sobral, 15th Nov., 1810. 20m. past 10 A.M. My Dear General, You will have observed that the enemy have retired from the ground they occupied with their right, about Sobral, and I think it most probable that they will have retired their whole army towards Santarem . . .

For three days Wellington contemplated attack but then, to Hill, 19 November 5.00 p.m.: . . . I did not attack Santarem this morning, as the artillery intended for the left missed its way; and I am rather glad that I did not make the attack, as the enemy have there undoubtedly a very strong post . . . *On the twenty-first, to Henry:* The French have a position at Santarem, compared with which Busaco is nothing. However, when it shall be fair weather, and the roads passable, I hope to dislodge them by moving on their flanks.

In just over four weeks the Lines had done their job. Masséna watched his army wither through starvation, sickness, and appalling weather from a host that could threaten Lisbon with an army at least 10,000 stronger than its defender's to one that was now outnumbered by about the same amount. He withdrew to one of the most naturally secure positions in the Peninsula, and sat it out there for a further three months, but unless or until he was very substantially reinforced, he was now very much the defender. The tide had turned, or at any rate, had reached that point where contending forces are so evenly matched as to create 'slack-water'.

Wellington was often criticised for not giving credit where credit was due, and is reputed to have said, when asked in old age if there was any thing he could have done better, 'Yes, I should have given more praise.' *But it is difficult to see in what way he could have improved on this encomium of Fletcher and the Engineers. To Liverpool, 21 November: . . .* Having advanced from the positions in which I was enabled to bring the enemy to a stand, and to oblige them to retire without venturing upon any attack, it is but justice to Lieut. Colonel Fletcher, and the Officers of the Royal Engineers, to draw your Lordship's attention to the ability and diligence with which they have executed the works by which these positions have been strengthened, to such a degree, as to render any attack upon that line occupied by the allied army very doubtful, if not entirely hopeless. The enemy's army may be reinforced, and they may again induce me to think it expedient . . . to resume these positions; but I do not believe they have it in their power to bring such a force against us as to render the contest a matter of doubt. We are indebted for these advantages to Lieut. Colonel Fletcher and the officers of the Royal Engineers . . .

Thus his public dispatch. In the private letter he wrote: My dispatch will give you a tolerably correct notion of the state of affairs here. At first I thought the enemy were off, and I am not certain yet they are not going . . . I am convinced there is no man in his senses who had ever passed a winter in Portugal who would not recommend them to go . . .

It is probable that we shall have another campaign in the Peninsula.

1811

—∿∿—

SLACK WATER

THE PURSUIT

SABUGAL

FUENTES DE OÑORO

ALBUERA

THE TURNING POINT

—∿∿—

SLACK WATER

G.O.   Alemquer, 16th Nov., 1810

The Commander of the Forces requests the officers commanding regiments will be very cautious in occupying the quarters in which the French troops may have been quartered; to make their men clean them well out before they sleep in them; and if possible to have fires lighted in them; but care must be taken not to burn the houses. These precautions will be found to contribute much to preserve the health of the soldiers.

Wellington

To the Right Hon. W. Wellesley Pole

My Dear William,   Cartaxo, 8th Dec., 1810.

. . . I am glad you approve of the battle of Busaço. I trust that you will approve equally of my subsequent proceedings . . . I feel I must not lose a great battle; and I believe Masséna has very much the same feeling respecting his situation . . . I have 60,000 men in their shoes, and he has 50,000. But this superiority of numbers is not sufficient to induce me to think it expedient to attack the French in a very strong position which they have got . . . I have determined to persevere in my cautious system, to operate upon the flanks and rear of the enemy with my small and light detachments, and thus force them out of Portugal by the distresses they will suffer and do them all the mischief I can upon their retreat.

Masséna is an old fox, and is as cautious as I am: he risks nothing. But it is astonishing what a superiority all our light detachments have assumed over the French . . . although I may not win a battle immediately, I shall not lose one; and you may depend upon it that we are safe, for the winter at all events . . .

Give my best love to Mrs Pole and the girls, and believe me,

Ever yours most affectionately,

Wellington

Masséna, it seems, wily though he was, or even because he was wily, did not want to move out of his impasse without further instructions on how it was to be done. The stalemate therefore continued for as long as it took him to send

119

General Foy to Paris to report to the boss, and the point is that took a long time, for such was the 'superiority of our light detachments' *and of the guerrillas beyond them that he needed to take 1,500 men with him to be sure of getting safely as far as Ciudad Rodrigo.*

The delay was too much for many of Wellington's generals, especially those who had seats in either of the Houses of Parliament. The King was mad again, a regency seemed likely, and there was just a chance there would be a new Government, even a whig one.

To Craufurd, who was still only a brigadier though he commanded a division: Our operations depend so much upon those of the enemy, that it is impossible for me to say at what period officers might with propriety go to England . . . Adverting to the number of General Officers senior to you in the army, it has not been an easy task to keep you in your command; and, if you go, I fear that I should not be able to appoint you to it again . . .

In Cadiz there were intrigues to drive a wedge between Wellington and Romana, for one faction wanted the Marques back there. They came to nothing for the Peer had come to respect, indeed love the Marques. It prompted this comment: It is difficult to understand the Spaniards exactly, they are such a mixture of haughtiness and low intrigue.

The blank, wet, cold, grey days trickled by. Masséna sat on his line between the Tagus and the craggy hills of Rio Mayor with water, marshes and earth works between. By shifting back he had opened up another area where a few peasants remained to be tortured into revealing walled-up stores of hams, sausages, vegetables, where ovens could again be repaired and mills set turning. To Liverpool, 21 December: It is certainly astonishing that the enemy have been able to remain in this country so long; and it is an extraordinary instance of what a French army can do. It is positively a fact that they brought no provisions with them, and they have not received even a letter since they entered Portugal . . . This time last year I was obliged to move the British cavalry only from the district they now occupy with their whole army because it could not be subsisted. But they take everything, and leave the unfortunate inhabitants to starve.

General Leith was the next to try to get home for a spell: I sincerely wish the war was over, that I might take leave myself, and give leave to all those who are desirous to taking it. But as that is not the case, I have been obliged . . . to make rules by which I am guided by the grants of leaves of absence.

Those who are obliged to go for the recovery of their health are compelled to appear before a Medical Board, and I shall be very much obliged to you if you will go through that ceremony . . .

Wellington of course was not idle during this time, and used some of it to complete his reorganisation of the allied armies. In the first place they were now completely integrated one with the other, apart from the militia under Trant, the Ordenanza who were always locally based, and light auxiliaries operating behind French lines. This meant that Beresford's rank as Marshal and Commander of the Portuguese army no longer conferred upon him an independent command, though he remained responsible for recruiting and training the Portuguese regiments.

The combined armies were now divided into eight divisions which remained basically unaltered for the rest of the war, though casualties and sickness meant that both commanders and regiments were constantly being changed, but usually only intermittently, so each division retained its own character, and continued to maintain the same specialities. Each was roughly divided into two thirds British regiments to one third Portuguese, and all but the Light and the 1st usually mustered around 6,000 men.

The Light division, often proudly known as 'The division', was, to begin with, commanded by Craufurd, but drew its traditions from Moore. Craufurd had been unpopular at first — he was a violent, even barbaric disciplinarian and so was at odds with the liberal regimen created by Moore. But by 1811 his men had come to respect him for his dash, his bravery, his competence, and were even developing a sort of affection for him which was no doubt a response to the obvious pride he took in them. Besides taking its place in the line during general engagements the Light was always in the front during advances and covered the retreat during withdrawals, especially in broken country where the cavalry could not perform these functions. It usually mustered only about 4,000 men, and this was perhaps the reason why Wellington was able to keep Craufurd, one of his most junior generals, in command.

The 1st was the largest division at 7,000 and was therefore usually commanded by the most senior — in spring 1811 by Brent Spencer. Because it contained regiments of Guards it was known as 'The Gentlemen's Sons'. The 2nd always operated on the right of the army and, with the 4th formed the nucleus of what was usually Hill's independent command. The 3rd, which usually included a battalion of the 88th, the Connaught Rangers, and, except when ill health intervened was commanded by Thomas Picton, was known as the 'Fighting Third', a reputation it very genuinely earned on the battlefield, but, less fortunately, off it as well. It is perhaps the case that its ranks were more completely drawn from the Irish peasantry than other divisions, and its men felt more at ease, more independent, more able to look after themselves if the urge to straggle, to plunder, or just take a few hours off in the countryside became irresistible. Picton was Welsh gentry by birth, and Wellington said of him that he was as 'rough, foul-mouthed a devil as ever lived, but he always

121

behaved extemely well on service.' *He affected a top hat, against regulations, to keep the sun out of his eyes, which, like those of many of his colleagues, were not good. As a divisional commander he was superb, but failed rather badly in 1813 when the topography of the Pyrenees left him momentarily in something like independent command. He was shot dead at Waterloo leading a decisive charge. When his body was stripped after the battle it was found that a chest wound he had received two days earlier would almost certainly have proved to be mortal. One further anecdote about him cannot be excluded. A Commissary failed to provide the 3rd with rations one day. Picton pointed to a nearby tree and said that if the rations had not arrived by twelve o'clock the next day, he would hang the Commissary on it at half past. The Commissary duly complained to Wellington, who remarked:* 'He said that he'd <u>hang</u> you, did he? Well, General Picton is a man of his word. I think you had better get the rations up in time.'

There is nothing particular to say about the 5th and 6th which usually also operated with the main army, but the 7th were the 'Mongrels', being largely made up of foreign regiments whose uniforms were odd, or by regiments newly arrived from England. It had a high rate of desertion because many of those foreigners were in fact prisoners of war from Napoleon's non-French armies who enlisted as a means of getting across the Channel and so on the first step of the way home.

The cavalry was a separate command, for the most part under Sir Stapleton Cotton, though of course detachments of up to brigade strength were often separated from the main body. Until late in 1811 it was badly under strength – often less than a quarter of what military theorists recommended. This was partly due to the conventional wisdom that British horses could not be kept in Spain, and that subsisting them and replacing them was too expensive. Apart from one regiment in the King's German Legion and auxiliaries like Trant's mounted militia and Sanchez's Lanceros, it was predominantly British.

The artillery came from both armies, and indeed the field artillery of Portugal had a high reputation. It operated not as a separate command but in batteries attached to each division. By French standards there were nothing like enough of them, but what they lacked in mass (Wellington was only ever to concentrate enough to put down a bombardment at Vitoria in 1813) they made up for in mobility. Each battery usually consisted of five six pounder guns and one five-and-a-half-inch howitzer. There was rarely more than one battery to each division, and never more than two.

Hill's health remained a worry. To him, on 30 December, 1810: . . . I have prevailed upon Sir W. C. Beresford to go over the Tagus and take

122

charge of affairs there till you shall have sufficiently recovered to join the army.

Although I am anxious that you should join again, I beg you will not think of moving until your health shall be firmly re-established . . . *But the sickness remained and Beresford kept the more or less independent command on the right until the Summer, with consequences that were almost disastrous. Hill set a precedent by remaining in Portugal, although obviously very poorly.* I am concerned to learn from several quarters that you do not regain your strength so fast as you could wish, and therefore I suggest to you another change of air to Cintra, which is, I believe a very healthy place. You may depend upon it that in such an attack as you have had there is nothing like complete and frequent change of air as a remedy; and I strongly recommend this change for your consideration. *All of which is touching in its concern. Wellington is often presented as cold and unfeeling, but these letters often show just how wrong this assumption is. Where he was convinced of an officer's commitment to the job in hand, to the 'service', he is always generous. When the man is competent too he becomes concerned. Add to commitment and competence, good manners, and affection soon appears.*

Cotton, however, after a mere six months, was attempting to get home, with far less excuse than Hill had, had Hill chosen to use it, and at a moment when a new threat had appeared. 12 January: You will have heard that the French crossed the Guadiana at Merida on the 8th; and it appears to me that they must immediately undertake some operation or other. You will, however, judge for yourself the priority of going home.

The immediate threat was to the Alentejo, which so far had been virtually untouched. However, the French, under Mortier, moved north, presumably intending to reinforce Masséna via Ciudad Rodrigo. Meanwhile the peasants in the Alentejo were failing to do their bit. To Stuart, 16 January: Gordon says that the country abounds in corn, cattle, and provisions of all descriptions. There is something very extraordinary in the people of the Peninsula. I really believe them the most cordial haters of the French, that ever existed: but there is an indolence and a want even of the power of exertion . . . which baffle all our calculations and efforts . . . The people will not sell us what they have, and what they have repeatedly been told will fall into the hands of the enemy, because they will not incur the risk of being obliged, at a later period of the year, to take the trouble of sending to Lisbon to replace for their own consumption that which might have been sold to us. *Which, for once, is naive. Sell now at one price, and buy at black market rates from Lisbon later? The Portuguese equivalent for 'not bloody likely'. The time to sell would be when the first French dragoons crossed the border south of the Tagus – a threat that never materialised.* In the same manner I might now collect at Elvas quantities of corn of all descriptions, but we cannot get in Alentejo carriages for its conveyance to Lisbon, because the lower orders will not work for hire, and the magistrates will not take the trouble of making them work. Can such a people be saved? Are they worth saving?

The Spanish too seemed to be lacking in commitment to the cause. Soult was threatening Olivenza and Badajoz. Instead of strengthening Badajoz, which was already a sound fortress and difficult to take, Cadiz ordered most of their remaining regulars outside the Isla de Leon into Olivenza. Actually they had their reasons. Olivenza was disputed between Spain and Portugal and had been ceded to Spain as a result of the first joint French and Spanish invasion of Portugal in 1804. With the Portuguese army now looking very strong indeed, there was every chance they would put back their own garrison and reclaim it. Nevertheless, under existing circumstances it was militarily speaking a silly thing to do. To Henry, 20 January: They have settled their concerns finely in Estremadura; and no arrangement was ever so completely Spanish than to have sent 3000 and 4000 of their best men into Olivença *(Portuguese spelling),* a place without artillery, ammunition, or provisions, under circumstances in which it is impossible, if they should be attacked, that they could be relieved! Then as usual they halloo to the whole world for assistance, and abuse if it is not immediately given to them. . . . the Marques de la Romana, who is very ill, settled yesterday that the divisions of Carrera and O'Donnell, which are with this army, should cross the Tagus and proceed to the relief of Olivença. However, it is nonsense to talk of these people as troops, or to reckon upon their operations in any manner whatever, excepting in defence of a strong post, from which they have no retreat. In this view the loss of their numbers is a serious one to me. *They had occupied the right of the Lines.*

Three days later, also to Henry: I am concerned to inform you that Marques de la Romana died here this day. He was attacked some days ago with spasms in his chest, and he had since been very unwell. But I have seen him every day, and yesterday he was much better . . . but he was again attacked with spasms, and he died about two o'clock.

His loss is irreparable: under existing circumstances I know not how he can be replaced; and we may expect that it will be followed by the fall of Badajoz.

The loss was not merely serious, it was personal too. As we have just noticed, competence, commitment and good breeding almost always inspired affection in the Peer, especially if combined with good spirits. Romana had all these qualities. To Mendizabal, Romana's successor: I have lost a colleague, a friend, and an adviser, with whom I had lived on the happiest terms of friendship, intimacy and confidence; and I shall revere and respect his memory to the last moment of my existence. *To Peacocke, commanding the Lisbon garrison:* . . . I am desirous that every honor which is in our power to pay should be paid to his remains . . . and you will dispose of the troops under your command on this occasion, in such a manner as will be most proper to mark the sincere respect and regard which we all feel for his memory, and to do him most honor . . .

Olivenza duly fell and Badajoz was invested. Still Craufurd and Cotton wanted to be off. . . . my opinion is that there is no private concern that cannot be settled by instruction and power of attorney (yet) I cannot refuse leave of absence to those who come to say that their business is of a nature that requires their personal superintendance . . . In the meantime who is to do the duty? How am I to be responsible for the army? Is Colonel —— a proper substitute for General Craufurd in the command of our advance posts? or General —— for Sir Stapleton Cotton in command of the cavalry? . . . I repeat that you know the situation of affairs as well as I do, and you have my leave to go to England if you think proper. *In a PS to a letter on recruitment where he reiterated his argument that family allowances should be paid to married volunteers to encourage a better sort of man to enlist, his feelings on the missing generals overflowed. To Torrens:* They come to me to ask leave of absence, under pretence of business, which they say it is important to them to transact, and indeed I make them go so far as to declare that it is paramount to every other consideration in life. At the same time I know that many of them have no business, and that there is no business which cannot be transacted . . . by . . . power of attorney.

The inconvenience of their going is terrible, and the detail it throws on me greater than I can well manage; for I am first to instruct one, then a second, and afterwards, upon his return, the first again, upon every duty. At this moment we have seven General Officers gone or going home; and, excepting myself, there is not one in the country who came out with the army . . .

Bad though things were for Wellington, they were worse for Masséna. Not only were his men starving, he was virtually cut off from the rest of the world since couriers could only reach him when escorted by large detachments. It was vital above all that he should not know about Soult's progress in Estremadura, yet, to Stuart, 6 February: I shall be very obliged . . . if you draw the attention of the Government to the communication carried on between Lisbon and the enemy's head quarters at Torres Novas. This correspondence has been carried on principally through the means of persons who go into the enemy's lines with coffee, sugar, &c., to sell, which goods they dispose of at large prices; and they generally carry a letter either to or fro . . . It is astonishing how accurately informed we find the enemy of everything. The Marques de la Romana's death, the King's illness . . . were well known to them. They say they get the newspapers; but I rather doubted that, till I found out the traffic in sugar, coffee &c. If they can get these articles, they can get not only newspapers, but anything else they please.

On the same day he dealt with another problem that had raised its, to him, ugly head. In a letter to the Adjutant General of the Forces he put in a plea for better pay and terms for the Chaplains. I believe Mr Briscoll is the only chaplain doing duty. *He had his reasons.* It has come to my knowledge that Methodism is spreading very fast in the army. There are two if not three Methodist meetings in this town, of which one is in the Guards. The men meet in the evening and sing psalms; and I believe a serjeant (Stephens) now and then gives them a sermon. Mr Briscoll has his eye on these transactions, and would give me notice were they growing into anything which ought to be put a stop to . . .

These meetings likewise prevail in other parts of the army. In the 9th regiment there is one at which two officers attend . . . Here, and in similar circumstances, we want the assistance of a respectable clergy-man. By his personal influence and advice, and by that of true religion, he would moderate the zeal and enthusiasm of these gentlemen, and would prevent their meetings from being mischievous . . . The meeting of soldiers in their cantonments to sing psalms, or hear a sermon read by one of their comrades is, in the abstract, perfectly innocent; and it is a better way of spending their time than many others to which they are addicted; but it may become otherwise . . . *What was the Peer frightened of? Enthusiasm, of course, always caused him to reach for his General Order book, but there may have been deeper suspicions too. Did not the Methodists preach Brotherly Love? Was that not a step away from Quakerish pacifism? Not a commodity an army requires, especially when the enemy makes, however hypocritically, a fetish out of Equality and Fraternity. Mainly, though, he simply distrusted any form of religion that was not properly administered by the representatives of the propertied classes. Which was why, of course, he insisted on proper respect for Catholicism where it was the established church, and why he thought it should be established, and therefore brought under control, in Ireland.*

It's interesting to note that of all his pleas to the Horse Guards for anything from curry-combs to family allowances for the men, and Generals who were not alcoholic or mad, this was the one that was most promptly attended to.

Chaplains' pay and terms were immediately improved and by the end of the year there were plenty of them with the army.

Stalemate continued in front of Lisbon, but on the Guadiana Soult extended his operations against Badajoz and Mendizabal, with Romana's army, moved to its relief. To Liverpool, 9 February: The enemy have broke ground . . . and have thrown some shells into the town . . . Mendizabal has not adhered to the plan which was ordered by the late Marques de la Romana. *A week later Foy at last got back to Masséna, having taken in Madrid and Seville on the way. He lost 500 men to the partidas and Ordenanza between Salamanca and Torres Novas. To Liverpool:* I have every reason to believe . . . that the enemy were on the move last week, and would have retired, had they not received Buonaparte's orders by Foy to remain. They are now anxiously looking to the siege of Badajoz, on the course of which they have no intelligence, excepting from Foy that it was to be undertaken . . .

Which was frustrating, and worse was to follow. With dreadful inevitability the Spanish army that was to relieve Badajoz was surprised in a position that should have been unassailable. To Henry, 28 February: This is the greatest misfortune which has fallen upon the allies since the battle of Ocaña, and in the existing state of the war more likely than that to affect their interests vitally; and it was not to be expected.

I could not imagine that an army having two rivers between it and the enemy, and knowing that the enemy was endeavouring to pass one of them, could have been surprised in a strong position . . . It is impossible to speculate on the consequences of this misfortune upon the garrison at Badajoz . . . *What, of course, he dreaded was that Masséna would hear of it and be induced to hang on until he received reinforcements.*

Yet Badajoz hung on – not for long, as we shall see, but for just long enough. To Beresford, 4 March: By the last telegraph of yesterday it appears that Badajoz had the best of it. The enemy's fire had ceased, and the fort's continued. *On the next day:* The reinforcements have arrived, and we shall in a few days be able to attack the enemy if he retains his position, or possibly to attack him in any other which he may take . . . *Masséna heard of the reinforcements too, possibly with his morning café au lait. And so, at last, it happened.*

To Beresford, 6 March, 5.00 a.m.: I have received an account from Lumley that the enemy have evacuated Santarem . . . I am just going up to Santarem, where I shall move head quarters this day. I shall desire Lumley to move the boats up, in order that we may communicate this way. *Santarem, 4.00 p.m.:* I am just now returned from Pernes. All is clear on this side of that river, over which the enemy have destroyed both bridges . . . I shall be obliged to if you will send an express to General Leite, and desire him to tell the Governor of Badajoz by telegraph that he must hold out to the last extremity, that Masséna has begun to retire, and that he may expect assistance as soon as it is in my power to give it to him.

THE PURSUIT

To Stuart, Thomar, 8th March: Having been on horseback almost ever since the morning of the 6th, I have not been able to write to you. The French retired from their position on that morning and they march literally night and day . . . We are close at their heels, and have taken some prisoners, and I mean to continue to press them so hard that they will not have time to do much harm . . .

To Beresford, 9 March, 8.00 p.m.: Our advanced guard found the whole army this day in front of Pombal . . . whether offering battle, or waiting for an opportunity to cross the Mondego, I cannot tell. However, it is desirable that in this case I should be a little stronger; and as Badajoz is certainly not pressed; and as, at all events, it would be desirable that you should not commence operations there till the boats shall have arrived at Elvas, I have sent to Cole to desire that his division and the dragoons would march to-morrow morning to Cacharias: I shall then be as strong as the enemy, very nearly.

To Liverpool, 14 March: . . . We found the whole army yesterday in a very strong position at Condeixa; and I observed they were sending off their baggage . . . From this circumstance I concluded that Colonel Trant had not given up Coimbra, and that they had been so pressed in their retreat, that they had not been able to detach troops to force him from that place. I therefore marched the 3rd division under Major General Picton, through the mountains on the enemy's left, towards the only road open for their retreat, which had the immediate effect of dislodging them from the strong position of Condeixa . . .

The result of these operations has been that we have saved Coimbra and Upper Beira from the enemy's ravages . . .

The whole country, however, affords many advantageous positions to a retreating army, of which the enemy have shown that they know how to avail themselves. They are retreating from the country, as they entered it, in one solid mass, covering their rear on every march by the operations of either one or two corps d'armée in the strong positions which the country affords; which corps d'armée are closely supported by the main body . . . They have no provisions, excepting what they plunder on the spot, or, having plundered, what the soldiers carry on their backs, and live cattle.

I am concerned to be obliged to add to this account, that their conduct throughout this retreat has been marked by a barbarity seldom equalled, and never surpassed. Even in the towns of Torres Novas, Thomar, and Pernes, in which the head quarters of some of the corps had been for four months, and in which the inhabitants had been invited, by promises of good treatment, to remain, they were plundered, and many of the houses destroyed, on the night the enemy withdrew from their position, and they have since burnt every town and village through which they have passed . . . This is the mode in which the promises have been performed, and the assurances have been fulfilled, which were held out in the proclamation of the French Commander-in-Chief, in which he told the inhabitants of Portugal that he was not come to make war on them, but with a powerful army of 110,000 men to drive the English into the sea.

So far so good. However . . . I am sorry to inform your Lordship that Badajoz surrendered on the 11th instant . . . *and he goes on to explain how, following Mendizabal's disgraceful defeat, there was really very little he could do to relieve the fortress until he had seen Masséna out of Portugal. In any case Badajoz should not have surrendered so soon – it was, as we shall see, betrayed.* It is useless to add any reflection to these facts. The Spanish nation have lost . . . Olivença and Badajoz, in the course of two months, without sufficient cause; and in the same period Marshal Soult, with a corps never supposed to be more than 20,000 men has taken or destroyed 22,000 Spanish troops.

The pursuit went on: . . . Cole joined Nightingall at Espinhal on the afternoon of the 13th; and this movement, by which the Deixa was passed, and which gave us the power of turning the strong position of Miranda de Corvo, induced the enemy to abandon it on that night. They destroyed at this place a great number of carriages, and burned . . . the ammunition which they had carried; they likewise burned much of their baggage; and the road throughout the march from Miranda is strewed with the carcases of men and animals . . . The destruction of the bridge at Foz d'Arouce, the fatigue which the troops have undergone for several days, and the want of supplies, have induced me to halt the army this day.

129

This was the sixteenth, and it gave Wellington a chance to catch up on his correspondence. To Lady Sarah Napier, Louzão, 16 March, 1811: I am sorry to have to inform you that your two sons were again wounded . . . but neither of them I hope seriously. William is wounded in the back; George in the right arm, which is broken. Both are doing remarkably well, and will, I hope, soon recover to return to their duty.

Your Ladyship has so often received accounts of the same description . . . and your feelings upon the subject are so just and proper, that it is needless for me to trouble you further. Your sons are brave fellows and an honor to the army . . .

William was one of the first formal historians of the war, and the only one who actually fought in it, and this is perhaps the moment to attend to his very characteristic voice, though the attentive reader will already have heard echoes of it.

Every horror that could make war hideous attended this retreat. Distress, conflagrations, death, in all modes, from wounds, from fatigue, from water, from the flames, from starvation! On all sides unlimited violence, unlimited vengeance. I myself saw a peasant hounding on his dog to devour the dead and dying, and the spirit of cruelty smote even the brute creation: for the French General, to lessen incumbrances, ordered beasts of burden to be destroyed, and the inhuman fellow charged with the execution hamstringed five hundred asses and left them to starve; they were so found by the British, and the mute, sad, deep expression of pain and grief visible in the poor creatures' looks, excited a strange fury in the soldiers: no quarter would have been given at that time: humane feelings would thus have led direct to cruelty. But all passions are akin to madness.

More details were now available on the fall of Badajoz. To Marquess Wellesley: Nobody entertains a doubt that Imaz sold Badajoz. He appears to have surrendered as soon as he could after he knew that relief was coming to him lest his garrison should prevent the surrender when they should be certain of the truth of the intelligence of Masséna's retreat. *Whether or not Badajoz was sold was never completely established, but, to quote Oman, 'It is impossible to deny that this was pusillanimity reaching into and over the border of treason.'*

Yet Soult's corps was a mere 12,000 and there was a chance that the damage done by Imaz might be quickly repaired. Beresford was to be put immediately into reverse. 18 March, 1811, 4.00 p.m.: You had better lose no time in moving up to Portalegre, and attack Soult, if you can, at Campo Mayor. I will come to you if I can, but if I cannot, do not wait for me. Get

Castaños to join you, from Estremoz, with any Spanish troops he can bring with him . . . *Two days later he mapped out Beresford's course in more detail:* The character of Soult's operations, I think is to detach a good deal. I recommend you to keep your troops very much <u>en masse.</u> I have always considered the cavalry to be the most delicate arm we possess, we have few officers who have practical knowledge of the mode of using it, or who have ever seen more than two regiments together . . . you will see the necessity of keeping the cavalry as much as possible <u>en masse,</u> and in reserve, to be thrown in at the moment when an opportunity may offer of striking a decisive blow.

The pursuit ran on, but there were problems. In the same letter to Beresford: We took yesterday three officers and 600 prisoners. Our divisions and their baggage make their marches (however short) so very ill that I am obliged to halt the greatest part of the army again to-day. However, I have now begun a new system with them, which is, to state in the orders at what hour each is to start and is to arrive at each place. By degrees I shall bring them to some system. *This, the ordering of the hour of arrival rather than departure, caused a lot of grumbling but was effective. Then, of course, two days later:* We have outrun our supplies so much, that we have been a little distressed for a day or two, and I have been obliged to halt all but the advanced guard this day; but the distress will be only momentary, and, I shall, I hope, be able to march the whole army to-morrow.

Nevertheless he found time next day to write a long letter to Liverpool analysing minutely the Treasury's calculations of the cost of the Peninsula campaign, showing how they had got it wrong, and arguing that a further 10,000 men in the winter would have saved money, for then there would have been no question of evacuation and the naval establishment and transports maintained at Lisbon could have been reduced or sent home. He concludes by arguing that if the Peninsula army was brought home, and Europe remained quiet, then the French would invade England.

Now, the history books that I was brought up on insisted Trafalgar had made this impossible, because the Channel would always be held by the Navy, but I think Wellington is right. According to the French system, as exemplified by Masséna over the previous six months, they only needed a few hours to get an army across – after that it would survive on its own. Then indeed would commence an expensive contest; then would His Majesty's subjects discover what are the miseries of war, of which, by the blessing of God, they have hitherto had no knowledge; and the cultivation, the beauty, and prosperity of the country, and the virtue and happiness of its inhabitants would be destroyed, whatever might be the result of the military operations. God forbid that I should be a witness, much less an actor in the same . . .

This came from the heart, with the obscene wilderness the French had created around him. This and horrors yet to come never left him, and the possibility of civil war both in Ireland and England led him to see through, against the instincts of his caste and the apparent interests of his class, the Catholic Emancipation Bill, and finally to withdraw his long and obstinate resistance to the First Reform Act.

SABUGAL

That he found time to write that last letter is extraordinary, with his generals still absent. The consequence . . . has been . . . I have been obliged to be General of Cavalry and of the advanced guard, and the leader of two or three columns, sometimes on the same day . . .

Up to this point the French had conducted their rearguard actions with brilliance under that specialist in the art, Marshal Ney. Now Masséna should have withdrawn past Ciudad Rodrigo and given his men time to recover and re-equip. However, he decided to make a final effort to retain a position in Portugal, and moved to his left into the mountains. Ney, who objected, was sent to the rear under arrest. To Spencer, 25 March: The French retired from Celorico yesterday, and they appear to intend to take up a line on the Coa. Their left has gone by Guarda, apparently for Sabugal. I enclose Graham's dispatches on his action.

These, indeed contained good news. To provide Soult with a corps to take to Badajoz, the French depleted their force in front of Cadiz. Graham, who led the English part of the garrison, and the Spanish general La Peña, led a sortie which, in spite of the failure of the Spaniards to support Graham at all, ended in a victory for the British. Wellington's approval was wholehearted and unconditional: I beg to congratulate you, and the brave troops under your command, on the signal victory which you gained on the 5th instant. I have no doubt whatever that their success would have had the effect of raising the siege of Cadiz, if the Spanish corps had made any effort to assist them, and I am equally certain, from your account of the ground, that if you had not decided with the utmost promptitude to attack the enemy, and if your attack had not been a most vigorous one, the whole allied army would have been lost . . .

A general who could act decisively and successfully when others would have

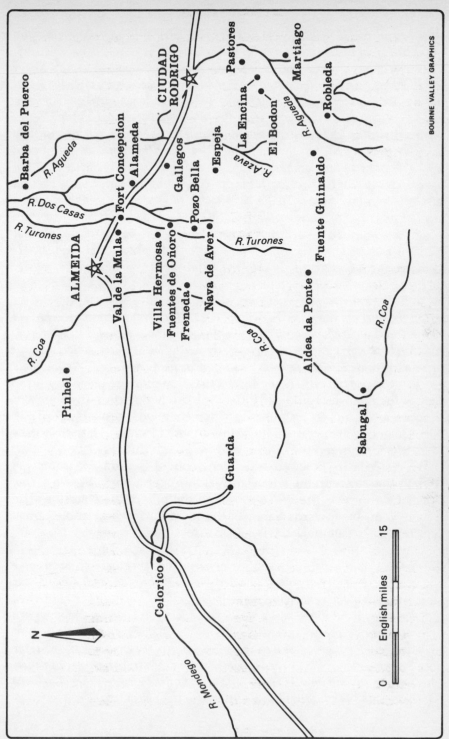

8. Between the Coa and the Agueda: April – September 1810; April 1811; May 1811; August 1811 – June 1812

BOURNE VALLEY GRAPHICS

N

English miles

0   15

Pinhel●

Guarda●

Celorico●

Sabugal●

R. Mondego

R. Coa

R. Coa

R. Coa

ALMEIDA

Val de la Mula●

Villa Hermosa●
Fuentes de Oñoro●
Freneda●
Nava de Aver●

Aldea da Ponte●

R. Turones

R. Turones

Pozo Bella●

Gallegos●

Fort Concepcion●
Alameda●

CIUDAD RODRIGO

Barba del Puerco●

R. Agueda

R. Dos Casas

Espeja●

Fuente Guinaldo●

La Encina●
El Bodon●

R. Azava

R. Agueda

Pastores●

Martiago●

Robleda●

been in a scrape was clearly someone to have closer at hand, and Wellington immediately set in train the procedures which would get Graham out of Cadiz. The victor of Barossa was a Scottish Laird, Graham of Balgowan, and by a very long way the oldest of Wellington's generals, having been born in 1748. It had not occurred to him at all to be a soldier until 1792 when he had a wretched experience with the Jacobin mob. His wife – the subject of one of Gainsborough's greatest portraits – had died of consumption on the Riviera. Graham wished to bury her in Scotland. On the way a mob, believing the coffin was filled with arms broke it open, and converted Graham from a mildly pro-French whig into a lifelong enemy. For the next fourteen years (beginning, as Napoleon can be said to have done, at the siege of Toulon) he attached himself to the army, though his position was never properly regularised. By 1809 he had seen action in Austrian and Italian campaigns as British Attaché to the allies, as well as in Minorca and Malta, for he was that very rare bird, a Briton who was a good linguist. He spoke six languages fluently. In 1809 he was promoted to be a full major-general on the regular establishment although until then he had technically never been more than a civilian with an honorary title.

On the thirtieth more good news came, this time from Beresford, who had recaptured Campo Mayor only days after the French had occupied it. However, the 13th Dragoons and the 1st Portuguese cavalry, 'that most delicate arm', lost control of themselves in what was still a far too typical way. Wellington's reaction was also typical: Their conduct was that of a rabble, galloping as fast as their horses could carry them over a plain, after an enemy to whom they could do no mischief when they were broken . . . If the 13th Dragoons are again guilty of this conduct I shall take their horses from them, and send the officers and men to do duty at Lisbon . . .

We yesterday manoeuvred the French out of Guarda. Masséna was there, some say with the whole army, I think certainly with two corps; but not a shot was fired. We ascended the hill in five columns. The enemy went off towards Sabugal, the rearguard in admirable order. Ney is gone to Salamanca, it is said in arrest.

The time has come to halt the narrative for a while and give an impression of the sort of countryside we are about to enter – for it will be the main scene of our story for much of the next eighteen months.

Salamanca, about ninety miles north east of Sabugal, is the central point in a high undulating plateau – indeed at 3,000 feet it is higher than almost any point in the whole of Portugal to the west, certainly south of the Douro. To its east, the even higher peaks of the Gredos separate it from Madrid, to the south these continue, lower, but just as impenetrable, into the Peña de Francia and the Sierra de Gata. These form a southern rim to the plateau, which now drops

*through them very suddenly and steeply into Las Batuecas and Las Hurdes,
deep, remote river valleys almost at sea level, which in turn feed the Tagus.*

*To the north Salamanca's plateau is bounded by the Duero (Douro in
Portugal) which swings south at Miranda do Douro and descends sharply
through ravines and gorges for forty miles, before swinging west again to
Oporto. The flattened oval of the Salamanca plateau is completed on the south
west by the rivers Agueda and Coa which run from the south into the
Duero/Douro. The first is the wider and, on its way, touches the fortress of
Ciudad Rodrigo; the second, which lies in Portugal, runs a couple of miles to the
west of the smaller fortress of Almeida.*

*Salamanca itself is surrounded by open country, down-like but with occa-
sional outcrops of reddish rock which become grey, limestoney to the west. In
1811 the parts nearest the larger centres of population were ploughed for wheat,
the rest was uncleared ancient ilex (ever-green oak) forest, which is astonishingly park-like. Each tree colonises the area around it, permits no undergrowth.
Grasses, poppies, wild lavender, daisies flourish. All of it of course was, and is,
owned – the trees are topped out, timber for building and charcoal is harvested
from them, and so they spread widely. Usually three large boughs are left which,
from most angles, give the trees the appearance of rustic crosses. Beneath them
roam fighting bulls, rated second only to those of the Las Marismas marshes
between Seville and Cadiz, and wild boar. Nearer the villages pigs roam at day,
finding their own way back to their pens each night. These are almost
exclusively acorn fed and produce the very best hams in the world. In
Wellington's time the hillier parts and especially the Gata supported wolves,
wild cats, and even bears.*

*To the west and south of Salamanca, the area we are immediately concerned
with, the plateau gradually breaks up. Rivulets, then rivers, and one large river
in particular, the Tormes, on which Salamanca lies, drive their way into the rock
on their way into the Duero or its tributaries. As you approach Portugal the
ground becomes more and more broken, the rock breaks more frequently through
the surface, often in dramatically piled boulders or as whale-like ridges; the oaks
become smaller, etiolated, there is more scrub, almost no wheat; thin sheep roam
over the area in tight flocks guarded by vicious dogs.*

*But in the valleys which, as you get nearer Portugal, and into Portugal,
become deeper, more gorge-like, there is cultivation – and, suddenly, it is
intense. From three thousand feet you have dropped to five hundred at the river
beds and these are sheltered from frost and wind alike. Thus on the top of a crag
nothing grows but thin pasture, a little lower, scrub oak. But down at the
bottom of a gorge, and only a matter of a mile or so from the top, ilex gives way to
its cousin cork, olive trees appear, arbutus (strawberry tree), juniper, figs,
vines, oranges and lemons.*

135

Sabugal

On the plateau the climate is continental – nine months of winter, three of hell, like Madrid. The valleys though are rarely cold, almost always humid, and in summer like greenhouses.

Sabugal is situated on a bend in the Coa, and at this apex Masséna stationed Reynier's corps. On his right the Coa ran into one of those deep ravines and was virtually uncrossable; but to his left, south, higher up, the valley was much shallower, the ground now part of the plateau – undulating, grassy, with outcrops of rock. At Sabugal, in the middle, there was a bridge.

To Beresford, Sabugal, 4 April: Yesterday morning we moved the whole army to the right in order to turn this position *that is in the uplands on Masséna's left* and force the passage of the river. The 2nd Corps could not have stood here for a minute; but unfortunately the Light division, which formed the right of the whole, necessarily passed first . . . *That is, ahead of the rest, and it was not necessary but the result of a blunder by Sir William Erskine who commanded them in place of Craufurd.* At this time came on a rainstorm, and it was as difficult to see as in the fogs of Busaço, and the troops pushed on too far . . . The light infantry fell back upon their support, which, instead of halting, moved forward. The French then seeing how weak the body was which had passed, attempted to drive them down to the Coa and did oblige the 43rd to turn. They rallied again, however, and beat in the French, but were attacked by fresh troops and cavalry, and were obliged to retire; but formed again and beat back the enemy. At this time the 52nd joined the 43rd, and both moved on upon the enemy to be charged and attacked again in the same manner, and beat back. They formed again, moved forward upon the enemy, and established themselves on the top of the hill in an enclosure, and here they beat off the enemy.

But Regnier was placing a body of infantry on their left flank, which must have destroyed them, only at that moment the head of the 3rd division, which had passed the Coa on the left of the Light division, came up and opened their fire on this column; and the 5th division, which passed the bridge and through the town, made their appearance.

The enemy then retired, having lost in this affair a howitzer *which changed hands several times* and I should think not less than 1000 men.

Our loss is much less than one would have supposed possible, scarcely 200 men . . . But really these attacks in columns against our lines are very contemptible . . . Our cavalry *(also under Erskine)* which ought to have crossed the Coa on the right of the Light division, crossed at the same ford, and therefore could be of no use to them. Besides they went too far to the right.

In short, these combinations for engagements *(separate divisions acting on their own)* do not answer, unless one is on the spot to direct every trifling movement. I was upon a hill on the left of the Coa, immediately above the town, till the 3rd and 5th divisions crossed, whence I could see every movement on both sides, and could communicate with ease with everybody, but that was not near enough. After this affair the whole French army retired from the Coa . . . and if they are not out of Portugal, they are, at the utmost, in the frontier villages . . .

You will be concerned to hear that Waters *(Oporto boat finder)* is at last taken prisoner. He crossed the Coa alone, I believe, yesterday morning, and was looking at the enemy through a spying glass, when four hussars pounced upon him. Nobody has seen him since yesterday morning; and we have the account from the prisoners, who tell the story of an officer attached to the staff, a Lieut. Colonel, blond, with a petit chapeau. They saw him with Regnier.

Of course, the daring Waters was not done for at all. As the French withdrew he looked for his opportunity to escape, and took it when almost at Salamanca. He was guarded by four gens d'arme, only one of whom had a horse as good as his own. Nature eventually intervened and the well-mounted gens d'arme alighted. Waters was off, galloping down the side of the French columns; his 'petit chapeau' fell off; some of the French cheered him, others loosed off their pieces; and always the gens d'arme, sword in hand were at his heels. At last he broke across the road between two columns, got into a wooden hollow, and so baffled his pursuers. Three days later he was back at headquarters where Wellington had his baggage waiting for him, observing that he had not expected him to be absent long.

Sabugal was botched in many ways. Erskine could not co-ordinate the movements of his troops and so left the Light division hopelessly exposed. Six months earlier Wellington had written to Torrens: I have received your letter announcing the appointment of Sir William Erskine, and General Lumley . . . The first I have generally understood to be a madman. I believe it is your opinion that the second is not very wise . . . and there are some in this army whom it is disreputable and quite unsafe to keep. Colonel Sanders . . . was sent away from Sicily by Sir John Moore for incapacity . . . Then there is General Lightburne, whose conduct is really scandalous. I am not able to bring him before a court-martial as I should wish, but he is a disgrace to the army which can have such a man as a Major General.

Really when I reflect on the characters and attainment of some of the General Officers of this army, and consider that these are the persons on whom I am to rely to lead columns against French Generals, and who are to carry my instructions into execution, I tremble; and as Lord Chesterfield said of the Generals of his day, 'I only hope that when the enemy reads the list of their names he trembles as I do.' . . . I pray God and the Horse Guards to deliver me from General Lightburne and Colonel Sanders.

With most of his best generals still absent – Hill, Cotton, Craufurd amongst them, and Beresford moving on Badajoz – it was surprising nothing worse than Sabugal occurred during those few weeks. Only Wellington's constant attention to every detail, his presence at every crisis point, ensured that it did not. It should not be forgotten that on this retreat the French, albeit sick, worn down, lacking sound equipment as they were, still had more men in the field than he did.

Cock-up though it was, Sabugal was enough to put Masséna out of Portugal, leaving only a garrison at Almeida. He was back at Salamanca on 11 April, 1811, eleven months after taking command with orders to drive the leopard into the sea. Throughout almost all the period he had outnumbered the English – once his retreat began Wellington reduced the numbers in front of him by sending two divisions into the Alentejo with Beresford. He had lost at least 25,000 men and vast quantities of guns, baggage, and transport. Yet he did well to get back at all – and Wellington continued to respect the 'old fox' as the greatest soldier he faced before Waterloo. Within a month, they were to fight their last, and most closely contested battle.

Meanwhile a Proclamation was in order.

To the People of Portugal

10th April, 1811
The Portuguese nation are informed that the cruel enemy who had invaded Portugal, and had devastated their country, have been obliged to evacuate it . . . The inhabitants of the country are therefore at liberty to return to their occupations.

Wellington

FUENTES DE OÑORO

The missing generals, who had not dared to come with the daffodils but had waited for the swallows, began to trickle back. Wellington wasted no ink on welcoming them – simply and curtly filled them in on the position as it then stood. To Cotton, 10 April: I have just received your letter of Thursday morning; and I write to let you know that the French have retired from the Agueda towards the Tormes. I don't mean to follow them any farther. *To Craufurd, 14 April:* I received this morning your letter of the 9th instant. You will find your division in your old quarters, Gallegos, and the sooner you can come up with them the better.

Meanwhile, with Masséna regrouping on the Tormes, and even as far away as the Duero, he felt he had time to go south, in spite of the fact that Erskine was still botching things on the Agueda. To Beresford, 14 April: Sir William Erskine did not send a detachment over the Agueda in time, as I had desired him, and the consequence was that the French got their convoy into Ciudad Rodrigo this morning . . . now it is useless to keep anybody on the other side of the Agueda, excepting for the sake of food and observation. I confine myself therefore to the blockade of Almeida, and as this is a simple operation, which I do not think the enemy have means or inclination to interrupt, I propose to go over to you, and, if I can, I shall set off to-morrow morning.

I see that Generals Stewart and Craufurd are arrived.

By 17 April he was half way, and obviously very worried at being at the furthest point from both his armies. To Spencer, Castello Branco, 17 April, 1811, 2.00 p.m.: I have not yet heard from you; and I conclude that you did not find it necessary to write to me till last night . . . In case you should wish to communicate anything to me, and to be quite certain that it reaches me as soon as it can, I recommend you to send a Staff Officer, on his own horses, to Sabugal, and to order him to proceed on with the horses of the guides by the following route from Sabugal . . . *which he then specifies, village by village at ten mile intervals.*

On the twentieth he was at Elvas. To Beresford: I congratulate you on the surrender of Olivença. and entirely concur in the directions which you gave that the garrison should have no terms; and I hope they were well plundered by the 4th division . . .

The conventions of siege warfare were quite clear. First, the attackers would issue a first summons to the garrison to surrender. It was rare that this summons was taken up, but if it was, terms of capitulation would be drawn up which would be favourable to the garrison: they might even be allowed to return to their own country with the right to fight again. A second summons would be issued once a practicable breach had been made, and, in the eighteenth century, this usually did end in a negotiated settlement. This was because to take a city or fortress by storm through one or more breaches almost certainly meant the attackers, and especially the 'forlorn hope' in the vanguard, were virtually doomed to suffer appalling casualties until they had gained a foothold at which point the defenders could withdraw and surrender having suffered comparatively slightly. So, to make up for this, a third convention insisted that a garrison that had refused a summons when the breaches were practicable, could, in the event of a successful storm, be put to the sword, and certainly the town could be sacked as a reward to those who had risked death in the breaches. As I say, because of this threat the convention in the eighteenth century was that a governor whose fortress was penetrated with breaches usually felt obliged to negotiate a bloodless surrender.

However, this relatively civilised convention had been undermined by Buonaparte who had issued an edict that made any Governor who surrendered a fortress on the issue of a summons chargeable with dereliction of duty and liable to be shot.

The consequence was a history of bloody assaults followed by horrendous sackings of the fallen cities. The British army in Spain 'enjoyed' this privilege on two major occasions — at Ciudad Rodrigo and Badajoz in 1812. On both occasions there was a public outcry, often directed against Wellington personally; on both occasions Wellington took steps, after a time, to bring the rioting troops back to order; and on both occasions he was reported as having suffered through the sack. One result of this is that those biographers who would, in spite of everything, try to make some sort of liberal humanist out of him, have said that he disapproved of this convention of the sack, that his humanitarian instincts rejected it, but that there was nothing he could do about it — his troops simply got wildly out of hand and nothing could stop them.

I do not think this is the case. If Buonaparte was such an oaf as to reject a civilised convention then the blame lay with him. Wellington did react personally to unnecessary suffering, and did all that he could to avoid it — but in this case the matter had been taken out of his hands by the intransigence of the foe. His fastidiousness too rebelled at the scenes of drunken licence that followed a sack; he hated the way innocents, often women and children, suffered appallingly; he disapproved of the way the men were ruined as a fighting force for up to a week after. But he did not repudiate the convention, indeed saw practical sense in it. Men who had survived a holocaust, who had, unnecessarily, *seen their comrades blown to bits beside them, needed the sack. On the other side, if there was no sack the ultimate threat to an intransigent governor was removed. So –* 'I hope they were well plundered' *encapsulates his attitude to the whole business.*

Back to his letter to Beresford: I hope that you will be able to return; but if you cannot, I shall write to you my opinion on the several points which occur to me, in regard to the siege of Badajoz, which is your principal object. I cannot venture to stay long away from the frontiers of Castille, and I shall return to that quarter as soon as I shall have looked about me here.

I cannot pretend to give directions at this distance. My opinion is, that you are too advanced for your object, and the sooner you come back the better . . .

Next day, 8.00 a.m.: I see that Soult is fortifying Seville, which is a serious event, as affecting our operations at Badajoz. It is therefore more urgent that not a moment should be lost in commencing them . . . *The point being that with Seville fortified Soult could release more troops for the relief of Badajoz.*

On the twenty-second he rode dozens of miles over the whole area, taking in a brief skirmish with a sortie party from Badajoz itself whose repulse he personally directed. He was back in Elvas on the twenty-third in time to write a detailed memorandum for Beresford on the coming siege. The important part deals with the likely event of an army coming to its relief. During the siege of Badajoz his object will be to place his troops in such situations as that they will be best able to carry on the operations, and to join, in case the enemy should attempt to relieve the place . . .

If Sir William Beresford should think his strength sufficient to fight a general action, to save the siege of Badajoz, he will collect his troops to fight it.

I believe that, upon the whole, the most central and advantageous place to collect his troops will be Albuera . . . *And thus was fixed the pattern that very nearly, but through no fault of Wellington's, produced disaster.*

On the twenty-fifth he was on his way back north – with one hundred miles of rough country to cover again. He left not a moment too soon. From Castello Branco he wrote to Beresford on the twenty-seventh: P.S. 3 P.M. It appears by letters which I have received from Sir Brent of the evening of the 25th, that the enemy are in motion towards the Agueda . . . I go on immediately, and shall be with the army to-morrow.   W.

142

On the twenty-ninth he was at La Alameda, almost exactly half way between Almeida and Ciudad Rodrigo, answering a query from Campbell who was blockading Almeida. The French Governor, the Brennier who had been taken at Vimeiro and released under the terms of the Convention of Cintra, wanted an exchange of prisoners. The truth is that this gentleman wants to get a little news. He has found that our men know little, or are but little communicative, and he wants to get some Frenchmen in exchange for them, from whom he thinks he will find out what is going on. It is as well to let him believe that we are good natured gulls who will easily swallow.

The rushing about had had its effect. To Stuart, on the thirtieth: I have unfortunately lost my keys, and many of your letters are locked up in boxes. If you should want answers to any, you must send me duplicates.

On 1 May he was at Villa Fermosa, the Portuguese border town, the Spanish equivalent being Fuentes de Oñoro. He reported the situation to Liverpool: They have collected a very large force at Ciudad Rodrigo. Marshal Masséna, and the head quarters of the army, are at that place; and it is generally reported in the country that they propose to raise the blockade of Almeida. I do not intend to allow them to relieve this place, unless I should be convinced that they have such a superiority of force as to render the result of a contest for this point doubtful.

From all accounts . . . I believe that they have still in that place provisions for the garrison, which is stated to consist of 1500 men, for one fortnight.

The enemy may be stronger than they were when they were obliged to evacuate Portugal, and they may be reinforced with detachments of troops, particularly the Guards under Marshal Bessières; but still I feel confident that they have it not in their power to defeat the allied army in a general action; and I hope to be able to prevent them from relieving this place, unless they should bring the contest to that issue in a situation unfavourable for us.

On 2 May Masséna advanced from Ciudad Rodrigo. He had 48,000 men to the allies 38,000, but, for the first time in the history of the war, actually had fewer guns – thirty-eight to forty-eight. One of Wellington's divisions, the 7th, was weak, being three quarters foreigners, and the two British regiments untried and untrained. There were 1,500 men in Almeida behind him. Worst of all he had only 1,864 regular cavalry and 600 of Sanchez's Lanceros against 4,662 French. Militarily speaking he should have withdrawn. To Busaço? To the Lines? To do so without a fight would have been immensely damaging to morale at home and abroad and in the army itself.

South of the village of Fuentes de Oñoro (see map overleaf) the ground is

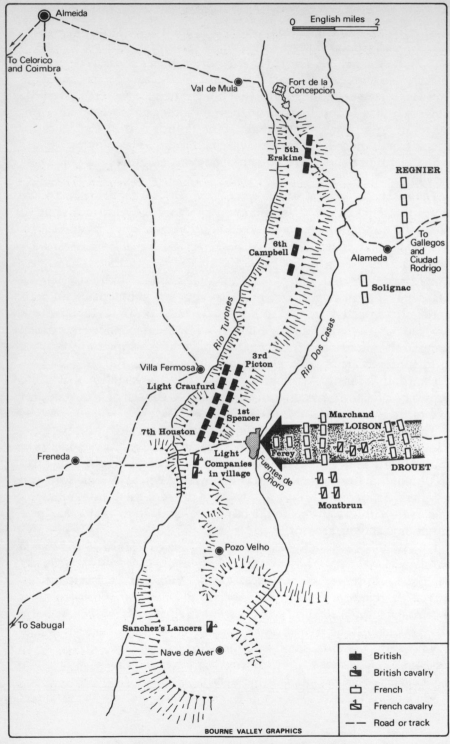

9. Fuentes de Oñoro: first day, 3 May 1811

basically upland, the edge of the plateau, but laced with rivulets that rise in marshy, partially wooded land before flowing into the rivers Dos Casas and Turones. At the beginning of May these quickly grow into mountain brooks prattling over brown flat boulders into rushing streams that are fast-flowing and knee deep at Fuentes and Villa Fermosa. From then on they bite into the hillsides; ravines, even gorges are formed before they pass Almeida, one on each side.

Between them, to the north, lies a fortified building on an eminence – Fort de la Concepcion – and the five miles from it to Fuentes form a virtually unassailable Busaco type position – ridges faced with a deep ravine. The village itself lies on a steepish hill and is a warren of narrow streets tumbling down to the river bed. It should not be confused with the modern ribbon development of ventas, restaurants, barracks and customs sheds along the road to the border. The old village is reached by turning south half a mile or so before the actual frontier.

To Liverpool, Villa Fermosa, 8 May, 1811: The enemy's whole army, consisting of the 2nd, 6th, and 8th corps, and all the cavalry which could be collected in Castille and Léon, including about 900 of the Imperial Guard, crossed the Agueda at Ciudad Rodrigo on the 2nd instant . . .

As my object in maintaining a position between the Coa and the Agueda . . . was to blockade Almeida . . . and as the enemy were infinitely superior to us in cavalry, I did not give any opposition to their march . . .

They continued their march on the 3d, in the morning, towards the Dos Casas, in three columns . . . The Light division fell back on Fuentes de Oñoro . . . , with the British cavalry, in proportion as the enemy advanced, and the 1st, 3d and 7th divisions were collected at that place. *In fact, behind the crest above the village. Detachments, mostly of light troops, occupied the village itself.* The 6th division, under . . . Campbell, observed the bridge at Alameda; and . . . Erskine, with the 5th division, the passages of the Dos Casas at Fort Concepcion. *This was the extreme left of the position, and because of the depth of the ravine in front, about the safest . . . Sir William was not, on this occasion, to be required to manoeuvre. Cotton was already back with the cavalry; Craufurd arrived to take over the Light division on the fourth, and, as we shall see, it was as well he did.* . . . Pack's brigade, with the German regiments from the 6th division, kept the blockade of Almeida; and I had prevailed upon Don Julian Sanchez to occupy Nave d'Aver with his corps of Spanish cavalry and infantry . . . *This too should have been a safe position: he was there to keep watch on the extreme right, rather than to protect it.*

Shortly after the enemy had formed on the ground on the right of Dos Casas, on the afternoon of the 3d, they attacked with a large force the village of Fuentes de Oñoro which was defended in a most gallant manner by Lieut. Colonel Williams . . . The troops maintained their position: but having observed the repeated efforts which the enemy were making to obtain possession of the village, and being aware of the advantage they would derive from the possession in their subsequent operations, I reinforced the village successfully with the 71st regiment *Highlanders* under Lieut. Colonel the Hon. H. Cadogan *(brother Henry's brother-in-law)* . . . who charged the enemy, and drove them from a part of the village of which they had obtained a momentary possession.

Nearly at this time . . . Williams was unfortunately wounded, but I hope not seriously . . .

The contest continued till night, when our troops remained in possession of the whole.

It had been a bloody, bitterly fought business, from cottage to cottage, from tiny garden, to pig-sty, to hen-run and back into the alleys, but generally the French, in spite of huge numerical superiority, failed to maintain footholds on the west bank in the village proper for any length of time. This in part was because they would mass, whereas the light allied troops, hand-picked as excellent marksmen and trained to use cover, kept open order, were ready to fall back and come on as opportunity arose.

On the 4th the enemy reconnaitred the position which we had occupied on the Dos Casas river; and during that night they moved the Duc d'Abrantes' *(our old enemy Androche Junot)* corps from Alameda to the left of the position occupied by the 6th corps opposite to Fuentes de Oñoro.

From the course of the reconnaissance on the 4th I had imagined that the enemy would endeavour to obtain possession of Fuentes de Oñoro, and of the ground occupied by the troops behind that village, by crossing the Dos Casas at Pozo Velho; and in the evening I moved the 7th division, under Major General Houston, to the right, in order if possible, to protect that passage.

For the rest, a truce occurred on the fourth and both sides buried their dead from the village, the French being allowed to cross the river to reclaim their own.

In the morning of the 5th the 8th *(Junot's)* corps appeared in two columns, with all the cavalry, on the opposite side of the valley of Dos Casas and Pozo Velha. *In the pre-dawn fog they had crossed the river, and were splashing through the marsh beneath the dripping oaks way out on Wellington's right. Don Julian Sanchez pulled back immediately to the west of the Turones, no doubt aware that the French cavalry were present in huge*

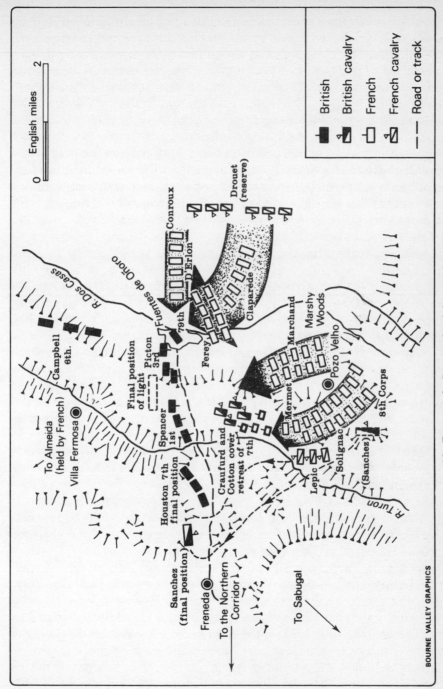

English miles

0   2

British

British cavalry

French

French cavalry

Road or track

Conroux

Drouet
(reserve)

D'Erlon

R. Dos Casas

Fuentes de Oñoro

Campbell
6th.

Clapardède

79th

Picton
3rd

Final position
of light

Ferey

Marchand

Marshy
Woods

To Almeida
(held by French)

Villa Fermosa

Spencer
1st

Mermet

Pozo Velho

8th Corps

Houston 7th
final position

Craufurd and
Cotton cover
retreat of
7th

Solignac

(Sanchez)

Lepic

R. Turon

Sanchez
(final position)

Freneda

To the Northern
Corridor

To Sabugal

BOURNE VALLEY GRAPHICS

10. Fuentes de Oñoro: third day, 5 May 1811

numbers, but also angered because his lieutenant had got so close to the enemy in the fog that he had been mistaken for a French officer by an English piquet who shot him dead. Yet the French cavalry continued to watch him for over an hour, and this gained valuable time. Meanwhile the news of the strength of the French on his right was rushed to Wellington who was shaving in one of the cottages at the top of the village. 'Oh! They are all there, are they? Well, we must mind a little what we are about.'

. . . and as the 6th and 9th corps also made a movement to their left, the Light division, which had been brought back from the neighbourhood of Alameda, were sent with the cavalry under Sir Stapleton Cotton, to support . . . Houston; while the 1st and 3d divisions made a movement to their right, along the ridge between the Turon and Dos Casas rivers, corresponding to that of the 6th and 9th corps on the right of the Dos Casas.

The 8th corps attacked . . . Houston's advanced guard . . . and obliged them to retire; and they retired in good order, although with some loss. The 8th corps being thus established in Pozo Velho, the enemy's cavalry turned the right of the 7th division, between Pozo Velho and Nave d'Aver, from which last place Don Julian Sanchez had been obliged to retire; and the cavalry charged.

One should try to imagine Liverpool reading this off the top as it were. He must have been sweating – his eye glancing ahead, trying to guess how it would turn out.

The charge of the advanced guard of the enemy's cavalry was met by two or three squadrons of the different regiments of the British dragoons, and the enemy were driven back . . .

Notwithstanding that this charge was repulsed, I determined to concentrate our force towards the left, and to move the 7th and Light divisions and the cavalry from Pozo Velho towards Fuentes de Oñoro, and the other two divisions.

I had occupied Pozo Velho and that neighbourhood, in hopes that I should be able to maintain communication across the Coa by Sabugal as well as provide for a blockade, which objects it was now obvious were incompatible with each other; *By making this withdrawal, and totally realigning his troops, he had not merely given up the route south via Sabugal but had also put at risk the main road to Lisbon via Guarda. If he had now been pushed back out of this position, and Almeida had been relieved, he would have had nowhere to go but Aveiro or Oporto. The point is that although Fuentes de Oñoro looks like a typically defensive battle, with the French attacking throughout, it was brilliantly and daringly offensive in effect. You cannot call the management of a battle defensive where the commander deliberately forgoes*

148

*his securest line of retreat in the confident knowledge that his men will not be
beaten, even in the face of superior numbers generally, and outnumbered two
to one in cavalry.* . . . and I therefore abandoned that which was the
least important, *(a safe retreat if beaten!)* and placed the Light division in
reserve in the rear of the left of the 1st division, and the 7th division on
some commanding ground beyond the Turon which protected the
right flank and rear of the 1st division . . .

The movement of the troops on this occasion was well conducted,
although under very critical circumstances . . . The 7th division was
covered in its passage of the Turon by the Light division under . . .
Craufurd; and this last, in its march to join the 1st division, by the
British cavalry.

*This was the Light division's finest hour, and one of the best for the cavalry.
But first it was marked by one of the most stirring moments in the campaign. In
the first assault on the 7th division, in which they were badly mauled, a battery
of horse artillery under Ramsay were cut off. Napier was there:*

Their troopers were seen closing with disorder and tumult towards
one point, where a thick dust arose, where loud cries and the
sparkling of blades and flashing of pistols indicated some extraordinary occurence. Suddenly the crowd became violently agitated, an
English shout pealed high and clear, the mass was rent asunder, and
Norman Ramsay burst forth, sword in hand at the head of his
battery, his horses breathing fire, stretched like greyhounds along
the plain, the guns bounded behind them like things of no weight,
and the mounted gunners followed close, with heads bent low and
pointed weapons in desperate career.

Craufurd covered the passage of the 7th over the Turones, and
then retired slowly along the plain in squares . . . *Four of them, square
by square, each covering the other.* Many times the strong cavalry made
as if it would storm them yet always found them too formidable, and
happily so, for there was not during the war a more perilous hour.
The whole of the vast plain was covered with a confused multitude of
troops, amidst which the squares appeared as specks, and there was
a great concourse of commissariat followers, servants, baggage, led
horses (the impedimenta left by the 7th), and peasants attracted by
curiosity, and all mixed with broken piquets and parties coming out
of the woods . . . The French horsemen merely hovered about
Craufurd's squares, the plain was soon cleared, and the British
cavalry took post behind the centre and the Light division formed a
reserve to the 1st division, the riflemen occupying the rocks on its
right, and connecting it with the 7th division, which had arrived at
Frenada and was again joined by Julian Sanchez. At the sight of this
new front, perpendicular to the original one and so deeply lined with

troops, the French army stopped and commenced a cannonade . . .
but twelve British guns replied with such vigour that the enemy's fire
abated.

Meanwhile the rest of the French army repeated its assault on the village. The
enemy's principal effort was throughout this day directed against
Fuentes de Oñoro; and notwithstanding that the whole of the 6th corps
were at different periods of the day employed to attack this village, they
could never gain more than temporary possession of it . . . on one of
these occasions the 88th, with the 71st and 79th, under the command of
Colonel Mackinnon, charged the enemy and drove them through the
village . . .

The contest again lasted in this quarter till night, when our troops
still held their post . . .

In the course of last night *the 7th, two days after the battle*, the enemy
commenced retiring.

*They had sat it out, hoping Wellington would go, planning another assault
and rejecting it when they saw the allies were digging in. They consumed the
provisions they had brought for Almeida and by the eighth they were hungry.
Again Wellington was told the news while shaving.* 'Aye, I thought they
meant to be off; very well.'

To Henry: We have had warm work in this quarter, but I hope we
shall succeed in the end. The French, it is said, lost 5000 men, we 1,200,
in the affair of the 5th: on the 3d we lost about 250; the French left 400
dead in the village of Fuentes de Oñoro. We lost prisoners by the usual
dash and imprudence of the soldiers.

*The French had decisively failed in their overall object of pushing the allies
back into Portugal. Apparently too they had failed to relieve the garrison at
Almeida, but by a mixture of guile, good luck, and allied incompetence,
Masséna still got them out – and so claimed Fuentes as a victory. His master
was not deceived: 'His Majesty is distressed to see his army retire before a British
force so inferior in numbers.'*

To Beresford, 12 May: I think the escape of the garrison of Almeida is
the most disgraceful military event that has yet occurred to us.

To Liverpool, 15 May: The 6th division resumed the duty of the
blockade of Almeida on that evening *(10 May)*; and Major General Sir
William Erskine was ordered to send a battalion to Barba de Puerco to
guard the bridge there . . .

The enemy blew up some mines which they had constructed at the
works of Almeida at a little before 1 of the morning of the 11th, and
immediately attacked the piquets by which the place was observed,
and forced their way through them. They fired but little; and they

appear to have marched through the bodies of troops posted to support the piquets; and in particular could not have passed far from the right of the Queen's regiment.

Upon the first alarm Brig. General Pack . . . joined the piquets, and continued to follow and fire upon the enemy, as a guide for the march of the other troops employed in the blockade; and Major General Campbell marched from Malpartida with a part of the 1st Batt. 36th regiment. But the enemy continued their march in a solid compact body, without firing; and were well guided between the positions occupied by our troops.

The 4th regiment, which was ordered to occupy Barba de Puerco, unfortunately missed the road, and did not arrive there till the enemy had reached the same place, and commenced to descend to the bridge . . .

The rest lays out excuses. In his private letter of the same day he is more blunt:
. . . although I believe we have taken or destroyed the greater part of the garrison, I have never been so much distressed by any military event as by the escape of even a man of them . . .

Sir W. Erskine was dining with Sir Brent Spencer at head quarters, and received his orders about 4 o'clock; and he says he sent them forthwith to the 4th regiment . . . and the 4th regiment . . . it is said did not receive their orders before midnight, and had only two and a half miles to march, missed their road, and did not arrive at Barba de Puerco till after the French . . .

The 8th Portuguese regiment, under Lieut. Colonel Douglas . . . marched when the explosion was heard, and arrived at Barba de Puerco before the French; but finding nobody there excepting a piquet of cavalry, they passed the Dos Casas again, and thus missed them . . .

Possibly I have to reproach myself for not having been on the spot; but . . . having employed two divisions and a brigade, to prevent the escape of 1400 men . . . the necessity of my attending personally to the operation, after I had been the whole day on the Azava *seeing Masséna across the Agueda*, did not occur to me . . .

I certainly feel, every day, more and more the difficulty of the situation in which I am placed. I am obliged to be everywhere, and if absent from any operation, something goes wrong. It is to be hoped that the General and other Officers of the army will at least acquire that experience which will teach them that success can be attained only by attention to the most minute details; and by tracing every part of every operation from its origin to its conclusion, point by point, and ascertaining that the whole is understood by those who are to execute it.

To William he added: I was then quite sure of having Almeida but I begin to be of opinion, with you, that there is nothing on earth so stupid as a gallant officer.

There is a sort of comedy in all this, but as we have noted before comedy or farce in war nearly always end with bitterness. Erskine, dining too well, stuffed Wellington's order in his pocket and forgot it. Later he proposed sending a piquet of a corporal and four men to the bridge, but his staff prevailed upon him to send a regiment. Nevertheless, Bevan, Colonel of the 4th, did not get the order until midnight when he took his officers' advice and decided to wait for daylight. Erskine lied when he said the 4th had received the order earlier but lost their way. Bevan was to face a Court Martial which would probably have exonerated him. Rather than face it he blew his brains out.

One other result of all this was that Liverpool did not recommend Parliament to move a Vote of Thanks for the Battle of Fuentes de Oñoro.

To William, 2 July: Lord Liverpool was quite right not to move thanks for the battle at Fuentes, though it was the most difficult one I was ever concerned in, and against the greatest odds. We had very nearly three to one against engaged; above four to one in cavalry; and moreover our cavalry had not a gallop in them, while some of that of the enemy was fresh and in excellent order. If Boney had been there we should have been beaten.

And to Prime Minister Spencer Perceval, 22 May: My soldiers have continued to show the Portuguese nation every kindness in their power, as well as the Spaniards. The village of Fuentes de Oñoro having been the field of battle the other day, and not having been much improved by the circumstance, they immediately and voluntarily subscribed to raise a sum of money to be given to the inhabitants as a compensation for the damage which their properties had sustained in the contest.

ALBUERA

I am obliged to be everywhere and if absent from any operation something goes wrong . . .

By the fifteenth Wellington felt confident that the northern corridor was safe. It was again time to turn his attention south. On the sixteenth he was at Sabugal and writing to Beresford: Unless I should see reason on the road to move more quickly I shall be at Elvas on the 21st . . . *Unfortunately he had every reason. To Spencer, from Elvas, 19 May, 4.00 p.m., having covered the distance in two and a half days less than he expected:* . . . Beresford had an action with the French at Albuera, on the 16th, in which he repulsed Soult, but suffered great loss. General Houghton and Sir William Myers killed, and General Cole wounded. I do not yet know the particulars of the action, nor the extent of the loss; but it is certainly very severe . . .

To Beresford, at 4.30 p.m.: Your loss, by all accounts, has been very large; but I hope that it will not prove so large as was at first supposed. You could not be successful in such an action without a large loss; and we must make up our minds to affairs of this kind sometimes, or give up the game.

To Peacocke, Governor of Lisbon, 20 May: You will have heard that Marshal Beresford fought a severe action on the 16th; in consequence of which it is necessary that all the medical and surgical attendance which our hospitals at Lisbon can afford should be sent as soon as possible, together with some 2000 sets of bedding . . .

To Major General Howarth: In consequence of the loss of artillerymen in the late action, and the want of them in this quarter, I have written to General Peacocke to desire him to send here a company of Royal Artillery . . .

To Beresford, 9.00 p.m.: . . . as I find you are at Albuera, and it appears desirable that you should remain there, I shall go straight there in the morning . . . My baggage will not be up till to-morrow or next day; therefore I must live upon you.

The same day he wrote to Berkeley and one now gets the impression that he has put together in his mind what the Battle of Albuera should be. This is not to say he was planning deceit, simply that Beresford's first reports had created an impression of disaster . . . it was now clear that bungling though there had been, and very serious losses, there was no defeat. The fighting was desperate, and the loss of the British has been severe; but adverting to the nature of the contest, and the manner in which they held their ground against all the efforts the whole French army could make against them, notwithstanding all the losses which they had sustained, I think this action one of the most glorious and honourable to the character of the troops of any that has been fought during the war . . .

To Stuart: I think it very desirable that if possible no flying details of the battle of Albuera should go home till Sir William Beresford's report shall be sent . . . where there are many killed and wounded the first reports are not favourable; and it is not doing justice to the Marshal to allow them to circulate without his.

To Spencer, 22 May: I went yesterday to Albuera, and saw the field of battle. We had a very good position, and I think should have gained a complete victory in it, without any material loss, if the Spaniards could have manoeuvred; but unfortunately they cannot . . . I think it appears that the enemy's loss cannot be less than between 8000 and 9000 men.

To Berkeley: I am about to send Colonel Arbuthnot home with the accounts of Sir William Beresford's action of the 16th instant; and I shall be very much obliged to you if you will send a ship of war with him, as it is desirable that he should arrive as soon as possible . . .

That is, before rumours or incomplete reports of the battle could reach England.

What had actually happened? Very briefly, 24,000 French under Soult marched to relieve Badajoz. At Albuera Beresford faced them with 20,000 Portuguese and British and 14,500 Spaniards. The country is a plain with only very slight rises or declivities. Beresford's position lay behind two rivulets which joined at the large village of Albuera and ran on as a river. He clearly expected the main assault to come at the town or on his left and so put his weak Spanish troops out on the right. Soult flanked these, Beresford ordered the Spanish General Blake to change his front, but he only managed to manoeuvre four battalions out of three divisions, and although the Spaniards fought with immense gallantry, he was soon in danger of being rolled up by what was in effect the largest single attack of the whole war – 8,400 infantry, 3,500 cavalry, and many guns.

Beresford sent in reinforcements and his generals independently added more. At one point 3,700 British faced 7,800 French in what became a stand-up fire-fight with the British under French guns firing grape at an oblique angle down the two-deep line – clearly one situation out of many that would not have occurred had Wellington been there. As men fell the survivors of each battalion moved into the colours in the centre and the gaps between each battalion increased. Polish lancers, armed with what was the most effective of cavalry weapons if used ruthlessly, and it was, swept through the allied lines, and a freak thunderstorm left the British rifles and muskets impotent against them.

In the confusion orders sent by Beresford did not reach his divisional commanders for the A.D.C.s carrying them were killed on the way. Beresford himself, who was big, burly, strong, and personally indomitably brave, escaped being skewered on a Polish lance by knocking the weapon aside, seizing the Pole by the neck and dashing him senseless to the ground. An unauthorised advance by Cole, posting squares on his flanks against the cavalry, held the French, who finally withdrew.

The British losses were unacceptably high. Of the units engaged 4,000 fell out of 8,700, and this is the reason why the 'victory' remained unpopular and a matter of dispute for many years. The total allied loss was 6,000 against 8,000 French. Beresford himself was clearly shattered by what had happened. When Wellington saw his original dispatch at Elvas on the 20th, he said to Colonel Arbuthnot who had brought it: 'This won't do. Write me down a victory,' which Beresford duly did. The tone of the original dispatch can be judged from a covering letter Beresford sent ahead of it.

> I feel much for the number we have lost, and I thank you for what you state; but I freely confess to you I can scarcely forgive myself for risking this battle, and I as freely confess that it was very unwise, and I am convinced I ought not to have done it . . . the more I reflect on the balance of good and evil from success or defeat, the more I am convinced the battle ought not to have been risked. I certainly risked all that you had been so long in gaining, and I cannot tell you how much that consideration oppressed me till all was safe. We have been fortunate and therefore all is well, and the risk we ran will not be known.'

There was a small deception in the re-written dispatch, which itself was entirely accurate, the improvements made were of tone only; the fact is that, like the first, it is dated 18 May, when in fact it could not have been written until at least three days later.

Among many letters of condolence Wellington wrote following Fuentes and Albuera, this, to his elder brother about a mutual friend, seems to me especially felt.

My Dear Wellesley,   Elvas, 22nd May, 1811
I am convinced that you will feel severely the loss of poor Houghton, whose last hours must have tended to raise him in the estimation of everybody.

I understand that it was impossible for any body to have behaved better than he did throughout the scene, to him novel, in which he was an actor. He was not only cool and collected as he ought to have been throughout the action, but animated and anxious . . . he actually fell waving his hat and cheering his brigade on to the charge.

I could not deny myself the satisfaction of communicating to you this last anecdote of our poor friend, whose loss I am convinced you will lament, on account of his private worth.

Believe me, my dear Wellesley,
Ever yours most affectionately,

Wellington

Beresford wrote of the British infantry:

It is impossible by any description to do justice to the distinguished gallantry of the troops; but every individual nobly did his duty; and it is observed that our dead, particularly the 57th Regiment, were lying as they fought, in ranks, and every wound was in front.

A cavalry officer who passed by a year later remarked their white bones, picked clean by kites and wolves, still lying where they fell, for the truth was there had not been enough survivors in some regiments to care for the wounded or bury their dead.

The last word on Albuera belongs to a sergeant of the 29th. Wellington made his rounds of the hospitals. 'Men of the 29th, I am sorry to see so many of you here.' *'If you had commanded us, my Lord, there wouldn't be so many of us here.'*

THE TURNING POINT

The French had been fought to a standstill twice. Both times they had brought superior numbers against the allies, and both times they had failed. But on both occasions it had been a near run thing. Both sides now looked about them to see how they could get the edge. On his side Wellington knew very well that he must have commanders on his right and on his left whom he could trust to act, at least to some extent, independently.

To Liverpool, 23 May, 1811: When Hill comes he must return to his command: and I must confine Beresford to the management of the detail of the Portuguese army, which has suffered from his employment in this campaign . . . I should like to have General Graham *to take the place of Brent Spencer on the right. Spencer was liked by Wellington as someone who did his best and was committed to the cause. His competence in a crisis was suspect, and his ability to attend to detail was negligible. Graham was the Victor of Barossa.*

I am glad to hear such good accounts of affairs to the north. God send they may prove true, and that we may overthrow this disgusting tyranny: however, of this I am very certain, that whether true or not at present, something of the kind must occur before long, and, if we can only hold out, we shall see the world relieved.

'Affairs in the north' *were the growing rift between Buonaparte and the Czar, and rumours of Buonaparte's plans to invade Russia.*

On their side the French, having failed to beat two separate allied armies with two separate armies of their own, naturally decided to combine. With Ciudad Rodrigo newly supplied, with Badajoz regularly threatened, and the desire on everyone's part to keep the riches of Andalusia under their control, the concentration was to the south.

To Spencer, at Alameda, 24 May: I think the French are about to do exactly what I expected, viz., collect their army about the Tagus . . . they are not so strong even as you are, and Marmont's movement is decidedly this way . . . Murray *(the Q.M.G. who, amongst much else, was responsible for planning just how any large portion of the army got from point A to point B)* sends you a route this day for the march here of General Howard's brigade and of Colonel Ashworth's Portuguese brigade . . .

I enclose a letter for Marshal Marmont, which I beg you to forward the moment you receive it: in order that he may believe I am still at Villa Fermosa, I date it the 25th . . .

Another step the French had taken to break the stalemate was to replace Masséna with Marmont. Even though Masséna was the only Marshal who kept Wellington awake at night, Napoleon's reception of him was less than gracious. 'I see the Prince of Essling. But where is André Masséna?' Marmont, Duc de Raguse, was young, educated, of 'good' family – which was something the Corsican Upstart had grown more and more to value – and reputed to be 'scientific' in his soldiering.

But how could Wellington be so sure of what the French were up to? To Spencer, 25 May: I understand that you have sent our friends at Salamanca 1000 dollars, and I shall be obliged to you if you will give direction that they may have 2000 more . . . *These 'friends' or 'correspondents' were a cell of spies whose information was regular, accurate, and of the greatest importance. They operated at tremendous personal risk by appearing to be collaborators or 'Afrancesados'. Among them was Patrick Curtis of the Irish College, of whom more later.*

Soult had withdrawn thirty miles to the south to regroup the army shattered at Albuera. Drouet was moving in reinforcements from the Army of the Centre. Marmont was edging the Army of Portugal towards them, and as he did Spencer marched on the west of the border, march for march, keeping pace. Knowing these concentrations were inevitable Wellington pressed on with the siege of Badajoz.

To Hill, 27 May: I am very glad to hear that you are returned in good health, and I hope that we shall see you soon.

You will have heard of events here, which I hope will enable us to obtain possession of Badajoz, upon which we are busily employed.

But things were not going well. Our old friend Fletcher, still Chief Engineer, was having problems (see map of Badajoz, page 192). To Wellington, 3 June: 'Much of the wall of the castle has fallen, but there is yet nothing like a practicable breach. On the whole I think the guns employed are so uncertain in their effects that it may become necessary to push yet further forward . . .' *(The guns were Portuguese, brass, and some over a century and a half old.) On the fifth: '. . . the breach in St Christoval was not considered . . . to be sufficiently practicable this evening to attempt an assault.' He repeated the warning on the sixth, but the French armies were closing in. Wellington ordered an assault. To Liverpool:* The men advanced under a very heavy fire of musketry and hand grenades from the outworks, and of shot and shell from the town, with the utmost intrepidity, and in the best order, to the bottom of the breach . . . but they found that the enemy had cleared the rubbish *that is the debris caused by the bombardment, which could have raised the level of the deep ditch* from the bottom of the escarp; and notwithstanding that they were provided with ladders, it was impossible to mount it. They retired with some loss.

Fletcher to Wellington, 7 June, 7.45 p.m.: '. . . the breach in the walls of the castle is somewhat improved.' Next day, 5.30 p.m.: '. . . the breach in the Castle walls, though much improved, is not in a state to justify sending the paper in possession of Major General Picton . . .' That is, the formal summons to surrender. But time had now really run out. Another assault went in on that night. They advanced at about 9 at night, in the best order, though opposed by the same means, and with the same determination . . . Ensign Dyas again led the service, and the storming party arrived at the foot of the breach; but they found it impossible to mount it, the enemy having again cleared the rubbish from the bottom of the escarp. The detachment suffered considerably . . . officers fell; but the troops continued to maintain their station till . . . Houston ordered them to retire.

Houston to Wellington, 10 June:

I have the honour to enclose General Philippon's reply to the flag of truce . . . The bodies of Major M'Geachy and Lieutenant Hogg have been brought in. Captain Nixon, severely wounded, Captain Budd, and Ensign Leslie are prisoners with the enemy. Money and clothes have been sent to them. Lieutenant Westropp has been brought in, I fear mortally wounded.

On the morning of the 10th instant I received the enclosed intercepted dispatch, from the Duke of Dalmatia *(Soult)* to the Duke of Raguse

(Marmont) which pointed out clearly the enemy's design to collect in Estramadura their whole force . . . on the same morning I received accounts . . . which left no doubt of the destination of the army of Portugal to the southward . . . I therefore ordered that the siege should be raised.

Slowly the armies drew together – 60,000 French plus the 3,500 garrison of Badajoz, 54,000 British and Portuguese. It could have been the most decisive confrontation of the whole war. To Liverpool, 20 June: The enemy's advance have appeared in the neighbourhood of Badajoz this day; and I conceive that their whole army will be collected to-morrow in the neighbourhood of Merida. *(See page 38.)*

The enemy have collected upon this occasion all their force from Castille, their whole force from Madrid, and what is called their centre army, and all the force from Andalusia, excepting what is absolutely necessary to maintain their position at Cadiz . . . *Much had been achieved. The partidas were reasserting their control over huge areas the French had abandoned in order to make this concentration.*

On that day Marmont and Soult met at Badajoz, but it was a gesture for the media rather than anything else. To enter the once beleaguered fortress with a parade and bands, to make an emotional reunion in front of vast crowds – of soldiers presumably, one imagines the inhabitants stayed indoors – looked good in the newspapers of the world. Soult could now claim Albuera for a victory, for had he not relieved Badajoz?

On the twenty-first Wellington completed his concentration on a fifteen-mile line between Elvas and Campo Mayor with the arrival of Spencer from the north. I am only three or four leagues from you, and dine every day at three, and shall be glad to see you any day that you will come over.

Three days later his request to have Graham received its clearance: I have great pleasure in sending you the accompanying orders to join this army. You will find us somewhere in this neighbourhood . . . Let me know by which road you will come, that I may have arrangements made to facilitate your progress.

And the next day, the twenty-fifth, the French appeared to be concentrating in front. To Hill, who held the left, midday: About 1600 cavalry, which were at Olivença, have come over to Badajoz, and at half past nine were still upon the esplanade of the fort on the left of the Guadiana. Send this intelligence to Cotton and Picton, as it is not improbable they make another reconnaissance on Campo Mayor.

To Cotton, from the atalaya (or watch tower, a feature of border villages) of Ponte de Caya, where he was up with the advance posts to see what was happening for himself, 25 June, 6.30 p.m.: 1600 cavalry . . . marched through Badajoz at 10, passed the river, and went into the woods on the Gevora, where I now see them.

I think it possible there may be a great reconnaissance to-morrow morning at Campo Mayor, and therefore I recommend that General de Grey's and Anson's brigades, and Le Fevre's troop of artillery, should be shortly after daylight behind the hill behind the town.

It was the last demonstration the French made. As Napier says: 'Marmont's army was conscious of its recent defeats at Busaco, at Sabugal, at Fuentes de Oñoro; the horrid field of Albuera was fresh; the fierce blood there spilt still reeked in the nostrils of Soult's soldiers.' The fact was the French only twice more, at Sorauren in 1813 and at Waterloo, attacked Wellington in a defensive position. Moreover they lost chances of what might have been substantial victories on occasions when they believed that a line of skirmishers below a hill crest concealed larger bodies of troops than were actually there. This is the point which Oman makes the turning point of the war. 'The offensive, though it was hardly realised yet, had passed to Wellington.' At all events it marked the end of the seven month period since Masséna's withdrawal from Sobral to Sabugal during which the scales had been nicely balanced.

The French hung around for another week. Wellington found time to catch up on less pressing business. A lady in England was in love, ready to die if her Major was not sent home to make an honest woman of her. To her protector, 27 June: But this fortunate Major now commands his battalion, and I am very apprehensive that he could not quit it at present . . .

We read, occasionally, of desperate cases of this description, but I cannot say that I have ever yet known of a young lady dying of love. They contrive, in some manner to live, and look tolerably well, notwithstanding their despair and the continued absence of their lover; and some have even been known to recover so far as to be inclined to take another lover, if the absence of the first has lasted too long. I don't suppose that your protegée can ever recover so far, but I do hope she will survive the continued necessary absence of the Major, and enjoy with him hereafter many happy days.

Again we are to look for a happy end in vain. Yes, the Major did eventually take leave to marry his lady – but returned to the army and was mortally wounded almost exactly two years later at Vitoria.

On 29 June Wellington welcomed His Serene Highness the Hereditary Prince of Orange, whose father was in exile in London, on to his staff. Once his initial suspicion of officers foisted upon him for reasons of politics or patronage had worn off, he quite took to the young man. On the thirtieth he learnt that a feud was ended. The Court of Common Council of the City of London had expressed its approbation of his Portuguese campaign. Samuel Whitbread, an old whig enemy, and hitherto one of his fiercest critics, wrote privately expressing his conversion, and received a most magnanimous letter back. It was not only with the French that he no longer needed to be defensive.

On the same day he wrote to Torrens, Military Secretary to the Commander-in-Chief: The last post brought us accounts of the Duke of York's appointment to be Commander-in-Chief, at which I rejoice most sincerely . . . *The nation had forgiven HRH for his indiscreet mistress, and most of the military establishment was glad to see the back of Sir David Dundas who was hidebound and resisted all change.*

On 2 July it was clearly over. To William: They don't like to attack us, and are now breaking up; Soult returning to Andalusia, and the other apparently across the Tagus. I am waiting to see whether I cannot give one of them a knock: if I can't, I must then wait till Soult will undertake something to the southward, when I shall be able to try my hand on the north of the Tagus. It won't do to keep our troops in the field in Estramadura in the months of August and September, by choice at least.

But both French marshals were entirely competent at this sort of withdrawal, and no chance for a 'knock' came.

To Beresford, 5 July: The enemy have drawn off entirely from this neighbourhood . . . I keep our troops still in their camps, meaning, if Soult leaves Marmont alone, to endeavour to give Marmont a blow. However, I doubt that Soult will leave that in my power.

The French have taken a great deal of cannon out of Badajoz. They have blown up Olivença.

12 July, 1811: The devil is in the French for numbers!!! A deserter came in yesterday, and told me that . . . the two armies had 60,000 infantry and nearly 10,000 cavalry! I made them . . . 50,000 infantry and 7000 cavalry. Our army continues very healthy, indeed more so since the nights have become warmer . . .

17 July: I see there are some troops in motion in Castille towards Ciudad Rodrigo, which is I believe with a view to provision the place, which Don Julian had kept tolerably closely blockaded . . .

As Marmont has moved . . . I shall go to Portalegre.

1812

(AUGUST 1811–JULY 1812)

———✦———

A BUSTLE

FRENEDA

CIUDAD RODRIGO

BADAJOZ

TWO BRIDGES

THE SALAMANCA CAMPAIGN

THE MASTER

———✦———

18 July he wrote a long letter to Liverpool summarising the situation and his intentions. The French could still overwhelm him if they chose to concentrate all their forces against him, but this was impossible – such concentrations could not be fed in a bitterly hostile countryside. Nevertheless Marmont and Soult alone, by abandoning Galicia to the north and the siege of Cadiz to the south could still field a substantially larger army than his. However, he goes on, with the fine and well-equipped army which we have, and with our cavalry in such good order as it is, and with the prospect of the renewal of hostilities in the north of Europe, I am most anxious . . . to improve the situation of the allies in the Peninsula.

He rejects the siege of Badajoz because of the heat and the disease, and the ease with which Soult could again march to its relief. He rejects an immediate attack on Marmont, then opposite him on the Tagus, because of Marmont's superiority in cavalry in the open plain. He rejects the relief of Cadiz: Marmont, Soult, and the besieging force would present him with overwhelming numbers. So . . .

The next operation which presents itself is the siege of Ciudad Rodrigo, for which I have so far prepared as to have our battering train on the Douro.

It would be necessary to leave . . . 12,000 men on the Alentejo *(under Hill)* to watch the 5th corps d'armée *(Soult)*, which would reduce our force to about 45,000 men, to which Marmont and Bessières would be equal and superior in cavalry . . . This enterprise, however, upon the whole promises best. We can derive some assistance from our militia in the north . . . , the climate is not unfavourable at this season. If it should not succeed, the attempt will move the war to the strongest frontier of Portugal; and if obliged to resume the defensive, the strength of our army will be centrally situated, while the enemy's armies of the north and south will be disunited. . . . I am tempted to try this enterprise.

However, a period of irritating inaction followed. Far from losing men for the Russian campaign, the French were reinforced in the north by a further 40,000 – Marmont could stay put on the Tagus. On the other hand Wellington's reinforcements were the sick troops from the Walcheren expedition. In the northern fens of Holland they had caught what came to be known as Walcheren

Fever, a particularly vicious form of influenza, which was often fatal, and appallingly difficult to shake off.

At this point, it is worth quoting one of the best memoirs of the war – that of John Green of the 68th Light infantry. An apprentice in a Louth carpet factory 'where in vain I tried to settle, having a disposition to wander', he ran away to sea, didn't like it, and enlisted in 1806. He went to Walcheren and caught the fever. In July his regiment sailed up the Tagus to Santarem and then marched along the north bank to join the army.

> On the 8th July, after receiving three days' bread and meat, three pints of wine, and sixty rounds of ammunition, we commenced movements towards Golegain: with this load on our backs, altogether amounting to little short of four stones weight – the hardships we endured from this, and the change of climate and provision, together with the abundance of fruit, and drinking cold water when exceedingly hot, our men began to be taken with fevers and fluxes [*diarrhoea*]. We have sent from ten to twenty a day to the general hospital, where many of them died, and others continued a long time.

Inaction led the lesser tacticians to believe that campaigning was over for the year, and, brought up on the morality of the absentee landlord, no-one saw much wrong in applying for leave to get back to England in time for the grouse shooting. While Private Green toiled on, suffering from fever and flux, as usual all the officers of the army want to go home, some for their health, others on account of business, and others, I believe, for their pleasure.

General Spencer is going, because General Graham has come from Cadiz; General Nightingall is gone; General William Stewart, General Lumley, General Howarth, and Colonel Mackinnon, likewise on account of their health . . . To this list add General Dunlop, General Hay, General Cole, and General Alexander Campbell who have applied to go to settle their affairs . . . I have also innumerable applications for leave from officers of the army of all ranks. Till we can get the minds of the officers of the army settled to their duty we shall not get on as we ought.

On 25 July Marmont at last moved north, and one officer at least was back and doing his customary duty with the advance guard. He had been promoted too. To Liverpool: The enemy's cavalry left Merida on the morning of the 17th, and Major Cocks' piquets were in that town shortly afterwards . . . *amongst the broken arches, the then unexcavated theatres and coliseum, the forum of the Roman capital of Estremadura.*

It was time to be moving. Craufurd and the Light division should have been to the fore, but apparently were not. Wellington's note to him of the twenty-fifth

166

suggests that he had not revealed even to his divisional commanders his designs on Ciudad Rodrigo. The orders were sent from hence two days ago for you to march . . . to a service which I think it probable you will be able to perform which I shall explain more fully when I see you. The fact is, that I am about to move the whole army farther to the left *(north)* . . .

On 6 August he was at Penmacor, about fifty miles south of Fuentes de Oñoro, sixty-five from Ciudad Rodrigo. To Beresford: I rather think I shall immediately close up Ciudad Rodrigo. It will depend on what I shall hear this day . . . *To Graham:* I have not yet received the intelligence which I expect at every moment, which will enable me to determine whether I shall move on upon Ciudad Rodrigo immediately or not. From the tenor of that which I have received, however, I think I ought to move on, and I therefore recommend you to come here tomorrow . . .

The intelligence he wanted was an estimate of how well provisioned the fortress was, and what he learned was confusing. A Spanish Colonel O'Lalor, who was scouting about the area with irregulars, reported that the fortress could last two months, but at the same time itemised what had gone in, and that added up to much less. And so Wellington moved on and was back at Sabugal the next day.

To Beresford: From what I have heard of the state of the provisions and of the garrison of Ciudad Rodrigo, I propose to shut it up as soon as I can, unless, before I can do so, I should receive positive intelligence that the information which I have already received is erroneous.

It must be expected that the enemy will adopt all the means in their power to oblige us to desist from our object and we must be prepared to adopt measures to resist them whenever they should attack us.

One of their plans will be to collect the whole of their force; that is Bessières' army of the north, the army of Portugal, and the fifth corps, and fight a general action, to oblige us to relinquish our object. If they do this I shall bring Hill's corps to this army . . .

And now, at last, he is becoming much more open about his real design. If Ciudad Rodrigo is provisioned as little as he hopes Marmont will be in a hurry to relieve it, might arrive with too weak a force . . . ; even if it is well provisioned he will still come, and troops, a large army, will be enticed away from the occupied areas of Spain. In short, Ciudad Rodrigo is not so much the object as the bait.

On the eighth he is more explicit to Liverpool, although now more certain that the fortress was well supplied: . . . the movement I am making may lead to some operation by the enemy which may afford an opportunity of striking an advantageous blow . . .

By the twelfth he had established his head quarters at Fuente Guinaldo where they were to remain for six weeks (see map page 133). It's a small hamlet in the uplands south of Ciudad Rodrigo. The river Agueda is the central feature of this area. Above Ciudad Rodrigo it meanders through open down-like country, now given over to wheat but in those days more grazed and with more scattered woods. As the river approaches the fortress town it cuts deeper, ravines are formed. Then it enters the small undulating plain, which, apart from rises and low hills, surrounds the town, extending on the north-west side and opening out towards Salamanca. Below the town the country breaks up in the way we have already described: the slopes become steeper, the ravines more gorge-like as the river drops away to its junction with the Duero/Douro forty miles away.

Wellington cantoned his army on an extended line from where a tributary of the Agueda, the Azava, joined the larger river a league or so west of the fortress, up into the uplands through Pastores, to El Bodon, Fuente Guinaldo and further south to Penmacor. All were behind the Agueda which is, for the most part, easily crossed in the uplands but is still an obstacle, and of course leaves ridges to its west that form good defensive positions. The Light division only was placed in front, that is east, of the river, with its headquarters at Martiago. From these positions any inadequately protected convoy could be swooped on and captured; in them he hoped to face out forces considerably larger than his own. But six weeks were to elapse before the French came.

In the meantime he had heard from Henry that there was a plot afoot in Cadiz to sell the place to the French. Now the Wellesleys liked to think of themselves as landowning aristocracy – though strictly speaking they had not been aristocrats for as long as they led people to understand, and had not yet acquired all that much land – yet that was very much their class and caste: tories, grandees. Yet Wellington's pragmatism, his unerring reading of almost any situation, led him to the culprits: My own opinion is, that several will be inclined to submit to the French as soon as they shall find them in possession of Valencia. Almost all the grandees have estates in Valencia, upon the rents of which they have subsisted since they have been deprived of their estates in the other provinces . . . , and they will of course feel sorely the loss of these their last means of subsistence; but their influence at Cadiz is not great, much less paramount, and I should think the merchants and people *(the bourgeoisie?)* would not submit on any account.

For news of what Marmont was up to he continued to depend on his people in Salamanca. To Beresford, 25 August, following his discovery that intelligence passed on from Marmont's headquarters had been leaked to the Portuguese papers: . . . from these papers it is copied in the English newspapers.

Our correspondents there will certainly be discovered if the practice is continued. Indeed they will be lucky if their own indiscretion does not bring some of them to the gallows.

What do you think of one of them going to Ledesma the other day and dining with Don Carlos de España and Don Julian, which was known publicly, and talked of in Salamanca; and having escaped hanging upon that occasion they wanted to have a meeting with Alava and O'Lalor. However, they are so very useful to us that we should take care that they are not discovered . . .

Ledesma is a delightful town on a hill above the Tormes about twenty-three miles by road north west of Salamanca. To Craufurd, 31 August: There is no convoy coming to Ciudad Rodrigo. The convoy which left Salamanca on the 27th . . . was one of artillery for the army of Portugal.

I have constant intelligence from Salamanca, the last letter dated the 27th; and there was no convoy for Ciudad Rodrigo then thought of.

To Liverpool, 11 September: A detachment of the Guards and of the lanciers de Berg, drove Don Julian's troops from Ledesma on the 4th . . .

Either these operations or increased vigilance of the police at Salamanca have prevented my receiving any intelligence from my correspondents in that town since the 3d instant . . . I am very apprehensive that the silence may be attributed to the latter cause, and even that some of them may have suffered for their attachment to us. . . . P.S. I have received a letter of the 7th from Salamanca, which has relieved me from the anxiety which I felt respecting my correspondents in that place.

While the pause continued there was time to see off an American horse-dealer who had seen the chance of a fast buck. To Berkeley, 16 September: . . . it would scarcely be worth while to make one *(a contract)* for such a saving as five guineas for each horse . . . There is also another objection to this plan, which is, that although horses might be very fit for the service in Passamaquoddy Bay *(on the border between Maine and New Brunswick)* upon their embarcation, the voyage would probably make such an alteration in their condition, particularly under American care, as might make them very unfit for service on their arrival here . . .

More important, Parliament and British charities had collected money for the poor and sick of Portugal. Wellington recommended to Stuart, 16 September, that this should be distributed along the Coa. These districts were the seat of war during the months of 1810 when the harvest of that year was reaped, the whole of which was consumed by the enemy; and again in the beginning of April this year, when the little they had sown began to appear above ground and was consumed . . .

The inhabitants of these villages are reduced to subsist upon a small quantity of millet which they have continued to save; but the food is not of a description, nor the quantity sufficient, to subsist them through the winter . . . the distressed state of these people deserves the attention of the managers of these charities.

It could be noted at this point that the Portuguese Regency had by now virtually collapsed through its internal intriguing. For the next two and a half years Stuart and Beresford were the effective government, and they took their orders from Wellington. That Lisbon coffee house owner, who about now petitioned to stay open at night, clearly knew who was top of the heap.

On 17 September Wellington wrote a routine letter to Cotton on cavalry returns and alluded to the expected <u>bustle</u>. *On the eighteenth he knew the army of Portugal was concentrating and had been reinforced by 4,000 from France. On the twenty-second he ended a letter to Hill:* The French have moved: and I think by to-morrow we shall have a very large army in our front. *Next day, to Stuart:* The French have not yet appeared, but I think they will before evening. I shall have my hands very full of business for the next three or four days . . .

On the same day at 7.00 a.m., he wrote his last letter for six days. It was a good one, had superlative results. To Hill: I do not think Girard has a force to annoy you. I reckon that you have about 11,000 men, and he cannot have 6000 of which 1100 or 1200 are cavalry.

If he moves forward, I beg you will fall upon him . . .

As the French came on their numbers became clearer. Marmont, the scientific general, was taking no chances. He had 54,000 infantry, 6,000 cavalry, and 125 guns against 46,000 allies who were deficient in both cavalry and artillery. There was clearly to be no big battle in the plain north east of Ciudad Rodrigo, but Marmont might be tempted into some foolishness in the hills behind the town. For this reason perhaps Wellington's line was very extended. On the left Graham, at Espeja on the Azava, was a day's march from the centre at Fuente Guinaldo. Craufurd was almost as far away again on the right, east of the Agueda, with outposts right out on the mountains that separate Castille from Estremadura.

To Liverpool, 29 September: On the morning of the 25th the enemy sent a reconnaissance . . . towards the Lower Azava, but having passed that river . . . were charged by two squadrons of the 16th and one of the 14th Light Dragoons and driven back. They attempted to rally and to return, but were fired upon by the Light infantry of the 61st regiment, which had been posted in a wood on their flank by Lieut. General

Graham . . . Major General Anson pursued them across the Azava, and afterwards resumed his posts on the right of that river.

But the enemy's attention was principally directed during this day to the position of the 3d division, in the hills between Fuente Guinaldo and Pastores. About 8 in the morning they moved a column, consisting of between thirty and forty squadrons of cavalry, and fourteen battalions of infantry, and twelve pieces of cannon, from Ciudad Rodrigo in such a direction that it was doubtful whether they would attempt to ascend the hills by La Encina, or by the direct road of El Bodon . . . and I was not certain by which road they would make their attack, till they actually commenced it upon the last.

El Bodon is a scrappy bit of a village on the first watershed of the hills that climb and drop and climb into the mountains along the road through Perales to Estremadura. By now the vine leaves would have turned to gold near the villages, and the poplars and birches too, planted as windbreaks along the edge of the settlement. The stubble in the wheat fields may already have been burnt and the red earth turned in the first ploughing. The nights were chill, even frosty, the days still hot at midday, the air clear and brisk in the uplands, hot and still in the ravines. Kites, Griffon's Vultures and Egyptian Vultures soared and wheeled, looked for starved sheep, or waited for more abundant supplies above the slowly shifting lines of red and columns of blue.

As soon as he saw what was happening Wellington reinforced the threatened area, but the distances were almost equal for both sides, and the French had a tiny advantage in time. In the meantime, however, the small body of troops in this position sustained the attack of the enemy's cavalry and artillery. One regiment of French dragoons succeeded in taking two pieces of cannon . . . but they were charged by the 2d batt. 5th regiment and the guns immediately retaken.

While this operation was going on on the flank, an attack was made on the front by another regiment which was repulsed in a similar manner by the 77th regiment, and the three squadrons of Major General Alten's brigade charged repeatedly different bodies of the enemy which ascended the hill on the left . . .

At length, the division of the enemy's infantry . . . were brought up to the attack and I determined to withdraw our post at El Bodon, and retire with the whole on Fuente Guinaldo . . . The enemy's cavalry immediately rushed forward . . . the 5th and 77th were charged on three faces of the square . . . but they halted and repulsed the attack with the utmost steadiness and gallantry.

During all this 1,000 British infantry, 500 cavalry and two batteries of artillery fought off and retired in the face of 2,500 French. Casualties were 149 to 200 in favour of the allies. Meanwhile Picton with the other half of the 3rd division, even further out on the left and nearer Ciudad Rodrigo at break of day, was also pulling back on the central position, across a wide, open down. Three brigades of cavalry and six light guns harassed them over six miles, but usually with Picton between them and his men, whom he repeatedly told to keep calm, and mind their distances. When they were at last within sight of Fuente Guinaldo it looked as if the French were about to make a general charge. Their front rank was half a pistol shot away, harnesses and heavy sabres jingled and clattered. Someone called out: 'Had we better not form square?' Picton lifted his top hat to shade his eyes from the sun, and replied, after a moment's examination of the French in front of him, 'No, it is but a ruse to frighten us, and it won't do.'

We then continued the retreat, and joined the remainder of the 3d division on their march to Fuente Guinaldo, and the whole retired together in the utmost order, and the enemy never made another attempt to charge any of them; but were satisfied with firing on them with their artillery, and with following them.

The position at Fuente Guinaldo was typically Busaco-like, with the added strength that Wellington actually ordered earthworks to be thrown up. As usual his main force was collected on the reverse slopes of the hills with only piquets and companies of light troops visible to the enemy. This was just as well. At this point he had only 14,400 men and 2,600 cavalry while Marmont, if he had fully understood the position, could have brought 40,000 against him without imperilling any of his other objects. Graham was still a day's march away on the Azava, which could be cut to half a day if they moved towards each other. But this they could not do without abandoning the Light division which was still way out on the right. At 3.00 p.m. on the twenty-fifth Wellington sent an order to Craufurd telling him to come in. Craufurd, not expecting to arrive before midnight stayed put until dawn of the twenty-sixth. All through the twenty-sixth Marmont gathered in his army and probed the allied outposts. A full scale attack at any time could have meant annihilation, certainly a withdrawal, and therefore the certain loss of the entire Light division.

The latter arrived at 3.00 p.m. on the twenty-sixth. 'I am glad to see you safe,' snapped the Peer. 'Oh! I was in no danger, I assure you,' said Craufurd. 'But I was, from your conduct.' Craufurd withdrew, muttering the immortal phrase: 'He's damned crusty today.'

That night they slipped away, leaving their camp-fires burning, linked with Graham, and by the twenty-seventh were in an even stronger position in Portugal, on the Coa. When Marmont realised that he had been faced with many thousands of troops less than he had expected, he commented, alluding to Napoleon's notorious good luck: 'Wellington also has his star'.

There was further skirmishing on the twenty-eighth during which Marmont realised that the British were now well and truly concentrated and safe . . . and as it appears that they are about to retire from this part of the country, and as we have already had some bad weather, and may expect more at the period of the equinoctial gales, I propose to canton the troops in the nearest villages to the positions which they occupied yesterday.

This dispatch of 29 September, 1811, concludes with lavish praise for all the units which had been involved in the fighting, but mentions the Light only once, to say it was ordered back on the 25th, and alludes to the danger he had been in by disclaiming that there had been any risk at all.

I did all that I could expect to effect without incurring the risk of great loss for no object: and as the reports as usual were so various in regard to the enemy's real strength, it was necessary that I should see their army in order that the people of this country might be convinced that to raise the blockade was a measure of necessity, and that the momentary relief of Galicia and Mina *a guerrilla leader who operated round Burgos* were the only objects which it was in my power immediately to effect.

He had also got the measure of Marmont – it was something he set high store by, knowing his enemy: and had found him . . . predictable.

On 2 October, when all was well and truly over, he issued a General Order that again recounted the events of those two days in the most glowing terms, ending: . . . it affords a memorable example of what can be effected by steadiness, discipline and confidence. *Why? As a snub to Craufurd? Perhaps. Because he knew he had been in a scrape and his men had got him out of it? Perhaps again. But mainly out of unconditional admiration for the courage and skill of his army. I emphasise this because on several minor occasions and on one or two notorious ones he denigrated, even slandered his men. Commentators forget how wholeheartedly he could praise them too.*

Autumn had come, and not all the fruits were mellow: The Commander of the Forces requests that *(all)* . . . officers will take measures to prevent the soldiers from eating unripe grapes and other fruit: the old soldiers must be aware how pernicious it is to their health; but those lately arrived are not aware of it, and he begs that measures may be taken to prevent their getting it. *Which is one of the very rare occasions that his sense of syntax let him down.*

To Campbell, Freneda, 6 October: I have been very well during the late bustle. Pray let me know how you are, and

Believe me, &c.

Wellington

FRENEDA

G.O.   Freneda, 7th Oct., 1811.
2. The Commander of the Forces requests that the General Officers commanding divisions will take the opportunity of the fine weather of the present moment to exercise the troops under their command. (*'Exercise' was drill and weapons training, not P.E.*)
3. It would tend materially to improve the health of the troops, and would keep them in the habit of marching, if, besides the exercise, they were to march a few miles on the road once or twice a week.
4. A Working Party . . . are to proceed to-morrow morning to Almeida, to be employed in the works of that place . . .
5. These men are to receive working money . . .
6. Such of the party as are bricklayers or stonemasons (*the unemployed of Britain*) will be employed as artificers, and will receive double pay.
7. It is to be clearly understood however, that those who do not work will get no pay.

Wellington

Freneda. Headquarters were there for three months in 1811, and for nearly six in the following winter and spring. It's the tiniest of hamlets, is not marked on the Kummerley and Frey tourist map of the Peninsula, so that makes it very small indeed. It lies two and a half miles west of Fuentes de Oñoro and Villa Fermosa, and you could, indeed I did, pass it without noticing. Stone hovels, cottages, and two or three two-storey buildings, a tiny church, a tiny square. The pigs were removed from the ground floor of one of the larger houses and the staff moved in with their tables, green baize cloths, maps, mapping instruments, and boxes and boxes of documents whose keys had presumably been found again. The other large buildings were occupied by the Adjutant General's department, and the Quarter Master General's department.

At this point I think a direct quote from one of the most useful books I have come across is in order. The book is Wellington's Headquarters *by S. P. G. Ward, who was himself a staff officer in the Second World War. It was published by the Oxford University Press in 1957.*

Unless active operations interrupted the routine it was Wellington's practice to see each of his heads of department daily. He rose at six every morning, wrote until breakfasting at nine, and immediately after was waited on by the Adjutant General, the Quarter Master General, the Commissary-General, the Inspector General of Hospitals, the Commanding Officer of Artillery, the Commanding Royal Engineer, and by any other officer he wanted to see on business . . . This occupied him until two, three, or four in the afternoon. He would then order his horse and ride until about six, or, when at Freneda, he might be seen walking up and down the little square in front of his quarter in his grey greatcoat, talking with anyone he wished to. Everyone who came to him found he dispatched business with remarkable facility, especially on the days he went hunting . . . *(pages 153 and 154)*

A tiny church, a tiny square . . . and, a tiny market. The following account of the Peer is based on that of authentic eyewitnesses.

It is mid-afternoon, shortly before dinner at three. Your Grace paused on the threshold, looked up and down, and then quite unattended strolled into the street and between the stalls, for all the world like a country squire among his tenantry. You were dressed, as I recall, in a grey frock-coat and grey trousers with a cape which shortly you removed and carried over your arm, for the sun was warmer perhaps than you had expected. On your head a small cocked hat – no plumes, no lace, no bullion, no sword, no pistol, not even a cane, and thus you took a little recreation from the cares of nations. Presently a small girl came up to you, a Portuguese, and taking you firmly by the hand with such familiarity as spoke of earlier meetings, indeed an established acquaintanceship, led you to the stall where the pedlar from Lisbon displayed his English wares. The girl was not above seven years, thin, dark, and a little pert – dressed cleanly in a white smock that set off her dark skin, and with her dark hair in braids tied with a red ribbon.

Anon, with easy familiarity, you addressed yourself to the pedlar who straight set up a pennyworth of wrapped butter-scotch which you offered to your companion. But perhaps she would not like these foreign dainties, and so to persuade her of their excellence you must draw one out, unwrap it and pop it in . . . not her, but your mouth. Miss frowned now. Perhaps a tear glistened. To forestall it a second piece was quickly exposed and this posted where it most properly belonged. A space while one might count twenty then smiles and glee on both sides, and two satisfied parties continued their perambulation, still hand in hand, of the tiny square. *(from Joseph by Julian Rathbone)*

Don Julian celebrated the feast of St Teresa of Avila, who is buried at Alba near Salamanca, and is venerated by all Charros, in typical style. A week later, on 23 October, to Liverpool: The Governor, General Renaud, had come out of the fort and across the Agueda, attended by some staff officers, and escorted by a party of about twenty cavalry, and he was surrounded by Don Julian's detachment as soon as he entered the hills, and was taken, with two of his escort, under the fire of the guns of the place.

Shortly afterwards Don Julian's detachments on the right of the Agueda drove off the greatest number of the cattle which had been sent out to graze, under the guns of the fort on that side of the river.

To Peacocke, 19 October: This letter will be delivered to you by General Reynaud, late Governor of Ciudad Rodrigo, who is going to Lisbon on his way to England, as a prisoner of war on his parole. *To Stuart:* I have recommended General Reynaud to you, you will find him a very intelligent fellow.

Wellington, as you will probably have gathered by now, had a clear scale of terms for people. 'Gentry' were scheming bastards; 'gentlemen' scheming bastards whose birth or position was privileged. 'fellows' were people he really liked; Alava, the Napiers, were 'fine fellows'.

The guerrillas were active everywhere. To Liverpool, 30 October: It appears from all accounts which I have received, that the guerrillas are increasing in numbers and boldness throughout the Peninsula. One party under Temprano, lately took, at the very gates of Talavera, Lieut. Colonel Grant of the Portuguese service . . . Both the Empecinado and Mina were very successful against some of the enemy's outposts and detachments, when their armies were lately collected for the relief of Ciudad Rodrigo; and Longa was likewise very successful in the neighbourhood of Vitoria . . .

Wellington, contrary to the opinion of modern Spanish historians, was never slow to acknowledge his debt to the guerrillas – the same historians, however, are very loth to acknowledge the guerrillas' debt to Wellington. Their activities always rose in direct proportion to the amount of troops the French were forced to draw off from the countryside to concentrate against Wellington and Hill. At these times the partidas raided magazines, carried off convoys, destroyed outposts and so on, and very materially assisted in bringing about the eventual outcome of the war. But in 'pacified' areas, policed by large garrisons of French, they quickly dwindled to bands of hill robbers who were little more than an irritant. It is nonsense to say, as at least one Spanish historian has, that they would have eventually driven out the French on their own.

The debt to Wellington goes further. Through Henry at Cadiz he pressured the Juntas and later the Cortes into recognizing the guerrillas and commissioning their leaders. They were armed by the British. And when Wellington became Supreme Commander their activities were co-ordinated by him. They could no more have affected the outcome without him than the Viet Cong could have got the Americans out of South Viet Nam without General Giap and the army of the North.

Not all the news on the sixteenth was good. To Liverpool: The French have seized Dr Curtis, of the Irish College, and the Providor of the Bishopric of Salamanca, who are two of the people with whom my correspondents there communicate. I suspect they have had orders from Paris to cut us off from all intelligence.

In 1811 Curtis was sixty-four, a good old age for those days, and had been attached to the Irish College since its foundation thirty odd years earlier. This came about when the Enlightened Despot Charles III closed the four Colegios Mayores of Salamanca University. These, much like Oxford and Cambridge today, had dominated politics, government, the church, indeed every corner of public life for a hundred and fifty years and had done as much harm to Spain as Oxford and Cambridge have to us. One of them, the Colegio de Santiago Apostol, was taken over by the Irish Catholic hierarchy as a seminary for Irish priests, and as such it soon became one of the ornaments of the university both for its learning and its liberalism. Curtis was in at its inception, soon became its rector, and also held the university chairs of astronomy and natural science. He did not, however, neglect his pastoral duties and was for a time a chaplain to the Spanish navy, in which capacity he was, like Alava, at the Battle of Trafalgar – on the wrong side. When Moore came through Salamanca he urged his seminarists to enlist, and many of them were later commissioned in the Portuguese and Spanish armies. As Catholics of course they could not be commissioned in British regiments.

Curtis was tall, though stooped, and had a charismatic shock of white hair. After the war he returned to Ireland and, partly on Wellington's recommendation, became Archbishop of Armagh and Primate. In 1811 he suffered no worse than house arrest.

The cooler weather improved the health of the troops but brought other problems. To Liverpool, 23 October: As the soldiers of the army frequently sleep out of doors, and as, even when in houses, they are obliged to sleep in their great coats, that article of their equipment wears out in a much shorter period of time than that specified by the regulations (three years) . . . I therefore request your Lordship that 10,000 great coats . . . may be sent . . .

There was another aspect to what the well-dressed soldier might or might not be wearing during the coming season. To Torrens, 6 November: I hear that measures are in contemplation to alter the clothing, caps, &c. of the army.

There is no subject of which I understand so little; and, abstractedly speaking, I think it indifferent how a soldier is clothed, provided it is in a uniform manner; and that he is forced to keep himself clean and smart, as a soldier ought to be. But there is one thing I deprecate, and that is any imitation of the French, in any manner.

It is impossible to form an idea of the inconveniences and injury which result from having anything like them, either on horseback or on foot. A piquet was taken in June, because the 3d hussars had the same caps as the French chasseurs à cheval . . . and I was near being taken on the 25th September from the same cause.

At a distance, or in action, colors are nothing: the profile, and shape of a man's cap, and his general appearance are what guide us; and why should we make our people look like the French? . . . I only beg that we may be as different as possible from the French in everything. The narrow top caps of our infantry, as opposed to their broad top caps, are a great advantage to those who are to look at long lines of posts opposed to each other.

'If he moves forward, I beg you will fall on him . . .' Wellington to Hill on 23 September, the 'he' being the French general Girard who operated between the Tagus and the Guadiana from Caceres. Hill duly obliged. Drouet withdrew to the Sierra Morena leaving Girard with only 6,000 men. Hill drove him south out of Caceres, and then by means of forced marches contrived to get his corps between Girard and Merida, where the French were hoping to cross the Guadiana and rejoin the French armies in Andalusia. All this was done in appalling weather, and on 27 October the British position was kept secret – no camp fires were lit. On the next day Hill fell on the French at Arroyo de Molinos – barely 600 escaped, and over 1,300 prisoners were taken with artillery, baggage, Commissariat, and a recently replenished military chest.

To Liverpool, 6 November: It would be particularly agreeable to me, if some mark of the favor of His Royal Highness the Prince Regent were conferred upon General Hill; his services have always been meritorious, and very distinguished in this country, and he is beloved by the whole army.

At the passage of the Douro *(1809, see pages 44–5)* he commanded the detachment which first crossed the river, after General Paget was wounded, which maintained itself against all the efforts of Soult's corps; and he commanded a division, distinguished himself, and was wounded at the battle of Talavera. He has since commanded a separate corps of this army; he has shown the greatest ability in all the movements he has made, and nobody could have been more successful than he has been in his late operation.

In recommending him, as I do most anxiously, I really feel that there is no officer to whom an act of grace and favor would be received by the army with more satisfaction than on General Hill.

Hill was the best of Wellington's generals. He and Graham were the only ones who never let him down, and, after Albuera, he was the only one to be trusted with an entirely independent command. Although never ready to take a risk (his commander would not have trusted him out of sight if he had been) he acted in the days leading up to Arroyo de Molinos and in the affair of the bridge at Almaraz with almost Napoleonic – no, Wellingtonian – swiftness and decisiveness.

He was a kind, generous man, who did all he could to soften the barbarous penal code, and always tried to reform rather than punish. He did not look after his men any better than Wellington did, that would have been impossible, but he added warm personal touches. Sydney-like he would pass up a can of water to a wounded soldier or fill a messenger's knapsack with bread and meat. The soldiers christened him 'Daddy Hill' and he is somehow always remembered as rather an elderly gentleman – yet he was three years younger than Wellington, and in 1811 just thirty-nine years old.

I stress: Wellington recognised how Hill was 'beloved' and where a lesser man might have felt envy, his magnanimity saw only an extra reason for praise. To Hill, 9 Nov.: Nothing could be more satisfactory to me than all that you did, and I am happy to send home your brother with the report of your transactions, before I had heard that it was your wish to do so. *Captain Hill, as bearer of victorious dispatches, would thereby gain a step in promotion.*

CIUDAD RODRIGO

To Liverpool, 6 November: The new governor . . . General Barrié moved from Salamanca on the 30th October . . . escorted by one division of infantry and 600 cavalry . . . The state of the fords at Agueda . . . prevented our troops from making any movement . . . and the enemy had marched on their return before daylight. *3,000 men to get one general across territory which the French claimed to occupy.*

Preparations for the siege of Ciudad Rodrigo went on: it was to surprise the French by coming in January, not in Spring; they were to be kept in doubt as to whether or not Wellington might choose to go for Badajoz first.

A new siege train had been put together (no more brass guns 150 years old) and shipped to Oporto. The Douro was navigable to Lamego which left a long, circuitous, mountainous route to Almeida. Therefore no siege train would be available until the end of May at the earliest. So thought the French. To

Pimental, a member of the Portuguese government, 28 November: Having lately sent an officer of the Engineers to survey the Douro . . . to Barca d'Alva, he has reported to me that the river is already navigable to that point for large boats, with some inconvenience, and at certain seasons of the year; and that it might be made navigable with convenience at all seasons, by a certain degree of labor . . .

Understanding that you have from His Royal Highness the Prince Regent *of Portugal* the power to destroy the mill dams in the River Douro, which are the principal obstruction to the navigation, I request you to co-operate with Captain Ross in the performance of this work.

This was in its way, as striking a move as the Lines of Torres Vedras. Barca d'Alva is right on the border, only twenty-five miles north of Almeida to which it is linked by a good road.

A monograph could be written on Wellington's dynamic, indeed dialectical use of rivers – he made them what he wanted them to be. They were means of communication and transport if he made them navigable. They could protect a front or a flank, which was admittedly the conventional wisdom, but when they were inadequate for that purpose he dammed them to form impassable floods. On the other side, however, he made sure that for the French they were hindrances to communication or movement by seizing bridgeheads and blowing up bridges; and in 1813 he even denied them their use as flank protection by discovering unsuspected routes round their head waters. Finally, he caused to be built a mobile pontoon – which was never quite as mobile as he hoped, but which still enabled him to move where the French did not think he could go; and on the same line but more efficiently his engineers produced to his design an extraordinarily effective and quick way of repairing the bridges the French, or even he himself, had blown up.

Two valued colleagues had to go, Campbell, who commanded the 6th division, and Admiral Berkeley. Campbell, in poor health and hard up too, was presumably being pressed by his wife. Wellington's letter to him seems to me to be a little masterpiece of domestic wisdom: I assure you, that I lament the chance which certainly exists that I may never meet you again. I acknowledge, that with this chance before your eyes, I am astonished that you should think, at your time of life, of returning to the East Indies . . . I do not think that any man's family have a right to expect that he should die a few years sooner to put a little more money in their pockets after his death: and I should think that your wife, who, in a pecuniary way, would be the person most interested in your return to the East Indies, would prefer your prolonged life to increase of pounds.

After their earlier differences over the navigability of the Mondego, and one or two later brushes when Berkeley had been just a little too forward in anticipating his wishes, Wellington was now most anxious to keep him. To Liverpool, 2 December: . . . it is impossible for two officers to be on better terms than we are. I have always found the Admiral not only disposed to give us every assistance in his power, but to anticipate and exceed our wishes in this way. *Unfortunately though, it was again the wife who was behind it all. What's more she was a very well connected lady indeed.* I know that the Duke of Richmond and Lord Bathurst are anxious that the Admiral should remain on station in a temperate climate for the benefit of Lady Emily's health; and I would submit to many inconveniences to gratify them . . . but he anticipates all our wishes . . . and we go on very well with him.

Nevertheless, Berkeley went, and Wellington did not get on at all with his successors, particularly in 1813, when, as we shall see, successful co-operation with the navy was a fundamental corner-stone of his strategy.

His awareness of the cupidity of the rich seems to have been particularly sharp at this time. On the probable fall of Valencia he again adverted to the Grandees. To Liverpool, 4 December: The greater number of grandees of Spain have estates in Valencia, upon the revenues of which they have subsisted since they have lost everything elsewhere. It may be expected therefore that the loss of this kingdom will induce many to wish to submit to the French yoke.

At a local level, too, the better-off were working the 'he who has' principle. To Stuart, Freneda, 8 December: I do not know what to do with the 15,000 dollars which the committee of charities have sent to me . . . I find that the rich persons, in easy circumstances, and the poor, are equally desirous, and claim a right to partake of the charity. The curates in the villages . . . declare that they are afraid to omit the names of any in a list of persons distressed by the war. They say that the rich and powerful insist upon sharing with others; and the curate of this very village says that a legacy of corn came into his hands . . . to be distributed to the poor of the village, in which rich and all insisted upon sharing alike . . .

On a larger scale, the harvest in England had, 'owing to a blight in the month of June' (Liverpool to Wellington) failed. To Stuart, 17 December: I recommend you to renew your measures in America, so far as to send there bills for 400,000l., to be laid out in purchase of corn; to adopt those which you propose for the purchase of rice to the amount of 200,000l. in the northern provinces of the Brazils; and further to make an effort to get grain from the coast of Africa . . . The merchants of England will of course send colonial goods and merchandise where they can sell it with advantage . . .

181

From macro-economics back to micro. To a spy, 14 December: I sent you by your messenger . . . fifty dollars, an ass, and baskets, according to your desire, and will pay it in such manner as you will point out; and I beg you to send me intelligence of all that passes that comes to your knowledge. It would be particularly desirable to receive it from the headquarters of the French army.

Only 50 dollars? An ass? Baskets? Following the closure of Salamanca the only way in was to go disguised as a peasant bringing produce to market.

Meanwhile he pushed on with what was necessary for the fall of Ciudad Rodrigo. Without explaining exactly why, he asked Hill to make a demonstration towards Merida. 18 December: In your movement . . . I would likewise beg to draw your attention to the position of the army of Portugal on the north side of the Tagus. There are at least two divisions within a short distance of the bridge at Almaraz . . . *and so on. The concealed point is that this was part of his design to convince the French that he is going for Badajoz first. With Liverpool he is more open. There was almost no chance of this letter falling into the wrong hands. 18 December:* As Almeida is becoming a place of security I have brought up there our battering train . . . I have directed materials for a siege to be prepared, and I propose to lay down our bridge on the Agueda. I am also making an effort to get up the stores of our train to Almeida, and if I can succeed, I shall be in a situation to attack Ciudad Rodrigo on any day I please, without risk or inconvenience . . .

The stores in question were those essential commodities powder and shot, but also cover for the troops who would have to leave their cantonments. For the Commissary General . . . and the Officer of the Ordnance Department in charge of the powder, 25 December: Six hundred barrels of the powder now in store at or near Lamego must be sent up the Douro in boats, as far as it can be brought: a careful person should accompany each boat, and see that the powder is preserved from the wet . . . Four hundred tents now at Coimbra must be sent up to Almeida as soon as may be practicable. They must be brought in boats to Raiva . . . *and so on. The stream of instructions went on, bringing in supplies as speedily as possible, but at the last moment, revealing nothing of his intentions, except where he had to.*

On New Year's Day the spies brought good news. Napoleon was at last withdrawing some troops for the proposed conquest of Russia. To Liverpool: I have received reports that the cavalry of the Guard had returned to France, and that the infantry of the Guard had likewise moved from Valladolid in a northerly direction . . . I propose therefore to make an attack on Ciudad Rodrigo . . .

To Henry, 3 January: I propose to invest Ciudad Rodrigo on the 6th, and to break ground if possible on that night. The weather, however, is now very bad; the whole country being covered with snow . . .

To Graham, Freneda, 6 January: The last of the engineers' stores left Almeida this morning, but it is impossible to say how far they will go this afternoon. If they reach Gallegos we may invest the place tomorrow. If they do not, it would be advantageous to defer the operation till the 8th.

I am going to Gallegos this day.

To Hill, Gallegos, the same day: I am about to attack Ciudad Rodrigo, in which enterprise I shall succeed, or I shall bring back to this frontier the whole army . . . If I should get this place, we shall, I hope, make a fine campaign in the Spring.

Ciudad Rodrigo (say thee-oo-dad) is one of the loveliest small towns in Spain. Set on a hill which rises in a small plain through which the Agueda enjoys a peaceful meander before tumbling down gorges to the Duero, it dominates the river and the important bridge that lie beneath its walls.

These remain. You can still make the complete circuit of the battlements without a break. Originally Moorish they were strengthened in the sixteenth century against the first cannon and again in the eighteenth century according to the principles of Vauban, the great French theoretician of siege warfare. In the simplest terms these amount to an outer system of fortifications with a very deep ditch separating them from the older, inner ones, and pronged with triangular bastions which always give the plans their characteristically sea-urchin look. Where the ground allowed it there was another ditch, then a steep, bare slope, the 'glaçis', which could be swept by enfilading fire from the bastions.

Ciudad Rodrigo would have been a difficult place to take but for one feature, a hill lying 600 yards due north with a ridge in front of it at 200. The crest of the further ridge, the Great Teson, is almost exactly as high as the fortress walls. If an attacking force could seize these and install an up-to-date battering train the fortress was doomed. Barrié had manned a redoubt on the Great Teson and named it after his predecessor. It was a fairly puny affair but covered by two convents outside the city walls, that of Santa Cruz to the west, of San Francisco to the east. These were also manned with artillery which could subject both Tesons to an enfilading fire.

I spent a night in Ciudad Rodrigo in the first week of February during the carnival festivities, and slept in an unconverted van in a sleeping bag on bare boards. The moisture in the van froze on the inside of the metal walls to such a degree that it got that tacky feeling an ice lolly straight from the freezer has, yet by two o'clock in the afternoon the sun was hot and I sat in shirt sleeves on the scaffolding terraces erected in the small city square for the Charro dancing and bull-fights. There was no snow. For Wellington's army there was.

On the south side of the walls above the river and the bridge, is a Moorish castle, now a 'parador' or luxury hotel for the well-heeled tourist. Towards the north-west angle stands the cathedral, and just by it, set into the walls in what was once a gun embrasure, a little, well, shrine is almost the right word, to Don Julian Sanchez, el Charro. The cathedral bell tower is still pitted where shot aimed high flew over the walls.

Instructions to General Officers
Commanding Divisions
employed in the Siege of Ciudad
Rodrigo.   Gallegos, 8th January, 1812.
The Commander of the Forces proposes to attack Ciudad Rodrigo, and in order that the troops may suffer as little as possible from exposure to the weather, he intends that the operation shall be carried on by each of the divisions of the army employed, alternately, for twenty-four hours . . .

When a division is ordered for duty . . . it is to march from its cantonments before daylight in the morning . . . The troops will be able to cross at the fords . . . *His bridge was needed only for the battering train.* The troops are to have with them a day's provisions cooked, and they are to be followed by two days' spirits, and no other baggage.

A sufficient number of men to cook the provisions for the day the division is relieved are to be left in the cantonments . . . *A hot meal waiting for them. Would a French Marshal have thought of that?*

Each regiment is to take along with it the intrenching tools belonging to it . . .

The Engineers will order to the ground a sufficiency of cutting tools to enable those men not immediately on duty to supply themselves with firewood.

To Major Dickson, R.A., Gallegos, 9 January, 1812, 5.00 p.m.: . . . You will have heard that we carried the redoubt on the hill of San Francisco *(the Great Teson)* last night; and we have opened our parallel within 600 yards of the place. Colonel Fletcher expects to be ready for the guns possibly by the 11th, at night, or 12th in the morning . . .

To Liverpool, 15 January: We opened our fire from twenty-two pieces of ordnance, in three batteries in the first parallel, yesterday afternoon, and we opened an approach to, and established ourselves in our second parallel, 150 yards from the place last night.

This measure has been facilitated by Lieut. General Graham having

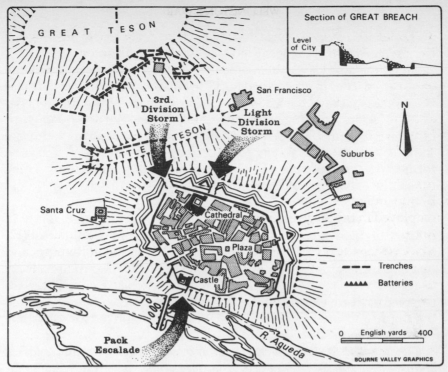

11. Ciudad Rodrigo, 8–19 January 1812

surprised the enemy's detachment in the convent of Sta Cruz . . . on the night of the 13th . . . Colville who commands the 4th division in the absence of . . . Cole, likewise attacked the enemy's post in the convent of San Francisco last night and obtained possession of that post, and of the other fortified posts in the suburbs, where our troops are now lodged . . .

We have had, till now, very fine weather, and the troops have suffered but little from exposure to it . . .

To Liverpool, 20 January: . . . the batteries . . . continued their fire . . . and yesterday evening . . . had not only considerably injured the defences of the place, but had made breaches in the <u>fausse braie</u> (*outer wall*), and in the body of the place, which were considered practicable; while the battery on the slope of the hill . . . had been equally efficient still further to the left (*east*), and opposite to the suburb of San Francisco.

Two breaches then and possible access by escalade, that is climbing long ladders. I therefore determind to storm the place . . . *The 3rd division under Picton took the main breach headed by Mackinnon and the Connaught Rangers, the Light division under Craufurd the San Francisco breach, and*

185

Pack, with his Portuguese was destined . . . to make a false attack upon the southern face of the fort . . .

All these attacks succeeded; and . . . Pack even surpassed my expectations, having converted his false attack into a real one . . . these regiments not only effectually covered the advance from the trenches of . . . Mackinnon's brigade by their first movements and operations, but they preceded them in the attack . . . in less than half an hour from the time the attack commenced, our troops were in possession, and formed on the ramparts of the place, each body contiguous to the other. The enemy then submitted, having sustained a considerable loss in the contest.

Our loss was also, I am concerned to add, severe, particularly in officers of high rank and estimation in this army. Major General Mackinnon was unfortunately blown up by the accidental explosion of one of the enemy's expense magazines close to the breach *not actually an accident, the French had laid a mine.* Major General Craufurd likewise received a severe wound while he was leading on the Light division to the storm, and I am apprehensive that I shall be deprived for some time of his assistance . . .

Craufurd died. Wellington visited him as often as he could but was saddened and embarrassed as Craufurd begged for forgiveness for intriguing with the 'croakers' in 1810. Years later he commented: 'Craufurd talked to me as they do in a novel.' *The Light division buried him in the breach, which remains, like almost all similar places in the Peninsula, an unmarked war grave. On their way back to camp they deliberately marched through water when a detour would have been reasonable – for Craufurd had taught them to waste no time on such niceties. The Light division was never again led with the same élan – nor with the occasional lapses into rashness.*

To Lady Sarah Napier, again: I am sorry to tell you that your son George was again wounded in the right arm so badly last night that it was necessary to amputate it above the elbow . . . I have seen him this morning, quite well, free from pain and fever, and enjoying highly his success before he had received his wound.

Having <u>such</u> sons, I am aware that you expect to hear of these misfortunes . . .

Towards the end of the long list of commendations comes this. The forlorn hope of the Light division was led by Lieut. Gurwood of the 52nd regiment, who was wounded . . . *To which Gurwood has added the following footnote, for he was the compiler of these Dispatches which form the basis of what you are reading. This is the only occasion on which he intrudes, and I think he should be heard this once.*

He *[i.e. Gurwood]* afterwards took the French governor, General Barrié, in the citadel; and, from the hands of Lord Wellington, on the breach by which he had entered, he received the sword of his prisoner. The permission granted by the Duke of Wellington to compile this work has doubtless been one of the distinguished consequences resulting from this service; and Lieut. Colonel Gurwood feels pride, as a soldier of fortune in here offering himself as an encouraging example to the subalterns in future wars.

The last word should be the Peer's. To Liverpool, 20 January, the 'private letter': You will receive with this the account of the successful termination of our operation, in half the time I told you it would take, and less than half that which the French spent taking the same place from the Spaniards . . .

Or should it? Well, yes, but not that last word. A week or so earlier, a detachment of Connaughts, driving a cart up from St João da Pesqueira, exchanged two fine white bullocks for two mediocre black ones. At the subsequent Court Martial, Private Charles Reilly pleaded: 'Wasn't the white beasts lazy, and didn't we beat them until they was black?' The Corporal with him was sentenced to 700 lashes, Reilly to 500.

G.O.   Gallegos, 22nd Jan., 1812
3. In consideration of the good conduct of the 88th regiment . . . the Commander of the Forces remits . . . the sentence . . . under which the prisoners are to receive corporal punishment.

BADAJOZ

Badajoz had no Grand Teson. The only time it had been taken, it had been 'sold', by the Spaniard Imaz, to the French the year before.

Over the next six weeks Wellington moved as quickly as he could, but not as quickly as he would have wished. In the first place he couldn't move at all until the breaches at Ciudad Rodrigo had been repaired, and the fortress properly provisioned and garrisoned; in the second he had to shift his battering train. The direct route by Castello Branco and Portalegre was out of the question at that time of the year.

Memorandum to Major General Borthwick *(i/c Royal Artillery)*, Major Dickson *(artillery siege expert)*, and J. Bissett Esq. *(Commissary General)*. 26th January, 1812.

1. . . . the sixteen 24 pounders carronades (howitzers) should be sent off to the Alentejo by eight bullocks each.

They might go by easy stages, and the 150 bullocks required to draw the bridge might accompany them, in order to assist in their removal.
2. Twenty 24 pounder guns and their carriages, and six spare carriages, with their necessary small stores, should likewise be removed from Almeida to Barca d'Alva. They should here be embarked in boats and sent down to Oporto and thence by sea to Setuval.

There were similar instructions for powder and timber, and when all had been brought from Ciudad Rodrigo, via Almeida, to the upper Douro . . . the bullocks should be turned to grass.

Memorandum to . . . *the same as above*, 28th January, 1812. Major Dickson will proceed to Setuval in order to arrange the removal of the ordnance and stores from Setuval to Elvas . . .

Mr Bissett will . . . order an intelligent commissary to Setuval . . . to make the preparations of boats to convey the heavy ordnance and stores from Setuval to Alcacer do Sol . . .

The same Commissary . . . to procure bullocks and carts to remove the ordnance and stores from Alcacer do Sol to Elvas . . . *and so it goes on, but with each move carefully plotted so this memorandum concludes . . .* in all, thirty-eight days.

To Henry, 29 January, 1812: I propose to attack Badajoz, and I think it probable that I shall be in readiness to invest the place in the second week of March. *In fact he made it on 17 March, only three days later, which was a remarkable achievement considering the factors involved: weather, sickness, the movements of the French, and so on. He explains why he feels able to go south to Liverpool:* We shall have great advantages in making the attack so early if the weather will allow it.

First, all the torrents in this part of the country *round Almeida and Ciudad Rodrigo* are then full, so we may assemble nearly our whole army on the Guadiana, without risk to anything valuable here.

Secondly, it will be convenient to assemble our army . . . in Estramadura, for the sake of the green forage, which comes in earlier to the south than here.

Having wound up the clock and set it going, he somehow contrived to find time to read books on the French economy and comment on them to a correspondent. The long and detailed letter that results encapsulates Wellington's views on why the Napoleonic wars were being waged. I am no expert in this sort of area, but it all seems very convincing . . . at least it pays no homage to the Great Man (Buonaparte) theory of History, and of course none either to France's mission to spread liberalism and the principles of the bourgeois revolution to a grateful continent. It's a tory document but pragmatically so – there is equally no Burkean rhetoric. Even a marxist might approve it – it at least, however crudely, places itself on the foundation of economic reality.

To Baron Constant, 31 January, 1812: I have long come to the conclusion . . . respecting the plunder resulting from the war being the cause of its continuance . . .

In the early days of the revolutionary war, the French . . . adopted a measure which they called <u>levée en masse</u>; and put every man, animal, and article in their own country in requisition for the service of the armies . . . It is not astonishing that a nation among whom such a system was established should have been anxious to carry the war beyond their own frontiers. This system both created the desire and afforded the means of success . . .

The capital and the industry of France having been destroyed by the Revolution, it is obvious that the government cannot raise a revenue from the people of France adequate to support the large force which must be maintained in order to uphold the authority of the new government, particularly in the newly conquered or ceded states; and to defend the widely extended frontier of France from all those whose interest and inclination must lead them to attack it. The French Government therefore . . . must seek for support for their armies in foreign countries. War must be a financial resource . . . *which is a lot nearer the truth than placebos like 'war is the continuation of politics by other means'.*

I have great hopes, however, that this resource is beginning to fail . . . the expense of collecting this resource becomes larger than its produce.

He argues that Napoleon's recent annexation of Rome, Holland, and the Hanse Towns, was promoted not by the dictate of wild and extravagant ambition, *but because he needed their resources for his treasury, and because* Spain is now plundered to its limit. The cultivation in some parts . . . is entirely annihilated . . . There is no commerce . . . *He goes on to analyse how the French in Spain subsist, but argues that it is now no more than subsistence, that their troops have to be paid, and even fed from across the frontiers. Hence the recent annexations.*

Back to Badajoz. To Liverpool, 5 February: The very bad weather which we had lately must have put an end to all our operations and communications by sea . . . and it must delay the execution of our plans in Estramadura.

But by the eighth it cleared and all was business again. To Graham: Hunting appears out of the question to-day . . . This delightful weather will, I hope, dry up the roads; and heavy ordnance carriages march tomorrow.

In the winters of 1811 and 1812 he kept a pack on the Coa and they were out whenever time allowed. He wore the sky-blue with black velvet trimming of the Salisbury Hunt, and it is still worn at Pau, in Béarn, where a hunt was founded in the 1820's by Peninsular War veterans who came back with their families to form the first generation of the English communities there and in Biarritz. Several sources suggest that the pack on the Coa raised far more foxes than they ever actually caught, but that was scarcely the point.

One lesson at least had been learnt at Ciudad Rodrigo. To Liverpool, 11 February, 1812: I shall be very much obliged to your Lordship if you will desire that the Storekeeper General may take some measures to insure the supply of articles by his department of a better description. *(Sic)* Everything in the way of intrenching and cutting tools supplied by his department is so bad as to be almost useless; and indeed all the stores supplied by this department are nearly of the same description. It would be cheaper for the public to pay larger prices, if that is necessary, in order to get better goods. The troops would be saved much inconvenience, and a vast expense would be saved, which is now incurred in transporting these stores to the army to replace those worn out in consequence of their being so very bad. It is really shameful that the public should be so badly served . . .

P.S. The cutting tools which we have found in Ciudad Rodrigo belonging to the French army are infinitely better than ours. Is it not shameful that they should have better cutlery than we have?

In spite of Wellington's efforts, Berkeley and Lady Emily were off to a 'temperate station'. To Liverpool, 12 February: Of the two persons proposed, I believe Admiral Martin would suit us best. I hope that it is not likely we shall have to embark; and even if we should . . . the Admiral on the station should be not only a man capable of making the necessary arrangements, but one of a conciliatory disposition . . . *Is that code for 'one who will do what I tell him'? I think so.*

Amongst endless correspondence about 'fascines' and 'gabions' came the news that the Cortes had made him a Grandee of Spain and Duque de Ciudad Rodrigo . . . it did not seem to make a lot of difference. Things, on a large scale, though, were going well. On the nineteenth, to Liverpool: All my arrangements preparatory to the attack of Badajoz are in train, and I believe are getting on well; some of the troops have marched for the Alentejo, and others will follow soon; and I intend to go myself the last, as I know that my removal from one part of the country to the other will be the signal for the enemy that the part to which I am going is to be the scene of active operations . . . Pray let us have plenty of horses for cavalry and artillery, and the reinforcements for our infantry, as early as you can. If we should succeed at Badajoz, I propose to push our success early in the year as far as I can.

At a more detailed level he still needed to have his eye on everything. 'Gabions' were wicker baskets filled with earth, which were placed on the parapets of trenches to provide cover. And Fletcher had got it wrong. 23 February: Probably it did not occur to you that a gabion eighteen inches in diameter would not cover a man. Every man, even the smallest, occupies twenty inches; and the gabion ought at least to cover him . . . I beg to hear from you before the post shall go on the morning of the 25th, whether you continue to think they should be one foot and a half.

Poor Fletcher! The success of the Lines had worn thin over the previous eighteen months, and in the interim Wellington had been inclined to blame him in part for the failure of the first siege of Badajoz.

On 6 March he left Freneda for Sabugal, having sent his hounds on ahead of him – for a day or two the French might think he had moved simply to find more foxes. On the tenth he was at Portalegre where he received directions to invest the victors of Barosa and Arroya de Molinos with the Order of the Bath, the 'Red Ribbon'. This was done at Elvas on the twelfth, with some briskness. Neither Graham nor Hill had time for feasts and junketing.

Wellington somehow always had time, in this case to revise his opinion of Shrapnell's shells. To Liverpool: My opinion in favor of these shells has been much shaken lately. First, I have reason to believe that their effect is confined to wounds of a very trifling description; and they kill nobody. I saw General Simon, who was wounded by the balls from Shrapnell's shells, of which he had several in his face and head; but they were picked out of his face as duckshot would be out of a face of a person who had been hit by accident while out shooting ... .

By the next day he had ridden over to Badajoz, and could report: The enemy have improved the works . . . very considerably since the place has been in their possession, and they have in the place a very sufficient garrison; but I hope I shall be able to obtain possession of it.

On the eighteenth, he wrote to Hill, who was covering the east approaches at Merida: We broke ground last night, and got on well, notwithstanding the rain. *On the twentieth, to Liverpool:* The work has continued ever since with great celerity notwithstanding the very bad weather . . .

The enemy made a sortie yesterday from the gate called La Trinidad, on the right of our attack, with about 2000 men. They were almost

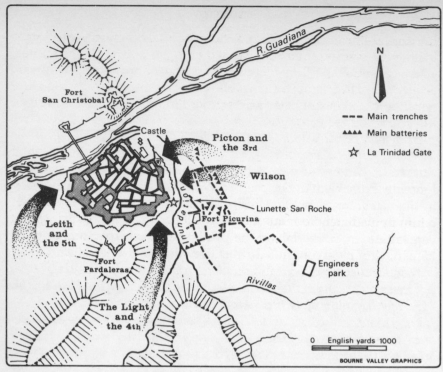

12. Badajoz, 17 March – 6 April 1812

immediately driven in, without effecting any object, with considerable loss. *Not quite true – the French carried off intrenching tools which Philippon, the Governor, knew were in short supply. He paid a bounty for all that were captured.* Lieut. Colonel Fletcher was slightly wounded but I hope he will soon be able to resume his duties . . . *A musket ball hit his purse, forcing a Spanish silver dollar an inch into his groin.*

On the same day Wellington wrote a more than usually affectionate letter to Richard, who had just resigned as Foreign Secretary. In truth the republic of a cabinet is but little suited to any man of taste or of large views . . . *and concludes:* We are getting on well with our operations here, although the weather is very bad. The soldiers swear that we shall succeed because we invested on St Patrick's eve, and broke ground on St Patrick's day.

To Henry, 24 March: The rain has been almost constant and has done us a good deal of mischief. *The Guadiana rose several feet, the trenches flooded and had to be evacuated, and, worse of all, the pontoon bridge broke loose so that for a time the army was cut in two.*

The next day fire was opened. To Liverpool: I directed Major General Kempt, who commanded in the trenches that afternoon, to attack La

192

Picurina by storm after it was dark that night, which service he effected in the most judicious and gallant manner.

Things should now have gone on more quickly, but Philippon was a resourceful and determined man, and every measure that might delay the siege was taken. The gap between the fortress and La Picurina was flooded, a constant and accurate fire was maintained on the allied trenches and batteries, and every move the allies made he contrived to counter. And he had his reasons. To Graham, 29th March: Soult broke up from before Cadiz on the 23rd and 24th, and commenced collecting his troops upon Seville . . . It is very desirable that you should come back to Villa Franca . . keeping your cavalry out in front; and that Sir R. Hill should come to Merida. I write to him immediately to request him to fall back . . . *And on 1st April:* I have letters . . . From Salamanca . . . Marmont was at Salamanca on the 28th, but it was expected he would move on the following day. They have collected about fifteen days' provisions, ladders, a bridge, &c., and I am inclined to believe they will attack Ciudad Rodrigo . . .

If Soult should move forward when your troops shall be in the stations mentioned in my letter of the 29th, I should wish you to collect them in the wood in front of the position at Albuera.

Against these two threats things had to be hurried along . . . Nevertheless one of the principle objects of the campaign had been achieved. The long blockade and siege of Cadiz was raised, and it was never properly resumed. This is the actual turning point, the general shift on the part of the French from offensive to defensive.

To Wellington at that moment, it might not have seemed like it. By the 5th April there was news that Soult was at Llerena, half way between Seville and Badajoz, and Foy was on the Guadiana above Merida. The attempt had to be made though the breaches were by no means practicable. But before drawing up his customary Memorandum, he had time to dash off a note to Henry, who had now got his K.B. You must be introduced by a Knight of some Order to the person who is to invest you . . . the person who is to invest you must knight you by passing his sword over your shoulder. He then puts the riband over your right shoulder, and the star on your left breast. The ceremony here generally ends in eating and drinking, &c., &c.

In all five attacks were made. The Light and 4th divisions stormed the breaches, Picton's 3rd escaladed the castle (again, as at Ciudad Rodrigo, this was meant to be a diversion. Fortunately it turned out to be the only entirely successful major assault.); Leith's 5th division was to escalade the walls on the north-west corner; and 1,000 men under Major Wilson were to attack the Lunette San Roche.

To Liverpool, 7 April, 1812: The attack was accordingly made at ten at night; Lieut. General Picton preceding by a few minutes the attacks of the remainder of the troops . . . notwithstanding . . . the obstinate resistance of the enemy, the castle was carried by escalade, and the 3d division established in it at about half past eleven.

While this was going on, Major Wilson carried the ravelin of San Roche . . . and established himself within that work.

The 4th and Light division moved to the attack from the camp along the left of the river Rivillas, and of the inundation. They were not perceived by the enemy till they reached the covered way; and the advanced guards of the two divisions descended without difficulty into the ditch protected by the fire of the parties stationed on the glaçis for that purpose; and they advanced to the assault of the breaches led by their gallant officers with the utmost intrepidity. But such was the nature of the obstacles prepared by the enemy at the top and behind the breaches, and so determined their resistance, that our troops could not establish themselves within the place. Many brave officers and soldiers were killed or wounded by explosions at the top of the breaches; others who succeeded to them were obliged to give way, having found it impossible to penetrate the obstacles which the enemy had prepared to impede their progress. *These include razor-sharp sword-blades fixed into enormous beams which had been chained to the ground.* These attempts were repeated until after twelve at night; when, finding that success was not to be attained, and that . . . Picton was established in the castle, I ordered that the 4th and Light divisions might retire . . .

In the meantime, . . . Leith pushed forward . . . and escaladed the face of the bastion of San Vicente . . . and our troops being thus established in the castle, which commands all the works of the town, and in the town; and the 4th and Light divisions being formed again for the attack of the breaches, all resistance ceased; and at daylight in the morning, the Governor, General Philippon . . . surrendered . . . and all the staff, and the whole garrison . . . General Philippon has informed me that it consisted of 5000 men at the commencement of the siege . . .

It is impossible that any expression of mine can convey to your Lordship the sense which I entertain of the gallantry of the officers and troops upon this occasion . . .

The losses were appalling, almost the highest of any single engagement in the war, nearly 5000, or as many French as there were actually in the garrison. On the morning of the 7th Wellington went amongst the dead in the breaches, and wept. Picton apparently exclaimed: 'Good God, what is the matter?' In his

*private letter to Liverpool, not in the Dispatches but quoted by Oman,
Wellington added:* The capture of Badajoz affords as strong an instance of
the gallantry of our troops as has ever been displayed. But I greatly
hope that I shall never again be the instrument of putting them to such
a test . . .

*As we already know, it was a custom, and not one which Wellington entirely
disapproved, to allow troops who had stormed a summoned fortress to loot it.
And they did. No attempt was made to stop them until dawn of the eighth.*

A.G.O. Camp before Badajoz, 7th April, 1812.
1. It is now full time the plunder of Badajoz should cease; and the
Commander of the Forces requests that an officer and six steady
non-commissioned officers may be sent from each regiment . . . into
the town to-morrow morning, at 5 o'clock, in order to bring away any
men that may be straggling there.
2. The Commander of the Forces has ordered the Provost Marshal into
the town, and he has orders to execute any men he may find in the act
of plunder, after he shall arrive there.

G.O. Camp before Badajoz, 8th April, 1812, at 11 o'clock, P.M.
1. The rolls must be called in camp every hour, and all persons must
attend till further orders.
3. The Commander of the Forces is sorry to learn that the brigade in
Badajoz, instead of being a protection to the people, plunder them
more than those who stormed the town.
6. The Commander of the Forces calls upon *(all)* officers . . . to assist
him in putting an end to the disgraceful scenes of drunkenness and
plunder which are going on at Badajoz . . .

*The losses occurred in the first place because the assault was ordered before the
breaches were practicable, and this because Marmont was threatening Ciudad
Rodrigo, and Soult was moving in to relieve the place from the south. However,
Wellington also insisted that his equipment was still sub-standard. To Torrens,
7th April:* The truth is that, equipped as we are, the British army are not
capable of carrying on a regular siege . . . *and that he had been ill-served by
his engineers.*
    *His final comment came later in a letter to his much-valued Quarter Master
General, Major General Murray, who was leaving to take up a post in Ireland.
28 May, 1812:* The siege of Badajoz was a most serious undertaking, and
the weather did not favour us. The troops were up to their middles in

mud in the trenches . . . The assault was a terrible business, of which I saw the loss when I was ordering it. But we had brought matters to that state that we could do no more, and it was necessary to storm or raise the siege. I trust, however, that future armies will be equipped for sieges, with the people necessary to carry them on as they ought to be; and that our engineers will learn how to put their batteries on (*i.e. to aim at*) the crest of the glaçis, and to blow in the counterscarp, instead of placing them wherever the wall can be seen, leaving the poor officers and troops to get into and across the ditch as they can . . .

TWO BRIDGES

To Hill, 11 April: I heard yesterday that some of Marmont's troops had crossed the Coa, and had appeared on this side of Sabugal on the 8th . . . It is therefore necessary that I should return to that side of the Tagus, and I have put some of the troops in motion this day . . .

My wish is to put Badajoz in a state of defence again as soon as possible, and Lieut. Colonel Fletcher is setting to work upon it, and that you should cover the place with your corps while the work will be going on . . .

Of course if the enemy should attempt to play tricks with small corps, you will fall upon them . . .

Let me have as soon as you can, returns of the number of masons, bricklayers, carpenters, sawyers, wheelwrights, miners, and smiths in each of the divisions . . .

To Liverpool, Niza, 16 April: Marshal Soult collected his army at Villa Franca in Estramadura on the 8th instant and having there heard of the fall of Badajoz, he retired before daylight on the 9th towards the frontiers of Andalusia. . . . Graham directed . . . Cotton to follow their rear with the cavalry, and he attacked and defeated the French cavalry at Villa Garcia . . . *Allied loss, 60; French loss 300, half of which were prisoners. The allied cavalry now equalled the French in numbers and were on the whole fighting with more skill and control. This meant that Wellington could at last consider a campaign in the plains.* The enemy retired on that day from Llerena, and since entirely from the province of Estramadura . . .

It appears that on the 3d instant the greatest number of the *(French)* troops in the neighbourhood of Ciudad Rodrigo broke up and marched towards Sabugal where I believe Marshal Marmont came himself. Major General *(Victor Alten – left blank in Gurwood's edition)* whom I had kept in front of Ciudad Rodrigo . . . I hope misunderstood, as he disobeyed my instructions in every point. He was followed, although at a distance, through Lower Beira, by Marshal Marmont's advance guard; and having quitted Castello Branco, contrary to orders, the advanced guard entered Castello Branco on the evening of the 12th. . . . having heard that *Victor Alten* had crossed the Tagus, I ordered him to cross that river again, which he did on the 12th, and the enemy retired . . . before daylight on the morning of the 14th . . .

To Alten, 10 April: I beg to refer you to my instructions of the 5th ultimo . . . in case the enemy followed your march . . . you were to move gradually, and you were not directed to proceed further than Castello Branco without further orders.

I cannot consider movements to be gradual which brought you from Val de Lobos to Castello Branco *(fifty miles)* in two days. . . . You are not to interfere in any manner with the bridge at Villa Velha . . . *Alten wanted to blow it up behind him. If he had, he would have destroyed a vital link between the north and south sections of the allied forces.*

The enemy have, as usual, in this expedition robbed and murdered the inhabitants of the country. But the injury which they have done, as far as I can learn, has been confined to these acts of atrocity . . . If my orders had been obeyed . . . it is probable that the enemy would never have passed the Coa . . .

As soon as I heard of Soult's retreat from Villa Franca I put the army in motion towards Castille . . . Hill remains with the 2nd division . . . and . . . Erskine's division of cavalry . . .

Not only Alten was in trouble in the Peer's absence, but Trant too got into a scrape that almost cost him his militia and Wilson his mixed corps of light troops. Wellington, who, as we have seen, liked the man, let him down very lightly considering what had happened. 21 April: . . . troops ought not to be put in a strong position in which they can be turned, if they have not an easy retreat from it; and if you advert to that principle in war, and look at the position of Guarda, you will agree with me, that it is the most treacherous position in Portugal.

I can only say that, as Marmont attacked you, I am delighted that you have got off so well; which circumstance I attribute to your early decision not to hold the position . . . *In fact it was Trant's men who took the decision, having been surprised in the night. For once the French were surprisingly merciful, driving them down the steep hill and only using the flats of their sabres.*

They had collected at Guarda, hoping to surprise Marmont at Sabugal. As to your plan to surprise Marmont . . . I would observe . . . that with such troops as we, and you in particular, command, nothing is so bad as failure and defeat. You could not have succeeded in that attempt; and you would have lost your division and that of General Wilson. I give you my opinion very freely . . . begging you at the same time to believe that I feel for the difficulty of your situation, and that I am perfectly satisfied that both you and General Wilson did everything that officers could do under the circumstances; and that I attribute to you the safety of the two divisions.

I shall be at Sabugal to-morrow or the next day; and I hope to see you before we shall again be more distant from each other.

Clearly, it was time to be back – the precious prize of Ciudad Rodrigo could be left at risk no longer. And as soon as he was back, Marmont withdrew: it had, after all, been no more than an expedition for plunder.

Wellington now set in motion the steps that would complete his preparations for the summer: the destruction of the bridge across the Tagus at Almaraz and the repair of that at Alcantara.

To Hill, 24 April: Marmont has retired and I shall immediately get provisions into Ciudad Rodrigo . . .

I think you might avail yourself of this opportunity to strike your blow at Almaraz . . . Make all your preparations in secret for this expedition. I shall watch from hence the course of the enemy's retreat, and will let you know if it should appear to me that you have anything to fear from any of the divisions of the army of Portugal going near Almaraz. Of course you will not march till you shall hear further from me.

First, Ciudad Rodrigo had to be secure, so he would be free to march to Hill if Hill got into a scrape.

To Graham, 27 April: I was yesterday at Ciudad Rodrigo, and I am sorry to say that the works are but little more forward than they were when I saw them last on the 5th March, yet the Spaniards had till the 1st April to work without any enemy being near them.

It is difficult to know what to do with these people. I have this day tried to excite them to work by feelings of national vanity and honor, but I fear I shall not succeed.

Two days earlier, one of the most significant events of 1812 had got a bare mention, also in a letter to Graham. I see in a paper of the 10th, that the Russians have declared war on the 19th March.

On 3 May the river strategy took a step further. To Graham: I have set

Sturgeon and Todd to endeavour to repair the bridge at Alcantara; in which I hope they will succeed.

At Alcantara, close to the Portuguese border, the Tagus enters a wide ravine between steeply terraced slopes (see page 50). A Roman bridge spans what is in effect a substantial chasm one hundred and forty feet deep, and the centre arch had been blown out. If this could be repaired then Wellington's internal communication with Hill, even with heavy artillery, would be enormously speeded up – just as by destroying the bridge at Almaraz the enemy's, between Soult and Marmont would be made immeasurably slower.

The builder was Colonel Sturgeon of the Royal Service Corps; the designer was, in effect, Wellington himself. A suspension bridge of timber and ropes of a type often used in India, it was soon carrying heavy loads. An added advantage was that it could be taken down and re-erected at very short notice.

In spite of a mutiny amongst the Spanish troops in Ciudad Rodrigo, which led Wellington to threaten 'I will destroy it entirely' rather than waste 5,000 of his own men in the place, it was time to send Hill off. To Graham, 7 May: I have desired Sir Rowland Hill to undertake the service which I have long had in contemplation for the destruction of the enemy's establishments at Almaraz, and I hope he will have marched by this time with 5000 or 6000 men for that object.

There followed a fortnight or so of anxious waiting, during which news came of the United States of America's growing involvement in the war. Napoleon had attempted to cut off all trade between Europe and Britain by the Berlin Decrees. In reprisal the British took all merchantmen who entered those ports closed to her, including American shipping. To Graham, 8 May: I have a paper from America, from which it appears that the Americans have laid a general embargo on all vessels. This is a measure of importance, as all this part of the Peninsula has been living this year on American flour.

To Henry, 10 May: Would it be possible to come to any arrangement with the Barbaresque powers to supply Cadiz, Lisbon, &c., with corn? It would be capital to turn the tables on those cunning Americans . . . *On 18 June the USA declared war on Britain.*

On 19 May Hill took Almaraz. Wellington wrote to Liverpool on the twenty-eighth when he had received Hill's full account. He attained the object of his expedition on the 19th instant, by taking by storm Forts Napoleon and Ragusa, and the têtes de pont, and other works by which the enemy's bridge was guarded, by destroying these forts and works, and the enemy's bridge and establishments, and by taking their magazines, and about 259 prisoners and 18 pieces of cannon.

I have the honor to enclose Sir R. Hill's report of this brilliant exploit

. . . Hill had threaded his small army through open though hilly country, never far from superior French forces commanded by Foy and Drouet, only to find that he could not easily get his cannon in range of Fort Napoleon. He resolved on a surprise assault which was completely successful. The only thing that marred the whole adventure was that Erskine (who else?) commanding the cavalry screen to the south misread French movements as being the quite fictional arrival of Soult with the entire army of the south. Hill withdrew unnecessarily early leaving one fortification standing. Nevertheless Wellington could conclude: The result then of . . . Hill's expedition has been to cut off the shortest and best communication between the armies of the South and of Portugal, which, under existing circumstances, it will be difficult, if not impossible, to re-establish.

THE SALAMANCA CAMPAIGN

With Ciudad Rodrigo, Almeida, Badajoz and Elvas all secure, with one bridge across the Tagus down, and the other nearly up, he was at last ready to move into Castille, and to endeavour, if possible to bring Marmont to a general action . . .

In respect to the general action, I believe there is no man in the army who entertains a doubt of its result, and that sentiment alone would do a great deal to obtain success. But we possess solid physical advantages over the enemy . . . Our infantry are not in bad order; our cavalry more numerous in relation to the enemy, and the horses in better condition than I have known them . . .

We have a better chance of success now than we ever had . . .

The campaign that was to reach its climax with the greatest battle he ever fought was under way. His optimism is there again in a most kind and appreciative letter to his departing Q.M.G. General Murray, 28 May, which concludes: As you have left us I will not tantalize you by entering on our plans for the rest of the campaign; I think it will be ours at all events, and I hope may be attended by permanent important consequences.

For reasons of subsistence the Army of Portugal was dispersed. If Wellington struck swiftly towards Salamanca he would find barely more than 20,000 bayonets against him, although Marmont would be able to pull in reinforcements quite quickly. Something therefore was needed to delay the allied advance until these could arrive. Of course there would be no problem for the French if Salamanca was a fortress, which most decidedly it was not . . .

Salamanca was, and still is, in spite of what was now happening, the most beautiful university city in the world – perhaps the most beautiful city. Roughly egg-shaped within its medieval walls, now mostly gone and replaced by boulevards that form an inner ring road, its centre is the rococo Plaza Mayor which really is the most beautiful square in the world, whatever you may think of the rest of the town. It is built in the honey-coloured stone of the region, honey made from roses, and is the most euphorically uplifting place I have ever been in.

From the Plaza the Rua, a fine ancient street of bookshops, souvenir shops, and bars, leads to the two cathedrals and the central university buildings which span the ages from the twelfth century to the late eighteenth and represent the best of every intervening style. Beyond the cathedrals the ground drops away towards the river and the marvellous Roman bridge, drops away through a shanty town of hovels, cheap housing and brothels which is now being cleared and filled with new university buildings which, though by no means the worst of their kind, don't quite match up to what remains of the old university.

Marmont had to hold up Wellington's advance. He fortified the three convents that controlled the bridge and razed to the ground three quarters of the university to provide materials and leave a wide swathe of open ground, a glaçis, in front of them. In the middle ages Salamanca was the greatest university in the world. It declined, as all Spain did, but Charles III's enlightened reforms built it up again into something like its original splendour as a seat of research and learning. Marmont put it back into the dark ages and the recovery did not really begin again until the 1890s. In this way it is a figure for what France generally did to the whole of Spain: not only by their total destruction of the internal economy, but also by leaving behind a deep and abiding hatred of what were taken to be the principles of the French Revolution: liberalism, enlightenment, rationalism. The Reaction that followed the Napoleonic Wars damaged us all . . . it ruined Spain.

Wellington's correspondents told him of what was going on. After two sieges it must have been a blow to have another on his hands so soon. To Dickson, in charge of the siege train now at Elvas, 31 May: We <u>must</u> have in this part of the country immediately the 6 howitzers, and as many spherical case as you can carry and . . . as many common shells. I shall have 24 pounder shot and powder ready here . . .

I want this equipment here now for a particular purpose . . . You know how many waggons you want, and you will give such directions as you may think necessary . . . It is absolutely necessary that you

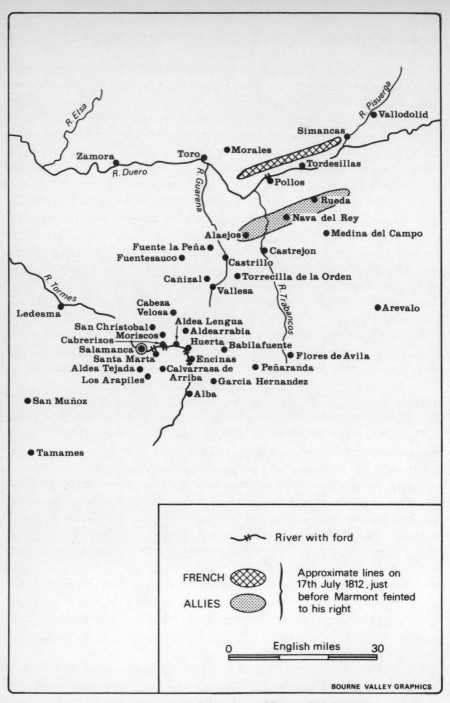

R. Elsa

R. Pisuerga

R. Vallodolid

Simancas

Morales

Toro

Tordesillas

Zamora

R. Duero

Pollos

R. Guarena

Rueda

Nava del Rey

Alaejos

Medina del Campo

Castrejon

Fuente la Peña

Fuentesauco

Castrillo

Cañizal

Torrecilla de la Orden

Vallesa

R. Tormes

R. Trabancos

Cabeza Velosa

Arevalo

Ledesma

Aldea Lengua

San Christobal

Aldearrabia

Moriscos

Cabrerizos

Huerta

Babilafuente

Salamanca

Santa Marta

Encinas

Flores de Avila

Aldea Tejada

Calvarrasa de Arriba

Peñaranda

Los Arapiles

Garcia Hernandez

Alba

San Muñoz

Tamames

River with ford

FRENCH

ALLIES

Approximate lines on
17th July 1812, just
before Marmont feinted
to his right

0   English miles   30

BOURNE VALLEY GRAPHICS

13. The Salamanca Campaign, 13 June – 24 July 1812

should cross the Tagus at Alcantara, as soon as the bridge there is ready.

By the eleventh everything was about ready. To Hill: The army is collected on the Agueda, and I intend to move forward on the 13th . . . *and there follows a list of meticulous instructions for a rather nervous Hill, on what he should do in any circumstances likely to arise. He concludes with a note on Alcantara.* We have repaired this bridge by a piece of machinery which can be taken up and laid down at pleasure, but it will require two days' notice to lay it down, as much time to take it up . . . *Obviously he was pleased with it.*

On the seventeenth he entered Salamanca, virtually unopposed. It was the first Spanish city he had liberated rather than stormed and the populace appreciated the fact. In spite of the presence of the fortified convents half a mile away he was mobbed in that glorious square by cheering crowds who decked him and the staff with flowers and sang and danced around the no doubt irritated horses. In the midst of it all Wellington contrived to scribble a note using his sabretache as a miniature desk – what it was I am unable to say for there is nothing in my sources with that date. Perhaps it was an answer to Rector Curtis's offer of his private house, for certainly that's where he stayed while he was in the city.

To Liverpool, 18 June: Their cavalry were immediately driven in by ours, and the enemy evacuated Salamanca on the night of the 16th, leaving a garrison of 800 men in the fortifications which they have erected on the ruins of the colleges and convents which they have demolished. By the fire from these they protect the passage of the Tormes by the bridge, and our troops crossed that river yesterday morning, by two fords which are in this neighbourhood.

The forts were immediately invested by the 6th division . . . and having been accurately reconnaitred it was found necessary to break ground before them. This was done last night, and I hope we shall commence our fire to-morrow morning from eight pieces of cannon, at the distance of 300 yards *such was the size of the area devastated from the principal of the enemy's works* . . .

It is impossible to describe the joy of the people of the town upon our entrance. They have now been suffering for more than three years; during which time the French among other acts of violence and oppression, have destroyed 13 of 25 convents, and 22 of 25 colleges, which existed in this celebrated seat of learning.

The euphoria was somewhat diluted by a report from Hill. His cavalry, now commanded by 'Black Jack' Slade, an impetuous Major General who clearly was in a hurry to make a name for himself, had come to grief in the usual way. This time they actually covered nine miles (nearly twice the distance of the Grand National) before running into fresh troops in superior numbers when their own horses were thoroughly blown. Wellington was furious, and it drew from him a letter that the Cavalry never forgave him for. I have never been more annoyed than by . . . Slade's affair . . . It is occasioned entirely by the trick of our officers of cavalry have acquired of galloping at everything . . . They never consider their situation, never think of manoeuvring before an enemy – so little that one would think they cannot man-oeuvre, excepting on Wimbledon Common . . .

What Wellington was up to during the next four and a half weeks to 22 July and especially the next few days, remains something of an enigma. He had marched into Castille with the declared purpose of bringing Marmont to a general engagement yet twice he refused opportunities to do so where success was apparently certain. Marmont hung about north of Salamanca as reinforcements reached him, until on 20 June he moved in again. Wellington shifted most of his army on to the heights of San Christobal, three miles or so north of the town. His right was above the river where the Don Quixote campsite now is, his left on the Zamora road above the declivity now occupied by the football ground. On the twenty-first Marmont's numbers were still inferior to Wellington's by 8,000 men – he could have been attacked and defeated.

Why not? The reasons Wellington gave at the time, here condensed, are as follows. The ground the French occupied in front of the heights was broken with villages, small-holdings, dry-stone walls, and orchards, and was therefore more easily defended than it looked. He knew Marmont was about to be further reinforced by corps under Clausel and Foy, and he did not know how far off they were. He did not like to leave Salamanca at the mercy of the garrison behind him. He knew Joseph was collecting an army of the Centre and he wanted to be sure that it was not to be directed against Hill before he himself moved any further north. Add up all these reasons and you have an answer.

Nevertheless I would supply another. If he had attacked on the morning of the twenty-first he would have driven Marmont out of his position and inflicted a 'newspaper' defeat at the cost of near equal casualties. Marmont would have fallen back on fresh reinforcements, possibly he would have enticed the British and allies into a pursuit which could have ended disastrously. But, yet more important, I think Wellington wanted Marmont to have those reinforcements and was prepared to wait for them so as to take him on equal terms and inflict the heaviest and most uncompromising defeat possible. If this was the case it was something he must of necessity never reveal . . . deliberately to wait until your opponent is on equal terms with you, when you could have taken him earlier at a disadvantage, could lead to a public enquiry – if not worse.

Distant Salamanca

By the afternoon Thomierès and Foy had arrived and now it was Marmont who wanted to attack, but Foy and Clausel knew too much about Busaço type positions and persuaded him to desist.

For almost three days the armies remained within artillery range of each other. The weather grew hot. There was no water on San Christobal apart from what could be brought from the brackish Tormes. Behind the position the guns thudded away at the forts in Salamanca. There was some skirmishing but to little effect. In open downy country, not unlike Salisbury Plain, the movements of both armies were clearly visible, and Napier could not help finding them rather beautiful. On the slopes of San Christobal the near-ripe wheat stood shoulder-high. In those days men were shorter and wheat taller. Flocks of Little Kestrels swooped after flies in the afternoon sultriness. Some French coming through the wheat surprised allied piquets but were driven in again.

In the night of the twenty-third Marmont moved east across the Tormes, perhaps hoping to relieve the forts from that side. To Clinton, who commanded the besieging force in town, on the heights above Aldea Lengua, 24 June, 1812, 6.30 a.m.: The enemy have crossed the Tormes in some force and are skirmishing with General Bock's brigade of dragoons which is in front of Calvarassa . . . I have ordered the 7th and 1st divisions to cross the Tormes at the ford of Sta Marta. You should send your baggage, except camp kettles, heavy guns and stores &c., across the Tormes at the ford of El Canto *on the road back to Ciudad Rodrigo.*

To Graham, who commanded the 1st, 6th, and 7th divisions: All the enemy's infantry on the plain on the left of the Tormes . . . appear to me to be about 10,000 men with cavalry . . . I shall observe their movements, and reinforce you as it may be necessary.

To Graham, 5.00 p.m.: The enemy's infantry and cavalry have moved to the rear as you will have observed; but I see they are getting under arms at Aldea Rubia and on the hill on the right of that village. I think it advisable that if the men of the 1st, 6th, and 7th divisions are not cooking they should move to the ford of Sta Marta. If they are cooking, the movement may as well be delayed till they have done, unless I should see reason to make it earlier, of which I will give you notice . . . *One reason for all this to Graham was that the poor man was almost blind. That 'as you will have observed' was tact.*

Meanwhile, to Liverpool: The siege of the forts of Salamanca has not advanced with the rapidity which I expected . . . Although, from the pains taken, and the expense incurred in their construction, and the accounts which I had received of them, I was prepared to meet with some difficulties, and provided an equipment accordingly, the difficulties are of a more formidable nature than they were represented and

the forts, three in number, each defending the other, are very strong
. . . and I have been obliged to send for more, which has created some
delay . . . Major General Clinton made an attempt to carry that work by
storm on the night of the 23d inst. . . . This attempt failed . . . Major
General Bowes was killed . . . after his first wound was dressed, he
returned again to the attack, and received a second wound, which
killed him . . . I expect that everything which is necessary to get the
better of these forts will arrive to-morrow . . .

And so it did. The last of the howitzers, powder and shot from Elvas arrived at
last. A red hot ball fired one of the convents and after failing to control the blaze
the gallant French 800, already much reduced, capitulated. To Hill, 28 June:
We took the forts of this place yesterday, two of them by storm, and the
third by capitulation . . . Marmont has retired and we march forward
to-morrow.

To Liverpool, 30 June: Marshal Marmont's army . . . broke up, and
retired in three columns towards the river Duero; one of them directing
its march upon Toro, and the other upon Tordesillas.

The allied army broke up the following day, and are this day
encamped upon the Guareña.

We have various reports of reinforcements on their march to join the
enemy, but none on which I can rely. I know from intercepted letters,
that Marshal Marmont expects to be joined by a division of the army of
the North . . . and it is reported that General Bonet had withdrawn
from the Asturias . . .

The position Marmont took up between Toro and Tordesillas with his left
extended to Simancas is significant. It encapsulated what had gradually become
a dominant feature of both strategy and tactics during the war. Before the war
the military text books had condemned a defensive line with an angle in it, a
formation 'en potence', since the troops in the corner could be caught in
enfilading fire, or cut off by a pincer movement on a large scale. But this failed to
take account of the enormous advantage of such a position, especially when faced
with superior numbers, the advantage that comes from having a far shorter line
of communication between right and left than the force on the 'wrong' side of the
dog-leg, who have nearly twice as far to go. You can see the enemy concentrat-
ing and respond immediately. Equally, if you want to take the offensive as
Marmont was about to, you can feint one way and then reassemble overnight at
the opposite end of the position. This was the basis of Wellington's position on
the second day of Fuentes de Oñoro where the village was strong enough to hold
the potentially weak angle; it was the principle, on a scale covering hundreds of
miles, that lay behind the destruction of the Almaraz bridge and the repair of

that at Alcantara. Finally it was most dynamically and devastatingly used, offensively, in the general action which was yet to come.

For a few days the position on the Duero remained static, and Graham took the opportunity to leave. His eyesight had been troubling him for months; on 3 June Wellington had written to Liverpool: I am very sorry to have to inform you that Dr M'Grigor has told me he has great reason to apprehend that Sir Thomas Graham will, in a short time, be obliged to quit the army. He has a disorder in his eyes, one of which it is most probable he will lose.

M'Grigor was the new Inspector General of Hospitals: an energetic and efficient man who made the hospitals more mobile and so able to be kept nearer the main army than hitherto. On 9 June: Since I wrote to you last I have seen General Graham. He complains of his right eye, for which he has been blistered on the temple, but he says with little effect. He certainly looks very ill, and is grown thin and is low spirited.

To Graham, 3 July: I have for some time been apprehensive that you would be under the necessity of confining yourself . . . I must . . . make up my mind to this loss; as, from what I have heard, I am apprehensive that no time is to be lost in applying the remedies to your eye, which are most likely to recover it. *And on the fourth:* I have written to Admiral Martin *(Berkeley's successor)* to request him to send a vessel to Oporto to take you home . . . Wishing you a pleasant journey, and the early recovery of your sight.

Also on the fourth he heard of the Government re-shuffle following the assassination of Perceval. Liverpool became Prime Minister and Earl Bathurst Secretary of State for War. To Bathurst, Rueda, 4 July: I assure you that the arrangement by which you have been placed at the head of the War Department is perfectly satisfactory to me, and you will find that I shall correspond with you with the same freedom and confidence as I have with your predecessors. *Actually, not quite. He was a personal friend of Castlereagh and Liverpool, and I think not so well acquainted with Bathurst. He was also beginning to feel the strength of his position as Britain's most successful general since Marlborough. At all events he more readily bullies Bathurst than he did the others, and the personal touch, the unguarded confidences, appear less frequently in the 'private letters'.*

Our principal and great want is money, with which I am afraid you cannot supply as sufficiently. But we are really in terrible distress; I am afraid in greater distress than any British army has ever been.

I hope I am strong enough for Marmont at present, whatever force he may bring from the Asturias or the army of the North; but I am anxious to establish myself well upon the Duero. If we cannot effect that object we may be obliged to fall back . . .

The deadlock continued for two weeks. Napier describes what this interlude was like:

> The weather was fine, the country rich, the troops received their rations regularly, and wine was so plentiful it was hard to keep the soldiers sober; the caves of Rueda, natural or cut in the rock below the surface of the earth, were so immense and had so much wine, that the drunkards of two armies failed to make any sensible diminution in the quantity and many men perished in that labyrinth. The soldiers of each army also, passing the Duero in groups, held amicable intercourse . . . and the camps on the banks seemed at times to belong to one general, so difficult is it to make brave men hate each other.

On the ninth Wellington wrote to Graham, keeping the old boy in touch as he made his way home: . . . the French have continued in their positions on the fords, which it is impossible to cross as long as they hold them in such strength. Indeed it would not answer to cross the river at all in its present state, unless we should be certain of having the co-operation of the Galician troops . . .

Bonet has joined; and on the evening of the 7th the enemy made a movement to their right, and Foy's division arrived at Toro yesterday . . . I see . . . Marmont was a little uneasy at the progress of the Galicians *following Bonet down from the north* . . . and it is probable these movements are the cause of Foy's; but, at all events, I propose to move two divisions to La Nava del Rey this evening, in case the enemy entertain any design of striking upon our communication . . .

Wellington was afraid Marmont would use the road from Toro to Salamanca to cut behind him on to the supply line back to Ciudad Rodrigo, but it seems likely to me that Marmont's move to the right on this occasion was, as Wellington had guessed, to strengthen his right rear against the Galicians. However, he must have noticed Wellington's nervous response, and that may have given him the idea for the larger feint he made a week later.

Meanwhile disquieting news was coming in from Madrid. To Hill, 1 July: The King, from accounts received last night, appears to be collecting a large force . . . , particularly in cavalry, and I am apprehensive that after all, the enemy will be too strong for me . . . *To Henry:* I have an intercepted letter stating that the King would collect 12,000 men, of which six regiments are cavalry. *To Bathurst:* In truth, the enemy's numbers are equal, if not superior to ours; they have in their position

209

twice the amount of artillery which we have, and we are superior in cavalry alone.

With Joseph on his way the safest thing for Marmont to do was to sit tight. When Joseph arrived in his rear Wellington would withdraw to the Agueda and all would be over for the year. But such was the effectiveness of the guerrilla control of the countryside Marmont almost certainly did not know of the King's intentions – to which one may add, he could certainly pretend not to know. It is likely he would have preferred to be the one to defeat Wellington, or at any rate get him back to the Agueda without the King's help. He had fought Wellington now for a year – had great respect for the allied troops, discipline and so on; but believed still that in a fight Wellington would not manoeuvre, that therefore in open country he remained vulnerable to Napoleonic stratagems and élan.

On the sixteenth he began his feint to his right. To Graham, from La Nava del Rey: Marmont has continued to reinforce his right to Toro, and at last, this morning, has moved everything from opposite Pollos. I came here last night . . . The enemy have continued to repair the bridge at Toro, and Marmont was there yesterday. *To Hill:* Marmont has collected his troops about Toro, with what object I do not know; but we have rather drawn in our right . . . *which was exactly what Marmont wanted him to do!*

To Clinton, commanding the 6th division on the allied left, 8.45 a.m.: . . . the enemy have withdrawn entirely from opposite Pollos a very large body of cavalry in the morning early, and their infantry at about half-past seven, and marched in the direction of Toro. *By 6.00 p.m. a vanguard had actually crossed the river. Again to Clinton:* General Picton has informed me the enemy, at half-past nine had sent a battalion and a few cavalry out of the wood of Cubillas to the heights opposite his left. *To Clinton, at 6.30 p.m.:* I have received an intercepted letter *(deliberate misinformation from Marmont or was it merely misinterpreted?)* which makes it clear that the enemy propose to cross the Duero. *At 7.00 p.m.:* I have just now heard that the enemy have crossed the Duero at Toro in strength . . . if you have not already moved, you should move immediately on Fuente La Peña . . .

But it was only a strong advance guard, or rather, a bait. The next few days were hectic and Wellington had no time for letters until the 21st. Then he wrote to Bathurst from Cabrerizos, near Salamanca: The enemy recrossed the river at Toro in the night of the 16th, moved his whole army to Tordesillas, where he again crossed the Duero on the morning of the 17th, and assembled his army on that day at La Nava del Rey having marched not less than ten leagues in the course of the 17th. *Which shows just how far to his left Wellington had moved on the 16th – Marmont must have felt he'd got him.*

The next paragraph describes in the coolest way the bustle of the seventeenth. Wellington galloped about his army with Beresford functioning as a sort of chief of staff behind him and those of the rest of the staff who could keep up somewhere near. He took personal command of one division after another in preference to sending orders to detached, nervous generals who knew something was afoot, but were not too sure just what. During one of these excursions, he was very nearly caught – he and Beresford had their swords out in the midst of a squadron of French cavalry – the British dragoons arrived in the nick of time.

The enemy attacked the troops at Castrejon at the dawn of the day of the 18th . . . *On the seventeenth these had been the extreme left of the army, now they were the rear and right as the rest of the army came back, but further south, behind them. It was the critical moment. . . .* and Sir Stapleton Cotton maintained the post without suffering any loss till the cavalry had joined him. Nearly about the same time the enemy turned, by Alaejos, the left of our position at Castrejon.

The troops retired in admirable order to Torrecilla de la Orden *where Napoleon had spent Christmas night, 1808, entertained by the reluctant abbess* having the enemy's whole army on their flank, or in their rear, and thence to the Guareña, which river they passed under the same circumstances, and effected their junction with the army.

There followed a sharp burst of fighting which warned Marmont that he had not after all gained any significant advantage. He lost a general, many casualties and 240 prisoners. For the next three days, the nineteenth, twentieth, and twenty-first, the armies continued to march south, the French always trying to get round Wellington's right and cut off his communication with Ciudad Rodrigo. It was hot; the French, because they marched lighter, were perceptibly quicker, but only just; often they were in artillery range of each other, occasionally within musket shot; the country was open wheat land though occasionally lightly wooded with ilex. It seemed like a massive parade, of over 100,000 men in two distinct columns, conducted with care and ceremony for no purpose except to exhaust them all. Wellington himself had had scarcely forty-eight hours sleep in a fortnight. On one occasion he stretched himself on the ground, put a newspaper over his face, and said to the future Lord Raglan: 'Watch the French through your glass Fitzroy . . . when they reach that copse near the gap in the hill, wake me . . .'

And in the copse the French would have heard the nervous chattering of one of the most extraordinary and beautiful birds in the area. If they were lucky they would have seen them. The azure-winged magpie, a bird from China, is presumed to be an escaped exotic from some Grandee's aviary. It can now be found in most woods between the Duero and the Tagus, but no where else in Europe. Their name exactly describes them. Not exotic, but equally pretty there

211

Salamanca

would, at this time of year, have been hoopoes with their fan-like crests, blue rollers, and jade bee-eaters.

By the evening of the twenty-first Wellington was back on San Christobal, Marmont at Huerta where there was a ford across the Tormes. Wellington's dispatch concludes despondently.

Your Lordship will have seen by the returns of the two armies that we have no superiority in numbers, even over that single army opposed to us; indeed I believe that the French army is of the two the strongest; and it is certainly equipped with a profusion of artillery double ours in number, and of larger calibres. It cannot be attacked therefore in a chosen position, without considerable loss on our side.

To this circumstance, add that I am quite certain that Marshal Marmont's army is to be joined by the King's, which will be 10,000 or 12,000 men, with a large proportion of cavalry, and that troops are still expected from the army of the North, and some are ordered from that of the South; and it will be seen that I ought to consider it almost impossible to remain in Castille after an action . . .

I have therefore determined to cross the Tormes, if the enemy should; to cover Salamanca as long as I can; and above all, not to give up our communication with Ciudad Rodrigo; and not to fight an action, unless under very advantageous circumstances, or if it should become absolutely necessary . . .

Two days later:

To Lieut. General   On the heights near
Sir R. Hill, K.B.   Alba de Tormes
My Dear Hill,   23rd July, 1812.
I write to let you know that we beat Marshal Marmont's army yesterday evening near Salamanca, and they are now in full retreat, and we are following them . . .
   Believe me, &c.,

                                                      Wellington

What happened?

THE MASTER

Most accounts of the battle present it as a chain of events, each producing an effect which in turn caused the next, or, in some cases, produced a response from Wellington or Marmont, which then caused the next. With this approach one arrives at the conclusion that shortly after two o'clock, Wellington realised he had a chance, which he then took.

My own interpretation of the events is that Wellington foresaw them from the early morning at the latest – may even have had something like them in mind for days or even weeks. One indication that this was so occurred two days earlier. Carlos de España was a French aristocrat, whose real name was Charles de Espagnac, Conte d'Espagne. He was in the service of the Spanish Cadiz government and commanded the Spanish division in Wellington's army. On 20 July Wellington ordered him to maintain unchanged the garrison in the castle of Alba whose guns covered the first bridge across the Tormes above Salamanca. But with the French already between the allied armies and Alba de España had already removed the garrison, seeing, quite correctly, that they were doomed if things went on as they were: the only possible way they could be saved, indeed the only way they could be any use at all, would be if the French suffered an overwhelming defeat, and needed the bridge for their retreat. Clearly he thought such an event so unlikely as not to be worth considering; equally clearly this was not something he was going to say to Wellington, so he did not tell him that the garrison had already been evacuated. What is equally clear, is that Wellington already knew that a famous victory was about to occur; for that is the only reason he could have had for wanting that garrison in Alba.

The next indication comes during the morning of the twenty-second . . . But before we go further it would be best to understand the lie of the land.

Start with Alba, about sixteen miles south-east of Salamanca. From it the Tormes flows in a more or less directly northward direction for about fifteen miles before turning at right angles to flow another twelve miles or so to Salamanca. On this bend there is a ford, and a village on the right bank, called Huerta. Round here the French army was grouped on the twenty-first. Six or seven miles downstream the allies were on or near their old position between San Christobal and Cabrerizos where the next ford was. Below Cabrerizos there is another ford at Santa Marta, and then comes the bridge at Salamanca itself.

South of Salamanca, and west of the Tormes before it makes its bend, the country rises into an undulating down-like plain, whose slopes are more broken

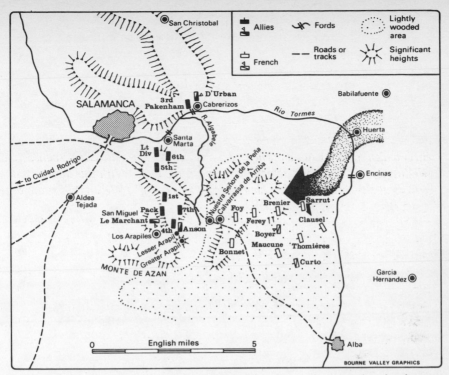

14. The Battle of Salamanca, 22 July 1812: positions of armies shortly after daybreak.

and steeper than they at first appear. These hills form into recognisable systems of ridges, the first, west of the Tormes, crowned by a village called Calvarassa de Arriba, with a hermitage, Nuestra Señora de la Peña half a mile west of it. The land then falls away into a winding valley with a brook in the middle, not quite dry even in July, called the Algabele. On the further western side, another, more distinct ridge of hills rises also running more or less south-north towards the ford at Santa Marta.

At the southern end of this system, it is too broken to be called a ridge, though militarily speaking it could act as one, come the two striking eminences of the region – two flat-topped hills which, because they are isolated, seem higher than anything else for miles around, though in fact this is not the case. They are the Dos Arapiles, the Lesser and the Grand. The epithets refer not to difference in height, which is negligible, but to area. The Lesser comes at the end of the western line of hills, and is a steep-sided hummock with rock and some scree near its top, but mostly covered in July with dried-up pasture and wild thyme. The flat summit is about sixty yards or so across and from it one can see Salamanca nearly six miles away slightly north of north-west, the village of Los Arapiles a mile or so to the west, and to the east the wooded hills between it and the Tormes.

215

Its southern side drops steeply into a declivity a couple of hundred yards wide, then the ground rises sharply again, almost precipitously to the longer escarpment of the Grand Arapil.

The ground east and south of the Arapiles was, in July 1812, lightly wooded with ilex, dried wild lavender, thyme, daisies, immortelles, and poppies; north and west of them it was cultivated – where wheat had grown there was now dry stubble, in places crops of flax still stood. There were almost no walls, the plots being separated by very shallow dry ditches occasionally marked by tooth-shaped splinters of rock standing three feet or so high. All the area is, as I said, hilly with hollows that are deep enough to have military significance, but two more rises stand out particularly – one to the west of the Lesser Arapil, immediately above the village, called San Miguel, and another further west still from the Grand Arapil called the Monte de Azan with a lump at its western end called the Pico de Miranda. But one must not imagine that these 'heights', 'montes', or 'picos' are more than gently swelling downs. They are enough though to give advantages of height and concealment.

The present main road to the south from Salamanca now climbs this last rise and near the crest is a lorry drivers' restaurant and hotel. Opposite there is what looks like a farm building, but is in fact an excellent little restaurant called, after the battle, Los Arapiles.

The Salamanca dispatch begins: In my letter of the 21st, I informed your Lordship that both armies were near the Tormes; and the enemy crossed that river with the greatest part of his troops, in the afternoon, by the fords between Alba de Tormes and Huerta, and moved by their left towards the roads leading to Ciudad Rodrigo, *the first of which ran south west from Salamanca, two or three miles west of the Pico de Miranda.*

The allied army, with the exception of the 3rd division and General D'Urban's cavalry, likewise crossed the Tormes in the evening by the bridge of Salamanca and of the fords in the neighbourhood; and I placed the troops in a position, of which the right was upon one of the two heights called Dos Arapiles, and the left on the Tormes, below the ford of Sta Marta. *That is, on the north-south ridge of hills in what must have looked to Marmont exactly typical of every defensive position Wellington had ever taken.* The 3rd division, and . . . D'Urban's cavalry were left at Cabrerizos . . . as the enemy still had a large corps on the heights above Babilafuente, on the same side of the river.

The crossing on the evening of the twenty-first was made in a horrendous thunderstorm. Men were struck by lightning in the fords, horses broke loose (one got into the French lines but, amazingly, was recovered by its owner the next day), but by midnight the sky was bright and clear, and, because of the rain, cold. Wellington later remarked that it was one of the coldest he

216

experienced in the Peninsula. Henry V-like he spent most of the night hacking through his lines checking that all was well. Dawn was crystal clear, the sparkling air rain-washed, and in the very early hours there was skirmishing in front of Nuestra Señora de la Peña, and columns of blue could be seen threading their way through the woods to the south.

And so at last, we come to our second demonstration of Wellington's prescience or forward planning. According to most accounts Colonel Waters came galloping up from the south and reported to Beresford that the French were heading for the Arapiles and that these eminences were important. Beresford apparently ignored him, and since he was the only man Wellington ever took completely into his confidence, I think we can guess why. Waters went on to Wellington himself, who apparently agreed with him and speeded up the movement to his right.

Now all this implies that this was the first Wellington knew of the Arapiles, and that is nonsense: he knew the ground very well indeed. To Graham, 25 July: I took up the ground which you were to have taken during the siege of Salamanca . . . We had a race for the <u>larger</u> Arapiles, *(my emphasis – the race was not, as commentators say, for both Arapiles: Wellington had made sure of the Lesser from the start)* which is the more distant of the two detached heights which you will recollect on the right of your position: this race the French won, and they were too strong to be dislodged without a general action. *Now, it is my contention that Wellington lost this race deliberately, in spite of Colonel Waters' possibly unwelcome intervention. He already knew the ground and he could have occupied it at dawn, long before the French got there. Again, it was not the sort of thing he could ever admit, except possibly to Beresford, for one simply does not allow an enemy to occupy points of obvious advantage if one can possibly help it.*

But what would have happened if Marmont had not got the Grand Arapil and Wellington had? Wellington's position would have been impregnable. To turn it Marmont would have had to bring his army right round in a wide sweep across broken low ground to the south of the whole position; with nearly equal numbers and an inferiority in cavalry that would have been unthinkable. He would simply have waited first for Clausel who was protecting his rear from the Galicians, and then for the King with his 12,000 men to come up, and Wellington would have been obliged by sheer weight of numbers to give up Salamanca and fall back to the Agueda, without fighting the general action he so much wanted. But with the Grand Arapil in his hands Marmont had a strong position which would protect his infantry as he pivoted round it on to what he took to be Wellington's right flank.

In the morning the light troops of the 7th division, and 4th caçadores belonging to General Pack's brigade were engaged with the enemy on the height called Nuestra Señora de la Peña, on which height they maintained themselves with the enemy throughout the day . . . *Though actually after a time their place was taken by the 1st division and the Light. The 7th were pulled back into the concealing hills, while Pack moved south to attack the Grand Arapil in what was essentially a diversion, though an expensive one. The choice of two crack divisions, the 1st and Light for the north-south ridge will be explained below.*

The possession by the enemy, however, of the more distant of the Arapiles rendered it necessary for me to extend the right of the army <u>en potence</u> to the height *(San Miguel)* behind the village of Arapiles and to occupy that village with light infantry; and here I placed the 4th division . . . *'En potence' means, as we have already noted, 'at right angles'. This then is the beginning of what looks like a Fuentes de Oñoro, a right-angled position with the point at the angle again being virtually invulnerable. In the earlier battle it had been the village that made it safe, now it was the Lesser Arapil. But there is more to all this than just that. The French could see clearly that the village of Los Arapiles was occupied, and that a division stood, and later when they bombarded it, lay, on the open ground behind the village and between it and the Lesser Arapil. And that, they thought, was the extent of the British position – a strongly held north-south line to the Lesser Arapil which had been reinforced on its right by a division 'en potence', whose own right flank was guarded by the small but occupied village.*

. . . from the variety of the enemy's movements . . . I considered that on the whole his objects were upon the left of the Tormes. I therefore ordered Major General the Hon. E. Pakenham *(his brother-in-law)*, who commanded the 3rd division in the absence of Lieut. General Picton, on account of ill-health, to move across the Tormes with the troops under his command, including Brig. General D'Urban's cavalry, and to place himself behind Aldea Tejada . . .

All this took several hours, and again Wellington's prescience or forward planning are clearly demonstrated. The order reached Pakenham as early as 10.30 a.m. He was on the move shortly after 11.00, and, to avoid bottlenecks, sent some of his force over Cabrerizos, some over Santa Marta, and some through the town and across the bridge. They assembled again at about 2.30 p.m., having marched twelve miles or more, at Aldea Tejada. The point is clear: Wellington was using the advantage of the <u>en potence</u> position to strengthen and extend his right long before Marmont began to move decisively in the same direction, and Marmont could not see what was happening. The movement of the 3rd was followed by movements of the 5th, 6th and 7th divisions across the inside of the same line, and these too were hidden by San Miguel.

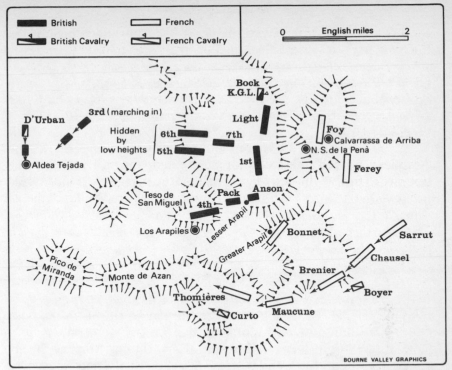

15. The Battle of Salamanca, 2.00 p.m. 'My Lord, the French are extending to their left!'

After a variety of evolutions and movements, the enemy appears to have determined upon his plan about two in the afternoon, and under cover of a very heavy cannonade, which however, did us but very little damage, he extended his left, and moved forward his troops, apparently with an intention to embrace, by the position of his troops, and by his fire, our post on that of the two Arapiles which we possessed, and from thence to attack and break our line, or at all events, to render difficult any movement of ours to our right . . . *that is, in the direction of Ciudad Rodrigo.*

The extension of his line to his left, however, and its advance upon our right, notwithstanding that his troops still occupied very strong ground, and his position was still defended by cannon, gave me an opportunity of attacking him; for which I had long been anxious.

At 2.00 p.m. Wellington was in a small farmhouse between Aldea Tejada and the Lesser Arapil, having a hurried lunch of cold chicken rather than the usual cold mutton. A staff officer rode up: 'My Lord, the French are extending to their left!' 'The Devil they are!' and then to Alava, with whom he conversed and corresponded in French: 'Mon cher Alava, Marmont est perdu.' He

219

mounted and galloped up onto the Lesser Arapil. The French cannon were falling into position in a long line on the ridge that ran on from the Grand Arapil and were bombarding the 4th division and the village. One division, commanded by Maucune, was threatening the village with skirmishers. This shortly developed into a full-scale assault which was gallantly repulsed by the fusilier companies of the Guards with which Wellington reinforced the light troops. Another, Clausel's, newly arrived from protecting Marmont's rear on the Duero, lay in reserve behind it. But to the west, to the French left, another division with cavalry, Thomières' and Curto's, were marching on to the Monte de Azan and showed every sign of continuing in that direction. It has been said that Marmont had mistaken the dust of the 3rd arriving at Aldea Tejada for that of the allied baggage moving off towards Ciudad Rodrigo, and he had it in mind to take it, or at any rate separate it from the allied army. It is more likely that he was occupying the height on his extreme left before continuing what he thought would be a flanking movement, but had perhaps not quite realised in the clarified air how far the height was from his main force.

At all events Wellington, suddenly pale, took in the situation, snapped up his telescope, and said: 'By God, that will do.' Briskly he gave his orders. It was 2.45 p.m. I reinforced our right with the 5th division, under Lieut. General Leith, which I placed behind the village of Arapiles, on the right of the 4th division, and with the 6th and 7th divisions in reserve. *The French could see the 5th, and would have expected a reinforcement to appear behind the threatened village, but the 6th and 7th were still concealed.* And as soon as these troops had taken their station, I ordered . . . Pakenham to move forward with the 3rd division and General D'Urban's cavalry, and two squadrons of the 14th light dragoons, under Lieut. Colonel Hervey, in four columns, to turn the enemy's left on the heights . . . *He rode over to Aldea Tejada himself to give that order.*

It was now a hot and sultry afternoon, the sky resuming the brassy look that in July, on the Spanish plateau, hints at thunder gone and thunder to come. As the long red lines wound in the men of the 3rd division unloaded the iron camp-kettles from the mules that carried them, gathered what wood they could find, and began to prepare their main meal of the day – boiled beef with whatever vegetables they had been able to buy in Salamanca market. In the distance the cannon fire thudded and thudded – louder, more unbroken with every moment. They looked a rough, tough lot. On campaign Wellington never bothered about uniforms beyond the point of being sure he could tell whose side a man was on and what regiment he belonged to. Their red jackets had faded to russet except where they were patched, their trousers were as likely to be French pantalons (the material was tougher) as regulation issue, their boots gaped, some went barefoot, all were caked to their knees in the fine, brick-red dust of the campo they had crossed. Only their pipe-clayed accoutrements, the straps fastened across the chest or on the shoulder with the large regimental badge, were relatively clean. Their firelocks, sixty rounds, and bayonets were immaculate. They were incredibly fit, and spoiling for the fight that had been denied them since Badajoz.

Two horsemen appeared, flying over the stubbled down, pumping up the red dust beneath their hooves. They reined in. Wellington touched Pakenham's shoulder with his crop: 'Edward, move on with the 3rd division – take the heights in your front – and drive everything before you.' *'I will, my Lord, if you will give me your hand.'*

. . . to turn the enemy's left on the heights, while Bradford's brigade, the 5th division . . . the 4th division . . . and the cavalry should attack them in the front, supported in reserve by the 6th . . . the 7th, and Don Carlos de España's Spanish division; and . . . Pack should support the left of the 4th division by attacking that of the Dos Arapiles which the enemy held. *The signal for this massive onslaught was to be the engagement of Thomierès' division by the 3rd on the far, allied, right.*

The 1st and Light divisions occupied the ground on the left and were in reserve. *They were also poised to pursue a defeated enemy, and were the best units for the job: the Light because it was one of their specialities and they were supported by Bock's German cavalry; the 1st because they were the most disciplined and least likely to break ranks and get out of control, go too far. And, and this is the point, they were ideally placed to inflict terrible losses, or take thousands of prisoners from a broken army that would, Wellington thought, be fleeing back almost across their front, to the ford at Huerta, since he still believed the bridge at Alba was covered by España's garrison's guns . . .*

The attack upon the enemy's left was made in the manner above described, and completely succeeded. . . . Pakenham formed the 3rd division across the enemy's flank, and overthrew everything opposed to him. These troops were supported in the most gallant style by the Portuguese cavalry, under . . . D'Urban, and . . . Hervey's squadrons of the 14th, who successfully defeated every attempt made by the enemy on the flank of the 3rd division.

Here is how the 'Fighting Third' went in. The infantry were formed up in two columns, with two columns of cavalry on their right flank and their light troops skirmishing on their left. The formation of both centre columns was 'open column of companies'. This meant that each company of a hundred men marched in double line abreast, forming a front of fifty men, with the next company sixty paces behind. There were slightly larger gaps between battalions. The senior officers rode in front of each colour company, the subalterns carried the colour in the centre of each battalion, or marched in the centre of each company.

221

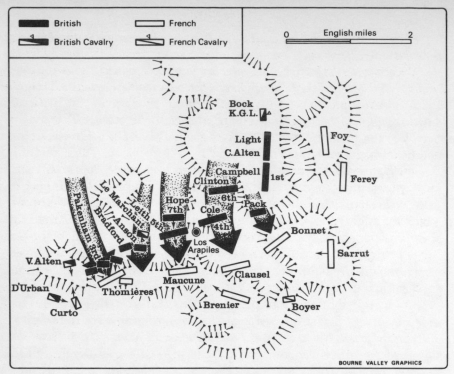

16. The Battle of Salamanca, 4.15 p.m. The 3rd 'bring up their right shoulders'.
The other assaults followed within minutes.

They were attacked by Curto's cavalry on the right, but the allied cavalry saw them off before much damage was done. They were shelled and bombarded and cannonaded from the heights, but a battery of artillery and a troop of Royal Horse Artillery found positions on low ridges behind them from which, firing over their heads, they managed to silence some of the French guns or draw their fire. The French sent down a cloud of voltigeurs against their left flank, but the light rifle companies neutralised them. Nevertheless they suffered losses, and the men moved in towards the centre of each company to replace them. Officers and N.C.O.s continually checked the lines and spacing.

At the foot of the slope, with the nearest of them two hundred and fifty yards from the French, they 'brought their right shoulders up', that is, in each company, the men on the right quickened their step, the men on the left shortened their stride right down to the anchor man at the extreme end who merely marked time: thus the right of each company swung round in a quarter circle to lock into the left of the company in front. In less than two minutes two long columns had changed their front and formation into that of two thin red lines, each two deep. Something similar can be seen to this day in the Trooping of the Colour — but not under heavy fire.

222

At this point French cavalry at last got through to the right flank of the rear line, and sabred many before being driven off. All then moved forward again, up the slope towards the French, their more junior officers in front, the generals and colonels on horses between the two lines. At fifty yards the French volleyed, the lines checked, a Major fell, his foot caught in the stirrup, the horse, wild with fright, dragged his corpse down the narrowing gap between the two armies. The French got in one more volley, but ragged and ill-aimed, and the troops went in – the Connaught Rangers in the centre.

Of Pakenham's part in all this Wellington later wrote, to Torrens on 7 September: I must say he made the manoeuvre which led to our success . . . with a celerity and accuracy of which I doubt that many are capable, and without both it would not have answered in its end. Pakenham may not be the brightest genius, but my partiality for him does not lead me astray, when I tell you he is one of the best we have.

Meanwhile . . . Bradford's brigade, the 5th and 4th divisions, and the cavalry . . . attacked the enemy in front, and drove his troops before them from one height to another, bringing forward their right, so as to acquire strength upon the enemy's flank in proportion to the advance . . . Pack made a very gallant attack upon the Arapiles, in which, however, he did not succeed, except in diverting the attention of the enemy's corps placed upon it from the troops under the command of . . . Cole in his advance.

Private Green, now back with the 5th division after a prolonged convalescence from recurring Walcheren fever, describes as vividly as any what this sort of thing was like.

We now came into an open plain, and were completely exposed to the fire of the enemy's artillery. Along this plain a division of the army was stationed . . . the men laid down in order to escape the shot and shells . . . I saw a shell fall on one of the men, which killed him on the spot, a part of the shell tore his knapsack to pieces, and I saw it flying through the air after the shell had burst . . .

As we were marching in open column to take our position a sergeant whose name was Dunn had both his legs shot from under him, and died in a few minutes. Shortly after, a shot came and took away the leg and thigh, with part of the body, of a young officer named Finukin: to have seen him, and heard the screams of his servant, would almost have rended a heart of stone.

The next thing I have to relate is of the company directly in our front . . . a cannon ball came, and striking the right of the company, made the arms gingle and fly in pieces like broken glass. One of the bayonets was broken off, and sent through a man's neck with as much force as if it had been done by a strong and powerful hand. I saw the man pull it out, and, singular to relate, he recovered . . .

We now took our position . . . About half-past four o'clock Lord Wellington came into the front of our position, and pulled off his hat; our army gave three cheers and advanced on the French who were ready to receive us . . . the firing of both armies commenced . . . it was like a long roll of a hundred drums without an interval . . . at last the enemy gave way in all directions, and we completely beat them out of the field with dreadful carnage.

The cavalry under Lieut. General Sir Stapleton Cotton made a most gallant and successful charge against a body of the enemy's infantry, which they overthrew and cut to pieces. In this charge Major General Le Marchant was killed at the head of his brigade; and I have to regret the loss of a most able officer . . .

Le Marchant was a 'scientific' general of cavalry who had thought carefully about the role of cavalry and how it could best be carried out. He was also a fair water colourist and had painted the view of Salamanca from the Santa Marta ford that very morning. His son was his A.D.C., and had just been sent to Wellington with a message when the charge was ordered. He returned to find his colleagues carrying the body of his father to the rear.

A charge by massed heavy cavalry on massed infantry, in the course of a general engagement, was a very rare event, and, when attempted, was rarely successful – especially if the infantry had time to form squares. But Wellington had placed his cavalry exactly, so they hit the centre of Thomierè's division just as it was striving to maintain good order with their left crumbling in front of the 3rd's assault. Furthermore the presence of so many heavy cavalry had been screened by the rises – only Le Marchant himself had gone forward earlier to examine the ground. Conscientious and thoughtful officer that he was, he was not going to risk the sort of hidden ditches that had done so much damage at Talavera.

A rare event, and one which should not, I think, be too readily celebrated. The curved sabre of the light dragoons slashed and maimed, but generally left wounds that would heal; the heavier broadsword of the heavy dragoons was a far more vicious weapon, and its cut, delivered from the back of a large horse, smashed collar bones and rib cages, severed limbs, and left its victims often horribly mutilated and dying . . . slowly. Grattan, with the Connaught Rangers at the front of the 3rd division described the effects of the charge.

His brigade pierced through the vast mass, killing or trampling down all before them. The conflict was severe and the troopers fell thick and fast; but their long swords cut through bone as well as flesh. The groans of the dying, the cries of the wounded, and the piteous moans of the mangled horses as they ran away from the terrible scene, or lay with shattered limbs, unable to move in the midst of the burning grass, was enough to unman men not placed as we were.

Hundreds of beings, frightfully disfigured, in whom the human form and face were almost obliterated – black with dust, worn down with fatigue, and covered with sabre cuts and blood – threw themselves among us for safety. Not a man was bayoneted, not even molested or plundered; and the invincible old 3rd division . . . actually covered their retreat, and protected them at a moment when without such aid their total annihilation was certain.

At the time, Wellington, perhaps excusably, was appreciative. He was riding with Cotton behind Le Marchant's charge, and in front of the reserve cavalry. 'By God, Cotton, I never saw any thing so beautiful in my life; the day is yours.'

After the crest of the height (*the long rise of Monte de Azan*) was carried one division of the enemy made a stand against the 4th division, which, after a severe contest, was obliged to give way, in consequence of the enemy having thrown some troops on the left of the 4th division, after the failure of . . . Pack's attack upon the Arapiles, and . . . Cole having been wounded.

This was the crucial moment. For twenty minutes it looked as if the French might recover from the initial shock, which had been aggravated by the loss first of Marmont, severely wounded, and then of his successor Bonet. But now Clausel, perhaps the best general on the French side, had assumed command. Courageously, Napoleonically even, he launched his remaining fresh, unscathed divisions into the weakest part of the British line, just west of the Arapiles, only to find himself countered far more quickly than he expected – for Wellington had foreseen the move and set in motion the troops that would relieve the 4th, even before Clausel had set the counter-attack going.

Marshal Sir William Beresford who happened to be on the spot, directed Brig. General Spry's *Portuguese* brigade . . . which was in the second line, to change its front and to bring its fire on the flank of the enemy's division; and I am sorry to add that, while engaged in this service, he received a wound which I am apprehensive will deprive me of the benefit of his counsel and assistance for some time. Nearly at the same time Lieut. General Leith received a wound which unfortunately obliged him to quit the field. I ordered up the 6th division, under Major General Clinton, to relieve the 4th, and the battle was soon restored to its former success.

The time had come, as the main French army broke and fled behind a last line of reserves and detachments that had gallantly reformed, to launch what should have been the coup de grâce – the moment Wellington had possibly, and I believe it to be so, contemplated at least as early as the time when he instructed Carlos de España to maintain the garrison at Alba.

The enemy's right, however, reinforced by the troops which had fled from his left, and by those which had now retired from the Arapiles still continued to resist; and I ordered the 1st and Light divisions, and Colonel Stubb's Portuguese brigade of the 4th division, to turn the right, while the 6th division supported by the 3rd and 5th, attacked the front. It was dark before the point was carried by the 6th division; and the enemy fled through the woods towards the Tormes. I pursued them with the 1st and Light divisions, and Major General Anson's brigade, and some squadrons of cavalry under . . . Cotton, as long as we could find any of them together, directing our march upon Huerta and the fords of the Tormes, by which the enemy had passed on their advance; but the darkness of the night was highly advantageous to the enemy, many of whom escaped under its cover who must otherwise have been in our hands.

I am sorry to report that, owing to this same cause, . . . Cotton was unfortunately wounded by one of our own sentries after we had halted.

His letter to Graham is more frank – he had not wanted to spoil his official dispatch with criticism of anyone and certainly not of a general officer of the Spanish army. I had desired the Spaniards to continue to occupy the castle of Alba de Tormes. Carlos de España had evacuated it, I believe before he knew my wishes; and he was afraid to let me know that he had done so; and I did not know it till I found no enemy at the fords of the Tormes. When I lost sight of them in the dark, I marched upon Huerta and Encinas, and they went by Alba. If I had known there had been no garrison in Alba, I should have marched there, and should probably have had the whole.

To Graham still, he goes on: Marmont, Clausel, Foy, Ferrey, and Bonet are wounded badly. Ferrey, it is supposed, will die. Thomierès is killed. Many generals of the brigade killed or wounded.

I need not express how much I regret the disorder in your eyes since this action.

Back to the dispatch for the pursuit on the following day.

We renewed the pursuit at break of day in the morning with the same troops . . . and having crossed the Tormes, we came up with the enemy's rear of cavalry and infantry near La Serna. They were immediately attacked by the two brigades of dragoons and the cavalry fled, leaving their infantry to their fate. *This time the French did have time to form – and this was the only occasion in the war when cavalry broke squares.* I have never witnessed a more gallant charge than was made on the enemy's infantry by the heavy brigade of the King's German Legion, under Major General Bock, which was completely successful; and the whole body of infantry, consisting of three battalions of the enemy's 1st division, were made prisoners.

The pursuit was afterwards continued as far as Peñaranda last night, and our troops were still pursuing the flying enemy . . . they are now considerably advanced on the road towards Valladolid, by Arevalo. They were joined yesterday . . . by the cavalry and artillery of the army of the North, which have arrived at too late a period . . . to be of much use to them.

The dispatch concludes with estimates of losses, and a long, long list of 'honourable mentions', but the battle was best summarised at the end of his letter to Graham. I am in great hopes that our loss has not been great. In two divisions, the 3rd and 5th, it is about 1200 . . . There are more in the 4th and 6th, but there are many men who left the ranks with wounded officers and soldiers, who are eating and drinking, and engaged in regocijos *(making whoopee)* with the inhabitants of Salamanca . . .

I hope that you receive benefit from the advice of the oculists in London.

Believe me &c.,

Wellington

P.S. Beresford's wound is not dangerous. Leith's arm is broken and his wound painful. Cole's wound is through the body, and it is apprehended will be tedious. Cotton's is through the fleshy part, and the two bones of his arm. It may be a bad wound, if there should be haemorrhage.

Wellington himself had a narrow escape – a ball pierced his cloak and pistol holster, and bruised his thigh.

The allied losses were eventually computed as something under 5,000. The French lost at least 14,000, 20 guns, eagles and colours, baggage.

Wellington's last word again carries the implication of what he could never openly state – that the whole thing had been foreseen in advance. From the private letter to Bathurst: I hope you will be pleased with our battle . . . There was no mistake; everything went on as it ought; and there was never an army so beaten in so short a time.

1812

(AUGUST–NOVEMBER)

MADRID

BURGOS

RETREAT

17. Northern Spain

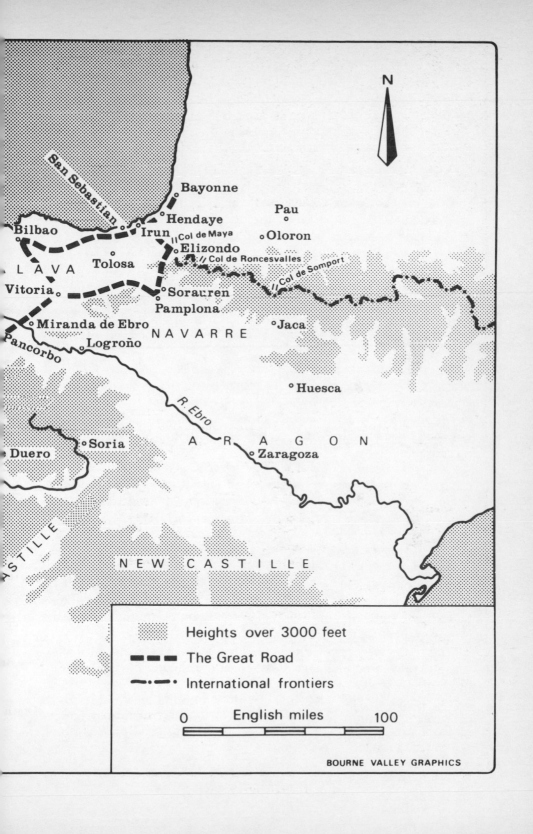

N

San Sebastian

Bayonne

Pau

Bilbao   Hendaye
            Irun   Col de Maya
L A V A   Tolosa   Elizondo   Oloron
                        Col de Roncesvalles
Vitoria   Col de Somport
                        Sorauren
                        Pamplona

Miranda de Ebro   N A V A R R E   Jaca

Pancorbo   Logroño

                        R. Ebro   Huesca

                  A   R   A   G   O   N
         Soria
Duero   Zaragoza

CASTILLE

N E W   C A S T I L L E

Heights over 3000 feet
The Great Road
International frontiers

0   English miles   100

BOURNE VALLEY GRAPHICS

MADRID

―∾∾∾―

The pursuit continued as far as Valladolid which the French abandoned on the thirtieth. To Bathurst, 4 August: Our advanced guard crossed the Duero, and our parties entered Valladolid on the same day: and I had the satisfaction of being received by the people in that city with the same enthusiastic joy as I had been in all other parts of the country.

The army of Portugal having thus crossed and quitted the Duero, it was necessary to attend to the movements of the army of the Centre *(Joseph's 12,000)*, and to prevent a junction between the two on the Upper Duero, which it was reported was intended. While therefore the advanced guard and left continued the pursuit of the army of Portugal, I moved the right along the Cegar to Cuellar, where I arrived on the 1st instant.

This is twenty-five miles south-west of Valladolid, pointing directly at Madrid and Joseph. The move had the desired effect. To Commodore Sir Home Popham, who was operating a squadron along the north coast and doing well: I have come here with our right, in order to look a little after the King, who had assembled the army of the Centre about Segovia, but he has retired upon Madrid.

Wellington stayed at Cuellar for four whole days during which his main preoccupation was the health of his troops. On top of everything else an epidemic of 'flux' swept through the army. Wellington ascribed this, almost certainly correctly, to the eating of unripe grapes. From my own experience as a traveller on a budget tight enough to make fields of grapes a temptation, I believe it is the yeasts that form the 'bloom' on the fruit that cause the sickness.

G.O.   Cuellar, 1st August, 1812.
1. The Commander of the Forces requests that (all) officers will take measures to prevent the soldiers from plundering and eating the unripe grapes.
2. The followers of the army, the Portuguese women in particular, must be prevented by the Provosts from plundering the gardens and fields of vegetables . . .
3. . . . to each soldier daily one eighth of a pound of rice, if it can be procured; if it cannot, the same quantity of wheaten flour, or of barley, or of wheat, which the officers are requested to see that the soldiers boil

up with their soup. If barley or wheat should be issued, the husk should be beaten off before it is boiled.

5. As much of the sickness of the troops is attributed to the use of raw spirits by the soldiers in the hot season . . . the officers will see that the men of each mess in their companies mix their spirits with four times the quantity of water as soon as the spirits are issued . . .

All of which may seem quaint, but the advice about rice, or de-fibred substitutes was sound – no doubt something Arthur Wellesley had learnt in India. And the situation was serious. To Bathurst, 4 August: I am sorry to say that the British troops are by no means healthy, notwithstanding the pains which have been taken to make moderate marches with them, and to encamp them in healthy situations, and they have never failed to receive their regular food . . . The soldiers are not able to bear the labor of marching in the heat of the sun . . . (*some*) officers have disobeyed orders . . . to have their men supplied with blankets . . . and they are consequently very inadequately protected, in comparison with the other soldiers, from the sun in the day time, and from the dews at night . . . it is melancholy to see the finest and bravest soldiers in the world falling down, owing to their own irregularities, and the ignorant presumption of those who think they know better what is good for them than those do who have been serving so long in this country.

'The finest and bravest soldiers in the world' – not, after all, the scum of the earth. He had another debt to pay as well. To Henry, 5 August: I believe you are aware that I have always had the best intelligence from Salamanca, which was given to me by persons residing there at the constant risk of their lives, who have uniformly refused to be rewarded for their services, which they very justly have considered to be rendered to their country. They have now applied to me to have their services considered and rewarded by the Spanish government . . . and I request you to use your utmost influence with the Government, that they may attend to the claims of these worthy individuals.

For four days he considered how best to make use of his victory. There were still four unbeaten armies in Spain. He could continue to pursue Marmont, even into the Pyrenees, but would surely have faced before long a combined force far bigger than his – reinforcements would come from France, Joseph would join or be in his rear, he would be separated from Hill, who in turn would be vulnerable to a combination of Soult and the French army that had gone into Valencia.

To General Santocildes, the commander of the Galicians, at that time with his army at Zamora, 3 August: Upon considering our situation in all its views, I have thought I should do most good to the cause by marching immediately upon Madrid . . . I propose to return . . . as soon as I shall have removed the King from Madrid.

It was a decision that has been criticised in the light of later events but cannot really be faulted. The taking of the capital was a tremendous morale-booster all over the world, not least to the Russians who were falling back towards Borodino and Moscow. It placed him within reach of Hill and allowed him to form an immense strategic bastion, or position 'en potence', with its point at Madrid and one line stretching north-west through the Escorial and Segovia to Valladolid, and the other south-west through Talavera, Almaraz, to Badajoz. This bastion formed, or would form, once he got to Madrid, a wedge between the French armies, and gave him the shorter line of communication so he could quickly concentrate wherever the French chose to menace him.

The immediate success of this plan, in spite of a hitch with the Portuguese cavalry on the way, is summarised in a letter to Cotton written almost as soon as he reached Madrid. 13 August: I have long intended to write to you, but I have really not had time to write to any body. I was much concerned to learn that you were so unwell; but I hope that you will soon be better, as I am very anxious to have you again with the army . . . We followed Marmont as closely as we could to the Duero, but he marched at such a rate, and our troops were so much fatigued, that after the first day we did him but little mischief. After driving him from Valladolid . . . he and the King . . . had thoughts of joining at Aranda de Duero, and I moved our right to Cuellar. I there gave the troops a day's halt, upon finding the King retired upon Madrid; and afterwards I thought that, upon the whole, the best thing I could do would be to move upon the King and fight him; or force him from Madrid, which I have carried into execution.

I could not go farther north without great inconvenience, and I could at the moment do nothing else . . .

The King has retired upon Aranjuez and Toledo, leaving a garrison in the Retiro.

We had a devil of an affair on the evening of the 11th. The French, 2000 cavalry, moved upon the Portuguese cavalry; D'Urban ordered them to charge the advance squadrons, which charge they did not execute as they ought, and they ran off, leaving our guns (Captain M'Donald's troop). They ran in upon the German cavalry, half a mile or more in their rear, where they were brought up; but they would not charge on the left of the Germans. These charged and stopped the enemy . . . We . . . lost three guns but the French left them behind. *He goes on to discuss the state of the cavalry, of which Cotton was over all commander, and his fears that* constant marches and skirmishes must wear them out. *He concludes:* I shall make every body shoe up while we shall be engaged on the siege of the Retiro.

No love was lost between Beresford and Cotton, and while Cotton commanded the cavalry, Beresford of course commanded the Portuguese. He was mortified at the failure of the Portuguese horse at Majalahonda, and wrote, also from his bed in Salamanca:

> I have ordered that they should not again mount a horse or wear a sword, till they may, by coming near the enemy, have an opportunity of redeeming their credit . . . till then, hanging their swords on their saddles, they lead their horses, marching themselves. The Portuguese have a good deal of feeling and pride, and it is the only way to work on them . . .

It was the only shadow on what was a splendid period. To Bathurst, 13 August: It is impossible to describe the joy manifested by the inhabitants of Madrid upon our arrival . . . *Well, not exactly. Every diarist and memoir writer had a go. Green's is perhaps the least often quoted, so here he is.*

> The 12th, we moved off early, and suffered much from the paved roads. This day Lord Wellington passed our division on his way to the capital; when we were within five miles of Madrid, the people came out in great numbers to meet us; the day being very hot, some of our men fainted, but the Spaniards immediately took them under their care, giving them wine or spirits; a great number of melons were also distributed to the men in the ranks. The people shouted and rejoiced as we marched along, and the bands of the different regiments enlivened the scene by frequently playing the 'Downfall of Paris'; the colours were displayed, and we frequently gave three cheers: indeed there was little else but shouts of approbation for the last two miles. We at length arrived at the gates; the streets were crowded with the populace, and the windows occupied by ladies; the tops of the houses near the gate were also crowded. We marched along the streets amidst the rending and exulting shouts of 'Viva los Ingleses!' The bells of the different churches rang, the ladies waved their handkerchiefs from the windows, and every countenance beamed with joy, welcoming their deliverers: in some instances the Spaniards embraced the soldiers. We halted in front of the new palace: here we shouted and cheered the people in return.

For a day Wellington thought the Retiro was going to be as much of a nuisance as the Salamanca forts, but, to Bathurst, 15 August: the 3rd division . . . drove in the enemy's posts from the Prado, and the Botanical Garden, and the works they had constructed outside of the park wall; and having broken through the wall in different places they were

235

Madrid

established in the palace of the Retiro . . . the troops were preparing in the morning to attack . . . when the governor sent out an officer to desire to capitulate.

All was 'alegría' beneath the Velasqueño skies, in what was still, in spite of four years of occupation, the Madrid of the early Goya. Indeed it was. For me there are three entirely great men of the period – Beethoven, Goya, and Wellington. And both artists celebrated the General – Beethoven in his Victory Symphony (for Vitoria), and Goya in the equestrian portrait he now did from life, together with the red chalk drawing that was the sketch for the National Gallery portrait. The equestrian picture, now in Apsley House shows our hero bareheaded, hat in hand, in his blue Spanish cavalry cloak. It should not bother us that under the exigencies of the moment, Goya, who was now sixty-six years old, and deaf, recycled a canvas he had already done . . . of Joseph.

There were embarrassments for Wellington. Invited to parties, balls, 'agasacos', and 'regocijos', it was incumbent upon him to return hospitality in style. He was also expected to subscribe handsomely to local charities. The result was this letter to Bathurst, Madrid, 24 August. I have been going on for more than three years upon the usual allowance of a Commander in Chief, that is ten pounds per diem, liable to various deductions, among others of income tax, reducing it to about eight guineas; but it will be necessary that Government should now either give me an additional pay under the head of table money . . . or that they should allow me to charge some of the expenses, such as charities, which I am obliged to incur, in the existing state of this country, or I shall be ruined . . . I should not have mentioned the subject, knowing that the public expect in these days to be well served at the lowest possible rate of expense, if I did not find I was in a situation in which I must incur expenses which I cannot defray without doing myself an injury . . .

The embarrassment was perhaps sharpened when he discovered, that, even as he was writing this, the Prince Regent was recommending Parliament to grant him the quite enormous sum of £100,000. To Bathurst, when he was back in Valladolid, 7 September: I am very much obliged to your Lordship for having averted to my expenses in this country and for having provided for them so handsomely. You will have received a letter from me on this subject . . . I should never have written upon it if I had not incurred an enormous expense at Madrid, which I could not bear.

Meanwhile, something Wellington had been urging for months, and which he had latterly given up all hope of, at last occurred – the landing of a British expeditionary force on the east coast of Spain, at Alicante, led by Lieutenant General Maitland. It lessened the danger of Soult joining the King to attack Hill from the south, and left him free to move back to the Duero. To Maitland, 30

237

August: I proceed to-morrow to join the detachment of this army collected at Arevalo, with which I shall march to drive the detachment of the enemy's army of Portugal from the Duero, which have advanced to that river since I have been in this quarter, and to establish a good communication between this army and the Spanish army of the North, to which Astorga has recently surrendered.

He left behind four divisions of infantry and two brigades of cavalry at Madrid and the Escorial to hold the angle of his bastion, leaving him free to join the Galician army and sweep up into the north-east out of the Duero and finish off or box in the army of Portugal on the upper Ebro. A central part of this design was that, once on the upper Ebro, he would be able to re-open his contact with the sea through Santander and the Basque ports.

On 7 September he wrote to Murray, his much-missed ex-Quarter Master General, from Valladolid. Murray had been replaced by Colonel Gordon, whose cock-ups were yet to reach their appalling climax, but had caused enough bother for Wellington to write: I assure you that I have every day fresh reason to regret your departure.

He went on: I hear that the siege of Cadiz is raised; and there is a storm brewing up from the south, for which I am preparing by driving the detachments of the army of Portugal away from the Duero; and I propose, if I have time, to take Burgos from them. In the mean time, I have ordered Hill to cross the Tagus by Almaraz when he finds that Soult moves out of Andalusia . . . By keeping this detachment at Alicante . . . I shall prevent too many of the gentlemen now assembled in Valencia from troubling me in the upper country.

Matters go on well, and I hope before Christmas, if affairs turn out as they ought, and Boney requires all the reinforcements in the North, to have all the gentlemen safe on the other side of the Ebro.

We should note that before he left Madrid, he again found time to advert to the good conduct of his men. His memorandum to Alten and de España, whom he had left in charge there, concludes: I have been much satisfied with the conduct of the allied troops since they have been in Madrid.

BURGOS

Matters continued to go on well, for a fortnight or so. The 'gentlemen' duly obliged by yet again abandoning the Duero before making a brief stand before Burgos on the seventeenth. Wellington (now a Marquess: 'What the devil is the use of making me a Marquess!' *found time to answer this letter from Lord Bathurst.*

> To General the Marquess of Wellington. Lord Wellesley has express-
> ed a strong wish that you should have an augmentation of arms . . .
> the augmentation he proposed was the French eagle. I think this
> would be objectionable . . . What I have submitted for the considera-
> tion of the Regent is, that the augmentation should be the Royal
> Union Flag of the United Kingdom. This is what no subject has
> hitherto enjoyed . . . I am sorry to detain you with what you may
> probably think not worth the trouble of reading.
>   The Duke of Newcastle has written me word that the Order of the
> Bath is an inadequate reward for Sir Stapleton Cotton's services; that
> he was second in command, and that to him, after you, the signal
> success of the day [Salamanca] was to be attributed. He says Sir
> Stapleton should be made a peer . . .

The first point Wellington dealt with briskly. To Bathurst, 7 September: The addition proposed to my arms is the last *(honour)* which would have occurred to me. It carries with it an appearance of ostentation, of which I hope I am not guilty, and it will scarcely be credited that I did not apply for it. However, I prefer the addition proposed by your Lordship to that proposed by Lord Wellesley.

The second point was far more complex. Following Graham's return to England Cotton was senior Lieutenant General and commander of the cavalry. To have given him alone a peerage would have confirmed him as Wellington's successor in the event of an accident, and also as second in command – a post Wellington saw no purpose in, and did his utmost to leave unfilled. Moreover, much though he valued Cotton's services, he knew very well he would be quite inadequate as Commander-in-Chief. The only person on the spot who could fill that post, in Wellington's judgement, was Beresford. Moreover Beresford, as Commander of the Portuguese, and on the field of Salamanca, had contributed as much, if less spectacularly, to the victory as Cotton. Peerages for both was the obvious solution, but there was prejudice at home against Beresford. Restric-

tions had until recently barred bastards from the peerage; the 'victory' of Albuera and its concomitant high losses remained unpopular.

I always thought the Order of the Bath that mark of the King's favour which it was most desirable to an officer to receive; and I mentioned it to you as I thought it likely it would be agreeable to Sir Stapleton . . . It might be very proper to make him a Peer; but I could not propose such an arrangement to government . . . Beresford . . . was much disappointed and hurt that this mark of the King's favour was not conferred upon him when the restrictions ceased; and I really believe his regard for me alone prevented him from resigning his situation. If Sir Stapleton had been made a Peer, I really believe Beresford would resign . . .

At Torquemada he paused on 13 September and wrote a note on what was becoming a quite severe interruption to the flow of intelligence. The French, who had at last cottoned on to the fact that almost every letter they sent to each other ended up on Wellington's desk, had begun to use a cipher. To Bathurst: I see that some person employed by Lord Castlereagh has made some discoveries approaching to the key of the Paris cipher . . . I shall be very much obliged to you if you will send me what has been discovered. *In fact the cipher never was completely broken.*

On the eighteenth his headquarters were at Villa Toro outside Burgos and in his despatch of the twenty-first he filled in what had happened in the interim. To Bathurst: The enemy had on the 16th taken a strong position on the heights behind Celada del Camino, and arrangements were made to attack them on the 17th; but the enemy retired in the night; and they were driven on the 17th to the heights close to Burgos. They retired through the town in the night, leaving behind them some clothing and stores, and a large quantity of wheat and barley; and have since continued their retreat to Briviesca, where it is reported they have been joined by 7000 conscripts . . .

The castle of Burgos commands the passages of the river Arlanzon in the neighbourhood and the roads communicating with them so completely, that we could not pass the river until the 19th . . . The enemy have taken considerable pains to fortify the castle *on Napoleon's orders. He inspected it in December 1808* and had occupied with a horn-work the hill of San Miguel, which has a considerable command over some of the works of the castle at the distance of 300 yards.

To Maitland: I doubt, however, that I have means to take the castle, which is very strong.

The country around Burgos is half-and-half land, not quite the campo, not quite the sierra and lacking the beauties of either. Burgos itself is a prosperous, indeed rich town with the glossiest and priciest bars in the Peninsula, for it commands the rich corn land to the south of it, the timber and pasture of the hills to the north, and the two most practicable passes to the sea. In the shadow of its castled hill a cathedral was built by the architect who built Cologne, but where Cologne towers like a tall ship above the flatlands of the lower Rhine, Burgos crouches below that hill and never remotely begins to soar.

Inside, it is one of the few Spanish cathedrals still filled with the junk of the nineteenth-century counter-reformation – where the rest are for the most part restored to Romanesque humanism, gothic exuberance, or neo-classical purity, Burgos cathedral is as dark and morbid, as filled with guttering candles and realistically tortured saints as any church that ever inspired satire from Browning.

The castle itself is now planted as a park and one can drive up the zig-zag road through pines to a car-park. All is neat, children play, people picnic; the main features of the fortifications can still be traced though most were blown up by the French in 1813. Yet the melancholy that seems to settle over any battlefield is as thick here as anywhere else.

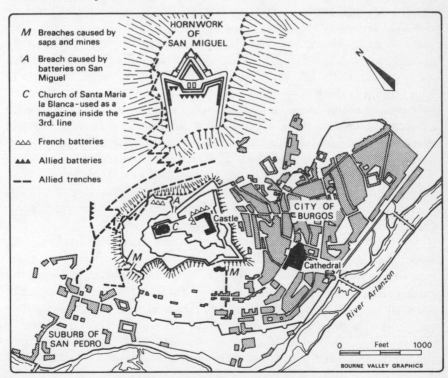

18. Burgos, 19 September – 21 October 1812

After a good beginning the siege of Burgos was near disaster for Wellington – the one military failure of his entire career.

As soon as the 1st division crossed the Arlanzon on the 19th, the enemy's outposts were driven in by the Light infantry battalion of Colonel Stirling's brigade, under the command of Major the Hon. C. Cocks *(The same Cocks Wellington had thought so well of since 1810, had had on his staff for a time, and had always trusted in the most exposed positions);* and the enemy's outworks on the hill of San Miguel, with the exception of the horn work, were occupied by our troops.

As soon as it was dark the same troops, with the addition of the 42nd regiment, attacked and carried by assault the horn work which the enemy had occupied in strength . . . *The main assault in fact failed – Major Cocks converted what had been intended as a diversion into a real assault and entered the horn work by the gorge at night.* Our loss was much greater than it ought to have been . . . If I had had here some of the troops who have stormed here so often, I should not have lost a fourth of the number. *This became a refrain during and after the siege. The fact was the Generals and/or the divisions he felt he could leave to themselves for a while were in his front watching the re-forming army of Portugal, or strung out from the Escorial through Madrid and back to Almaraz. Under his own eye he kept those who needed him to be there.*

It was impossible to ascertain the exact state of the works of the castle of Burgos till we had obtained possession of the hill of San Miguel; and as far as I can judge of them, I am apprehensive that the means which I have are not sufficient to enable me to take the castle. I am informed, however, that the enemy are ill-provided with water; and their magazines of provisions are in a place to be set on fire. I think it possible therefore, that I may have it in my power to force them to surrender, although I may not be able to lay the place open to assault.

He should have backed off now – but how could he having come so far? How explain an apparently pusillanimous withdrawal after such successes? How give up the prize – the withdrawal of all the French in the Peninsula to a line behind the Ebro with the Pyrenees at their backs?

Already that day he had pushed things on. To Clinton, 21 September, 1812, 9.00 a.m.: I am anxious to confine the enemy a little more to the castle; and I have it in contemplation to take possession this evening of the exterior line of their works. As I understand that Colonel Brown was of great service, at the siege of Salamanca, in keeping down the enemy's fire . . . by the possession of neighbouring houses, I shall be obliged to him if you will leave him in charge of the troops of the 6th division in the town, and direct him to make arrangements for placing the troops under his command in the houses close to the walls, and for keeping possession, as soon as we shall be prepared to lodge ourselves in the exterior line.

With the dispositions made an escalade was launched on the outworks on the night of the twenty-third. The covering fire proved to be inadequate after all – they were firing up for a start, whereas at Salamanca they had been on a level or even on a rise above the forts. To Bathurst, 27 September: The Portuguese troops were so strongly opposed that they could not make any progress on the enemy's flank; and the escalade could not take place. *There were 153 casualties.* We have since established ourselves close to the exterior wall, and have carried a gallery *that is a tunnel – 'gallery' as in mining –* towards it; and I hope that a mine under it will be completed in the course of to-morrow.

To Bathurst, 5 October: One of the mines which had been prepared under the exterior line of the castle of Burgos was exploded at midnight of the 29th, and effected a breach in the wall, which some of the party, destined to attack it, were enabled to storm; but owing to the darkness of the night, the detachment who were to support the advanced party missed their way, and the advance were driven off the breach . . . *Only twenty-nine casualties but a continuing drop in morale.*

Meanwhile shortages of almost everything were becoming more and more serious.

To Popham, who was on the north coast at Santander, 26 September: I am much in want of 40 barrels of gunpowder, each containing 90 pounds, for the attack of this place; I shall be very much obliged if you will let me have this quantity from the ships under your command . . .

27 September: I shall be very much obliged to you if you will let me know whether you can let me have from the squadron under your command at Santander one hundred or one hundred and fifty thousand pounds of biscuit for which I will send to Santander.

A.G.O.   27th Sept., 1812.
1. From the quantity of musket ammunition called for by the several divisions since the commencement of the siege of the castle of Burgos, the Commander of the Forces is persuaded that his orders on this subject have not been obeyed . . . the object of these orders is to prevent the waste or sale of ammunition.

On top of everything else it was now raining heavily for long periods almost every day.

For a moment, on 4 October things looked up. A second assault was made on the outer works. To Hill, 5 October: We carried the exterior line of the castle yesterday evening, without material loss. But this is altogether the most difficult job I have ever had in hand, with such trifling means. God send that they may give me a little more time! *The deity appears in these pages more often in the next two months than ever before or after – and is occasionally invoked with something like sincerity.*

To Bathurst: . . . another mine had been placed under the wall, which was ready yesterday, and a fire was opened yesterday, from a battery constructed under cover of the horn-work.

The fire from this battery improved the breach first made, and the explosion of the mine, at 5 o'clock yesterday, effected a second breach. Both were immediately stormed . . . and our troops were established within the exterior line of the works of the castle of Burgos . . .

It was the last good thing he had to report from the place. On the fifth and eighth the French launched sorties from the interior walls against the hold he had on the outer wall. To Beresford, 9 October, 1812: We have a practicable breach in the second line, notwithstanding that all our guns and carriages are what is called destroyed, – and I am now endeavouring to set on fire the magazine of provisions. I cannot venture to storm the breach. We have used such an unconscionable amount of ammunition particularly in two <u>sorties</u> made by the enemy . . . I have sent to the rear and to Santander; and we are making some. But I have not yet heard of any approaching. I fear therefore we must turn our siege into a blockade.

I am sorry to say we lost poor Cocks in the <u>sortie</u> of yesterday morning. He is on every ground the greatest loss we have yet sustained.

To Bathurst: . . . the Hon. Major Cocks . . . was killed in the act of rallying the troops who had been driven in . . .

To Hill: I am sorry to say we lost poor Cocks, which has grieved me much.

At the funeral he looked so overcome no-one dared speak to him. To Lord Somers, 11 October: Your son fell as he had lived, in the zealous and gallant discharge of his duty . . . and I assure your Lordship that if providence had spared him to you, he possessed acquirements and was endowed with qualities to become one of the greatest ornaments of his profession . . .

I have no hope that what I have above stated to your Lordship will at all tend to alleviate your affliction on this melancholy occasion . . . I was highly sensible of the merits of your son, and I most sincerely lament his loss.

I have the honour to be, &c.,

Wellington

Soult was coming out of Andalusia to threaten Hill, the armies of the North and of Portugal, much reinforced, were gathering in his front. On 18 October he launched his last assault, prematurely and with inadequate troops. To Bath- urst, 26 October: Having at that time received a supply of musket ammunition from Santander, and having . . . completed a mine under the church of San Roman, which stood in an outwork of the second line, I determined that the breach . . . should be stormed that evening, at the moment this mine should explode; and that at the same time the line should be attacked by escalade.

The mine succeeded, and Lieut. General Brown lodged a party of the 9th Caçadores and a detachment of Spanish troops . . . in the outwork. A detachment of the King's German Legion under Major Warmb carried the breach, and a detachment of the Guards succeeded in escalading the line; but the enemy brought such a fire on these detachments from the 3rd line and the body of the castle itself, and they were attacked by numbers so superior . . . that they were obliged to retire, suffering considerable loss. Major Warmb was unfortunately killed.

On the twentieth, the French concentrated in front of Monasterio, thirteen miles up the great road to the north-east; and he moved up to join the 1st division, leaving Pack with detailed instructions for the blockade of the castle – but a day later harder news came from the south. To Popham: It seems evident that Soult . . . is about to move on Madrid with the whole of the troops of Valencia and Murcia *plus his own from Andalusia* . . . under these circumstances I propose to raise the siege of Burgos, and withdraw across the Arlanzon.

To Pack, 21 October, 1812, 1.30 p.m.: The troops in the trenches should evacuate the horn work first. They should then evacuate the other part of the trenches . . . Your brigade should be across the bridge before the trenches are evacuated, leaving only the sentries necessary to prevent the enemy from coming out of the castle . . . shortly before 5 o'clock . . . the mines in the horn work must be exploded by an officer, who must be mounted and ride away.

The failed siege of Burgos cost the allies 2,000 casualties.

He made a measured withdrawal as far as Cabezon, eight miles north of Valladolid, which he reached on 27 October without mishap. By then he knew more about the forces opposing him: they were far larger than he had thought possible. In short, from now on he was retreating not to support Hill, but because he had to. To Hill, 27 October, 9.00 p.m.: We halted the day before yesterday at Dueñas, and this day at this place; but the enemy are infinitely superior to us in cavalry, and from what I saw to-day, very superior in infantry. We must, retire, therefore, and the Duero is no barrier for us. If we go, and we cannot hold our ground beyond the Duero, your situation will become delicate . . . it appears to me therefore, to be necessary that you, as well as we, should retire . . .

The problem was this: could he hold up his own retreat for long enough to give Hill time to come via the Escorial to combine with him, or should he advise him to get back into Portugal by the quickest and safest route, along the north bank of the Tagus? It needed seven extra days to give Hill the time he'd need to make the conjunction – and those he managed to provide. It was, though, a near run thing, and not at all helped when a party of Brunswicker Oels set to guard the already destroyed bridge at Tordesillas, allowed themselves to be driven out by a daring detachment of French who swam across the river naked, swords in their mouths, pushing their other weapons and accoutrements on a raft before them. They thus established a bridge head on the southern bank and the possibility of repairing the bridge.

To Beresford, who was still recovering from his wound but at Lisbon now, from Rueda on 31 October: . . . you will see what a scrape we have been in, and how well we have got out of it. I say we have got out of it, because the enemy show no inclination to cross the Duero. I have the army posted on the heights opposite the bridge of Tordesillas, of which they have possession. *Since Busaco the French had never attacked Wellington on heights. It's possible their infantry would refuse to do so, or at any rate those who remembered the rolling volleys, the lines enfolding their flanks. No, they would rather work their way round him, and Wellington had made that as difficult for them as he could.*

The bridge of Toro is destroyed and I hope that of Zamora; and at all events they cannot cross at either before Hill and I shall join . . . I am sorry to find that your wound is not healing as it ought. You must have patience. Poor Alava's was in a bad way this morning, and Gunning (*a surgeon?*) was not to be found. He soon stopped it however, and he is now doing well.

He held the line on the heights between Tordesillas and Rueda for those seven precious days. In a very frank letter to his friend Cooke, written four weeks later from his old quarters at Freneda, he wrote: I ought not to have remained so long at Burgos, and ought to have withdrawn Hill earlier from Madrid . . . I was deceived respecting the numbers in my front in the north. I had no reason to believe that the enemy were so strong till I saw them. Fortunately they did not attack me: if they had I must have been destroyed. *It was one of the rare times his intelligence sources failed him – because of those ciphers?* I ordered Hill to move; and I fairly bullied the French into remaining quiet upon the Douro (*sic*) for seven days in order to give him time to make his march.

One problem during this agonising wait was that it took three days for a letter to get to Hill and an answer back. To Hill, Rueda, 1 November: . . . I have not heard from you since you received my letter of the 27th . . . Have you given the orders about taking up the bridge at Almaraz? That should be done now, particularly if you have passed the Escorial. Send an officer into the valley of the Tagus, to observe the enemy's movements in that quarter . . .

In situations like this Wellington never wasted time pacing up and down, chewing his nails. He simply got on with his letters and often more expansively than usual. A cortes or parliament had been elected to serve at Cadiz in place of the Juntas – it pretended to be a popular assembly and had drawn up a liberal constitution which Wellington was obliged to have read in every town he liberated. Of course he hated it, but his criticisms were always couched in pragmatic rather than ideological terms – he thought it could not work. Compassion as well as pragmatism led him to condemn the Cortes' ruthless treatment of collaborators. His good sense, not to say magnanimity, is never more apparent than when he puts himself in the position of someone who is apparently at fault – a bungling general, or a Spanish magistrate who continued to maintain law and order under the French. To Henry, 1 November: Nothing can be more cruel, absurd, or impolitic than their decrees respecting the persons who have served the enemy. In fact it deprives the state of some of the ablest and most honest of its servants, and submits to enquiry the conduct of persons who have rendered the most important services of a secret and therefore an invidious nature.

It is extraordinary that the revolution in Spain should not have produced one man with any knowledge of the real situation of the country. It really appears as if they were all drunk, and thinking and talking of any other subject but Spain. How it is to end God knows!

And then Russia – where both sides had claimed Borodino (Mojaisk) as a victory. At that distance, and in ignorance of that wiliest of old men Marshal Kutusov and the imminent Russian winter, Wellington can be forgiven for fearing that 1813 would yet see the return of the victorious eagles pouring into Spain. Buonaparte was at Moscow the 19th September. The Emperor of Russia deceived . . . the people of Petersburgh *(sic)*, and pretended that the battle of Mojaisk was in his favour . . . the truth was not known at Petersburgh on the 10th, although Buonaparte was at Moscow and Moscow burnt on the 14th. The French in our front have two reports, one that the Russians are making peace; the other that Buonaparte is marching to Petersburgh.

Things began to move on the fifth. To Hill, 1.00 a.m.: I sent the 5th division of infantry and General Ponsonby's brigade of cavalry, to Alaejos this morning, the enemy having appeared in that quarter from Toro; and I propose to move to-morrow to Nava del Rey. If your troops at Arevalo should have marched . . . we shall be tolerably well connected. *(See map page 202.)*

An hour later he heard from Hill, who was nervous as to how near Soult was to him. Midday: I received about two hours ago your letter of two this morning. *Only nine hours now separated them – a day and-a-half's march for an army.* I think you had better make a movement to-morrow morning, and place your troops behind the Trabancos river, behind Flores de Avila. I propose to place this army behind the same river at Castrejon, Carpio &c.

Do not allow the enemy to come too near you with a small advanced guard. Move upon them immediately, and make them keep at a proper distance.

By 2.00 p.m. on the seventh the position seemed safe. To Hill: I shall take up the position in front of Salamanca to-morrow and you will do well to march in the morning upon Alba de Tormes. Occupy the castle of Alba with 200 men, which I understand commands the bridge effectually . . . *It was like a film re-wound. Wellington's position was to be on the heights of San Christobal, Hill's on the Calvarassa de Arriba ridge. A* P.S. *passes on news from Alicante of the estimated strength of the armies that had marched out of Valencia.* About 20,000 are following you. The King went into Madrid on the third instant, and it was supposed was to remain there . . . I have not heard of the enemy's movement to his right; if so it must be to join the army of Portugal.

Early next morning he reported to Bathurst: The two corps of this army, particularly that which has been in the north, are in want of rest. They have been in the field, and almost constantly marching since the month of January last; their clothes and equipment are much worn, and a short period in cantonments would be very useful to them. The cavalry likewise are weak in numbers, and the horses rather low in condition . . . I should prefer the cantonments on the Tormes to those further in the rear . . . It still remains to be seen what number of troops can be brought to operate against our position . . . I propose therefore to wait . . . till I shall ascertain more exactly the extent of the enemy's force; and if they should move forward I will either bring the contest to a crisis in the position of San Christobal, or fall back on the Agueda.

Not for the first time Wellington had underestimated the numbers the French would concentrate against him, and the sacrifices they were prepared to make in order to do so. On 9 November the first signs of what he and Hill were up against began to appear on the right bank of the Tormes. Remember, he already had the armies of Portugal and the North in his front. To Hill, 2.00 a.m.: . . . the enemy are moving in force on the fords of Huerta and Encinas, and I believe the troops are Soult's . . . Have a good garrison in the castle of Alba . . . If the enemy should attempt to cross either of the fords at Huerta, fall upon the first who cross.

I order my troops to remain at Calvarassa de Arriba in the morning, till I shall see how matters turn.

5.45 p.m.: I have just come in from the front; the enemy have two divisions of infantry and some squadrons of cavalry at Pituegua and Cabeza Vellosa . . . I saw a body of infantry at Morisco, Babilafuente . . . from the baggage . . . I should suppose them to be a division . . . All agree that the fords are not now practicable . . . and the best proof that they are not practicable is that the people of the country have their cattle grazing on the left bank . . . *if they were practicable the French would cross and make off with them* . . . I have never been at Alba *(which finally nails the myth that Goya did the red chalk drawing there on the night of the Battle of Salamanca)*, and shall be very much obliged to you if you will let me know what garrison ought to be in the castle. I should think 200 men . . .

9.30 p.m.: If the enemy can pass the Tormes at too many fords . . . your troops and those at Alba . . . must fall back on the heights of Arapiles.

10 November, 4.30 p.m.: I am sorry that I did not meet you at Alba . . . When I call a ford practicable for troops, I do not mean to say that a single horseman cannot get over; but that cavalry, infantry and artillery cannot. The river has certainly fallen since yesterday evening; but I believe no infantry soldier can get over, even if a cavalry soldier can . . .

And so it went on for four more days – constant anxieties about the fords, about Soult's strength, and, on Wellington's part, a determination not to give up the Tormes in the face of a steadily worsening situation, and the obvious nervousness of Hill. Soult was in touch with further reinforcements, could now put 80,000 in the field against the allies 60,000, yet only very slowly, very cautiously had he begun to move round the allied right, always keeping his distance. He was not going to be caught with an extended left in almost the same place as Marmont.

At about 1.00 p.m. on the fifteenth Wellington wrote to Hill: I have been out all morning, and have only now received your letter of twelve at noon. You must have the motions of the corps which has marched up the river well observed . . . The French have evacuated Madrid on the 7th. I do not yet know where the troops have gone.

An hour later he knew. They had communicated with Soult's left, way out on the allied right, and were threatening his communication with Ciudad Rodrigo. It was time to be off. It looked bad, and felt bad after the glory of Salamanca to be abandoning it four months later – but much had been achieved. Madrid too had been abandoned by the French only a week after they had re-occupied it, and they were never there again except when corps passed through. There was not a French soldier in Andalusia, and none ever went there again either. Joseph wintered first in Valladolid, and then in Valencia.

At two in the afternoon Wellington ordered the retreat, in three columns, to Ciudad Rodrigo, and as he did a sky that had been pitch black for hours opened and torrential rain, that was to make the next four days utterly intolerable, began.

Nothing went right. His Q.M.G. Colonel Gordon routed the supply train wrongly, so the men got no rations for three days. Naturally they plundered, particularly shooting the herds of pigs that wandered in the oak forest outside the villages. Sir Edward Paget, who had returned to command the cavalry in Cotton's continuing absence, got caught in too large a gap between divisions. Since he had lost an arm at Oporto there was little he could do to defend himself. Three generals re-routed one column and got lost.

To Torrens, 6 December, 1812: It is likewise necessary that General Dalhousie should be under the particular charge of somebody, and he wishes to be with Hill . . . on the night after poor Paget was taken, he and certain other general officers commanding divisions (new-comers) held a council of war to decide whether they would obey my orders to march by a particular road. He, at the head, decided he would not . . . *Wellington went to look for them and came across the officer in charge of the baggage.* 'What are you doing, Sir?' *'I've lost my baggage.'* 'Well, I can't be surprised . . . for I cannot find my army.' . . . they marched by a road leading they did not know where, and when I found them in the morning they were in the utmost confusion, not knowing where to go or what to do. This with the enemy close to them, and with the knowledge that, owing to the state of the roads and weather, I felt the greatest anxiety respecting the movement . . . With the utmost zeal, and good intentions and abilities, he cannot obey an order.

Some accounts of the actual confrontation say that a white-faced Wellington said nothing to the generals when he found them, simply got on with sorting out the mess; others that he remarked in a voice like cold steel: 'You see, gentlemen, I know my own business best.'

For the plunderers of pigs:

G.O.   16th Nov., 1812.
1. The Commander of the Forces requests the General Officers commanding divisions will take measures to prevent the shameful and unmilitary practice of soldiers shooting pigs in the woods, so close to the camp and the columns of march as that two dragoons were shot last night; and the Commander of the Forces was induced to believe this day on the march that the flank patrols were skirmishing with the enemy.
2. He desires that notice may be given to the soldiers that he has this day ordered two men to be hanged who were caught in the act of shooting pigs.

To Paget, written on the nineteenth: I did not hear of your misfortune till more than an hour after it had occurred . . . That which must now be done is to endeavour to obtain your exchange . . . I send you some money – 200 *l.* I will take care of your friend Marlay.. You cannot conceive how much I regret your loss . . . but God knows with what pleasure I shall hear of your being liberated, and shall see you with us again. . . .

To Bathurst, Ciudad Rodrigo, 19 November: We continued our march successively on the 16th, 17th and 18th, when part of the army crossed the Agueda, and the whole will cross that river to-morrow, and canton between the Agueda and the Coa . . . The troops have suffered considerably from the severity of the weather: which, since the 13th, has been worse than I have ever known at this season of the year. The soldiers as usual, straggled from their regiments in search of plunder,

251

and I am apprehensive that some may have fallen into the enemy's hands.

To Bathurst, from his familiar quarters at Freneda – how did he feel when he entered them again after such a year of glory and misery? – 25 November; the greater part of the enemy's force which had crossed the Tormes, have retired across that river, and it is reported have directed their march towards the Duero; and it is reported that the King has gone to fix his quarters at Valladolid, and that those of Soult are to be at Sala-manca . . .

Many men who were missing have returned to their regiments; but I am sorry to say that several who had straggled from their regiments, and strayed behind, have died from the extreme severity of the weather and the want of food which they experienced, all the villages having been plundered by the soldiers in hospitals who first passed *(they had been evacuated from Salamanca a week before the general retreat, and probably behaved worse than any),* and abandoned by the inhabitants.

He wrote a notorious epilogue to the retreat from Burgos – a Memorandum to Officers Commanding Divisions and Brigades, dated 28 November. It upset many people, first, because it was read as a blanket condemnation of all, and many units had behaved perfectly; secondly because Gordon's failure to give the Commissariat an accurate route had still been kept from him, and he therefore was not aware of how most of his army had starved for two days; and thirdly because it was leaked to the press in England where the hysterical abuse it provoked was far worse than anything he got from his own army.

The discipline of every army, after a long and active campaign, becomes in some degree relaxed . . . but I am concerned to have to observe that the army under my command has fallen off in this respect in the late campaign to a greater degree than any army with which I have ever served, or of which I have ever read. Yet this army has met with no disaster; it has met with no privations which but for trifling attention on the part of the officers could not have been prevented . . . nor has it suffered any hardships excepting those resulting from the necessity of being exposed to the inclemencies of the weather at a moment when they were most severe.

It must be obvious however to every officer that from the moment the troops commenced their retreat from . . . Burgos . . . and Madrid . . . the officers lost all command over their men. Irregularities and outrages of all descriptions were committed with impunity, and losses were sustained which ought never to have occurred. Yet the necessity for retreat existing none was ever made on which the troops had such short marches; none on which the retreating armies were so little pressed on their rear by the enemy . . .

I have no hesitation in attributing these evils to the habitual inattention of the Officers of the regiments to their duties, as prescribed by the standing regulations of the Service, and by orders of this army . . .

He goes on to suggest remedies – it is by no means an entirely negative document.

These then are the points to which I most earnestly intreat you to turn your attention . . . The Commanding officers of regiments must enforce the orders of the army regarding the constant inspection and superintendance of the officers of the conduct of the men . . . ; and they must endeavour to inspire the non-commissioned officers with a sense of their situation and authority . . .

(They) must likewise enforce the orders of the army regarding the constant, real inspection of the soldiers' arms, ammunition, accoutrements, and necessaries in order to prevent at all times the shameful waste of ammunition, and the sale of that article and of the soldiers' necessaries. With this view both should be inspected daily.

In regard to the food of the soldier, I have frequently observed and lamented . . . the facility and celerity with which the French soldiers cooked in comparison with those of our army.

The cause of this disadvantage is the same with that of every other description, the want of attention of the Officers to the orders of the army . . . Certain men of each company should be appointed to cut and bring in wood, others to fetch water and others to get the meat &c. to be cooked . . .

You will of course give your attention to the field exercises and discipline of the troops. It is very desirable that the troops should not lose the habits of marching . . .

But I repeat the great object of the attention of the General and Field Officers must be to get the Captains and Subalterns to understand and perform the duties required for them.

And the fourth reason why this document caused such distress must now be apparent. This time not a mention of the 'scum of the earth', oh dear me no. It's actually the officers who are at fault, and the upper classes back home found that very difficult to accept.

1813

(NOVEMBER 1812–JUNE 1813)

———❦———

INTERLUDE

CADIZ

FAREWELL TO PORTUGAL

IN FORTUNE'S WAY

VITORIA

———❦———

INTERLUDE

On 22 November Wellington wrote two letters to Henry.

Sir,   Ciudad Rodrigo, 22 Nov., 1812.
I have the honor to enclose the copy of a dispatch which I have received from the Secretary of State, from which I understand that His Royal Highness the Prince Regent approves of my acceptance of the command of the Spanish armies.

I request you therefore to signify this approbation to the Spanish Government, and to request them to signify to me their pleasure respecting the period at which I shall take upon myself the command.

I have the honor to be, &c.,

                                         Wellington

My Dear Henry,
If matters remain quiet, I think I should do some good by going to Cadiz for a little while, and I have some thoughts of going there. Let me know as soon as you can, whether you could send any tiros from Cadiz to meet me at Badajoz or Merida, and on the road from those places, to draw my carriage. This would greatly facilitate my journey. Do not mention to any body that I have thoughts of going to Cadiz.

Ever yours most affectionately,

                                         Wellington

The main purpose of the trip to Cadiz was of course to assert his new authority over the Spanish military, both its training and supply systems, and of course its generals. But a carriage!? He had ordered a landau from England some months earlier – had it been pointed out to him that he was the only Commander in Europe who rode everywhere, always? Did he feel the Spaniards would expect it of their new 'Capitan General'? Or was it perhaps that after all the man of iron was a little tired and, in the cold and wet, susceptible to lumbago?

Nearly three weeks were to elapse before he set off, and the routine concerns of an army in cantonments reasserted themselves.

G.O.   Freneda, 25th Nov., 1812.
4. The Commander of the Forces has taken the precaution of having

the grass mowed and saved as hay in many parts of the country in which the troops are now or may be cantoned, which resource is ample for all the food for all the animals of the army during the winter, if only taken care of and distributed under the regulations of the Service.

To Peacocke, 1 December, 1812: It has been stated to me that the horses of the Life Guards have landed at Lisbon in very bad condition; and . . . that the men have come unprovided with currycombs and brushes . . . *By now the reader will guess the rest.*

The 'second in command' situation refused to go away. To Beresford, 2 December: I have always felt the inutility and inconvenience of the office of second in command. It has a great and high-sounding title, without duties or responsibility of any description; at the same time that it gives pretensions, the assertion of which are, and I believe you know I found them in one instance to be, very inconvenient. Every officer in an army should have some duty to perform, for which he is responsible; and I understand a General Officer commanding a division or larger body of troops to be in this situation. The second in command none that any body can define; excepting to give opinions for which he is in no manner responsible, and which I have found one at least most ready to relinquish, when he found they were not liked in England.

To Bathurst, same day: You'll see from a dispatch which I send you from Sir William Beresford that he is not in a very good temper, and I hinted in the summer what was the cause. I have received a private letter from him . . . written in much more angry terms . . . I don't know how you will settle this question. All that I can tell you is that the ablest man I have yet seen with the army, and that one having the largest views, is Beresford.

They tell me that when I am not present, he wants decision; and he certainly embarrassed me a little with his doubts when he commanded in Estramadura; but I am quite certain that he is the only person capable of conducting a large concern.

What about Hill, you may ask, who at Arroyo de Molinos and Almaraz had most certainly not wanted decision. The answer lies in 'largest views' and 'large concern'. Wellington knew only too well that his successor, if the worst should happen, would have to be somebody who could handle the Portuguese and Spanish governments, as well as their combined armies – somebody who could take a view so large that it encompassed everything from the relevance of what was happening in Russia to the supply of currycombs and brushes. Beresford, who had built up the Portuguese army from nothing into a military machine as good as the British or French and had cajoled and threatened the weak-willed and intrigue-ridden Portuguese Regency into continuing to support him over three and a half years, was the only man of large views around.

Another old problem raised its ugly head as soon as the campaign was over – the constant change of officers in charge of every important department – *and it drew the full rolling volley directed at the Horse Guards via Colonel Torrens.* No man can be aware of the extent of this inconvenience who has not got this great machine to keep in order and direct . . . No sooner is an arrangement made, the order given, and the whole in a train of execution, than a gentleman comes out who has probably but little knowledge of the practical part of his duty in any country, and none whatever in this most difficult of all scenes of military operation. Nobody in the British army ever reads a regulation or an order as if it were to be a guide to his conduct, or in any other manner than as an amusing novel; and the consequence is, that when complicated arrangements are to be carried into execution (and in this country the poverty of its resources renders them all complicated), every gentleman proceeds according to his fancy; and then, when it is found that the arrangement fails (as it must fail if the order is not strictly obeyed), they come upon me to set matters to rights, and thus my labor is increased ten fold.

Suppressing momentary pique at this slur on amusing novels, one admits to knowing what he means.

This 'crusty' mood, perhaps the sign of a convalescent getting over a very nasty turn indeed, continues. Poor Daddy Hill is in the firing line this time. 8 December, 1812, 4.00 p.m.: I was in hopes I had put your troops in a plentiful country. I know that part of it had supplied the consumption of Marmont's army last year from July to December, and that in this year they had not a single soldier near them . . . I knew there was plenty of barley in this year . . . all that I can say is, that I placed the army in cantonments for its convenience, in order that the horses might recover their condition, and the men their discipline, and it is nearly a matter of indifference to me where they are cantoned . . . *He then describes how his part of the army are managing well enough in a poorer area, and crushingly concludes:* But I must do the General Officers of the cavalry the justice to say that they are desirous of overcoming, and not of making difficulties.

Another letter, next day, also 4.00 p.m. – just after dinner so perhaps dyspepsia lay behind it all, was almost as sharp.

On the tenth his mood improved, or he was writing before dinner. To Beresford: Matters being quiet here, and having put everything in train for the re-equipment of the army, I am about to go to Cadiz to see what I can do there . . .

I propose to get into fortune's way if I should be able to assemble an army sufficiently strong; and we may make a lucky hit in the commencement of the next campaign. *This is the first hint that he had already worked out in outline the consummate strategy of 1813. As with Torres Vedras, when he so quickly learnt the lessons of 1809, so now both the successes and failures of 1812 had already produced in his mind what he would do in 1813. Only to Beresford was he ever so open; but even with him, on paper at least, never specific.*

I am quite convinced that some of the crustiness of the previous week or so, came not from dyspepsia, and not only from reaction to the events of October and November, but also because his strategy for the next campaign had come to him with the suddenness and completeness that characterises all ideas touched with genius. At such a moment a commander's generals may find themselves bemused by a suddenly pre-occupied and irritable commander.

His letter concludes: But it is obvious that we cannot expect to save the Peninsula by military efforts, unless we can bring forward the Spaniards in some shape or other, and I want to see how far I can venture to go, in putting the Spanish army in a state to do something. In your life you never saw any thing so bad as the Galicians. Yet they are the finest body of men and best movers I have ever seen.

God knows the prospect of success from this journey of mine is not bright; but still it is best to try something.

To Henry, Freneda, 11 December, 1812: I propose to leave this place tomorrow morning, and to sleep at Moraleja . . . 17th at Seville; 18th at Cadiz.

Possibly you may find it convenient to meet us at Seville, as we shall have many things to talk over . . . I bring no body with me excepting Alava and Lord Fitzroy Somerset.

To Colonel De Lancey, who was now acting Q.M.G., 14 December: We were detained at Payo by the swelling of the rivulet in the Puerto de Perales . . . I cannot now arrive at Seville till the 18th. But the lumbago is not worse.

Acting Q.M.G.? Yes. To Vice Admiral Martin, 10 December: Colonel Gordon, the Quarter Master General has requested me to apply to you to facilitate his return to England in a ship of war. *He was generous to Gordon, as he always was to failures who had done their best. To Torrens, from Badajoz, 20 December:* . . . notwithstanding his zeal and his acknowledged talents, he has never in fact performed his duties and I do not believe he ever can or will perform them . . . At the same time I am anxious that Colonel Gordon should not be mortified . . . in consequence of my opinion of his want of qualifications for his office. If he is wise he will not return, as he must feel what is notorious to the whole army. Besides which his health and the habits of his life render him in some degree incapable of performing the active and laborious duties of his office in the field.

To Gordon, 31 January, 1813: . . . The truth is, that your health is, if possible, too robust; and I was frequently apprehensive that you would have had fever in the hot weather. Indeed, it was probable that you were saved only by the painful disorder which at last obliged you to go home. I sincerely hope that you may soon recover.

I beg to take this opportunity of returning you many thanks for the assistance you gave me while with this army; and wishing you success.

And that's the last word on the retreat from Salamanca to the Agueda – a general or so sent home; one put in the care of someone reliable; a bad Q.M.G. retired tactfully on account of his health; and a couple of fine fellows hanged for shooting pigs. By modern standards it is not harsh. But one can't help regretting the hangings – and blaming Gordon's failure with the Commissariat for them.

Let's put all that behind us. Wellington had. He concluded his letter to Torrens: I am going to Cadiz to endeavour to make some arrangement of the Spanish army . . .

CADIZ

Cadiz welcomed him as a hero. They dragged his landau through the cheering crowds, fêted him with balls, receptions, theatres. And everywhere there was a band, and even where there was not, they played and sang the hit 'jota' of the season, which, freely translated, can come out something like this:

> Hey there, Marmont, where are you off to?
> Hey there, Marmont, where are you going?
> Wellington said to Marmont, Come and eat with me:
> I've dressed at Arapiles a dish for two or three!
> The Frenchman brought his friends, but neither three nor two
> Had stomach for my Lord's tomato stew:
> Perforce they had to scarper, and tell Napoleon –
> So long life to our nation, and the same to Wellington!

Wellington was not at all averse to this sort of thing, and for some time after was not above asking the band to play 'Ahe Marmon'.

He was quickly down to serious business. To Don J. de Carvajal, Minister of War, Cadiz, 25 December, 1812 (not for the first time did he work on Christmas Day, which of course had not then been Germanised into the mess it is today): The Government and Cortes have done me much honor to confer upon me the command of the Spanish armies . . . It is impossible to perform these duties as they ought to be performed, unless I shall possess sufficient powers . . . First; that officers should be promoted and should be appointed to commands solely at my recommendation . . . *which was pushing things a bit, right at the start: the Horse Guards never allowed him these powers with British troops;* Secondly; I require that I should have the power of dismissing from the service those whom I should think deserving of such punishment. Thirdly, I require that the resources of the state which are applicable to the payment or equipment, or supply of the troops, should be applied in such manner as I might recommend . . .

A formal address to the Spanish army, dated 1 January, 1813, is full of good resolutions: . . . without discipline and good order, not only is an army unfit to be opposed to an enemy in the field, but it becomes a positive injury to the country by which it is maintained . . . The Commander in Chief assures the General and other Officers . . . that at the same time that he will be happy to draw the notice of Government, and to extol their good conduct, he will not be backward in noticing any inattention on the part of the officers of the army to the duties required from them . . . or any breach of discipline and order by the soldiers.

Other problems caught up with him at Cadiz. Castlereagh's half brother Charles Stewart was officially Adjutant General, but had been away for some time. He now wanted to return, but to command a cavalry brigade. Unfortunately, as Wellington had earlier pointed out to Torrens, he labours under two bodily defects, the want of sight and of hearing. *Nevertheless he had to be handled with tact. Wellington explained how the cavalry was to be re-organised into one corps under the sole command of Cotton, from which detachments would be made as necessary, that there could therefore be no independent command of a division or brigade as such. No doubt with relief he was able to conclude:* Under these circumstances, although it might be more agreeable to you to take a gallop with the Hussars, I think you had better return to your office. *He goes on:* I have made some progress; but the libellers have set to work, and I am apprehensive that the Cortes will take the alarm, and that I shall not be able to do all the good I might otherwise.

He left on the tenth but paused at Jerez to send off a last flurry of advice, instructions and requests to Carvajal, which end thus: I have to apologise for having written you several dispatches this day in the English language, and on paper of a small size, but none of the Staff are with me at present, and I have with me no paper of a large size; and I hope your Excellency and the Government will excuse me.

Charles Stuart, the Minister at Lisbon, had got his K.B. and had been badgering Wellington to come to Lisbon to invest him. Rather grumpily the Peer agreed to do it on the way back. 14 January, 1813, Estremoz: I should wish to invest you, as usual, before dinner; there should be many of the principal people present, who should be invited to dinner, and there should be a ball and supper in the evening, to which all society should be invited. I hope that, for all this, you will have given the preparatory orders . . . as I think there are symptoms of the enemy's moving, I cannot stay at Lisbon one day after I have invested you with the Order.

To Bathurst, Lisbon, 18 January: Having been travelling constantly from the tenth to the sixteenth, and feasting ever since, I cannot transmit by this mail an account of affairs at Cadiz . . .

The grumpiness continues – and again I feel it is not unconnected with his preoccupation with his grand strategy for the coming campaign. A hint that this is so lies in the fact that following news of Napoleon's retreat from Moscow he sent a special envoy of his own to the Austrian Emperor to inform him of . . . my expectation that I should at least be able to give employment to between 150,000 and 200,000 French troops in the next campaign. *Most of Europe at this time was striving to separate the Emperor from his yet more imperial son-in-law.*

But grumpy he remained: a long letter to Torrens written on the way back on the subject of what was to be done about incompetent officers ends: What a situation then is mine! It is impossible to prevent incapable men from being sent to the army; and when I claim that they are sent, I am to be responsible. Surely the responsibility or odium for the removal of such persons ought not to attach to the person to whom it belongs officially to represent that they are not capable of filling their stations.

And to Beresford, now that he is back in Freneda, 26 January: I have to mention to you that I found the road from Castello Branco to Alpehindra . . . absolutely impracticable for wheel carriages; and I was informed its state was owing to the neglect of the magistrates in repairing it . . . I beg leave to recommend that the Camera of Alpehindra may be called before the Special Commission to answer for this neglect. Generally speaking the roads throughout Portugal are in a very bad state . . . which is to be attributed very much to the practice of throwing the stones from the walls on each side of the road, from whence they are never removed.

Of course the continuing bad temper may now have been the result of his experiences in Cadiz, particularly of the Cortes, the 1812 Constitution, and the press. His report to Bathurst, 27 January: I got on tolerably well till unfortunately the trumpet of alarm was sounded in a libel in one of the daily newspapers, respecting the danger to be apprehended from the union of powers in the hands of military officers at the suggestion of a foreigner; and then I could get the Cortes to do nothing more than you will see in their decree of the 7th instant. It appears to me, however, that this decree goes sufficiently far to enable me to act . . . and if the system should fail, the responsibility will rest with them, and I have given them to understand that I shall take care to let Spain and the world know why it has failed.

I trust, however, that it will not fail; and that I shall still be able to place in the hands of the generals of the Spanish armies those powers which must secure the resources of the country for their troops.

It is impossible to describe the state of confusion in which affairs are at Cadiz. The Cortes have formed a constitution very much on the principle that a painter paints a picture, viz., to be looked at . . . The Cortes have divested themselves of the executive power, and have appointed a Regency for this purpose. This Regency are in fact the slaves of the Cortes; yet Cortes and Regency have so managed their concerns as that they have no communication or contact . . . neither knows what the other is doing, or what will be done on any point that can occur. Neither Regency or Cortes have any authority beyond the walls of Cadiz; and I doubt if the Regency have any beyond the walls of the room in which they meet . . . The Regency suspect that the Cortes intend to assume the executive power; and the Cortes are so far suspicious of the Regency, that although the leading members admit . . . the necessity of their removal from Cadiz, the principal reason alleged for remaining there is that they know the people of Cadiz are attached to them; but that if they were to go elsewhere, to Seville or Granada for instance, they are apprehensive that the Regency would raise the mob against them!!!

I wish that some of our reformers would go to Cadiz to see the benefit of a sovereign popular assembly, calling itself 'Majesty', and of a written constitution; and of an executive Government called 'Highness' acting under the control of 'His Majesty' the assembly! In truth there is no authority in the state, excepting the libellous newspapers, and they certainly ride over both Cortes and Regency without mercy . . .

It appears to me, however, that we must not allow these people to go to ruin as they are doing . . . I propose to try if I cannot prevail upon some of the leaders to propose an alteration to the Constitution, so as to connect the legislative assembly with the executive government, as our House of Parliament are, by the Ministers of the Crown being members.

To Henry, 28 January: . . . our shirts being at the wash, <u>as usual</u>, we did not leave Lisbon till the 20th . . .

FAREWELL TO PORTUGAL

To Lieut. General Sir T. Graham, K.B.

My Dear Sir   Freneda, 31st January, 1813.

I was happy to learn from Lord Fitzroy Somerset that you were able to return to us; and I hope that we shall make a good campaign of it.

Affairs are exactly in the state in which they were at the end of November . . .

I propose to take the field as early as I can, and, at least, to put myself in Fortune's way.

Many of the regiments are already very healthy; others, particularly the newcomers, remarkably otherwise. We have, as usual lost many men in the last two months of cold weather; but the troops are all well cantoned; and I hope that a continuation of rest for a month or two in the spring will set us up entirely . . . I think I shall have 40,000 British and possibly 25,000 Portuguese; and I shall be better equipped in artillery, and much stronger in cavalry than we have yet been.

I have been at Cadiz, where I have placed military affairs on a better footing than they were in the way of organization; and I have provided some means to pay and subsist the armies; and we are beginning with discipline. I am not sanguine enough, however, to hope that we shall derive much advantage from Spanish troops early in the campaign . . .

I believe that, upon your arrival, you had better direct your steps towards this village, which we have made as comfortable as we can, and where we shall be happy to see you. The hounds are in very good trim, and the foxes very plentiful.

Believe me, &c.,

Wellington

Another good old man had already arrived in Ciudad Rodrigo, before Wellington's return from Cadiz. The Reverend Dr Curtis to General the Marquess of Wellington:

The entrance of the French troops into Salamanca on the 15th November last was peculiarly marked with examples of barbarity and plunder, of which all those whom they looked upon as ill-disposed towards them or their cause became victims, in which number of course I was included; and about a month after, an order of banishment was issued . . . in consequence of which I was obliged to quit that city, and, by a long detour, to seek for an asylum in this place under your Excellency's protection . . .

He went on to explain how the French were destroying the fabric of the Irish College, how he had secreted all over Salamanca the College Library which he hoped one day would be passed on to the Irish Roman Catholic National College of Maynooth, how the Irish Church had lost the revenue that went with the College, and that he thought this would be a charge on the Spanish government. Finally:

My wants are few; but as I have nothing, I expect that after my long services . . . the Spanish Government will allow me some part at least of my stipend as Rector of the Irish College and Professor of Salamanca University . . . of which I neither received nor demanded anything these last seven years . . . I only demand . . . just so much . . . that I may not in my old age be exposed to want, or become a burthen to my friends and relatives.

To Curtis, 26 January: If you will do me the favor of coming over here some day, General O'Lalor tells me he will lodge you; and I shall be happy to see you at dinner . . .

To Curtis, 2 February: When you think it proper to go to Cadiz to present yourself to the Government I will recommend you to their notice and attention . . . and when you go to Ireland, I shall be happy to give you letters of introduction and recommendation to the principal persons there . . .

The first of these was written to the Spanish Minister of Grace and Justice on 22 February.

266

Preparations for the spring were under way and as usual Wellington concerned himself with every detail. Should portable forges be carried on mules, in carts, or on horses? Mules were best but should be bought not hired, for hiring meant employing the muleteer as well. I should think that the business of saddling and loading a mule with a forge is not a trade of such intricacy that our dragoons cannot learn it; and if pains are taken to teach it to them, and care is taken that they do as they are taught, that they take care of these mules, and above all do not load them with women, and with baggage besides forges, I shall not be under the necessity of giving up this useful establishment in order to resume the forge-cart.

In fact there is more to all this than one might think. The grand strategy of 1813 turned upon his ability to use unmapped roads and mountain tracks which even then, way up in Tras os Montes and even the Asturian mountains, officers from the appropriate departments were mapping, sketching and preparing detailed reports on. Any arrangement which cut down the amount of wheeled vehicles needed was a good one.

On a larger scale he was forced to lift a corner of his grand design. To Bathurst, 10 February: As it is possible that the events of the next campaign may render it necessary for the army to undertake one or more sieges in the north of Spain . . . I beg leave to recommend that the ordnance and stores contained in the enclosed lists should be embarked at Alicante in transports and sent to Coruña . . .

At last it seemed the vexed business of who should be interim successor and soi-disant second in command was sorted out by the expedient of persuading Graham to waive his claim. If the oldest and most senior of the Lieutenant Generals agreed that Beresford should have the coveted position then Cotton and Hill must fall in line. To Beresford, 12 February: I received yesterday a letter from Lord Bathurst, from which I judge that every thing in regard to your situation in this country has been settled to your satisfaction, by the consent of Sir Thomas Graham.

But no! Beresford was not yet happy – he was proud, slightly touchy in a society which already had begun to look on bastardy with proto-Victorian eyes, and he still did not have the peerage he knew he deserved.

This time Wellington was forced to be sharp, and, I am afraid, devious. To Beresford, 16 February: I enclose you an extract of Lord Bathurst's letter regarding the command, from which you will see the business is settled as you supposed it would be. However, being settled, I do not conceive that it is any business of yours to inquire in what manner, or on what principles.

As far as I have any knowledge of the sentiments of the King's Ministers, I believe them to be well disposed towards you; and the omission to which you advert, unaccountable as it is, must be attributed to that kind of negligent, slovenly mode of doing business, which is too common among public men in England.

Now this is clearly calculated to say 'you and I are military men and a cut above politicians', but if the 'omission' is the failure to give Beresford a peerage, then it is also a fib, and one can see why Beresford got only a copied extract of Bathurst's letter, the complete version of which ends: 'If we carry this question of command for Sir William Beresford, that will perhaps for the present satisfy him. Do you know of any mark of favour (not a peerage) which he would look to and receive with satisfaction?'

And that really is the end of that tedious little saga, though one should perhaps add that Graham, Cotton, Hill and Beresford got their peerages in 1814.

On the twentieth the first shots of the year were fired at Béjar where Hill's outposts guarded the main pass between Castille and the south. It's a lovely little town, a spa, with acacia-lined streets. To Bathurst, 24 February: . . . and on the morning of the 20th, a body of about 1500 infantry and 100 cavalry, under the command of the General de division, Foy, endeavoured to surprise the post at Béjar . . . The surprise did not succeed; and the enemy were repulsed with loss.

A good start to the year.

Much remained to be done.

To Bathurst, 24 February: It is desirable that 20,000 sets of black accoutrements should be sent to Lisbon as soon as may be convenient for the use of the Spanish army . . . *To distinguish those who were to march in British uniforms with Wellington's army* . . . I likewise request your Lordship to send out horse appointments to Lisbon for 4000 cavalry for the Spanish army in addition to the 4000 already arrived at Coruña . . .

Treasury bills were being redeemed for guineas, a novel coin in Spain. Some difficulty, however, has occurred in circulating guineas in Spain . . . and I shall be much obliged to you if you will request the Spanish Government to issue a proclamation to authorise the circulation of guineas in Spain at the rate of four dollars and four-sixths of a dollar, or at ninety-three reales twelve maravedis. *Would Hill have been able to cope with this sort of thing? Cotton? Graham even? But Beresford, yes.*

For an army that was preparing to make long marches over difficult country the advantages of the tin kettle were now obvious. The old iron one held sixteen helpings, but took a long time to heat up, had to be carried on a mule and often got separated from the men it was supposed to serve.

G.O.   Freneda, 1st March, 1813.

1. The Commanding Officers of regiments of infantry are immediately to make requisitions on the Commissariat . . . for tin camp kettles, to be substituted for the iron camp kettles . . .

2. The numbers are to be one for every six non-commissioned officers and soldiers . . . the kettle of each mess is to be carried on a march alternately by the men of the mess instead of on a mule as heretofore . . .

There is a delightful description in Kincaid's Random Shots of one of these messes at the end of a long day's march. First a fire would be built from the twigs and branches of the park-like oak forest, over which the kettle, a stew-pot really, would be suspended from a tripod of ram-rods. Then, beside it, two small trenches would be dug a yard or so apart so the men could sit facing each other as at a table. The sharpest shooter would go out under the oaks, through the wild lavender and thyme, to bag a rabbit or a brace of red-legged partridges to add to the pot or grill on the ends of bayonets. Soon the canteens of wine, a pint per man, and the bread, pure white, dense, with a powdery crumb and a teeth-shattering crust if they were still on the Campo, would be brought round. Both wine and bread are the best in the world for the price in Charro country. And if it was late, and the night still, candles would be set in the rings of bayonets stuck in the middle of the 'table' . . .

And the mules that had carried the iron kettles?

6. It is the intention of the Commander of the Forces that the mules hitherto provided . . . for the carriage of camp kettles shall hereafter be applied to the carriage of tents for the non-commissioned officers and soldiers . . .

9. Whatever may be the strength of a company, the mule provided by the Captain is to carry three tents, with their poles, pins, &c., . . . for the purpose, however, only of giving cover to the non-commissioned officers and soldiers.

10. The mule provided to carry the tents for the soldiers must be employed solely on that service, according to the orders heretofore issued in regard to camp-kettle mules. *Not for ladies, not for officers' baggage.*

From now on the men would eat every day, cook as quickly as the French, sleep under cover, and all this without adding to the amount of wheeled vehicles.

The Stewart problem hung on. No doubt the Adjutant General sensed victories ahead and a good time for the cavalry in particular, and he put pressure on through mutual friends. The trouble was, he had to be handled with tact – there was nothing to be gained by feuding with a bunch of Grandees like the

Castlereaghs' and their connections. To E. Cooke, Esquire, 16 March: Charles Stewart has unfortunately a defect of sight and another of hearing, both acquired by a wound . . . which in my opinion render him quite incapable of managing a large body of cavalry in front of the enemy in the field.

Our cavalry is the most delicate instrument in our whole machine. *This repeated use of the machine metaphor must be one of the first examples of what was to become the hegemonic classes' favourite way of describing almost everything from the workings of government to those of the brain, and has only been replaced a hundred and sixty years later by the computer metaphor. It shows what a thoroughly modern man Wellington was.* Well managed, it can perform wonders, and will always be of use, but it is easily put out of order in the field . . . if any serious accident were to happen to a large body . . . while we should be forward in the plains, we are gone, and with us our political system, our allies, &c., &c . . . The General Officer of a brigade or division of cavalry must have his eyes and ears about him . . .

Stewart, and the Horse Guards at last got the message. On 10 April Wellington heard that the Foreign Secretary's half brother had accepted the post of Ambassador to the King of Prussia, and on the twenty-fifth the whole matter was settled amicably. So Stewart's effects in Portugal had to be disposed of. To Stewart: I have sent to buy two of your horses for £400; and I believe Wood is to send me the hounds . . . I am besides indebted to you for a mare . . . which I have been keeping up for you, and she is now in excellent condition. Wood says you intended to give her to me; but I say all officers of dragoons are horse dealers, and that I cannot take her from you.

One of these horses had been dropped by a mare who had actually been on the Copenhagen expedition. The foal was named . . . Copenhagen. Wellington rode him through much of the coming campaign, in 1814, and, of course, at Waterloo. The soldiers learned to keep away from his hind-quarters – he kicked out. And years later – he lived to be over thirty – he still neighed at the sight of a red-coat.

Lower down the social scale, but still no doubt in the same class, if not the same caste, the young gentlemen were getting themselves, and others, into trouble. To Cole, 19 March: The Mother of the lady carried off by Lieutenant Kelly . . . having complained to me of his conduct, and having desired my assistance to remove her daughter from the disgraceful situation in which she is now placed, I consented to grant it, on the condition of a promise on her part, that the daughter should not be ill-treated, and, above all, should not be confined in a convent . . . I beg that you will call upon Lieutenant Kelly to restore the young lady to her family. If he should decline to do so upon your order, I beg you to put him in close arrest . . .

Kelly, however, was resourceful, and not merely a seducer. He and his lady were married by a Portuguese army Chaplain and that was that.

An uglier side of this period was the continuing stream of Courts Martial following the retreat of November. Wellington was convinced that brutal punishment acted as a deterrent which was why regiments were always paraded to witness floggings and hangings. Again and again he disclaimed any belief in punishment as retribution. He was also deeply aware of the inhumanity of the whole business, seeing it as an ugly necessity, and again and again he protested at the time the trials took and the time that thus elapsed between crime and punishment. Effectually, on 11 April, he put a stop to it all. If the execution of the sentence be postponed, and the man be allowed to return to his duty, a military irregularity is committed. No soldier should be put on duty having hanging over him the sentence of a Court Martial.

I recommend that all men whose punishment has been postponed may be pardoned; and that the practice of postponing punishment may be discontinued in future.

In spite of the steady progress of the Provost Marshal and the Judge Advocate through each of the offending regiments, in spite of the hardship of training and route-marches, in spite of all the day to day grind of pulling the army together again, there were good times too. In fact all the memoirs and diaries, whether of officers or men, agree that this winter was a good one. Some, writing from the middle of the nineteenth century or even later look back on it with nostalgia, as to a golden age, almost one of innocence. As indeed in a way it was – compared to the Britain of the industrial revolution, or compared to soldiering in the Crimea or India in the 1850s.

Here is Green again, now a servant to a Captain in his regiment who had been seconded temporarily to the Staff.

Lord Wellington and his staff officers used to hunt during the winter season; and on one occasion the hounds started a large wolf, which was hunted several miles: at length he got into a large hole and thus escaped. Another day a wild cat was started, and the hounds with difficulty succeeded in taking her . . .

The fifth of January being the anniversary of the taking of Rodrigo . . . [*not actually, but of the investment*] . . . there was to be a great ball given in honour of that memorable event . . . After dinner, the servants and several of the Spaniards danced what is called the fandango, one of the most obscene and immodest dances that

271

possibly can be: they have two wooden rattles, with which they beat time: this is the favourite dance of the Spaniards and Portuguese.

In spite of more than one biographer's attempts to have it otherwise, Wellington was then, of course, in Cadiz – perhaps, like Monty, he had his double. But he would have been back for Carnival, celebrated notably at Ciudad Rodrigo, with Charro dancing to fife and rattled drum, the ladies in heavy black dresses embroidered with silver buttons turning, in more stately fashion than the fandango allows, to rustic, less gypsy rhythms. There were bull-fights too – against 'becerros', young bulls, in rings improvised from whatever farmcarts the army had not requisitioned; and the local majos, with perhaps the odd Connaught Ranger, had a go.

The Light division put on 'The Rivals' with drummer boys playing the ladies' parts, and every regimental band was as good at quadrilles, two steps, and even waltzes as they were at marches. Again, and one is not quite sure whether to raise an eyebrow or not, drummer boys and the younger ensigns were dragooned into taking the ladies' side of the dances. I've not actually been able to find out whether or not they dressed the part.

One gathering Wellington did attend at Ciudad Rodrigo occurred early in March. To Cole, Freneda, 7 March, 1812: . . . you are made a Knight of the Bath . . . The box containing the insignia is here, and I will invest you with them with the greatest satisfaction on any day you will come over here.

We are not very roomy at Freneda . . . I am not quite certain that it would not be best to adjourn head quarters to Ciudad Rodrigo for the occasion.

Back to those all important details.

G.O.   Freneda, 25th April, 1813.
12. As the English and German infantry of the army will be provided with tents during the ensuing campaign . . . the great coats of the soldiers should be left behind, in order to relieve them from a part of the weight which they would otherwise be obliged to carry, and that they should carry only their blankets. *There were long, swift marches ahead.*
19. . . . the officers commanding regiments should have the corners and outside selvage of the soldiers' blankets strengthened, in order that the soldiers may pitch them, without injury to the blankets, in case it should . . . be necessary in order to shelter them from the sun. *Did Julius Caesar know what a selvage is? Marlborough? Earl Haig? Eisenhower?*

Peninsula muleteers were important people. They lived in clans, were clannish, ran their mule-trains up and down the sierras and across the plains

from one end of Iberia to the other, and most good mules in both countries belonged to them. They worked for hire, to the highest bidder, and never sold their beasts. Wellington discovered he was competing for their services with . . .
To Bathurst, 30 March: I must also inform your Lordship that our debts to the muleteers attached to this army are becoming a very serious evil. There was lately a desertion . . . produced, I believe, in a great measure, by the <u>sharks,</u> called British merchants, residing in Lisbon . . . who are ready to do anything to gain a little by the public distresses. In proportion as the success of the army may clear the country of the enemy's troops, and the inland traffic will revive, we must expect the desertion of this class of people, unless we can pay them a part of what we owe them . . .

Throughout the winter he hoped to move on the 1 May: not earlier, because he was heading north, moving ahead of his supply trains, and so would require the green forage of spring to feed his horses and cattle. In the same letter he still hoped . . . to take the field in the first week of May, *but a week later things were looking more doubtful.* We have not yet had the rain which usually falls at the period of the equinox; and there is as yet no appearance of grass. *And now, in the same letter, we get the first reference to what was to be a recurring worry throughout the summer and early autumn. The keystone of his strategy was British control of the sea, particularly on the north coast ports, from which he would be supplied once he was past Burgos.* I am sorry to say we have had some privateers on the coast, which have taken and destroyed some ships off Oporto, and others are missing . . . I cannot express how much we will be distressed if the navigation of the coast should not be secure from Coruña, at least, to Cadiz . . . the loss of one vessel only may create a delay and inconvenience which may be of the utmost consequence. *That 'at least' is significant, for really he has his eye on Santander, Bilbao, and Pasages.*

What then was the grand design? On St George's Day (also the birthday of Cervantes) he began to take the wraps off – but still with an almost arch coyness.
To Graham: I have just heard of your arrival at Lisbon on the 20th instant . . . I propose to move as soon as I can after the beginning of the month, and rather think, between ourselves, I shall direct my march across the Lower Duero, within the Kingdom of Portugal.

And to Beresford on the next day: . . . I am likewise much obliged to you for the artificers and pontoniers *(important ingredients, as we shall shortly see).* I am glad to find you are coming up. I propose to put the troops in motion in the first days of May. My intention is to make them cross the Douro in general within the Portuguese frontier, covering the movement of the left by the right of the army towards the Tormes, which right shall cross the Douro, over the pontoons . . . I then propose to seize Zamora and Toro, which will make all future operations easy to us . . .

To Admiral G. Martin, 28 April, 1813: I hope that in a few days we shall commence our operations, and I think it is not impossible that we may hereafter have to communicate with the shipping in one of the ports in the North of Spain. Under these circumstances, the communication along the coast becomes of the utmost importance, and I acknowledge I feel a little anxious upon the subject, adverting to the weakness of the squadron under your command, and that you have to attend to the southern coast and Cadiz, as well as to Lisbon and the western coast . . .

Sir G. Collier is now at Coruña with the Surveillante, and, I believe, two other frigates, and he is destined to cruize *(sic)* off the northern coast during the summer. I have now recommended him to take his station between Santona and Bayonne *note how far east this is* and to prevent the enemy from communicating along the coast by sea; but if you cannot get any reinforcement from England, I shall apply to him to station one of his frigates off Cape Finisterre.

And there you have it. He had learnt from 1812 that the French in retreat would stop at each river – the Duero, the Esla, the Ebro, in apparently secure positions; he knew the centre of Spain was devastated, that Madrid had suffered a second and even more appalling famine; and at Burgos in 1812 he had been successfully supplied by the navy through Santander. Put these together and the grand design emerges. Instead of making the Great Road (Salamanca, Valladolid, Burgos, Vitoria) the centre or even left of his movement, it would mark the extremity of his right. His left would be concealed from the French first by moving up within the Portuguese frontier to cross the Douro within that country, and then by swinging wide through mountains the French believed to be impassable. Thus by a succession of forced marches he would turn the French positions on the Duero, the Esla, and the Upper Ebro and within three weeks would be able to communicate with the Spanish armies of the north, and the sea. The movement would then strike straight towards the huge magazine and military centre at Bayonne; the French would be drawn like pus to a poultice from all over the rest of the Peninsula; and into the vacuum would come the reorganised Spanish armies from the south. The French would be further embarrassed by an allied landing at Tarragona on the north-east coast.

The remarkable thing about this plan is that it is not compromised by any defensive element at all, as his August/October position 'en potence' with Madrid at the angle had been: it depended solely on a sweeping dynamic movement aimed straight into the south-west corner of France, forcing the French to choose between a general action if they wished to stay, or a defensive line on the Pyrenees and the loss of the whole Peninsula. In the event, of course, they tried both and both failed.

Two problems remained at the outset, rain and the pontoons. To Henry, 28 April: We have at last got some rain in earnest, and the whole army will be in motion directly – *but grass does not grow that quickly, and anyway the rain created problems as well as solving them. In the mud the pontoon would not move. To Bathurst, 5 May:* The rain which has fallen plentifully, and some other trifling circumstances, have retarded our march for two or three days. But we shall have our bridge, which is what we wait for, by the 8th, when all the troops shall move.

I never saw the British army so healthy or so strong . . . We have gained in strength 25,000 men since we went into cantonments . . . and infinitely more in efficiency.

Two problems? Three. How to supply a fast-moving army with booze. The Portuguese government was peeved that he was importing colonial rum instead of buying Portuguese brandy or wine. To Stuart, 3 May: When we purchase wine or Portuguese brandy in this country we are obliged to pay for it at an enormous price, all in specie. When we purchase colonial rum, we pay for it by bills drawn upon England; and I believe that we are enabled to deliver the ration to the soldier at one third of the price at which we could procure wine or Portuguese brandy . . . and we give him an wholesome, instead of an unwholesome spirit. *Once, out of indigence, I bought the cheapest bottle of Portuguese gin I could find. Not only was it not drinkable, but when we used it to light charcoal the taste lingered and ruined the goat cutlets.* But this is not all. A soldier's ration of wine is one pint, of rum one third of a pint; of a Portuguese soldier, one sixth of a pint *(they were smaller!)*. Supposing then, that we are obliged to draw the wine from a distance . . . it may fairly be stated that the issue of spirits to the troops is made at the expense of one fourth of the land carriage required for the issue of wine . . . *In short, and labouring the point in order to justify what may seem to some a frivolous matter, everything was arranged to accommodate a lightning strike, involving fast, long marches.*

Graham arrived, and brought with him the Garter. To Sir Isaac Heard, Garter King of Arms, 10 May: I shall be very much obliged to you if you will let me know whether the riband of the Order is worn over the right or the left shoulder.

The main problem remained the bridge. Eventually the Peer went along to see just what was the trouble. To Colonel Sir R. Fletcher, Bart., Camp of the Pontoon Train, 14 May: It is clear that the train will not be ready to move until the day after to-morrow, on which day I wish it to move by the road fixed upon by General Murray, and which you were to reconnaitre this day.

There is one pontoon quite rotten, which it would be desirable to leave behind here.

Twenty pairs of wheels, if Colonel Dickson can spare as many, would set the train up in that respect completely . . .

Lieut. Piper appears to be of opinion that the bullocks answer equally well with the horses . . . the pontoons should in general be drawn by the oxen, and the horses should be used only when absolutely necessary.

In case the train can march to-morrow, it had better move a short distance by the proposed road . . .

Murray's contribution as Wellington's favoured Quarter Master General was vital. He rarely left Wellington's side during the next six months, and his importance becomes clear when they were unavoidably separated during the battle for the Pyrenees, for there was immediately a flood of correspondence between them. When he became Prime Minister in 1828 Wellington made him a member of his cabinet. With Murray back as Q.M.G., with Graham on his left and Hill on his right, Pakenham as Adjutant General, Picton back with the 3rd, Cotton with the cavalry, and Beresford at his side, it looked like the right team for once. There were, however, new generals in charge of divisions, and some old ones too, like Dalhousie, who were, to say the least, not quite reliable. Charles Alten too would never lead the Light division with quite the élan Craufurd had brought to the job.

On the eighteenth Graham got his orders. He was to take almost the whole allied army up the right of the Douro to Miranda where a magazine had been prepared, then to move by his right to Barca de Villal Campo a mile below the junction of the Esla and Duero. There, on the thirtieth, the pontoon bridge would be laid and communication would be made with the column on the right. This, consisting only of the 2nd and Light divisions and most of the cavalry, would come up the great road through Salamanca, and Wellington with them – for where Wellington was, the French expected the main army to be.

The object of these movements is first to turn the enemy's positions on the Duero, and next to secure the junction of the right of the army with the left, as far up the river as may be practicable.

On the nineteenth Graham moved. Wellington hung on at Freneda for two more days. To Henry, 20 May: I just write to let you know that we shall move head quarters the day after to-morrow. All the troops are in motion. Our confounded bridge has delayed us many days, but I hope before the end of the month we shall be established beyond the Duero.

He crossed the border, riding on Copenhagen, in the middle of the afternoon of 22 May, 1813. He turned in his saddle, and flourished his small cocked hat: 'Farewell, Portugal! I shall never see you again.' *Nor did he.*

IN FORTUNE'S WAY

To Graham, Ciudad Rodrigo, 22 May, 1813, 3.00 p.m.: I arrived here this day; and the Light division and cavalry are encamped on the river of Santi-espiritus in front. I go to-morrow to Tamames.

To Graham, Tamames, 23 May, 1813, 8.00 p.m.: The Light division and cavalry are at San Muñoz . . . Sir R. Hill has moved from Bejar.

To Graham, Matilla, 25 May, 1813, 8.00 p.m.: I arrived here this day. Our right will be to-morrow: the Spaniards at Alba and Hill and de Amarante close to Aldea Tejada. The Light division and the household brigade on the Valmusa, and Victor Alten's brigade on the heights, between that stream and Salamanca. I shall throw them into Salamanca if I can . . .

To Henry, Salamanca, 26 May: The enemy waited for us this day rather longer than they ought, and we did them a good deal of mischief on their retreat. I propose to join the left of the army immediately, in order to push that forward.

To Hill, who had come up the Camino Real from Béjar, Salamanca, 28 May: I intend to go to Miranda do Douro to-morrow in order to join the left of the army . . . *there follow detailed descriptions of where all the units of the right of the army were, and of his latest information of the dispositions of the French.* The object of the position given at present to the troops composing the right of the army is to secure their junction with those on the right of the Duero . . . *and, if Hill should be threatened by a superior force, he was to move on to Zamora to make that junction rather than fall back on Ciudad Rodrigo. Indeed the Agueda, the Coa and Portugal were things of the past.*

On the next day he rode fifty miles over rough country to Miranda where the Duero enters a gorge and becomes the Douro (see map page 230–1). Here he was swung across in a wicker basket suspended from ropes and wound in on a capstan. Immediately he moved the main part of the army on to the Esla, making his headquarters at Carvalajas.

To Hill, 30 May, 9.00 p.m.: I arrived here this day and the troops will cross the Esla to-morrow morning.

The enemy are still in Zamora, but in small numbers; and I understand they have destroyed the bridge there.

We have not the bridge over the Duero at the Barca de Villal Campo, as I think it will be required for the Esla; but this will make no difference in your instructions for the present. We can always remove the bridge in time if you should require it. *That is if Hill was threatened from the south or east.*

To Hill, 31 May: The greatest part of the army crossed the Esla this day, the cavalry in particular. The enemy have evacuated Zamora, and I shall be there to-morrow.

To Henry, Zamora, 1 June: We are getting on fast. I shall be at Toro to-morrow.

Zamora is a delightful town. There is a spot on the old walls near the cathedral from which one overlooks a convent tower whose top is slightly below you and no distance away and there nest a family of storks. On 1 June the chicks would have been putting on weight and flapping their stubby, nearly-feathered wings while their huge parents circled and glided in with small fry from the Duero. Their descendants are still there. The French overcharged the bridge when they blew it up and damaged a fair bit of the town too. No doubt they gave the storks a fright.

The French at last knew what a pickle they were in. To Graham, Toro, 2 June, 2.30 p.m.: I have received yours by the peasant of 10.A.M.; and I am obliged to you for the intelligence it contains. I was aware that the enemy had crossed the Duero; but not of the exact spot in which the army was likely to be concentrated. I have likewise heard that the troops from Segovia have crossed the Duero. I do not think we are so close up or so well concentrated as we ought to be, to meet the enemy in the state in which he will appear on the Horniza, probably to-morrow; and, therefore, I propose to halt the heads of the various columns to-morrow, and to close up the rear of each, and to move Hill in this direction preparatory to our farther movements.

The 10th have had a very handsome affair this morning, between this and Morales. Their loss is small; but they must have destroyed the enemy's dragoons . . .

He paused, and his men needed the rest. 40,000 of them had marched one hundred and fifty miles through 'regions thought to be impracticable even for small corps . . . and been suddenly placed as if by a supernatural power upon the Esla . . .' (Napier). All together he now had 12,000 cavalry, 70,000 infantry, 100 guns, swarms of Spanish partidas (Sanchez among them) on his flanks and in the front, and the Galician army coming in on his left. The French had about equal numbers of horse and guns, but so far could concentrate no more than 35,000 foot, though Joseph was moving up from Madrid, and more were moving up the Ebro towards Logroño.

On the second, then, they paused, and to be sure discipline had been properly maintained on the marches Wellington reviewed his two most suspect divisions, the 6th and 7th. Here's Green:

> Lieutenant General the Earl of Dalhousie gave the word of command . . . for a general salute: he and all the other generals in the division were uncovered during the time that the bands of the different regiments were playing the national air 'God Save the King' . . . After his lordship was satisfied with our manoeuvres, he ordered us to proceed to our encampment.

On the fourth they were on the move again. Lieut.-General Sir Thomas Graham will be so good as to move the left column of the army upon Villa Frades . . . The centre column will march upon La Mota . . . the right column to Villa Sexmir.

6th June: Right column . . . will move forward at daybreak by Cigales towards Dueñas – *home of the best wine on the Campo, reputed to promote dissension and much favoured at Salamanca University* – and halt in the neighbourhood of that place. Right column of the centre . . . to Villamuriel; Left column of the centre . . . towards Palencia; Left column to Villa Martin, and thence towards Palencia . . . General Giron's corps *the Galicians* will be to-morrow at Becerril. *And the French fell, almost scuttled, back before him.*

By the tenth he could write to Lieutenant Colonel Bourke at Coruña from Melgar on the Pisuerga: There are at Coruña certain ships loaded with biscuit and flour, and certain others loaded with a heavy train of artillery and ammunition; and I shall be very much obliged to you if you will request any officer of the navy who may be at Coruña when you receive this letter to take under his convoy all the vessels loaded as above mentioned, and to proceed with them to Santander. If he should find Santander occupied by the enemy, I beg him to remain off the port till the operations of this army have obliged the enemy to abandon it.

On the eleventh he was again in front of Burgos. To Bathurst, written on the thirteenth: I found the enemy posted with a considerable force on the heights of Hormaza, with their left in front of Estepar *in front of Burgos* . . . we turned their right with *basically the left column* . . . and the remainder of the troops under the command of . . . Hill threatened the heights of Estepar.

279

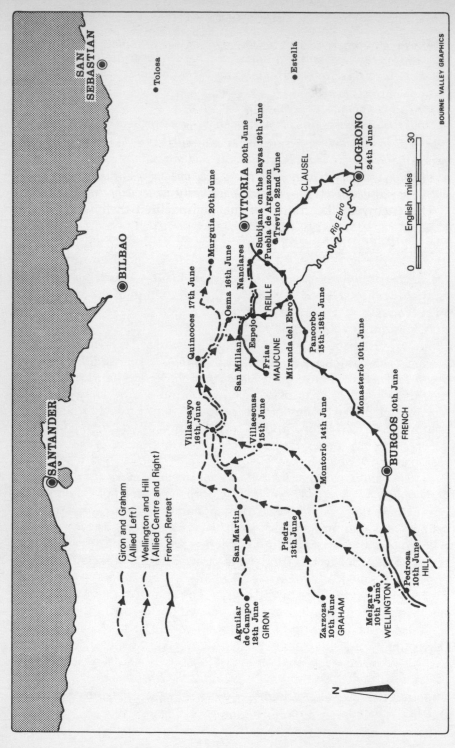

19. The Allied Advance, 10–20 June 1813

SAN SEBASTIAN

BILBAO

SANTANDER

• Tolosa

• Estella

Murguia 20th June

Subijana on the Bayas 18th June
Puebla de Arganzon
VITORIA 20th June
Trevino 22nd June

Nanclares

CLAUSEL

LOGROÑO
24th June

Rio Ebro

Osma 16th June

Quincoces 17th June

Espejo

REILLE

San Millan

Frias

MAUCUNE

Miranda del Ebro

Pancorbo
15th-18th June

Villarcayo
16th June

Villaescusa
15th June

Monasterio 10th June

Montorio 14th June

BURGOS 10th June
FRENCH

San Martin •

Piedra
13th June

Aguilar
de Campo • 12th June
GIRON

Zarzoza
10th June
GRAHAM

Melgar •
10th June
WELLINGTON

Pedrosa
10th June
HILL

Giron and Graham
(Allied Left)

Wellington and Hill
(Allied Centre and Right)

French Retreat

N

English miles

0   30

BOURNE VALLEY GRAPHICS

These movements dislodged the enemy from their position immediately. The cavalry of our left and centre were entirely in the rear of the enemy, who were obliged to retire across the Arlanzon by the high road towards Burgos . . . *I think he could have caught a substantial part of the French army at this point but he refused the opportunity. He would have suffered losses, the retreating French would have got off anyway, and he would have needed the inevitable three or four days to pull things together again during which the French as a whole would have had a breathing space. As always Wellington wanted one battle, and that a good one, disposing of as many of the enemy as possible in one go. The real opportunity was exactly ten days away.*

The enemy in the course of the night retired their whole army through Burgos, having abandoned and destroyed as far as they were able, in the short space of time during which they were there, the works of the castle which they had constructed and improved at so large an expense; and they are now on their retreat towards the Ebro . . .

The biggest bang of all:

The mines under the castle exploded outwardly at the moment a column of infantry was defiling beneath, several streets were laid in ruins, thousands of shells and other combustibles were driven upwards with a horrible crash, the hills rocked . . . and a shower of iron, timber, and stony fragments . . . in an instant killed more than three hundred men! *(Napier).*

Now the Ebro too could be turned – In the meantime the whole of the army of the allies made a movement to the left this day; and the Spanish corps of Galicia under General Giron, and the left of the British and Portuguese army under . . . Graham, will, I hope, pass the Ebro to-morrow at the bridges of Rocamunde and San Martin . . .

We keep up our strength, and the army are very healthy, and in better order than I have ever known them. God knows how long this will last. It depends entirely upon the officers . . .

He was, of course, relieved about Burgos. Probably he had planned to by-pass it leaving a blockade of Galicians, even so . . . To Henry: I consider the evacuation of Burgos a very important event.

So, pushing round the French right into the supposedly impassable mountains they went. They are not as high or as grand as some in Spain, but thickly wooded with steep slopes crowned with crags and very narrow valleys.

G.O.   Quincoces, 17th June, 1813.
2. In the defiles through which the army is likely to march, it is very desirable that great attention should be paid to the march of the

baggage, the hour at which it is to set off, and the order in which it is formed . . .

8. . . . when the names of several villages are marked in the route to be passed through, the Staff officer leading the column will enquire from his guide for each of them successively.

To Henry, same day: The whole army have crossed the Ebro, and we are in march towards Vitoria and the high road to France, of which I hope we shall be in possession in a day or two.

Via Osman, San Millan (ancient monastery, well worth a visit) and Espejo the left and centre swung through the hills towards Subijana, on the Bayas, and on the way they ran into the army of the North which was, like all the French now, pouring back into a position in front of Vitoria. To Bathurst, Subijana, on the Bayas, 19 June: The enemy assembled a considerable corps at Espejo . . . They had likewise a division of infantry and some cavalry at Frias . . . *which* marched yesterday upon San Millan . . . and that from Espejo on Osman.

The Light division, nominally under Alten but at that moment commanded by Wellington himself, drove the enemy from San Millan, and afterwards cut off the rear brigade of the division, of which he *(Alten, but really Wellington)* took 300 prisoners; killed and wounded many, and the brigade was dispersed in the mountains.

Our hero then rode through the mountains to Osman where Graham too was in difficulties. The corps from Espejo was considerably stronger than the allied corps under Sir Thomas Graham . . . The enemy moved on to the attack, but were soon obliged to retire, and they were followed to Espejo, from whence they retired through the hills to this place. *These two brilliant actions, fought on the same day, and both under the direct command of Wellington himself, completed the turning of the French right, and destroyed or demoralised an important section of the French army which was endeavouring to concentrate on the plain before Vitoria.*

The main French armies now poured across the Ebro and up through the defile north east of Pueblo into the plain of the Zadorra. A motorway runs through this defile now but Griffon's Vultures still soar above it. The army moved forward this day to the river *the Bayas, west of Pueblo.* I found the enemy's rearguard in a strong position on the left of the river . . . We turned the enemy's left with the Light division, while the 4th . . . attacked them in front; and the rearguard was driven back upon the main body of the army, which was in march from Pancorbo to Vitoria . . .

VITORIA

To Earl Bathurst
My Lord,   Salvatierra, 22nd June, 1813.
The enemy commanded by King Joseph, having Marshal Jourdan as
the major General of the army, took up a position on the night of the
19th instant, in front of Vitoria; the left of which rested upon the
heights which end at La Puebla de Arganzon, and extended from
thence across the valley of the Zadorra, in front of the village of Ariñez.
They occupied with the right of the centre a height which commanded
the valley to the Zadorra. The right of the army was stationed near the
city of Vitoria, and was destined to defend the passages of the river
Zadorra, in the neighbourhood of that city. They had a reserve in the
rear of their left, at the village of Gomecha. The nature of the country
through which the enemy had passed since it had reached the Ebro,
had necessarily extended our columns; and we halted on the twentieth
to close them up, and moved the left to Murguia, where it was most
likely it would be required. I reconnaitred the enemy's position on that
day, with a view to the attack to be made on the following morning, if
they should still remain in it.

*What he saw as he hacked along the crest of hills that separates the valley of the
Zadorra from that of the Bayas, was a long, broad valley, shaped like a meat dish
with wooded hills around its rim. It is threaded from the distant north-east by
the silver ribbon of the Zadorra, first passing through meadows with occasional
villages and hamlets, and small stone bridges, then meandering into the more
broken ground at the western end of the valley. Here it takes two sharp hairpins,
the first just below the village of Tres Puentes, the second below that of Villodes,
before entering the gorge-like defile that takes it out of the valley and so to Puebla
de Arganzon.*

*The first hairpin takes it round ground that rises unevenly to the hill or knoll
of Ariñez. The second feature which would have presented itself to Wellington's
spy-glass would have been the great road, the 'Camino Real' that links Burgos,
Valladolid, Salamanca and Lisbon to Vitoria, San Sebastian, Bayonne and
Paris. This runs on the southern side of the valley before meeting the river at the
Puebla defile.*

*In the distance, ten miles off, he would have seen the walls and spires of
Vitoria itself, perhaps, on that Midsummer's Eve, hazy with the dust and*

283

smoke from King Joseph's baggage park on the far side of it. The ground between Vitoria and Ariñez, where the later stages of the battle were fought, was broken with orchards, woods, fields, hamlets and farms. When Wellington looked over it he would have seen it filled with column upon column of blue, white and black, set out in three distinct corps. First Gazan's four and a half infantry divisions behind the hairpin bends of the Zadorra, covered by artillery on the hills of Ariñez, on which he could see the glittering staffs of three French armies with the King amongst them. Behind the hills came d'Erlon's army of the Centre, and finally Reille's three infantry divisions in front of Vitoria.

Behind Vitoria was that baggage train, one of the biggest caravans ever seen in Spain, or perhaps anywhere: carriages carrying thousands of àfrancesado Spaniards who had serviced the bureaucracy of Joseph's rule, with their families (their frenchified surnames still fill the telephone directories from Bayonne to Bordeaux); waggons stuffed with the loot of an empire – plate from every cathedral in Spain except Cadiz, so:ne of the greatest paintings in the world, robes, statues, furniture, jewels, gold; and to cap it all five 'fourgons' containing five million dollars in gold coin – the overdue pay for the entire collection of armies. For that is what they were – 70,000 of them, the armies of the South, Portugal, and the Centre, just about all the French first-line, combatant troops in the Peninsula bar those under Suchet facing the British expeditionary force in Catalonia, and a further corps under Clausel which had been at Pamplona. Wellington learnt on the twentieth that this force had marched south-west to Logroño intending to link with Joseph on the Ebro. But Joseph's retreat had been too quick and now it was making its way back. However, it would not be able to reach Vitoria before the twenty-second.

'. . . if they should still remain in it,' Wellington wrote, knowing that he had a numerical advantage of over 12,000 men which would be wiped out when Joseph made contact with Clausel. Surely they would not stay put. But they had to: first, because, now they had fallen back onto that convoy, to move at any sort of speed or in any sort of order would have meant abandoning it; second, because they believed that the hills to the north and south protected their flanks and that the only way they could be attacked was from the south-west where they had a river in their front and the hills of Ariñez and their guns behind. If Wellington came through the narrow Puebla defile, and across the river in their face they would have him pinned in detail against it and the hills to the west. He would be annihilated. Of course, he would do no such thing. Never mind, they simply had to wait until Clausel came up and then the whole awful business of the preceding four weeks would be put into reverse.

We accordingly attacked the enemy yesterday, and I am happy to inform your Lordship, that the Allied army under my command gained a complete victory, having driven them from all their positions, having

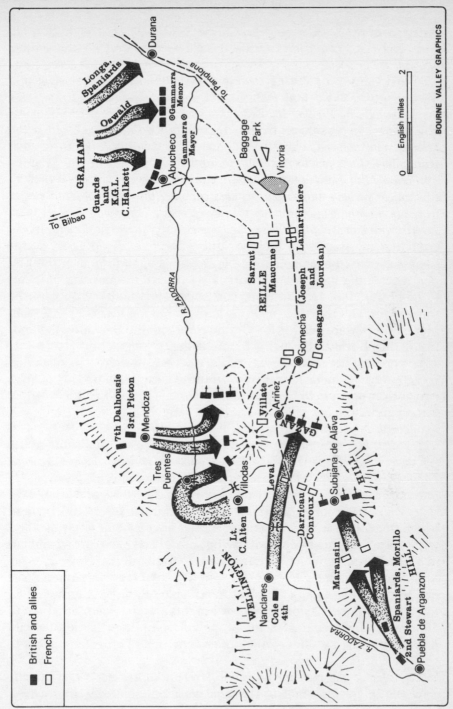

20. The Battle of Vitoria, 21 June 1813

BOURNE VALLEY GRAPHICS

British and allies
French

English miles
0   1   2

GRAHAM

Longa,
Spaniards

Oswald

Guards
and
K.G.L.
C. Halkett

To Bilbao

Durana

Gammarra
Menor

Abucheco

Gammarra
Mayor

To Pamplona

Baggage
Park

Vitoria

Sarrut

REILLE

Maucune

Lamartiniere

(Joseph
and
Jourdan)

Gomecha

Cassagne

R. ZADORRA

7th Dalhousie
3rd Picton

Mendoza

Tres
Puentes

Villodas

Lt.
C. Alten

WELLINGTON

Nanclares

Cole
4th

Villatte

Ariñez

Leval

GAZAN

Darricau
Conroux

Subijana de Alava

HILL

Maransin

Spaniards, Morillo
2nd Stewart

HILL

Puebla de Arganzon

R. ZADORRA

taken from them 151 pieces of cannon, waggons of ammunition, all their baggage, provisions, cattle, treasure, &c., and a considerable number of prisoners.

The operation of the day commenced *at about half-past eight of a Midsummer's Day morning that was cold, misty, with rain threatening on a north-westerly off the Bay of Biscay* by Lieutenant General Sir Rowland Hill obtaining possession of the Heights of La Puebla, on which the enemy's left rested, which heights they had not occupied in great strength. He detached for this service one brigade of the Spanish division under General Morillo . . .

And what a change was there! At the vital outset of a battle he uses Spanish troops in an attack in open order up steep slopes broken with boulders, then covered with thorns, juniper and gorse. The enemy, however, soon discovered the importance of these heights, and reinforced their troops there to such an extent, that . . . Hill was obliged to detach the 71st regiment and a light infantry battalion under the command of Lieut. Colonel the Hon. H. Cadogan, and successively other troops to the same point; and the Allies not only gained, but maintained possession of these important heights throughout their operations, notwithstanding all the efforts of the enemy to retake them.

The contest here was, however, very severe, and the loss sustained considerable. General Morillo was wounded, but remained in the field; and I am concerned to have to report, that Lieut. Colonel the Hon. H. Cadogan has died of a wound which he received.

Cadogan was Henry's brother-in-law, and a very good friend of the Wellesleys. When his sister ran off with Lord Henry Paget, he did his utmost to persuade her to return to Henry Wellesley, and even challenged Paget to a duel. To Henry Wellesley, 22 June: His private character and his worth as an individual were not greater than his merits as an officer, and I shall ever regret him. It is a curious instance of his devotion to his profession, and of the interest in what was going on, that after he was wounded and was probably aware that he was dying, he desired to be carried and left in a situation from which he might be able to see all that passed.

Back to the official dispatch: Under the cover of the possession of these heights, Sir Rowland Hill successively passed the Zadorra, at La Puebla, and the defile formed by the heights and the river Zadorra, and attacked and gained possession of the village of Subijana de Alava, in front of the enemy's line, which the enemy made repeated attacks to gain.

Now this is the moment when most commentators do not sufficiently emphasise the point. All Hill's movements were essentially diversionary, fulfilling what Wellington justly supposed would be Jourdan's and Joseph's expectations. Hill's attack on the south-west heights followed by the movement of the rest of his corps up the defile to a line that would stretch north from Subijana towards the river, a line which would duly be filled by the allies crossing the river north of Subijana to fill in the gap between the river and Hill's left, is precisely what they would have expected. And they allowed it to happen, even left the bridges up so it could happen, and as they saw it happen they weakened their right in preparation for the artillery supported onslaught that would pin Wellington against the river and the hills behind.

What the French did not realise was that the 3rd and 7th divisions were threading their way through the hills to the north which they supposed to be impassable to large bodies of men with artillery. The decisive and crippling attack was to be on the right flank they had already weakened.

However, for Wellington, momentarily, something had gone wrong: though you would scarcely guess it from the dispatch. The difficult nature of the country prevented the communication between our different columns moving to the attack from their stations on the river Bayas . . . and it was late before I knew that the column of the 3rd and 7th divisions, under the command of The Earl of Dalhousie, had arrived at the station appointed for them. *Picton and the 3rd reached their station, a village called Mendoza, a mile or so above the hairpin, on time, but Dalhousie was once again . . . lost!*

Meanwhile . . . The 4th and Light divisions *under Wellington's direct command* passed the Zadorra immediately after . . . Hill had possession of Subijana de Alava, the former at the bridge of Nanclares, and the latter at the bridge of Tres Puentes. *If the French had attacked at this moment the battle would have been drawn at best – but they waited, perhaps for the rest of the allied army to march into the trap they thought they had set.*

Wellington realised he was perhaps, after all, in a scrape. An A.D.C. was despatched with some haste to order Dalhousie to attack, or at any rate to discover why he had not. He found Picton and the 3rd waiting impatiently at Mendoza. 'Have you seen Lord Dalhousie?' he cried. 'No, Sir! I have not seen his lordship: but have you any orders for me, sir?' 'None!' 'Then, pray, sir, what orders do you bring?' 'Why, that as soon as Lord Dalhousie with the 7th shall commence an attack upon that bridge, the 4th and Light will support him.' 'You may tell Lord Wellington from me, sir, that the 3rd division under my command shall in less than ten minutes attack the bridge and carry it, and the 4th and Light may support if they choose.' Minutes later, when the brief instructions necessary had been passed on, he turned to the Connaughts, who were, as usual, the centre of the 3rd, lifted the wide-brimmed top-hat he affected to keep the sun out of his eyes, and cried: 'Come on, ye rascals, come on ye fighting villains!'

This has been described as 'grave and grand insubordination', but I hardly think so. Picton, like all the generals, would have been properly briefed, he would have known how precarious the situation of the 4th and Light was until the attack from the north was launched, and he knew very well that Dalhousie had gone astray again.

. . . and almost as soon as these *(the 4th and Light)* had crossed, the column under the Earl of Dalhousie arrived at Mendoza; and the 3rd division, under . . . Picton, crossed at the bridge higher up, followed by the 7th division under . . . Dalhousie. *Oh yes, he got there – his front files emerged from a defile just as the Connaughts went in.*

These four divisions, forming the centre of the army, were destined to attack the height *of Ariñez* on which the right of the enemy's centre was placed, while . . . Hill should move forward from Subijana de Alava to attack the left. The enemy, however, having weakened his line to strengthen his detachment on the hills, abandoned his position in the valley as soon as he saw our disposition to attack it, and commenced his retreat in good order towards Vitoria . . . *falling back on what was a very substantial reserve commanded by Reille, and possibly still hoping to end things in a stalemate.*

Our troops continued to advance in good order, notwithstanding the difficulty of the ground . . . *Dalhousie got it wrong again. This time he was too far ahead! Here's Green:*

> We then came to a certain height, where the enemy had twelve pieces of cannon placed, with which they opened a most destructive fire upon us; our brigade-major's horse had both his forelegs shot from under him: the poor creature began to eat grass, as if nothing was the matter with him . . . we were obliged to take shelter in a deep ditch, not more than two hundred yards from the muzzles of their guns . . . It was now reported by some of our timid soldiers that the enemy was advancing, and that we should all be taken prisoners . . . I looked to see whether the enemy was advancing or not. I had scarcely raised my head above the ditch, when a grape shot struck the top of my cap, and carried away the rosette, with part of the crown: had it been three inches lower, I should have been no more . . . I observed to the Brigade Major that it was sharp work. 'Aye,' said he; 'yet we are well off, if we can only keep so . . .' It appeared that we had advanced about fifteen minutes too soon for the Light division, which was to have supported us . . .

The French, with Reille's three divisions in broken country still behind them, still no doubt hoped for a drawn battle. But Wellington also still had three

Vitoria

divisions. The sixth were in reserve back at Puebla under Pakenham, but Graham's . . .

In the mean time, Lieut. General Sir Thomas Graham, who commanded the left of the army, consisting of the 1st and 5th divisions *and Pack's Portuguese and Longa's Spaniards* who had been moved on the 20th to Murguia *(the French were told of this movement by a renegade, but they refused to believe him)*, moved forward from thence on Vitoria, by the high road from that town to Bilbao. *Graham has been accused of unnecessary caution, but he was instructed not to engage until ordered to. It seems certain to me that if things had gone wrong Wellington intended to retreat not south-west but north to Bilbao and the safety of the coast and the Navy – Graham's column would then have covered the retreat. So, of course, Graham was not to advance until Wellington was sure nothing awful could happen to his right and centre. The order to Graham is timed 2.00 p.m.; it would not have reached him until shortly before three.* Sir Thomas Graham will be so good as to move forward and press the enemy . . . *but if the enemy resisted obstinately he was not to* undertake any movement which separates our corps too much. If on the contrary, the enemy seem decidedly in retreat . . . Sir Thomas Graham will in that case make a wider movement, and endeavour to cut off the retreat of the enemy by gaining possession of the great road beyond Vitoria *that is, the one to Pamplona.*

The main French army was not yet decidedly in retreat, and the resistance in front of Graham was obstinate.

The enemy had a division of infantry with some cavalry advanced on the great road from Vitoria to Bilbao, resting their right on some strong heights covering the village of Gamarra Mayor. Both Gamarra and Abechuco were strongly occupied as têtes de pont and the bridges over the Zadorra at these places . . . Pack and . . . Longa were directed to turn and gain the heights . . . Colonel Longa being on the left, took possession of Gamarra Menor.

As soon as the heights were in our possession, the village of Gamarra Mayor was most gallantly stormed and carried by . . . Robertson's brigade of the 5th division, which advanced in columns of battalions, under a very heavy fire of artillery and musketry, without firing a shot . . .

The Lieut. General then proceeded to attack the village of Abechuco with the 1st division, by forming a strong battery against it . . . and under cover of this fire, Colonel Halkett's brigade advanced to the attack of the village, which was carried . . .

During the operation at Abechuco the enemy made the greatest efforts to repossess the village of Gamarra Mayor, which were gallantly repulsed . . . The enemy had, however, on the heights on the left of the Zadorra, two divisions of infantry in reserve; and it was impossible to cross by the bridges till the troops which had moved upon the enemy's centre and left had driven them through Vitoria, *and that was not possible until those last two divisions of Reille's reserve had been moved out of the centre to plug Graham's advance. In short, with very little communication after the battle had started, and separated by hardly ever less than ten miles and often more, the co-operation between Graham and Wellington was perfect, the simultaneous pressure of each combining to break the French and produce their complete rout. This would not have happened if Graham had been further east.*

The movement of the troops under . . . Graham . . . intercepted the enemy's retreat by the high road to France. They were obliged to turn to the road towards Pamplona – *the modern road from Vitoria to San Sebastian via Alsasua and Tolosa was no more than a smugglers' track in 1813; the best route to France was via Bilbao* . . . but they were unable to hold any position for a sufficient length of time to allow their baggage and artillery to be drawn off. The whole, therefore, of the latter . . . *were taken.* I have reason to believe that the enemy carried off with them one gun and one howitzer only . . .

Believe me, &c.,

Wellington

The allies suffered 5,000 casualties, of which less than 800 were killed. The French at least 8,000, probably many more, and three armies smashed.

1813

(22 JUNE–1 NOVEMBER)

———✦✦✦———

THE PARTY AND AFTER

APOTHEOSIS OF OUR HERO

SORAUREN

SAN SEBASTIAN

JUSQU'AUX GENOUX DANS LA NEIGE

———✦✦✦———

THE PARTY AND AFTER

Between the allied army and their fleeing foe stood that caravan of treasure and coin, that 'bordel ambulante' as one French officer described it. In the light of past history what followed has about it all the inevitability of a banana-skin joke.

The anecdotes of what went on that night would fill a book on their own, and since this is Wellington's book, and not a compilation of Peninsular War sketches, I'll restrict myself to just two quotations, to give the flavour and some clue as to what lay behind Wellington's reaction.

Several men of our regiment obtained a great deal of money: one named Sullivan, found one thousand dollars amongst the baggage of the enemy; another, called Kenneville, who now lives at Scotton near Lincoln, obtained one hundred and eighty doubloons . . . amounting in all to seven hundred and twenty pounds sterling . . . A gown-piece, some children's frocks, two flutes, an English bible, and a few other small articles, were all that fell to my share. I fancy some one had had the bible in his possession who could not carry all his treasure, and therefore threw it aside . . . *(Green)*

Alongside Green's 68th, were the 51st among whom was Private Wheeler.

I had not proceeded far when I met one of the 68th regt. with a handkerchief full of dollars [Kenneville's doubloons perhaps]. He was followed by about a dozen Portuguese soldiers, one of these fellows ran in and cut the handkerchief and down went the dollars, a general scramble followed. As the Portuguese were down on their hands and knees picking up the money, we paid them off in stile [sic] with the sockets of our bayonets. After this fracas was over I proceeded on until my ear caught the welcome sound of Brown's voice, he was singing his favourite song 'When wild war's deadly blast was blown'. I knew there was luck, for he never sang this song but when he was elevated with the juice of the grape . . . I soon found him, he had been in a flour cask and was as white as a miller . . . I soon learned that the extent of his treasure was two canteens of brandy, three loaves, two haversacks of flour, one ham, and two dollars and a half. I took a good swig of brandy and half a loaf. Brown went home to make dumplings and I started off in the direction I heard most noise, soon came to the place where the money was. After much difficulty I secured a small box of dollars and was fortunate enough to get back safe to camp . . . the place was all in ablaze, I knew of nothing to compare it with but an Arab camp after a

295

successful attack upon some rich caravan . . . Dame Fortune had distributed her gifts in her usual way, to some money, others bread, hams, cherries, tobacco, etc. This of necessity soon established a market. Now the camp represented a great fair and the money and the goods soon became more equally distributed. 'Who will give fifty dollars for this pipe?' 'Here is a portrait of Napoleon for one hundred dollars.'

To Bathurst, 29 June: We started with the army in the highest order, and up to the day of the battle nothing could get on better; but that event has, as usual, totally annihilated all order and discipline. The soldiers of the army have got among them about a million sterling in money, with the exception of about 100,000 dollars, which were got for the military chest. The night of the battle, instead of being passed in getting rest and food to prepare them for the following day, was passed by the soldiers in looking for plunder. The consequence was, that they were incapable of marching in pursuit of the enemy and were totally knocked up. The rain came on and increased their fatigue, and I am quite convinced that we now have out of the ranks double the amount our loss in the battle; and that we have lost more men in the pursuit than the enemy have; and have never in one day made more than an ordinary march.

This is the consequence of the state of discipline of the British army. We may gain the great victories, but we shall do no good until we shall so far alter our system, as to force all ranks to perform their duty. The new regiments are, as usual, the worst of all.

A week later he wrote what became his most notorious letter because of one phrase that is almost never quoted in context, not even by biographers who pretend to accuracy, and of course it is used by anyone whose simplistic view of army life sees all generals always as bullying, cowardly ingrates, and all men always as pathetic cannon fodder. So here is the letter virtually complete – I have only cut some of his breakdown of how the army has been depleted by stragglers.

To Earl Bathurst
My Dear Lord,   Huarte, 2nd July, 1813.
I enclose a letter from the governor of Vitoria, which shows how our men are going on in that neighbourhood. These men are detachments of the different regiments of the army who were sent to Vitoria the day after the battle, each under officers, in order to collect the wounded and their arms and accoutrements. It is quite impossible for me or any other man to command the British army under the existing system. We have

in the service the scum of the earth as common soldiers . . . *and there it is: but chop it about as you like it simply does not mean that he thought the soldiers of his army were all the scum of the earth, but that the scum of the earth were amongst them. It does not seem to me to be inappropriate language for men who have not fired a shot, who have been instructed to tend the wounded, but prefer instead to rob and molest the dead, the prisoners, and the inhabitants of the town their colleagues had liberated* . . . and of late years we have been doing everything in our power, both by law and by publications, to relax the discipline by which alone such men can be kept in order. The officers of the lower ranks will not perform the duty required of them *(amongst the looters of the baggage train on the night of the 21st were many officers of the cavalry who were meant to be in pursuit)* for the purpose of keeping their soldiers in order; and it is next to impossible to punish any officer for neglect of this description. As to the non-commissioned officers, as I have repeatedly stated, they are as bad as the men, and too near them, in point of pay and situation, by the regulations of late years, for us to expect them to do anything to keep the men in order. It is really a disgrace to have anything to say to such men as some of our soldiers are. *Not to labour the point, notice he writes, 'some of our soldiers'.*

I now beg to draw your attention to the mode in which these irregularities affect our numbers . . . The loss of British rank and file in the battle was 3164 . . . from irregularities, straggling, &c., since, for plunder, 2733. The loss of Portuguese rank and file in the battle was 1022 . . . and their diminution from the same causes is 1423. *Now even if these also were the 'scum of the earth', and I still think it was those who neglected the wounded for plunder at whom the phrase was directed, it still only comes to ten per cent of the British force.*

While we were pursuing the enemy by the valley of Araquil towards Pamplona, finding so many men straggling from their ranks, I ordered that an hospital might be established to receive them; and although there are so many absent from their regiments, there are only 160 in that hospital. The others are plundering the country in different directions.

Believe me, &c.,

Wellington

APOTHEOSIS OF OUR HERO

The French armies, apart from Clausel's corps, were dispersed and making their way, unencumbered by discipline or baggage, to France. Only part of Foy's division continued any sort of resistance. Graham was brought up by him at Tolosa. Hill blockaded Pamplona, and Wellington himself tried to get between Clausel and Jaca, but Clausel was too quick for him and got his corps safely over the central Pyrenean passes to Pau.

To Bathurst, 3 July: . . . finding the enemy had already advanced so far upon their march as to render it impossible for me to cut them off from Jaca . . . I discontinued the pursuit with the allied British and Portugese troops; and they are on their return to Pamplona. *The Spanish horse under Mina and Sanchez were left to watch the French up into the Pyrenees and over the border.* In the meantime the troops under . . . Hill have kept up the blockade of Pamplona, and have moved through the mountains to the head of the Bidasoa, the enemy having entirely retired into France on that side . . .

The General *Graham* has continued to push on the enemy by the high road *from Tolosa to San Sebastian and so to the border* and has dislodged them from all strong positions which they have taken; and yesterday a brigade of the army of Galicia under the command of General Castanos, attacked and drove the enemy across the Bidassoa, by the bridge of Irun. Sir Thomas Graham reports that in all these affairs the Spanish troops have conducted themselves remarkably well.

Only two French garrisons remained – San Sebastian, and Pamplona. Both were now blockaded. In the east, however, in Catalonia, things had not gone well. General John Murray (who did not do well at Oporto in 1809) had given up the siege of Tarragona under disgraceful circumstances leaving behind artillery and stores. In the next months Wellington had to spend a lot of time and cover a lot of paper over this, but since it had no material effect on his own campaign, I intend to ignore it.

He now determined to turn the blockade of San Sebastian into a siege – and, though he was never directly in charge, like most other sieges he was involved in, it would not go right. The old firm of Dickson R.A. and Fletcher R.E. were called in.

To Graham, Lanz, 4 July, 1813: From the account which I have received from Major Smith of the state of San Sebastian, and in view to the

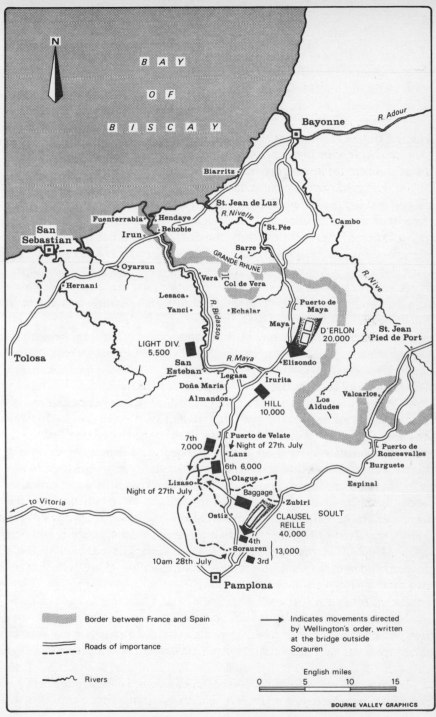

N

BAY

OF

BISCAY

Bayonne   R. Adour

Biarritz

St. Jean de Luz   R. Nivelle

Fuenterrabia   Hendaye   St. Pée   Cambo

San   Irun   Behobie
Sebastian

Sarre
LA
GRANDE RHUNE

Oyarzun   Vera   Col de Vera

Hernani

Lesaca   Echalar   R. Nive

Yanci   R. Bidassoa   Puerto de
Maya

LIGHT DIV.   Maya   D'ERLON   St. Jean
5,500   20,000   Pied de Port

Tolosa   San   R. Maya   Elizondo
Esteban   Legasa   Irurita   Valcarlos

Doña Maria   Los
Almandoz   HILL   Aldudes
10,000

Puerto de Velate   Puerto de
7th   ↓ Night of 27th. July   Roncesvalles
7,000   Lanz   Burguete

6th 6,000   Espinal
Olague

Lizaso   Baggage   Zubiri
Night of 27th July   Ostiz   CLAUSEL   SOULT
REILLE
to Vitoria   40,000

4th
Sorauren   13,000
10am 28th July   3rd

Pamplona

Border between France and Spain   Indicates movements directed
by Wellington's order, written
at the bridge outside
Roads of importance   Sorauren

English miles
Rivers   0   5   10   15

BOURNE VALLEY GRAPHICS

21. The Battles for the Pyrenees, June–November 1813

general situation of our affairs I feel very anxious to attack that place
. . . Sir R. Fletcher is now employed in the arrangement and construction of the works for the blockade of Pamplona; but as soon as these are
arranged, I will send him to San Sebastian . . . I shall likewise send
Lieut. Colonel Dickson, and all the means in artillery, sappers, &c.

*Meanwhile the rest of the army moved up into the mountains, covering the
principal passes. It was a countryside quite unlike anything they had ever been
in before. The last thirty miles or so of the Pyrenees from Roncesvalles to St Jean
de Luz and Biarritz are not particularly high but they rise on spectacularly steep
but well-timbered slopes from narrow but fertile valleys. These wind in and out
of France and Spain in a bewilderingly confused and twisting network of rivers
and gorges, crags and watersheds. One moment you feel sure you are about to
cross into Béarn, then at the last moment the valley or road twists back, and then
back again. And each valley is, to the naïve eye, exactly the same as the one
before. Even now, with roads well sign-posted, it is easy country to get lost in –
especially if the weather is bad, and, this being Atlantic country, it usually is.
Even in August, Roncesvalles is often smothered by drenching, cold cloud that
reduces visibility to a hundred yards or less.*

*There are a hundred galloping trout streams, but only one large river on the
Spanish side – the Bidassoa. Its gorge is fantastic, cutting through red cliffs as it
approaches the sea and you feel it must mark the border – but it does not, or only
at its estuary in the last few miles to Irun and Hendaye.*

To Bathurst, Irurita, 9 July: . . . I do not know what measures to take
about our vagabond soldiers. By the state of yesterday, we had 12,500
men less under arms than we had on the day of the battle. *7,000 plus
were unaccounted for.* They are not in the hospitals, nor are they killed,
nor have they fallen into the hands of the enemy as prisoners; I have
sent officers with parties of the Cavalry Staff corps in all directions after
them, but I have not yet heard of any of them. I believe they are
concealed in the villages in the mountains.

*Well, yes. Drunk first then lost. I once got drunk in Pamplona and ended up
in Les Aldudes (Los Alduides). Had I thought there was a Provost Marshal
behind me, I might well have stayed there too.*

*Wellington rarely got lost, and, since India, was never drunk, but this was a
confusing time for him too. Napoleon, having held the allies in Europe with a
series of bloody but more or less drawn engagements, was striving to save his
empire by a skilful diplomatic campaign of divide and survive. A sort of
armistice was in force while the crowned heads tried to sort something out. As
far as we are concerned two futures for Spain were on the table, and a move to
transfer our hero to the eastern front.*

To Bathurst, 12 July: In regard to my going to Germany, I am the Prince Regent's servant; but nobody would enjoy the same advantage here, and I should be no better than another in Germany. If a British army should be left in the Peninsula, therefore, it is best I should remain with it . . .

I recommend you not to give up an inch of Spanish territory. I think I can hold the Pyrenees as easily as I can Portugal. I am quite certain I can hold the position which I have got more easily than the Ebro, or any other position in Spain. I will go farther; I would prefer to have Joseph as *independent* King of Spain, without any cession to France . . . than to have Ferdinand with the Ebro as frontier. In the latter case Spain must inevitably belong to the French.

There were degrees of anti-Buonapartism in England. Radicals, even some whigs, were still almost wholly for him (what a thing it must have been to live in a truly pluralist society); many thought that, properly curbed, he might yet prove to be a good thing. The 'wets' amongst the tories were prepared to talk, and they included Prinny himself, and so when Wellington received the following from that august hand he took the opportunity, tactfully, to put backbone into his master, by raising 'The Cause' into an abstraction above both of them.

To Field Marshal the Marquis of Wellington, K.G.
My Dear Lord,   Carlton House, 3rd July, 1813.
Your glorious conduct is beyond all human praise, and far above my reward, I know no language the world affords worthy to express it. I feel I have nothing left to say, but devoutly to offer up my prayer of gratitude to Providence, that it has, in its omnipotent bounty, blessed my country and myself with such a General. You have sent me, among the trophies of your unrivalled fame, the staff of a French Marshal [*Jourdan's, found on the battle-field of Vitoria*], and I send you in return that of England. [*No such thing existed. One was quickly improvised.*]

The British army will hail it with enthusiasm while the whole universe will acknowledge those valorous efforts which have so imperiously called for it.

That uninterrupted health and still increasing laurels may continue to crown you through a glorious and long career of life, are the never ceasing and most ardent wishes of, my dear Lord, your very sincere and faithful friend,

G. P. R.

To His Royal Highness the Prince Regent.

Sir,   Lesaca, 16th July, 1813.

I trust your Royal Highness will receive graciously my humble acknow-
ledgements for the honour which your Royal Highness has conferred
upon me by your approbation, for the terms in which it is conveyed,
and for the last distinguished mark of your Royal Highness's favor.
Even if I had not been supported and encouraged as I have been by
your Royal Highness's protection and favor, the interest which I feel for
the cause which your Royal Highness so powerfully supports would
have induced me to make every exertion for its success. I can evince my
gratitude for your Royal Highness's repeated favors only by devoting
my life to your service.

I have the honour to be, &c.,

Wellington

*His confidence in his position had been assumed to bolster the allies. The French
were re-grouping behind the Pyrenees and real uncertainty was beginning to
trouble him. Two days earlier he had written to Hill:* It would appear that the
enemy have reinforced their left, towards St Jean Pied-de-Port; and I
should besides conclude that Clausel has by this time passed Oloron.

I ordered Clinton . . . to march to Lanz with the 6th division . . . and
I have ordered Sir L. Cole, with the 4th . . . to move towards Ronces-
valles . . . Sir Thomas Picton with the 3rd division will march to
Olague.

The truth is, that having two objects in hand, viz., the siege of San
Sebastian and the blockade of Pamplona, we are not so strong on any
point as we ought to be. These movements, when effected, will render
us fully strong enough for anything.

. . . Considering how ticklish our affairs are to the right, I think you
had better not yourself quit Elizondo.

*Another nagging worry, about which he was later to become almost frantic,
was the weakness of the Navy in the Biscay. To Bathurst on the nineteenth:* I
must again draw your Lordship's attention to the naval concerns off
the coast. Nothing has arrived but two or three small vessels to carry
dispatches, and we have nothing for the blockade excepting the
Surveillante, from which we have got six guns *for the siege of San
Sebastian, thus weakening her,* and a few Spanish boats fitted out by
General Giron.

Any thing in the shape of a naval force would drive off Sir G. Collier.

*Nevertheless things remained quiet for a few more days, and the siege
progressed.* We established a battery of four 18 pounders against a

302

convent, which the enemy had fortified and occupied in force, about 600 yards from the works of San Sebastian, the possession of which was necessary, previous to the commencement of any further operations against the place. This battery opened on the morning of the 14th, and the convent was so far destroyed that . . . Graham ordered that the building, and a redoubt which protected its left flank, might be stormed on the 17th . . . our troops were established at the convent . . . and our works have since been continued with great activity; and I understand from Sir Thomas that the batteries will open to destroy and enfilade the defences of the point of attack on to-morrow. The same batteries will answer to effect a breach in the town wall.

To Graham, 20 July: I did not summon Badajoz or Burgos, and the reason for not doing so has been confirmed in the King's papers *taken at Vitoria*, viz., that French officers are ordered not to surrender a place before it has been stormed. But as I hope the men will, on this occasion employ themselves, when they get in, in destroying the enemy, rather than, as usual, in plunder, I think this place should be summoned. But as it is desirable that the summons should be given at a period when it will not convey notice to the enemy of our intentions, you had better send it in to-morrow morning.

I believe the storm ought to take place by daylight, particularly if the defences are effectively destroyed; and as the enemy have their retreat open to the castle, and the means of sortie from thence when they please, the officers and men ought to be particularly warned of the danger of wandering about the town in search of plunder.

The date for the storm was set – 25 July.

Meanwhile Marshal Soult had returned to command the French. Recalled from the Peninsula in March he had successfully commanded Napoleon's centre at the battles of Lützen and Bautzen which had won for the French the truce in northern Europe. His proclamation to his troops dated 23 July first vilifies Joseph as an incompetent coward – they had quarrelled throughout the previous four years – and concludes:

Soldiers! I partake of your chagrin, your grief, your indignation. I know that the blame of the present situation of the army is imputable to others – be the merit of repairing it yours. I have borne testimony to the Emperor of your bravery and zeal. His instructions are to drive the enemy from those lofty heights which enable him proudly to survey our fertile valleys, and chase them across the Ebro. It is on the Spanish soil that your tents must next be pitched, and from thence your resources drawn . . . Extensive but combined movements for the relief of the fortresses are upon the eve of taking place. They will be completed in a few days. Let the account of our success be dated Vitoria – and the birth of his Imperial Majesty [*15th August*] be celebrated in that city . . .

It's a revealing document, as those composed bombastically out of spite and ambition usually are. As well as the unashamed implication that the plunder of Spain, or even mere subsistence from Spain, will be a motive for his troops, there is also the reference to the heights from which the British looked down: it reveals what Wellington would dearly have liked to know – from what quarter the counter offensive would come. Soult had three options – to march along the coast directly to the relief of San Sebastian, to combine that move with a thrust up the Bidassoa towards Wellington's centre, or to thrust through the passes of Maya and Roncesvalles on his right. Effectually Wellington's dispositions covered all three possibilities – but only if the commanders on the spot did their bit properly. The trouble was that his extreme left was separated from his extreme right by forty-five miles of rugged, confusing, unfamiliar countryside.

The twenty-fifth of July turned out to be a bad day for the allies and it is almost as if Wellington had a presentiment of this for in a letter he must have written very early in the morning to Liverpool, now Prime Minister, he offers a far franker estimation of the situation than the one he had previously sent to Bathurst. I do not think we could successfully apply to this frontier of Spain the system on which we fortified the country between the Tagus and the sea. That line is a very short one, and the communication easiest and shortest on our side. The Pyrenees are a very long line; there are not fewer than seventy passes through the mountains, and the communication, as far as I have been able to learn hitherto, is on the side of the enemy . . . *On 1 August he put the same point again to Bathurst in his dispatch which covered the next very hectic week.* The defect of the position was that the communication between the several divisions was very tedious and difficult, while the communications of the enemy in front of the passes was easy and short; and in the case of attack those in the front line could not support each other, and could look for support only from the rear.

One must ask why Wellington chose to remain in such a position. And the answer at first sight is obvious enough – he had no choice. To retire to the Ebro would have been politically disastrous while Napoleon was conducting his war of diplomacy in the north. And because of the truce he could not press into France. From a military point of view this would have been the right thing to do, for he had, to begin with at any rate, a dispersed and demoralised army ahead of him and he would have quickly achieved good defensive positions on the Nive, Nivelle, or even the Adour at Bayonne.

304

Roncesvalles

Obvious, but I believe too, as always, that he knew what he was about: that although he expected Soult to come at him through Hendaye and then perhaps up the Bidassoa, it did not much matter where he came, so long as he did. The point was, to lure him back on to non-French territory, where the war could be legitimately carried on again. What went wrong was that when the attacks came the English generals, from whom Wellington was cut off by those steep, twisting valleys, and rain-soaked forested crags, panicked and pulled back a very great deal more quickly than they should have done.

But the first bad news of the twenty-fifth came from San Sebastian. Graham to Wellington, St Sebastian, 25 July, 1813, 5.30 a.m.:

> My Lord, The attack has failed, owing to the quantity of musketry and hand-grenades the enemy brought upon the column in its advance and on its arrival at the breach. I cannot now form an estimate of the loss, but there is a number of officers wounded, and probably from two to three hundred men. Sir R. Fletcher has received a contusion on his leg . . .

Wellington received this at about ten o'clock at Lesaca, where, apparently, he was pacing in a churchyard. Immediately he rode off to San Sebastian and perhaps missed by minutes the sound of gun-fire in the hills behind him. I went to the siege on the 25th, and, having conferred with . . . Graham . . . it appeared to me that it would be necessary to increase the facilities of the attack before it should be repeated. But, upon adverting to the state of our ammunition, I found that we had not sufficiency to do anything effectual till that should arrive for which I had written on the 26th June, which I had reason to believe was embarked at Portsmouth, and to expect every hour. I therefore desired that the siege should for the moment be converted into a blockade, a measure which I found to be the more desirable when I returned to Lesaca in the evening.

When things go fairly wrong, Wellington's prose begins to approximate to that of a bank manager turning down an overdraft facility having adverted to the insufficiency of collateral. But when they go badly wrong, especially on account of his generals' blunders, he presents nothing but the very barest facts without comment, praise, or blame. It makes dull reading of what were often the most nail-biting events in the war – so here is what happened on the twenty-fifth and twenty-sixth, but pieced together from the historians for the most part rather than from our hero's pen.

The passes of Maya and Roncesvalles were held by the right and centre right of the army under Hill's overall command. But because of the difficulty of communication between the two passes and the fact that he was also in charge of the blockade of Pamplona his headquarters were well to the rear. Soult had marched most of his army from where they had been seen collecting near

306

Hendaye back into the Pyrenees. At dawn or a little after he attacked Roncesvalles with 40,000 men and Maya with 21,000. This was against Hill's 40,000, but initially the odds were far more in his favour, for the actual passes were held by far fewer – Roncesvalles by 13,000 under Byng, and later Cole; Maya initially by 6,000 led by Pringle who was a new and untried replacement for Cadogan, and eventually by S. Stewart, 'who never obeyed an order'.

At Roncesvalles the attack came on the mile wide saddle that marks the watershed. On the left Clausel was held by 500 riflemen on a 300 yard plateau of rocks and ridges and etiolated pasture until about 10.00 a.m. Both sides pushed in more troops, but the French still had enormous numerical superiority. However, the front was a short one, and neither side gained any material advantage. Wet cloud descended at 4.00 p.m., thick wet cloud reducing visibility to five yards. It's hell driving in it. One cannot imagine fighting in it. It is also horribly eery. The trees drip icy water, somewhere you can hear the prattle of a stream but is the drop to your left five feet or five hundred? Are you walking up hill or down? And didn't we pass that boulder ten minutes ago? Cole was frightened – not for himself but for his men – how hold on in this fog when a whole army who probably have guides with them knowing every inch of the way, might get round behind you? In spite of Wellington's specific orders to face out an attack he pulled back on to the high road to Pamplona. Wellington's dispatch sounds the tiniest note of disapproval: Cole considered it to be necessary to withdraw in the night. *Once below the fog the retreat was well handled and took him to Zubiri; Picton and the 3rd had been ordered up to support him there as soon as Wellington had heard of the attack on Roncesvalles.*

At Maya the basic position was held, but at the cost of unnecessary casualties. Here from 10.00 a.m. to 6.00 p.m. 6,000 allies held 20,000 French and only conceded a bare half mile, but they lost 1,500 men because the inexperienced Pringle fed in small units piecemeal instead of reinforcing his line convincingly. Stewart was equally indecisive when he arrived – indeed the pipe-major of the 92nd at one point took affairs into his own hands and piped the regiment back into the battle when Stewart had ordered them to retire. Moreover the allies lost three guns, spiked and thrown into a valley – the only ones lost under Wellington's command that were not immediately retaken.

I was not apprized of these events till late in the night of the 25th and 26th; *and inaccurately at that; at this point he did not know of Cole's withdrawal, nor the extent – 1500 out of 6,000 – of the losses at Maya,* and I adopted immediate measures to concentrate the army to the right, still providing for the siege of San Sebastian, and for the blockade of Pamplona.

He pulled back the 7th and Light divisions to back up the troops on the Maya, leaving the Light on his left so it could, if necessary, make forced marches down the Bidassoa to support Graham. Nevertheless Graham, at San Sebastian, was now exposed. To Graham, 26 July (wrongly dated as 24 in Dispatches X, p. 570) 4.00 a.m.: I think it desirable that you should carry into execution the arrangement proposed in my note last night so much farther as to embark the guns and stores which you will take out of the batteries, leaving only sufficient to keep up the fire.

I am going towards San Estevan and Elizondo . . .

He met Hill at Elizondo and found that 'Daddy' had everything under control – he was taking up a strong defensive position at Irurita, and the French had stayed put in the Col de Maya.

At 8.00 p.m. Wellington was at Almandoz where he heard at last of Cole's withdrawal, but he knew that Picton was now up with him and he ordered them both to hold the position at Zubiri, thus completing his 'concentration to the right' and consolidating a new line which, though withdrawn, had the advantage of bringing his divisions into closer communication with each other.

However, Picton and Cole had already decided otherwise. Picton to Wellington, Zubiri, 26 July, 8.30 p.m.:

The enemy . . . extended himself much to our right . . . which was easily turnable . . . and the country offering no post between this place and Pamplona . . . I agreed with . . . Cole that it was advisable to retire . . . on Vitoria Road, where we shall take up a position at as short a distance as practicable from Pamplona.

This withdrawal could have been catastrophic. It gave the French the opportunity to pin them down with their vastly superior numbers, nearly two to one, while they relieved Pamplona and added that garrison to their force. They then might have driven them west out of the line altogether. And almost immediately it gave them the chance to cut the road from Pamplona to Olague and Almandoz, in fact to the Bidassoa, and so prevent or very materially delay the arrival of reinforcements; whereas if they had remained at Zubiri, a mountain track a mere five miles long as the crow flies communicated them with the 6th division, which equally was placed to reinforce Hill. But by this movement they had actually put the 6th at risk (see map page 299).

Wellington reached Olague at 10.00 a.m. on the twenty-seventh, and there received Picton's note. Immediately he saw the danger. By their withdrawal Cole and Picton had given the French a chance to destroy the allied army in detail. Later he said: 'All the beatings we have given the French have not given our generals confidence in themselves and in the exertion of their troops. They are really heroes when I am on the spot to direct them, but when I am obliged to quit them they are children.'

He galloped south accompanied only by Lord Fitzroy Somerset. As they approached the northern end of the village of Sorauren he could see the French massing on the ridges of hills to his left and even behind him. A patrol was moving down the slopes with the obvious intention of taking him. In front Cole's 4th division was spread thinly, far too thinly, along the ridge south-east of the village, and there was no sign of the 3rd. He weighed up the situation with astonishingly cool accuracy, and scribbled this note to Murray, his Q.M.G., who was back at Olague.

At the bridge near Lairasoana, 27th July, 1813, 11 A.M.

Our troops are formed on the heights on this side of Pamplona, the enemy in the front. The enemy's right is close to the road to Ostiz, near this village. The road therefore by Ostiz can no longer be used.

The artillery and other carriages at Ostiz *in what had been the protected rear of the 6th* must march immediately to Olague.

As soon as the 6th division have cooked, they, and all the artillery at Olague, and now at Ostiz, are to march to Lizaso . . . Hill should march this night, if possible to Lanz, leaving a post at the head of the Pass, which he should withdraw in the morning.

I will send orders to Lanz and Lizaso for further proceedings.

The 7th division should also march on towards Lizaso.

Wellington

It is a marvellously precise and clear document. The 6th and 7th to Lizaso to wait orders. Thereby the 6th was removed from the extreme danger it was in, and both were placed on the alternative route to Pamplona, one the French could not cut. They could reach Sorauren, even by this roundabout mountainous route in a day, if that turned out to be the best thing. Or they could take the French in flank, if Hill was threatened up the road to Lanz. Or, if the worst happened, they could cover Cole and Picton's retreat towards Vitoria if that turned out to be necessary. But most probably one or both would come in to support Cole and Picton in what already looked like a sound defensive position in the old style. The only thing was . . . somehow he would have to frighten the French into holding back their assault for the rest of the day if possible, certainly for as long as he could . . .

Somerset took the note and galloped back off north. Wellington, no doubt with an anxious if calculating glance behind and to his left, clattered through the single street. As he left it the French patrol came over the bridge where a moment earlier he had rested his notebook on the parapet.

Coming out of the village he could see how a shoulder came down from Cole's ridge towards him. A white chalky track curled up past a hermitage where a Portuguese regiment held the left of the position, a track in full view of both

309

armies, in cannon shot of the French, but out of musket range . . . so long as those fellows behind kept their distance.

It was a calculated risk with a clear purpose. To those in the allied lines a solitary horseman appeared on the track below them. From a distance the silhouette was already familiar, then the short, grey coat buttoned to the chin, the small plumeless cocked hat. Nearer they knew for sure the nose, the high-arched brows, the firm set of the mouth that did not smile much, but smiled a little as reaching the crest, he reined in in an easy little pirouette and briefly doffed his hat – as much to the French across the way as to his own troops.

'Douro, Douro, Douro,' cried the Portuguese, using the title that country had conferred on him.

'Viva el Velintón, y viva la Nación,' cheered the Spaniards.

'By Jasus, it's Atty,' called out an Irish voice, 'the long-nosed bugger that licks the French.'

Later he said: 'Why, at one time it was rather alarming, certainly, and it was a close run thing.'

SORAUREN

Through his telescope Wellington could see that the French army was by no means fully up. Clausel's three divisions, 17,000 or more, were there, but Reille's corps, of about equal numbers, was only just coming in. Clausel wanted to attack but Soult, who could see Wellington as clearly as Wellington wanted to be seen, had had his mind made up by the presence of that spare figure across the way. He would wait, certainly until Reille's corps was fully in, preferably until he had made contact with d'Erlon, whose 20,000 should be pushing Hill down the Maya to make contact with his left.

'I saw him,' said Wellington later, 'spying at us – then write and send off a letter – I knew what he would be writing, and gave my orders accordingly.'

Both ridges are about a mile long, linked by a saddle at the eastern end which itself is marked on the southern side by a turfy hillock. The gap between them is very deep and very steep, grown over with brambles and littered with quartzy boulders that look like melting blocks of ice. Just below the saddle the slope up to Cole's ridge is at its steepest, at times almost a climb. As you near the top it levels a little and there are signs of terracing, also of the flattened ramparts of an iron age fort. On the top there is turf and a low cover of sage, thorns, scabious, some clover, and a box-like shrub that is faintly aromatic. In July there are cinnamon butterflies with black spots, frittilaries of some sort, Marbled Whites and Chalkhill Blues. There is a hot wind everywhere except in the valley, which, at midday and in the afternoon, becomes an oven. A lot of men died on the slopes and the wind in the brambles which are as fierce as barbed wire still seems to have something to say about it.

To Bathurst, the dispatch of 1 August again: I joined the 3rd and 4th divisions just as they were taking up their ground on the 27th, and shortly afterwards the enemy formed their army . . .

In a short time after they had taken up their ground, the enemy attacked the hill on the right of the 4th division which was then occupied by one battalion of the 4th Portuguese regiment, and by the Spanish regiment of Pavia. These troops defended their ground, and drove the enemy from it with the bayonet. Seeing the importance of this hill to our position, I re-inforced it with the 40th regiment, and this regiment, with the Spanish regiments El Principe and Pavia, held it from this time, notwithstanding the repeated efforts of the enemy during the 27th and 28th to obtain possession of it.

Nearly at the same time that the enemy attacked this height on the 27th, they took possession of the village of Sorauren on the road to Ostiz, by which they acquired the communication by that road, and they kept up a fire of musketry along the line till it was dark.

That night there was the usual horrendous thunderstorm that preluded so many of Wellington's victories. There are, of course, thunderstorms in any of the mountains of Spain two or three times a week in July and August. They may or may not have presaged Wellington's victories: they certainly presaged Rathbone's attempts to sleep in a tent or a camping car on or near the battlefields one hundred and sixty-five years later. This one passed before midnight when the men on Cole's ridge could look back to see Pamplona illuminated by the garrison in celebration of the relief they were sure would come next day.

The rain delayed the movement of the 6th, Hill's withdrawal to Lanz, and the French attack.

We were joined on the morning of the 28th *(the fourth anniversary of Talavera)* by the 6th division of infantry, and I directed that the heights should be occupied on the left of the valley of the Lanz *(Ulzana)* and that the 6th division should form across the valley in rear of the left of the 4th division . . .

The 6th division had scarcely taken their position when they were attacked by a very large force of the enemy which had been assembled in the village of Sorauren.

311

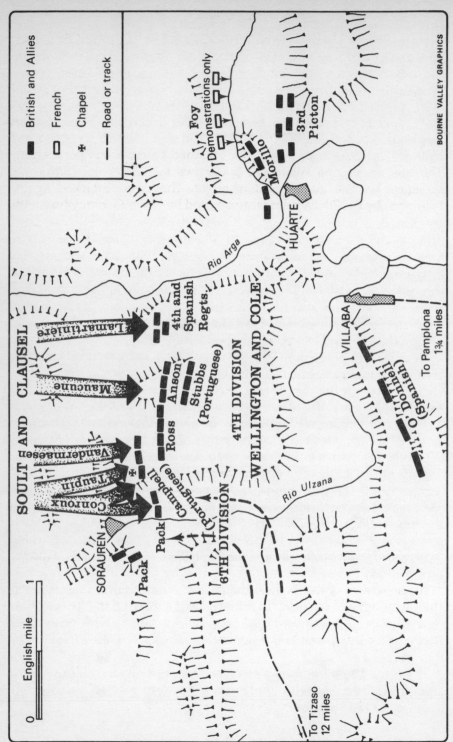

22. Sorauren: first day, 28 July 1813

Their front was however so well defended by the fire of their own light troops from the heights on their left, and by the fire from the heights occupied by the 4th division and . . . Campbell's Portuguese brigade, that the enemy were soon driven back with immense loss from a fire on their front, both flanks, and rear.

In order to extricate their troops . . . the enemy now attacked the height on which the left of the 4th division stood, which was occupied by the 7th caçadores, of which they obtained a momentary possession. *This was up the path Wellington had arrived by. The French reached the hermitage but that was as far as they got.* They were attacked again, however, by the 7th caçadores, supported by Major General Ross with his brigade of the 4th division, and were driven down with great loss. *This was the pattern of the whole day. Although outnumbered by two to one over the whole area, and by three to one or more where the actual fighting took place, Wellington always anticipated the attacks, and, as usual using the reverse slopes, was almost always able to meet the actual onslaughts on more or less equal terms.*

The battle now became general along the whole front of the heights . . . and in every part in our favour excepting where one battalion of the 10th Portuguese regiment of Major General Campbell's brigade was posted. This battalion having been overpowered, and having been obliged to give way immediately on the right of . . . Ross's brigade, the enemy established themselves on our line and . . . Ross was obliged to withdraw from his post. *This was at the very most western end of the land bridge, and a critical moment for, for a time, the allies actually faced the real odds of three to one.*

I, however, ordered the 27th and 48th regiments to charge, first, that body of the enemy which had first established themselves on the height, and next, those on the left. Both attacks succeeded, and the enemy were driven down with immense loss; and the 6th division having moved forward at the same time to a situation in the valley nearer to the left of the 4th, the attack upon this front ceased entirely, and was continued but faintly on other points of our line.

In the course of this contest the gallant 4th division . . . surpassed their former good conduct. Every regiment charged with the bayonet, and the 40th, 7th, 20th, and 23rd, four different times. Their officers set them the example, and Major General Ross had two horses shot under him.

The Portuguese troops likewise behaved admirably; and I had every reason to be satisfied with the conduct of the Spanish regiments . . .

To Bentinck, who was overall commander now in the east of Spain, 5 August:

I never saw such fighting as we have had here . . . the battle of the 28th was fair <u>bludgeon</u> work . . . and the loss of the enemy was immense. Our loss has likewise been very severe, but not of a nature to cripple us.

To William: I escaped as usual unhurt, and I begin to believe that the finger of God is upon me . . . *He used the same phrase once more – after Waterloo. To us now it sounds like the onset of delusions of grandeur, but that cannot be the case since he was already, in every possible way, rather grand. In fact, it was the sheer wonder of it that bothered him – as we have already seen, Generals in those days were often wounded, quite often killed; Wellington himself was badly bruised on six occasions. There cannot have been many men under his command whose chances of survival, computed by a modern insurance company, would have been worse than his – he was always there, no-one else was throughout the six years. So this apparently large claim that the deity had a special interest in his survival does not arise from any source other than the response of his sceptical, pragmatic mind to a phenomenon that was extraordinary and required explanation.*

On the twenty-ninth nothing happened on Cole's ridge. Both sides were waiting for reinforcements – Dalhousie and the 7th were called in from Lizaso to strengthen Wellington's left, Soult waited for d'Erlon to come down from the Maya on his right. The heat built up from the valley floor and the corpses between the two positions, and those caught in the brambles, stems an inch thick, thorns an inch long, began to blacken. The French had lost 4,000, the allies 2,500.

Soult made his calculations soundly enough. Although the allies were concentrating at Sorauren, Clausel and Reille would still outnumber them, and Hill's force now barely numbered 10,000 against d'Erlon's 20,000. The allied army was still split, Graham, and the Light division covering him, accounting for a third of the total. He left Clausel and Reille to hold a position which was stronger than the allied one had been, and joined d'Erlon, who also had behind him a convoy of supplies and ammunition which would give him three or four more days before he would have to either get into the Spanish plains for subsistence or withdraw into France.

What he could hardly have expected was that Wellington would seize back the initiative at Sorauren by launching a combination of storming attacks, brilliantly planned, and perfectly executed.

I, however – *an astonishing 'however' – because the numbers in front of him were still greater than his own and the French held a position stronger than his had been, because Sorauren was now fortified, and because he had a garrisoned fortress in his rear –* I, however, determined to attack their position and ordered Dalhousie to possess himself of the top of the mountain in his front, by which the enemy's right would be turned; and . . . Picton to cross the heights on which the enemy's left had stood, and to turn their left by the road to Roncesvalles. All the arrangements were made to attack the front of the enemy's position, as soon as the effect of these movements on their flanks should begin to appear . . . Pakenham *replacing Pack who had been wounded on the twenty-eighth* turned the village of Sorauren as soon as . . . Dalhousie had driven the enemy from the mountain *to the west of the Ulzana* by which that flank was defended; and the 6th division and . . . Byng's brigade . . . instantly attacked and carried that village . . . Cole likewise attacked the front of the enemy's position . . . *down through those brambles and quartzy rocks that look like melting ice but are too hot to touch, and up the other side.* All these operations obliged the enemy to abandon a position which is one of the strongest and most difficult of access that I have yet seen occupied by troops.

Considering that position, and the numbers they had, if the French had fought as well as they had at Salamanca, it would not have done . . . but our hero had an eye for such things: many of the French were adolescent conscripts, they had been beaten two days earlier, they were hungry.

It was now a question of pursuit – and for once it went well.

In their retreat from this position the enemy lost a great number of prisoners . . . and the movement made by Sir Thomas Picton merited my highest commendation. The latter officer co-operated in the attack on the mountain, by detaching troops to his left . . . *The twenty-eighth must have been the most humiliating day in the history of the 'Fighting Third'. While the 4th held Cole's ridge they had been kept in reserve. And not only that – when Foy did demonstrate against them, Morillo's Spaniards were in front of them to hold him off. No-one I have read suggests that this was Wellington's rebuke for Picton's failure to hold the Zubiri position, but I believe it was. Anyway he now came storming up the Arga so fast that he all but surrounded Foy who scuttled back up to Roncesvalles to escape instead of falling back with the rest of the French towards Olague. In some sense this was a desertion of Soult, but he got more of his corps back into France than any of his colleagues.*

While these operations were going on, and in proportion as I observed their success, I detached troops to the support of Hill.

The enemy *d'Erlon and Soult* appeared in his front late in the morning and . . . obliged him to withdraw from the height which he occupied before Lizaso to the next range. He there, however, maintained himself . . .

I continued the pursuit of the enemy after their retreat from the mountain *of Sorauren* to Olague, where I was at sunset immediately in the rear of their attack upon . . . Hill. They withdrew from his front in the night; and yesterday *31 July* took up a strong position with two divisions to cover their rear on the pass of Doña Maria. *This was in virtually trackless mountains to the west of Almandoz.*

. . . Hill and . . . Dalhousie attacked and carried the pass notwithstanding the vigorous resistance of the enemy, and the strength of their position . . .

In the meantime, I moved with . . . Byng's brigade, and the 4th division, by the pass of Velate, upon Irurita, in order to turn the enemy's position on Doña Maria . . . Byng took in Elizondo a large convoy going to the enemy, and made many prisoners.

We have this day continued the pursuit of the enemy in the valley of the Bidasoa *(sic),* and many prisoners and much baggage have been taken . . . Byng has possessed himself . . . of the position on the Puerto de Maya and the army will be this night nearly in the same positions which they occupied on the 25th July.

He sums up: The enemy having been considerably re-inforced and re-equipped, after their late defeat *at Vitoria,* made a most formidable attempt to relieve the blockade of Pamplona . . . This attempt has been entirely frustrated by a part only of the allied army . . .

The enemy's expectations of success beyond raising the blockade of Pamplon were certainly very sanguine. They brought into Spain a large body of cavalry, and a great number of guns; neither of which arms could be used to any great extent by either party in the battle which took place.

To Graham, 1 August, 1813, 8.00 p.m.: I imagine there are none of the enemy in Spain this night . . . *A pardonable exaggeration – two garrisons and an outpost remained in the west, Suchet in the east.*

The week 25 July to 1 August is one of the greatest in Wellington's career, but because the operations were confused, began with serious mistakes on the part of his generals, and were spread over a wide area, they never quite caught the public's, or the media's attention in the way that Salamanca, Vitoria and Waterloo did. Of the 60,000 French engaged only 45,000 got back into France, while only 40,000 allies took part of which 7,000 were lost. The effect on the morale of the allies – Russia and Prussia, and neutral Austria – in the north of Europe was incalculable.

Of the difference between the marshals and himself, Wellington later said: 'They planned their campaigns just as you might make a splendid set of harness. It looks very well, and answers very well, until it gets broken;

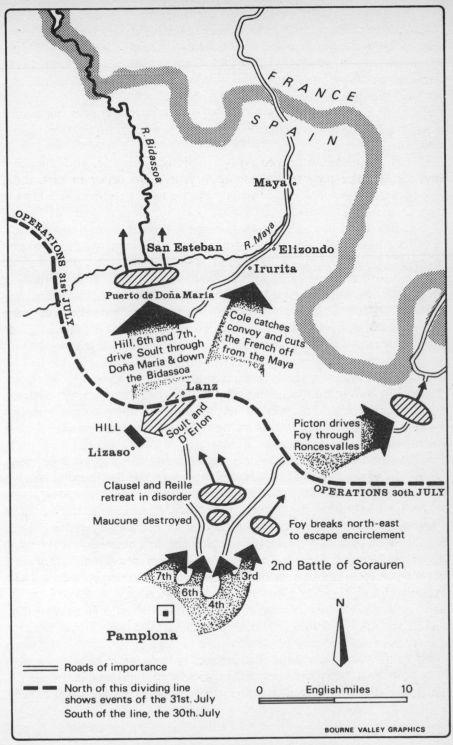

FRANCE

SPAIN

R. Bidassoa

Maya °

OPERATIONS 31st JULY

San Esteban

R. Maya
° Elizondo
° Irurita

Puerto de Doña Maria

Hill, 6th and 7th,
drive Soult through
Doña Maria & down
the Bidassoa

Cole catches
convoy and cuts
the French off
from the Maya

Lanz

HILL

Soult and
D'Erlon

Lizaso °

Picton drives
Foy through
Roncesvalles

Clausel and Reille
retreat in disorder

OPERATIONS 30th JULY

Maucune destroyed

Foy breaks north-east
to escape encirclement

2nd Battle of Sorauren

N

7th   3rd

6th   4th

Pamplona

Roads of importance

North of this dividing line
shows events of the 31st. July
South of the line, the 30th. July

0   English miles   10

BOURNE VALLEY GRAPHICS

23. The Battles for the Pyrenees: final stages

and then you are done for. Now I made my campaigns out of ropes. If anything went wrong I tied a knot; and went on.'

He was surely thinking of the battles for the Pyrenees.

SAN SEBASTIAN

On 4 August Wellington's headquarters were in Lesaca, above the west bank of the Bidassoa and a little more than ten miles inland. He spent the day catching up on his correspondence.

To Graham, 9.00 a.m.: The troops are of course a great deal fatigued, and we have suffered very considerably . . . which, with the existing want of shoes and musket ammunition, induces me to delay for a day or two any forward movement, and to doubt the expediency of making one at all. I keep everything in readiness, however. I am perfectly aware of the objections to our positions in the Pyrenees; but if we should not be able to advance from them without incurring more loss than we ought, or than we can well afford, I am afraid that we cannot well retire from them . . . as it is, I hope that Soult will not feel an inclination to renew his expedition on this side at least. *The 'other' side would have been Catalonia in support of Suchet.* The French army must have suffered terribly . . . I understand that their officers say they have lost 15,000 men. I thought so, but as they say so, I now think more . . . It is strange that our diminution of strength does not exceed 1500 men; although I believe our casualties are 6000. *But then all those who 'straggled' after Vitoria, or got lost in the Pyrenees later, had been steadily, quietly, without drawing too much attention to themselves, slipping back into the ranks.* I propose to resume the operations of the siege as soon as the train and stores shall arrive from England . . .

But there were problems, which Graham had been at pains to point out to him. To Bathurst, same day: Sir Thomas Graham reports that there is a daily communication between San Sebastian, and the French army by sea; and, in fact, boats go in and out as they please.

The siege was much delayed; and in case it should be necessary to raise the siege, the loss of guns and stores would be infallible . . . *sic – his prose is breaking down because he knows he is special pleading if not actually fibbing. He knows there is no real chance of the siege being raised, but he does want more and better naval support, and this threat might produce results . . .* owing to the want of naval means, the harbour boats at Passages being

San Sebastian

excessively bad, and all navigated by women, who are unequal to the labor of loading and unloading them; and the greatest number of boats are already destroyed by the weights we have put in them.

I entreat your Lordship to consider these points, and to let me know whether Government will or not send a sufficient naval force to co-operate with the army in this siege. The place has nine months' provisions, and there is no chance of getting it except by siege.

All of which is a bit crusty. On the same day he wrote to Beresford: My rheumatism still keeps me at home.

It's perhaps the strongest indication of how the battles for the Pyrenees had taken it out of him – he was the fittest of men, and that rheumatism could well have been psychosomatic . . . After the retreat from Burgos nine months earlier, he copped a bout of lumbago.

San Sebastian was to be no push-over. In 1813 the town was at the end of an isthmus with the estuary of the Urumea on the eastern side and a nearly land-locked bay to the west. The Urumea had silted up and then, as now, the actual port was Passages, two miles to the east. The town itself had Vauban-style fortifications and was dominated by an old castle on a rocky hill. The population of 10,000 were Basques – that is they spoke the same language, had the same customs, and were racially the same as the Basques in Hendaye and Biarritz. They had been occupied by the French for five years, and expected, indeed wanted the border to be re-drawn to place them in France. The garrison included front-line infantry that Foy had put in on the retreat from Vitoria. The guns on the castle could carry a mile and a half which was a fair bit of the distance, only twelve miles, to Hendaye and the French coast – the blockade therefore was not easily maintained by one frigate only.

Fortunately Wellington was in no hurry, in spite of pressure from both Government, who wanted him in France to stiffen the allies against Napoleon, and the media who could not see why one success should not be immediately followed by another.

To Bathurst, 8 August: It is a very common error, among those unacquainted with military affairs, to believe there are no limits to military success. After having driven the French from the frontiers of Portugal, it is generally expected that we shall immediately invade France; and some even here expect that we shall be in Paris in a month . . .

An army which has made such marches, and has fought such battles . . . is necessarily much deteriorated . . . The equipment of the army, their ammunition, the soldiers' shoes &c., require renewal; the magazines for the new operations require to be collected and formed, and

320

many arrangements to be made, without which the army could not exist a day, but which are not generally understood by those who have not had the direction of such concerns in their hands. Then observe, that this new operation is only the invasion of France, in which country every body is a soldier, where the whole population is armed and organised . . .

He might have added: 'and where our Commander is mentally and physically pretty exhausted himself.' It's an odd mood this, that Wellington got into after extreme exertions – there's a vulnerability about it, and a desire it seems at times almost to chat in his letters. To Bathurst, 9 August: I have not had a great deal of reason to complain about the conduct of the troops since the last battles; but we are pulled up on the frontiers of France, and they are getting into good order again. As we are getting men out of hospital, I hope we shall soon have in the ranks within 2000 or 3000 men of the number we had before the late battles. But our soldiers are terrible fellows for everything but fighting with their regiments. *'Fellow' is always a term of commendation, even affection – perhaps that spontaneous acclamation as he rode on to Cole's ridge had revealed to him something that he had not been fully aware of: the respect and even affection the men felt for him.* What do you think of 70 or 80 of them, having wandered from their regiments during the late operations, and having surrendered themselves to some of the French peasantry who accompanied the French army, and whom they ought, and would at other times, have eaten up?

Our having so much money *from Vitoria* has enabled me to adopt a plan for paying every non-commissioned officer and soldier a day's pay every day, which will, I think, produce a reform in their conduct. Many of their outrages are certainly to be attributed to want of money. *Not so much then 'the scum of the earth' as poor souls who could not buy an extra pint of wine or some veg to add to the stew, but had to . . . well, find such commodities.*

He found time to show his gratitude to Prinny for his baton and his Garter. To Colonel Bloomfield, an aide of the Prince Regent, 10 August: I send by Colonel Blanckley a sword of very curious workmanship, which belonged to King Joseph, and was taken by a Spanish officer in the battle of Vitoria, and he has since given it to me; probably His Royal Highness may deem it worthy of a place in his armoury, and I shall be very much obliged to you if you will lay it at his feet, with my most dutiful respects.

Next day he took a look at the French outposts at Vera and met Hill. To Bathurst: I wish to draw your attention to the situation of Sir Rowland Hill and Sir John Hope *who had commanded the 7th in 1812 and was now about to return to replace Graham who was ill again.* They each of them

321

command very large corps, and great expenses must be incurred by them; and I know that the former, and I believe the latter, has not the means of defraying those expenses.

The General Officers of the British army are altogether very badly paid, and, adverting to the deductions from their pay they receive less than they did fifty years ago, while their expenses are more than doubled . . . while, from the custom of the British army, they are all obliged to keep tables for their staff . . .

I would beg your Lordship to observe likewise that the expenses of an officer who spends more than he receives here are vastly increased by the disadvantageous rate at which he is obliged to draw his money; and I believe in this way even Sir Thomas Graham, who has a large private fortune, has been frequently in distress here.

The days trickled by and there was little to do but wait for shoes and the ordnance that was being collected at Portsmouth. Amazingly, the French in 'blockaded' San Sebastian were better served. To Bathurst: You will scarcely believe . . . that shoes and sandbags have been sent into that place by sea from St. Jean de Luz.

To Graham, 13 August: The season is wearing away fast, and every point to give protection to our shipping becomes of importance.

It is to be hoped that the British Government will at last discover the nature of the element by which they are surrounded; and will in future have their preparations made in time, particularly when the earliest notice is given them. *So much for the way our masters maintained the maritime power that had conquered at the Nile, Copenhagen, and Trafalgar. However, a dispatch vessel, the Polly, got through with news of the negotiations between Napoleon and the allies. The news of Vitoria had been kept from the French, but had put heart into the Russians and Prussians; nevertheless Napoleon was still playing off one against the other, and nothing was being properly considered or decided. It provoked straight comment from Wellington, who was perhaps becoming properly aware of his potential influence on world affairs. He was no longer a Sepoy General, but a Marquess, a K.G., a Field Marshal, and the only unbeaten commander in the world.*

To Bathurst, 14 August: There appears therefore, no concert or common cause in the negotiations for peace; and as for the operations of the war . . . there does not appear to exist any thing, in writing or any where, excepting in loose conversations among Princes. For my part I would not march even a corporal's guard upon such a system . . .

The object of each *ally* should be to diminish the power and influence of France, by which alone the peace of the world can be restored and maintained; and although the aggrandizement and security of the power of one's own country is the duty of every man, all nations may depend upon it that the best security for power . . . is to be found in the reduction of the power and influence of the grand disturber . . .

For my part, I repeat what I told you before, I shall enter France or not, (unless I am ordered) *and who, in Europe, was going to order Wellington in 1813?* according to what I think best for my operations as I have no reliance whatever upon what is doing in the north.

Graham's health had cracked again. 'The great increase of stomach complaints . . . as well as the aggravation of the symptoms which affect my right eye, warn me that it is time to relinquish the duties of active service.' To Graham, 15 August, 1813, 8.00 p.m.: I was very much concerned to find . . . that your health was in such a state as to induce you to think of returning to England. However much I regret this circumstance, I cannot but think you are right in giving up, if you find your health not equal to the calls upon your exertions; and I can only return my thanks for returning to us when you did. . . . *His own rheumatism was perhaps a little better:* I have been on horseback to-day. *To Beresford, same day, same time:* I am glad to find you are better. I am so likewise, but not yet quite free from pain when I move, and even sometimes when sitting still.

Which no doubt increased the testiness of his letter to Bathurst on the eighteenth: Your Lordship will see by my report, that we are still waiting for the battering train . . . This is a most important period in the campaign, particularly for the attack of a place in the Bay of Biscay *(he is thinking of the equinoctial gales).* How we are to attack Bayonne afterwards I am sure I do not know. A British Minister cannot have too often under his view the element by which he is surrounded . . .

We hear from France that peace is concluded. All that I am apprehensive of is that . . . Buonaparte may be enabled to detach a large force against us. I hope they *(Prussia, Russia, etc.)* understand that if he should do so, and we should by accident be overpowered, . . . he will not fulfil any expectations of favorable terms which he may have held out to them . . .

We have as yet no increase of naval force, excepting in dispatch vessels. It is curious that all the intelligence I have of San Sebastian comes from the French head quarters, they getting it by sea! *And curious too, of course, that his own intelligence depended on a spy or two operating out of Bayonne.*

The convoy arrived at last, the very next day, the nineteenth. But even then someone (the Senior Service?) cocked it up and infantry reinforcements were landed in the wrong place. To Captain Sir George Collier, R.N., 19 August, 9.00 p.m.: . . . I shall therefore be very much obliged to you, if you will take measures to have this infantry transported by sea from Bilbao to Passages.

His criticisms of the Navy had begun to tell. From Lord Melville, the First Lord of the Admiralty he received a touchy letter on the subject to which he replied in his most lapidary style on 21 August: What I have written has been founded upon my own sense of want of naval assistance on this coast . . . and I assure you that I neither know nor care what has passed, or may pass, in Parliament or in the newspapers on the subject.

I complain of an actual want of naval assistance and co-operation with the army. I know nothing about the cause of the evil . . . *there were several, but the most obvious was the war with America* . . . I state the fact, which nobody will deny; and leave it to Government to apply a remedy or not as they think proper, hoping only that they will let me know whether they propose to apply a remedy or not . . .

If the insecurity should be of any considerable duration . . . it will affect the army in its bread and corn; . . . the delay of any one ship affects the operations of the army . . . For instance, we have done literally nothing since the 2nd of August, because there was a mistake regarding the preparation of an ordnance equipment, which was afterwards delayed by contrary winds . . . But besides these facts I assure you that there is no hour in the day in which some statement does not come before me of the inconvenience resulting from the want of naval means; and even while writing this letter the Commissary General has been here to complain that his empty provision ships are detained at Santander for want of convoy!

Still, the ordnance had arrived, and things could get under way. Graham to Wellington, 26 August, 2.00 p.m.: 'The batteries opened this morning as was proposed . . . The arrangements are made with Sir G. Collier for the attack of the island (Santa Clara) about 2 A.M. to-morrow morning.' *This operation went off as planned and at last Wellington had something good to say for the sailors:* The conduct of Lieut. —— Arbuthnot of the Royal Navy, who commanded the boats, was highly meritorious, as likewise that of Lieut. Bell of the Royal Marines.

The bombardment from sea, the island, and the land continued for several days, and it is important at this point, for reasons which will become apparent, to quote from a letter Wellington wrote to Graham on the twenty-third: I am quite certain that the use of mortars and howitzers in a siege, for the purpose of what Colonel Dickson calls general annoyance, answers no purpose whatever against a Spanish place occupied by the French troops, excepting against the inhabitants of the place; and eventually

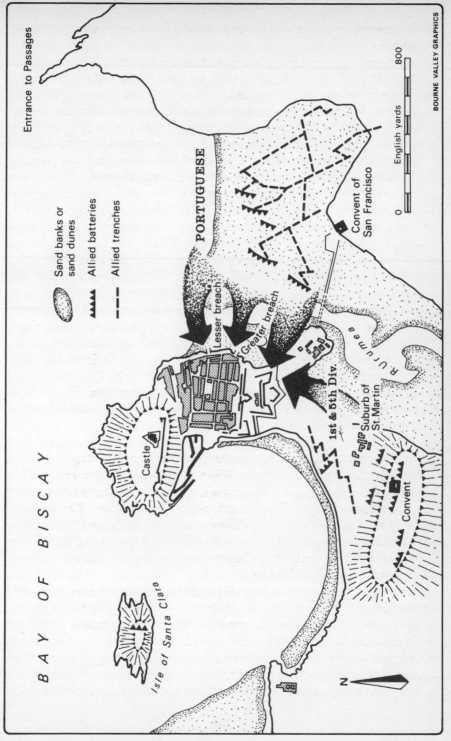

BAY OF BISCAY

Entrance to Passages

PORTUGUESE

Castle

Isle of Santa Clara

N

Sand banks or
sand dunes

Allied batteries

Allied trenches

Lesser breach

Greater breach

1st & 5th Div.

River Urumea

Suburb of
St. Martin

Convent

Convent of
San Francisco

English yards

0   800

BOURNE VALLEY GRAPHICS

when we shall get the place, against ourselves, and the convenience we should derive from having the houses of the place in a perfect state of repair . . .

On the twenty-eighth the key troops for the assault were moved in. To Graham: I have ordered 300 men of the 4th and Light divisions to march to Oyarzun to-morrow morning; and I shall be obliged to you if you will order 400 of the 1st division to assemble at the same place. I should hope these and some of Lord Aylmer's brigade would be enough to show the way to the breach . . .

I shall go over to Passages in the morning, to talk to Sir George Collier respecting an attack from the sea.

The assault on the town followed three days later. It was launched up the isthmus, and, by the Portuguese, across the estuary at low tide between 11.00 a.m. and noon on the thirty-first. The French placed undamaged field artillery (Foy's from Vitoria) into the breaches and almost brought the allied assault to a halt, with terrible losses, especially amongst the Portuguese who were in three feet of water. Graham now did a remarkable thing: with his troops almost in the breaches he re-opened the bombardment, but now firing grape, canister, and huge shrapnel shells fired from sixty-eight pounder carronades. The guns were new and of British manufacture – carronades were mortars built at the new works on the River Carron in Stirlingshire – and not a single missile was misplaced although some of the guns were firing from 1,200 yards. A few of the allies were wounded, but only by richochets and flying masonry.

The troops went in and there followed a short but bitter episode of street fighting before Rey, the Governor, withdrew what was left of his garrison, about a third, to the castle. Although many of the Spanish/Basque inhabitants fought with the French, and had traded with Bayonne throughout the war, it was only during this street fighting that any were molested at all. They suffered far less than the inhabitants of Ciudad Rodrigo or Badajoz. However, the town caught fire, perhaps as a result of Graham's second bombardment, and the Spanish press, indeed the world's press, accused Graham and Wellington of deliberately firing it – and therein lies the importance of that letter of the twenty-third. The town could have been set ablaze from any time after the carronades arrived and Wellington firmly rejected the option. To have set it burning on purpose when his troops went in would have been absurd: burning houses at that point could have served no purpose but did give cover to the garrison withdrawing to the castle. Indeed it's by no means unlikely that Rey set the fire going himself for that very purpose. Nevertheless, the British Government later paid for its reconstruction, which, though generous, was silly, for it seemed like an admission of guilt.

The dispatch which relates all this, is, of course, Graham's. Wellington's covering letter is brief: The place was stormed at 11 o'clock in the day of the 31st, and carried. The loss on our side has been severe . . . Generals . . . Leith, . . . Oswald, . . . and Robinson, were unfortunately wounded in the breach; and Colonel Sir Richard Fletcher was killed by a musket ball at the mouth of the trenches . . . In this officer . . . His Majesty's service has sustained a serious loss.

They had had their differences: over the first siege of Badajoz particularly, not to mention the proper width for gabions. But Fletcher had been Wellington's entirely competent and reliable instrument in the making of the Lines of Torres Vedras. Three weeks later he wrote directly to the Prime Minister, Lord Liverpool: I enclose a letter addressed to me by the late Sir Richard Fletcher, which was found among his papers, but which your Lordship will see by the date was written on the very date the head quarters broke up from Freneda . . . *21 May 1813. I don't know what was in Fletcher's letter, but it may well have been the same sort of appeal against low pay that Hope and Hill had more recently put in.*

I have had such frequent occasion to bring Sir Richard Fletcher's merits and services under the view of Government, that I have only to recall your Lordship's recollection to them, and earnestly to recommend his family to your favor and protection.

Liverpool replied: 'I will recommend such a pension for Colonel Fletcher's family as may be conformable to former precedents and due to his memory for his distinguished services.'

Convention demanded that Soult, in spite of the mauling he had suffered, should make some move towards the relief of San Sebastian. He timed the attempt well: it came the day before the assault.

The enemy crossed the Bidasoa by the fords between Andaya *Hendaye* and the destroyed bridge on the high road, before daylight on the morning of the 30th, with a very large force, with which they made a most desperate attack along the whole front of the position of the Spanish troops on the heights of San Marcial *which is a low but dominating ridge that runs parallel with the river in front of Behobie but a little less than a mile from it.* They were beat back, some of them even across the river, in the most gallant style by the Spanish troops, whose conduct was equal to that of any troops I have ever seen engaged, and the attack, having been frequently repeated, was upon every occasion defeated with the same gallantry and determination. The course of the river being immediately under the heights on the French side, on which the enemy had placed a considerable quantity of cannon, they were able to throw a bridge across the river three quarters of a mile above the high road, over which, in the afternoon, they marched again a considerable body, who, with those who had crossed the fords, again made a desperate attack upon the Spanish positions. *At this point General Freyre asked Wellington to deploy the English troops on his wings in support. Wellington later described the incident in conversation:* 'Well, I said, if I send you the English troops you ask for, they will win the battle; but as the French are already in retreat you may as well win it for yourselves. So they accordingly did; and now I see that in their accounts this is represented as one of their greatest battles – as a feat that does them the highest honor.'

At the time Wellington was more generous; his dispatch goes on: Notwithstanding that . . . I had a British division on each flank of the Spanish army, I am happy to be able to report that the conduct of the latter was so conspicuously good, and they were so capable of defending their post without assistance in spite of the desperate attempts of the enemy to carry it that . . . neither of them were in the least engaged in the action.

There were further engagements throughout that day and the next, all along the frontier between Vera and the Puerto de Maya, but in spite of the fact that Dalhousie at one point moved the 7th further forward than he had been instructed, Soult nowhere penetrated the allied line. A huge storm raised the level of the fords on the Bidassoa above six feet and brought the business to a halt.

Green, of the 68th rifles, was again in the front of Dalhousie's too-forward position, and gives us a good idea of what skirmishing in front of the line was like, and of other matters too.

It was now thought prudent to retire before this column to the next range of hills. We kept up a constant fire as we retired . . . there being several trees each man posted himself behind one . . . With firing so often, my flint became worn out, and I retired about fifteen yards to the rear . . . I . . . resumed my place; but had only fired one shot, when a ball struck me, entering my left side, a little below the heart. At first I felt nothing; in about ten seconds, however, I fell to the ground, turned sick and faint, and expected every moment to expire, having an intolerable burning pain in my left side. I thought it was all over with me . . . the sergeant-major ordered two of the men to take me to the rear . . . but I begged of them to let me alone, saying, 'For God's sake, let me die in peace!' The sergeant-major . . . said in a loud tone, 'Take him to the rear, for he is not dead.' They then raised me up, and loosed the straps of my knapsacks, and took off my belts. I opened my coat and waistcoat, and putting my hand against my side, found a lump occasioned by the ball nearly as large as a hen's egg. My shirt and trousers were drenched with blood . . .'

After further misadventures during which his life was saved by the Captain of his company, he reached the field hospital:

At length a surgeon began to examine me: he took off my shirt and ran his probe in the wound. In the meantime the Colonel of the Chasseurs Britanniques was brought to this spot wounded in the head; and the surgeon left me in my naked state to attend on him. In a few seconds, however, Mr Reid, our regimental surgeon, came to me, and ran his little finger into my side, to clear it of any substance that might be lodged in the wound. I cried aloud by reason of the pain it occasioned. 'Silence!' said the surgeon, 'it is for your own good.' The ball could not be extracted. A little dry lint was put over the wound, and a bandage bound tight round my body: my clothes were put on, and I was laid on the ground, but was so full of pain, that I could not rest more than two minutes in any one posture . . .

The ball was still in his body when he was discharged a year later. As far as I know he carried it with him to the grave, many years later. He wrote his memoirs in 1827, by when he was married, had children and a small business purchased out of his share of the Vitoria bounty, his discharge money, and so on.

Thus fizzled out Soult's last attempt to relieve the two French garrisons that remained. Extraordinarily though he did carry off one prisoner of note – F. S. Larpent, Wellington's Deputy Judge Advocate General, whose memoirs have provided me, and indeed all the chattier of the historians of the war, with some of the better anecdotes you have been reading. He was a civilian, a lawyer, and to him Wellington wrote: In former wars, a person of your situation would have been considered a non-combatant . . . but in this war, which, on account of the violence of enmity with which it is conducted, it is to be hoped will be the last, for some time at least, every body taken is considered a prisoner of war . . . I send you with this letter the sum of 200 dollars, of which I request you to acknowledge the receipt, and that you will let me know whether I can do any thing else for you.

Meanwhile the town of San Sebastian continued to burn, and Governor Rey, in the castle, resorted to tactics of a ferocity that indeed surpassed those normally current in the eighteenth or early nineteenth centuries – tactics very properly speaking more typical of our own period. Wellington to Graham, 5 September, 1813: I observe . . . that the prisoners are kept in the yard of the magazine 'sans blindages' *(without protection),* and many have been killed and wounded by the fire directed against that building.

I do not know that I have ever heard of such conduct, and the pretension founded upon it, viz., that we should not direct our fire against the place, is too ridiculous.

I request you to send in to General Rey a protest against his keeping prisoners in the yard of this magazine 'sans blindages' and likewise against his making them work under fire.

Rey capitulated as soon as the main batteries opened on the castle walls which were still basically medieval. To Graham, 9 September, 1813, 7.00 a.m.: I have received the capitulation, and sincerely congratulate you on your success . . . *and at 9.30 a.m.:* I shall be much obliged to you if you will give the following orders to the officer in charge of the Engineer Department . . . *which of course conceals a note of pathos. Truly Sir R. Fletcher was no longer there.* The pontoon train must be got together . . . and . . . assembled somewhere near Oyarzun . . . *and so on, particularly making sure that San Sebastian could not be retaken by a coup-de-main . . . but the important thing was the pontoon – not only was the Bidassoa in his front, but the Nivelle, the Nive, and the Ardour.*

JUSQU'AUX GENOUX DANS LA NEIGE

Of course that pontoon train did not arrive on time, as it had not at the start of the year in May. But this time the reasons for the delay were absurd. To Graham, 17 September, 1813, 9.30 a.m.: Fletcher's successor . . . is really too bad: This is the eighth day since he received the orders to collect the pontoon trains on the high road; and he is not now certain that the orders he sent have reached the officers in charge of them . . . He put his letter into the Spanish post office, I conclude directed in English . . . and there he left the matter. This is the way all our arrangements fail. The officers charged to send an order will not attend to that essential part of their duty, the mode of transmitting it.

Other vital preparations for the invasion of France were in hand. To Colonel Bunbury, Under Secretary of State, Lesaca, 19 September, 1813: I am very much obliged to you for the map of France, which, however, is of a shape I cannot conveniently carry, as we have no wheel carriages with the army, excepting the artillery. I have therefore had cut out the sheets . . . containing the maps of the country immediately in my front, which I have had pasted upon linen by the Staff corps and made to fold up . . .

Well! Such a burst of merry sarcasm – no wheel carriages, indeed – shows how the post-battle tristesse is at last lifting, and perhaps the psychosomatic rheumatism too. The news from Europe was good again. The allies had definitely refused Napoleon's offer of the Rhine as a frontier, fighting had broken out again with the battle of Dresden, and the way ahead for Wellington was clear. And if he was to move, why then, even the most humdrum things must be looked to. Humdrum perhaps, but very close to his Lordship's person. To Bathurst, 19 September: It is very desirable that some arrangement should be fixed and made public soon, under which officers will be able to get from England those equipments which they want. We can get nothing in these countries; and those who have been here as long as I have *(none had)* feel very uncomfortable for want of a variety of articles of their equipment, which they can get only from England. I cannot understand why the rule regarding the packets should have been made more strict lately; and I know that I among others, am suffering from it, not having even a second saddle.

Tin kettles inevitably cropped up again. A new batch were too heavy and . . . I beg leave to remark that there ought to be a canvass bag with each kettle.

More seriously, no – on a wider scale – he completed that day's volley of letters to Bathurst with this: . . . I acknowledge that I feel a great disinclination to enter the French territory under existing circumstances.

The superiority of numbers which I can take into France will consist in about 25,000 Spaniards, neither paid nor fed, and who must plunder, and will set the whole country against us . . . *Soult's army was still several thousand stronger than the British and Portuguese on their own.*

However, I shall put myself in a situation to menace a serious attack, and to make one immediately, if I should see a fair opportunity, or if I should hear that the Allies *in north Europe* have been really successful, or when Pamplona shall be in our possession.

To Graham, 24 September 1813, 1.00 p.m.: . . . it may be as well to move the 5th division and Wilson's brigade to their place in the line as soon as the weather holds up, as I intend to make the movement across the Bidasoa as soon afterwards as the state of the fords will allow . . .

To Graham, 24 September, 1813: Sir John Hope is to come out to succeed you . . .

I have received orders to invest Lord Dalhousie &c., with the Order of the Bath, and have fixed on the 27th for the ceremony, if you could make it convenient to come over here. The pontoons will not be ready till that day; and I doubt the river being low enough in these parts for our operation before that time.

On the same day he wrote to Bathurst on the subject of recruiting. It demonstrates, for the last time in this volume, that superior quality of his mind, his ability to see every problem in the wider context in which it existed. It also

331

shows how, in spite of his apparent aloofness, he was a lot closer to Green and Wheeler and the Connaught Rangers than might be supposed. I entirely concur with you in thinking that the best measure you can adopt to aid the recruiting of the army is to give an allowance to the wives and children, particularly of the Irish and Scotch soldiers. *There is a tactful irony here, he had been urging such a step for years.* When I was in office in Ireland, I had an opportunity of knowing that the women took the utmost pains to prevent the men from volunteering to serve in the line, and from enlisting; naturally enough, because from that moment they went not upon the parish, but upon the dung hill to starve. *This is no figure of speech. The dung hill is the refuse tip on which scraps of food might be found.* Indeed it is astonishing that any Irish militia soldier was ever found to volunteer; *the militia were raised for the defence of the country only, and to suppress riot. They were paid a family allowance which they lost as soon as they entered one of the regular regiments* . . . and they must certainly be the very worst members of society; and I have often been induced to attribute the frequency and enormity of the crimes committed by the soldiers to our having so many men who must have left their families to starve for the inducement of a few guineas to get drunk. *Again,* 'scum of the earth' *does not seem inappropriate language for this minority within his army.* A provision, however, for the wives and children of the soldiers will probably revive the spirit of volunteering, and we shall get better men than we have at present . . .

What had become a feud with the Navy was given a further twist in yet another letter to Bathurst written on the twenty-fourth. Wellington's criticisms had produced testy responses; yet more testily, but with touches of abrasive humour, he again lists the consequences of the Navy's failure to rule the waves off the Peninsula: Not a day passes that I don't receive an account of some capture at sea. Only yesterday . . . a Portuguese vessel, laden with 20,000 pairs of shoes . . . was run on shore by a French privateer, between Passages and Fuenterrabia *that is on allied held coast*; and this morning a report has arrived of the capture of two vessels off Viana. Your Lordship is also aware that the 77th regiment and 1200 Portuguese drafts are detained at Lisbon . . . for want of ships of war to give them convoy, Admiral George Martin's flag then flying in the <u>Wellington</u> tender. *Whether or not he was pleased to have had a mere tender named after him, I do not know. But it must have provoked that whooping laugh that so startled strangers, and even familiars, when he learnt that Martin was reduced to using it as his flagship.*

He goes on to describe again how San Sebastian was supplied right up to 31

332

August, and how the Navy could have blockaded it as early as June. Finally: Notwithstanding my ignorance of naval affairs in preferring the boats of the fleet to the harbour boats of Passages, navigated by women, for performing the services of landing the ordnance and the stores . . . I am happy to have to report that it was found practicable to give us this assistance in the second part of the siege . . . and that none of the difficulties referred to by the Secretary of the Admiralty were experienced.

On 5 October he decided he could wait no longer. To Graham, 5.00 p.m.: As the tide serves us on the 7th, and the weather is fair and settled, I propose that we should establish ourselves on that day on the right of the Bidasoa. Murray will send you the arrangements this day.

From what we can make out from an intercepted letter in cipher, from the Governor of Pamplona, I judge that he can hold out till the 20th or 25th; and till that time we certainly cannot move our right. But the heights on the right of the Bidasoa command such a view of us that we must have them, and the sooner we get them the better.

Anyone who knows that angle of France and Spain, and that must mean most people who have toured Spain in a car, must know the height he means. La Grande Rhune is a steep conical sort of a mountain, nearly 3,000 feet high with a nipple of rock on top that supports, inevitably, a hermitage. Although it has spurs and ridges running for the most part east and west from it, it appears from a distance to be independent of anything but itself. And it certainly does dominate the whole area – I have sat on a beach twenty miles north, at Capbreton, and found that it filled my painting of the coast line, and then again, on another beach twenty miles west, and there it was again. From its top you can see every movement of shipping from San Sebastian and Passages right round to Bayonne, and most of the main roads are clearly visible too. Now, it is entirely in France. In 1813 the border ran through its summit, so the movement Wellington was to make against it began in Spain, which is possibly why he used Spanish troops for it. The attack across the Bidassoa, which was into France, was made by British and Portuguese, the Spanish columns going no further than Behobie.

To Graham, 6 October, 1813, 11.00 a.m.: I received this morning your note of yesterday. We certainly shall not be able to do more than establish ourselves on the right of the Bidasoa, before the fall of Pamplona . . . I have therefore written to Sir George Collier, to be prepared to give you a passage in the President.

I shall be on the heights near Irun to-morrow morning at 7, and shall see you; in the mean time, I beg you will accept my best thanks for all

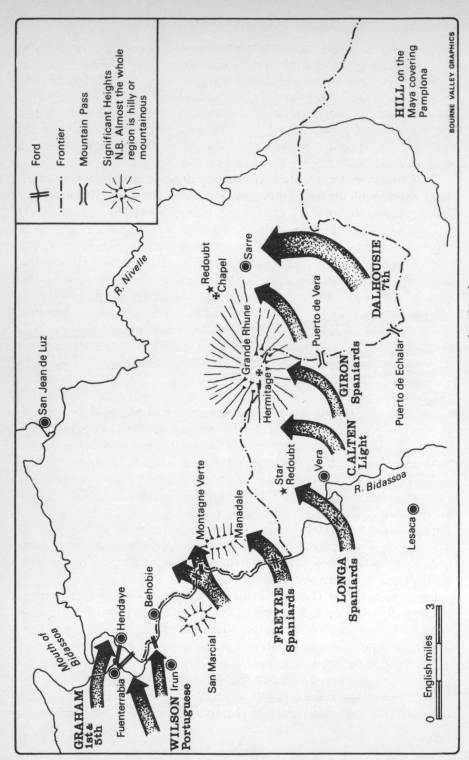

25. Operations on 7 and 8 October 1813

Map labels:

Ford
Frontier
Mountain Pass
Significant Heights
N.B. Almost the whole
region is hilly or
mountainous

R. Nivelle

San Jean de Luz

Redoubt
Chapel
Sarre

Grande Rhune

Puerto de Vera

DALHOUSIE
7th

Hermitage

GIRON
Spaniards

C. ALTEN
Light

Puerto de Echalar

Star
Redoubt

Vera

R. Bidassoa

Montagne Verte

Manadale

Lesaca

HILL on the
Maya covering
Pamplona

Hendaye

Behobie

GRAHAM
1st &
5th

Fuenterrabia

WILSON
Portuguese

Irun

San Marcial

FREYRE
Spaniards

LONGA
Spaniards

Mouth of
Bidassoa

English miles

0   3

the assistance I have received from you, and my sincere regret that your health does not permit you to stay longer.

Everything, naturally, went well. A pearly dawn with a sea mist, the wide estuary with flattish headlands, mud flats, sea marshes; the mewling of sea-gulls and the more tuneful calls of waders, among which avocets, like elegant little men in black formal wear over white shirts, strutted and nodded. The mist lifted, and along the ridge above Irun, where Wellington took his leave of Graham, the flashes, white smoke, and the roar of guns.

To Bathurst, 9 October: My Lord, having deemed it expedient to cross the Bidasoa with the left of the army, I have the pleasure to inform your Lordship that that object was effected on the 7th instant.

Lieut. General Sir Thomas Graham directed the 1st and 5th divisions, and the 1st Portuguese brigade under Brigadier General Wilson, to cross that river in three columns below and in one above, the site of the bridge; and Lieut. General Don Manuel Freyre directed that part of the Spanish army under his immediate command to cross in three columns at fords above those at which the allied British and Portuguese troops passed. The former were destined to carry the enemy's entrenchments about and above Andaye, while the latter should carry those on the Montagne Verte, and on the height of Manadale, by which they were to turn the enemy's left.

The fords nearest the sea, which the 5th division used, were found for them by shrimp-fishers. The British movement was shielded at first from view by the fortifications of Fuenterrabia, and they got across, sometimes above their waists, in flat, glaucous water, without a shot being fired at them. In the middle, on the site of the bridge, there was some resistance, but the 1st division here had covering fire from the artillery on the hills behind Irun. The Spaniards encountered the worst opposition round Behobie, but the French withdrew as the 1st division got onto their flank.

The operations of both bodies of troops succeeded at every point; the British and Portuguese troops took seven pieces of cannon in the redoubts and batteries which they carried, and the Spanish troops one piece of cannon in those carried by them . . .

Lieut. General Sir Thomas Graham, having thus established within the French territory the troops of the allied British and Portuguese army, which had been so frequently distinguished under his command, resigned the command to Lieut. General Sir John Hope, who had arrived from Ireland on the preceeding day.

While this was going on upon the left, Major General Charles Baron Alten attacked, with the Light division, the enemy's entrenchments in the Puerto de Vera, supported by the Spanish division under Brigadier

General Longa; and the Mariscal de Campo Don P. A. Giron attacked the enemy's entrenchments and posts on the mountain called La Rhune, immediately on the right of the Light division, with the army of reserve of Andalusia.

The Light division took 22 officers, and 400 prisoners . . . On the right, the troops of the army of reserve of Andalusia attacked the enemy's posts and entrenchments on the mountain of La Rhune in two columns, under the command of Spaniards only.

These troops carried every thing before them in the most gallant style, till they arrived at the foot of the rock on which the hermitage stands; and they made repeated attempts to take even that post by storm; but it was impossible to get up; and the enemy remained in possession of the hermitage during the night . . . Some time elapsed yesterday morning before the fog cleared away sufficiently to enable me to reconnaitre the mountain, which I found to be least inaccessible by its right, and that the attack of it might be connected with advantage with the attack of the enemy's works in front of the camp of Sarre. I accordingly ordered the army of reserve to concentrate to their right, and as soon as the concentration commenced, . . . Giron ordered the battalion de las Ordenes to attack the enemy's post on the rock on the right of the position . . . which was instantly carried in the most gallant style. These troops followed up their success, and carried an intrenchment on a hill, which protected the right of the camp of Sarre; and the enemy immediately evacuated all their works to defend the approaches to the camp, which were taken possession of by detachments from the 7th division, sent by Dalhousie through the Puerto de Echalar for this purpose.

. . . Giron then established the battalion of Las Ordenes on the enemy's left, on the rock of the hermitage. It was too late to proceed farther last night; and the enemy withdrew from their post at the hermitage, and from the camp of Sarre, during the night . . .

The allies were in France, at the cost of 800 casualties of whom half were Spaniards. The French, driven from heavily fortified but static positions (Soult attempted nothing at all of the sort of dynamic defence his adversary would have employed) lost 1,200, and a great deal of morale.

G.O.   Lesaca, 8th October, 1813.
1. The Commander of the Forces is concerned to be under the necessity of publishing over again his orders of the 9th July last, as they have been unattended to by the officers and troops which entered Frence yesterday . . .

which were:

The officers and soldiers of the army must recollect that their nations are at war with France solely because the Ruler of the French nation will not allow them to be at peace . . . they must not forget that the worst of the evils suffered by the enemy, in his profligate invasion of Spain and Portugal, have been occasioned by the irregularities of the soldiers, and their cruelties, authorised and encouraged by their chiefs, towards the unfortunate and peaceful inhabitants of the country.

To revenge this conduct on the peaceable inhabitants of France would be unmanly and unworthy of the nations to whom the Commander of the Forces now addresses himself; and at all events would be the occasion of similar and worse evils . . .

The rules, therefore . . . in requiring, and taking, and giving receipts for supplies from the country are to be continued in the villages on the French frontiers . . . *These rules were those first drafted in August, 1808 between the landing at Mondego Bay, and the battle of Vimeiro.*

This almost completed the expulsion of the French from Spain. Pamplona remained. To Hope, 17 October: . . . We heard from Pamplona yesterday that they were mining the works, which looked like an intention to escape. But they are at work in too public a manner, and I imagine a garrison living upon eight ounces of bread and four ounces of horseflesh are too low in condition to try to run 10 or 12 leagues over the mountains, even if they could expect to break through the blockade . . . *The memory of the escape from Almeida still rankled.* I have ordered up a reinforcement to the blockade, and our cavalry to show themselves on the plains near Pamplona.

Meanwhile, although Arthur's Spanish soldiers were improved out of all recognition, Henry's Spanish politicians and the libellous press in Cadiz, were as troublesome as ever. Enemies of the Wellesleys, and 'The Cause', were making capital out of the accidental firing of San Sebastian; even those better disposed could see no reason why Arthur should remain 'Capitan General' of all Spanish armies once the war had moved into France. Indeed some even doubted the necessity of any Spanish units going with him. Arthur was, for once, quite relaxed about it all, gave Henry this brotherly advice: From Vera, 23 October: I would recommend to you, if you find the new Cortes act upon the same democratical system as the last, to quit them, and travel about, and amuse yourself. You might go to my place near Granada . . . I am told that the place is quite beautiful.

Pamplona held on. To Hope, 27 October, 1813, 1.00 p.m.: They were

Pamplona

negotiating at Pamplona on the 25th, and I think it probable the place surrendered yesterday, and that Hill will move to-morrow, or possibly he may have moved this day. If that is the case, we shall make our attack on the enemy's left on the 29th; if he does not move until to-morrow it will be the 30th. Murray will have sent you the detail of the plan.

But the negotiations were protracted – the Governor wanted to march his men to France and threatened to blow up the fortifications if this was refused. Wellington held out for unconditional surrender and did not get it until the very end of the month.

One may now perhaps recall that letter from Castlereagh to Wellesley, 30 June, 1808:

> The occupation of Spain and Portugal by the troops of France . . . has determined His Majesty to direct a corps of his troops . . . to be employed under your orders . . . in affording to the Spanish and Portuguese nations every possible aid in throwing off the yoke of France . . .
> The entire and absolute evacuation of the Peninsula by the troops of France (is) the only security for Spanish independence . . .

Mission accomplished!

With Pamplona gone Hill could now move the right of the army down the north side of the Col de Maya to join Wellington and Hope at St Jean de Luz, in front of the Nivelle. Or could he?

Let's, of course, close with our hero's words. But it is not unfitting that they should be written in his own special brand of French, to a Spanish General. But first the same letter in English.

To Lieut. General Sir John Hope, K.B.   Vera, 1st Nov., 1813.
My Dear Sir,
I have the pleasure to inform you that Pamplona surrendered yesterday, the garrison being prisoners of war. Hill, however, being up to his knees in snow, it is absolutely necessary to defer our movement for a day or two; and I beg that every precaution be taken to prevent communication to the enemy.
   Believe me, &c.

                                                              Wellington

To General Don Manuel Freyre.   à Vera, ce 1 Nov., 1813,
Mon cher Général,   a 4 heures d'après midi.
J'ai le plaisir de vous faire savoir que Pampelune s'est rendu hier par capitulation, le garnison étant prisonnière de guerre. Il est très important, s'il est possible, d'empêcher l'ennemi de savoir cet évènement.

Quel terrible temps! Le General Hill ne peut pas se mettre en mouvement, étant jusqu'aux genoux dans la neige.

Agréez, &c.

                                          Wellington